SOUTH DAKOTA'S BLACK HILLS

LAURAL A. BIDWELL

Contents

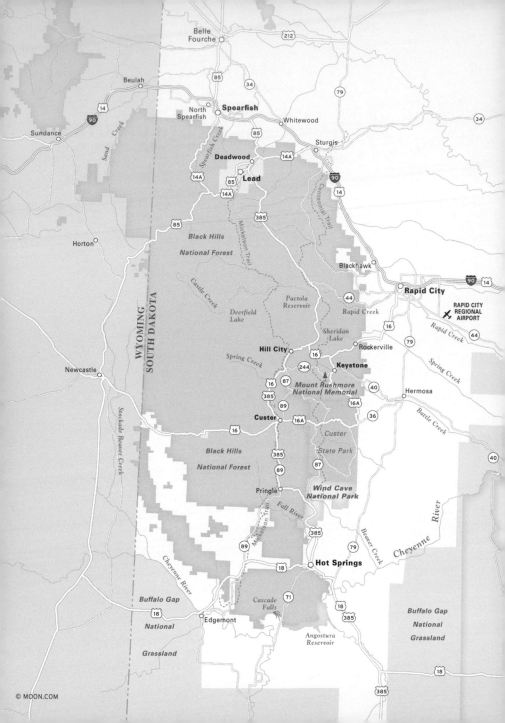

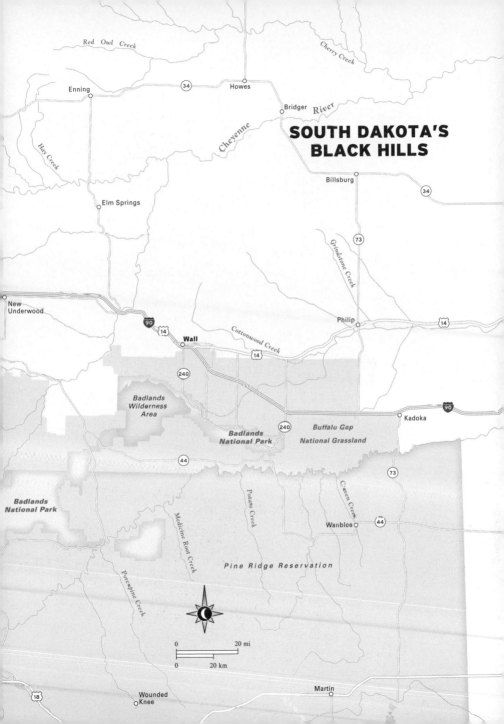

DISCOVER

South Dakota's Black Hills

I am a road warrior by nature. My first visit to South Dakota was more accidental than intentional. Wandering north and east through the plains of Colorado and Nebraska I stopped to study a map. I noted the South Dakota border was just an hour away. I'd never been there, which made the decision easy: head to Ardmore, South Dakota, get gas, and find a place to stay for the night. The buildings in Ardmore were in the process of tumbling to the ground. No gas, no people, and no place to stay. I continued north with fingers crossed and arrived in Hot Springs, the next town on the map. I got gas, got a room, and even better, discovered a landscape that captured my heart: the breathtakingly beautiful Black Hills of South Dakota.

Mount Rushmore, located in the hills, is one of the most recognizable monuments in the country. Close by, out in the plains, the eerie and strikingly beautiful Badlands are a landscape like no other.

The change from plains to hills is subtle. Miles of flatland transform into rolling swells of sparsely covered sand. One sharp incline and the view to the south is suddenly vast, empty, and as calming as staring out to sea. To the north, the soft hills are covered in dark ponderosa pine, the canyons are red, and the sky is

Clockwise from top left: fire tower at Black Elk Peak; Rapid Creek in Rapid City; Abe Lincoln by sculptor James Michael Maher at the City of Presidents; the Prairie Berry Winery; sunflower; South Dakota bison.

an azure blue. This edge—this meeting of two worlds, the best of everything—is what the hills are all about. Farmland turns into ranchland here. Warm springs flow into cold rivers. Eastern birds and western birds mingle. Just 100 miles (161 km) from north to south and 65 miles (105 km) from east to west, this "Island in the Plains" offers remarkable landscapes, wildlife, history, and recreation.

From points on the perimeter to peaks in the hills, storms are visible for miles before they arrive. Lightning streaks sideways across the sky, and rain falls but never reaches the earth. Electric summer afternoon clouds crack open and pour white beads of hail over the grasslands, striking with just enough power to release the prairie scent of sage.

While the weather can be dramatic, this is not harsh country. The Black Hills are old and round and soft. Home to the American bison, this is a land sacred to Native Americans. Its history is steeped in gold, greed, gambling, gunfights, and broken treaties. It is a land of homesteading and healing waters.

Bestowed with great natural beauty, it has always been a rewarding road-trip destination. Remnants of the 1950s' love affair with the automobile remain. Look for old hotels and diners that sport neon signs with names like the Rocket Motel. Roadside attractions abound. Pan for gold, visit a vineyard, pet wild burros, or attend a powwow. Bike, boat, ride a horse, or explore a cave. Hike the highest peak in North America east of the Rockies, or relax in the warm springs of a historic spa town. It's all here.

Clockwise from top left: aerial view of the Black Hills; Iron Mountain Road; Pactola Reservoir; wild burro.

9 TOP EXPERIENCES

1 **See the Stars Like Never Before:** Marvel at the stars in a truly dark sky at **Badlands National Park,** an out-of-this-world experience (page 210).

2 **Go Underground:** Descend into dramatic, otherworldly depths at **Jewel Cave National Monument** (page 102) and **Wind Cave National Park** (page 144).

3 **Appreciate Native American Culture:** An ongoing mountain carving of the Oglala Lakota warrior, **Crazy Horse Memorial** sets the stage on the grounds below for Native American artists, performers, and scholars (page 99). Attending a **powwow** in the hills is a celebratory way to learn more about the culture (page 226).

4 **Take a Scenic Drive:** Soaring granite pillars, spires, and towers loom over the **Needles Highway** (page 115). High canyon walls and waterfalls abound along **Spearfish Canyon Scenic Byway** (page 167). And vast views of buttes, pinnacles, and spires amid the plains line the **Badlands Loop Road** (page 205).

5 **Visit the Massive Monument:** It took 14 years and 400 men to sculpt **Mount Rushmore National Memorial,** nestled into the side of the mountain and surrounded by pines and pathways (page 35).

6 **Hike and Bike:** Experience the hills with a pair of hiking boots or a set of wheels. The **Flume Trail** (page 59), **Black Elk Peak Trail** (page 120), **Centennial Trail** (pages 61 and 122), and **Mickelson Trail** (pages 60 and 177) are all great options.

7 **Get a Taste of the West:** Spend an afternoon on horseback in Custer State Park with **Blue Bell Stables,** then walk across the street to **Blue Bell Lodge** for the **Hayride and Chuck Wagon Cookout** (page 128).

<<<

8 **Go Wildlife-Watching:** See buffalo and pronghorn on the **Wildlife Loop** (page 117) and sheep and prairie dogs along **Sage Creek Rim Road** (page 208). Get up close to creatures at the **Reptile Gardens** (page 76).

>>>

9 **Walk on the Wild Side:** Head to **Deadwood Social Club** (page 195) for lunch, then downstairs to **Saloon No. 10** (page 192) to take in gunfights, gambling, and outlaws (191).

<<<

Planning Your Trip

Where to Go

Mount Rushmore and the Central Hills

Mount Rushmore is a symbol of American exploration and expansion, a testimony to the visionary dreams of our founding fathers, and a tribute to individual effort and collective achievement. It's also at the heart of local tourism. Served by urban and transportation center **Rapid City** and supported by the old mining communities of **Hill City** and **Keystone,** this mountainous region is the hub of a Black Hills visit.

The Southern Hills

It's all about wildlife, warm water, and history in the soft rolling landscape of the Southern Hills. **Custer State Park** provides the best wildlife-viewing opportunities in the state, with accommodations that range from rustic to luxurious. **Hot Springs** originated as a place to travel to "take the cure" in the warm mineral springs that gave the town its name. It's also home to beautiful sandstone buildings and the **Mammoth Site. Wind Cave** and **Jewel Cave** are both in this region, and **Custer,** where gold was first discovered in the hills, provides easy access to all of the Southern Hills attractions, including the ongoing mountain carving of **Crazy Horse,** which honors the famous chief and the Lakota people who hold the Black Hills sacred.

The Northern Hills

Outdoor beauty and recreational opportunities grace every corner of the hills, and the northern region is no exception. Waterfalls,

at Crazy Horse Memorial

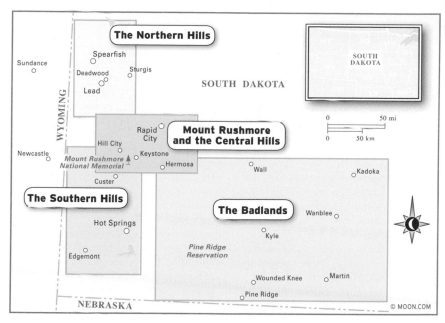

The Northern Hills

SOUTH DAKOTA

Spearfish
Sundance
Deadwood   Sturgis
Lead

WYOMING

Rapid
Hill City   City   **Mount Rushmore and the Central Hills**

Newcastle   Mount Rushmore ▲ Keystone
National Memorial   Hermosa   Wall   Kadoka

Custer

The Southern Hills

The Badlands   Wanblee

Hot Springs

Kyle

Pine Ridge
Reservation

Edgemont

Wounded Knee   Martin

Pine Ridge

NEBRASKA

© MOON.COM

hiking trails, and biking trails abound in the **Spearfish Canyon Scenic Byway,** which connects **Spearfish** to the historic mining town of **Lead.** There is plenty of wildlife in this region, though the definition of wildlife includes more than the local fauna. Once the stomping grounds of Wild Bill Hickok and Calamity Jane, this is a place where the raucous spirit of the Wild West flourishes. Gambling, gunfights, and rodeos set the ever-active stage in **Deadwood,** and the roaring bikes of the **Sturgis Motorcycle Rally** guarantee that the lights are always on in the Northern Hills.

The Badlands

Set in the midst of the vast plains, a wall of tall spires, flat-topped grassy buttes, and craggy eroding cliffs present an **otherworldly landscape** to visitors. Some 70 million years of environmental change are exposed to the eye, a product of the relentless and creative forces of wind and water. Each layer of time is different in color. When the sun is just right, the landscape of **Badlands National Park** turns into a wonderland of pastel yellow, dusty pink, burgundy, gray, green, and black. The town of **Wall** is the northern gateway to the park and home to **Wall Drug,** the ultimate roadside attraction. The **South Unit** of the park is located on the **Pine Ridge Reservation,** home to the Oglala Lakota. The tribe offers visitors access to recreational opportunities, art galleries, and historic sites to learn about Lakota culture.

Know Before You Go

High and Low Seasons

In old-fashioned vacation style, the Black Hills of South Dakota are fully open and ready for business between **Memorial Day** and **Labor Day,** which constitutes the **high season** for tourism. In the "shoulder season" (May 1-Memorial Day and Labor Day-mid-Oct.), most attractions are open and there is still plenty to do. If the purpose of your visit is primarily scenic and recreational in nature, there are hotels open year-round in every region. National monuments and national parks (including Mount Rushmore) are open year-round; however, **winter** is the slowest time, when hours of operation are reduced and fewer programs are offered. While Rapid City is still in full swing in the off-season, many hotels, shops, restaurants and activities shut down between November and May in smaller communities. If you're set on a particular site, hotel, or restaurant, call ahead.

The weather in the hills is unpredictable, but **spring** is the season during which cooler temperatures and rain are likeliest. It is also the season when the region is at its greenest. **Early summer** tends to be warm and dry, and brief afternoon thundershowers are not uncommon. **Mid- and late summer** can be anywhere from comfortable to extremely hot, and temperatures vary greatly between the warmer Southern Hills and the cooler mountain towns. For travelers not tied to a school schedule, **early fall** can be the best season to travel, with warm days and cool nights. It is my favorite season here.

The **Sturgis Motorcycle Rally** begins on the first Friday in August and lasts 10 full days. During the rally, hundreds of thousands of bikers flock to the hills and fill the campgrounds and hotels. **Traffic congestion** in the parks and on the roads is common during the rally, and room rates are at their highest. For some, it's the perfect

the Central Hills

week to come, but if the constant roar of motorcycles is not for you, it might be a week to avoid. If you've come to the hills inadvertently during the rally, rooms are generally available and the environment is a little quieter in the Southern Hills, particularly in Hot Springs.

Reservations

It is always possible to find rooms in the hills, with the probable exception of the Northern Hills during the **Sturgis Motorcycle Rally.** If you desire to stay in the **Custer State Park** cabins or lodges during peak summer season, however, reservations are strongly recommended—particularly if your heart is set on a specific lodge. Reservations in the park are allowed as much as one year in advance. Note that many of the chains practice pricing their rooms the way that airlines price their flights: the earlier the reservation is made, the less it is likely to cost. So if you know where you want to stay, make reservations early.

Reservations at a few other extremely popular sites and activities are also highly recommended. If you are traveling with children who might be interested in digging for mammoth bones, the programs at the **Mammoth Site** in **Hot Springs** are in high demand and require reservations early. The **1880 Train** in **Hill City** takes reservations for assigned seats and departure times. Also in Hill City, **Prairie Berry Winery** requires reservations for their very popular free wine-tastings during the busiest days of summer. Finally, for history buffs, there are three sites involved when visiting the **Minuteman Missile National Historic Site.** Of those sites, the tour of **Launch Control Facility Delta-01,** home to the missileers and the location of the control keys to launch the missiles, requires reservations; again, the earlier, the better. The other two Minuteman sites are open to the public with no reservations required.

Activities

It's a good idea to check the websites of the government agencies that manage the public lands in the Black Hills. The National Park Service,

the U.S. Forest Service, and, locally, the Black Hills National Forest and the South Dakota Department of Game, Fish, and Parks each sponsor **summer activities** and generally post information on summer events beginning in late spring. If you happen to be here during a full moon, for example, you won't want to miss a midnight hike in the Badlands.

Getting around the hills is not difficult, but if you didn't arrive by car and don't mind driving, plan on renting one. There are many **tour companies** that provide day trips into each region of the hills, but more options are available if you drive. There are also many small airports in the region, but the only commercial **airport** is in **Rapid City.**

What to Pack

Be prepared for unpredictable weather in the Black Hills. While summers are generally pleasant and dry, temperatures can soar to over 100°F by afternoon and fall to 50°F in the evening. Caves maintain a temperature hovering in the mid-50s no matter the outside temperature. Wind on the plains can be brisk and strong. Given these weather possibilities, be sure to **think in layers** when you pack. Cotton T-shirts work well on hot afternoons and can be layered with a long-sleeved shirt in the evening. Bring a windbreaker and pack a sweatshirt for cave tours and cool evenings. Layers are also key to comfortable hiking. Be prepared for afternoon thundershowers and bring rain gear. Even the shortest of hikes can be hard on the feet, and this is especially true in the Badlands. Bring **sturdy, ankle-supporting footwear.** Another must is **sunscreen and sunglasses.** And don't forget **binoculars.** While a **bathing suit** might seem out of place in this landlocked region, many lodgings feature outdoor pools and hot tubs, a very relaxing way to end a day, and there are many small lakes for swimming.

Dress is casual everywhere in the hills. You can dress up if you like, particularly in the finer restaurants, but jeans are welcome most everywhere.

The Best of the Black Hills

From a Western perspective, the Black Hills region is small, but in reality, the hills blanket an area about the size of the state of Connecticut. The outstanding variety of experiences includes stunning scenic beauty, fascinating Indigenous and Western history, and fabulous roadside attractions. From the longest caves to the largest mountain carvings, from wildlife-viewing in Custer State Park to the wild life of historic Deadwood, there is something for everyone.

Day 1: Rapid City, Mount Rushmore, and Hill City

Rapid City makes a good starting point for your exploration of the region. Begin your day with breakfast at **Tally's Silver Spoon** downtown and then head for the hills. The most scenic approach to **Mount Rushmore** is **Iron Mountain Road** (U.S. 16A). Head south on Highway 79 (Campbell St.) and take a right on Highway 40 at Hermosa. About 13 miles (20.9 km) in, take a left on Playhouse Road. Four miles (6.4 km) later, take a right and head north on Iron Mountain Road, wind through the hills, and enjoy the gorgeous views, the pigtail bridges, and the narrow tunnels that frame the monument.

Spend the morning at Mount Rushmore and then head down the mountain to **Hill City.** Stroll the compact boardwalk of downtown, visit **Jon Crane Gallery & Framing, Warrior's Work & Ben West Gallery,** and **The Museum at Black Hills Institute,** and then head back toward Rapid City on U.S. 16. If the timing and your mood match, call the **Prairie Berry Winery** and make reservations for a late afternoon wine-tasting (free!) and a light snack on the patio.

Spend your evening exploring Rapid City. Start at **Prairie Edge Trading Company and Galleries,** then enjoy an evening microbrew and a designer pizza at the **Independent Ale House.** If you prefer quiet fine dining, stop in at the **Delmonico Grill.**

Mount Rushmore

Badlands National Park

Day 2: Badlands National Park

Today is a day of contrasts with a trip to Badlands National Park and Wall Drug. Start the day early, heading east on I-90 and taking exit 110 at the town of Wall. (If visiting off-season, stop by Subway and pick up a picnic lunch.) Drive south to the main entrance of **Badlands National Park,** and begin the journey along the **Badlands Loop Road.** At **Sage Creek Rim Road,** take a right for a quick detour. Stop at the **Hay Butte Overlook;** there is usually a good-size herd of Rocky Mountain sheep in this area. Continue on for a glimpse of **Roberts Prairie Dog Town,** then turn around and head back to the Badlands Loop Road. There are several overlooks along the loop; don't miss the **Pinnacles Overlook.** Continue meandering along the loop, stopping whenever the mood strikes. Take the short **Fossil Exhibit Trail** and stop at the **Ben Reifel Visitor Center** at the southern end of the park. Enjoy lunch at the **Cedar Pass Lodge.**

Just north of the visitor center on Highway 240 are two easy hiking trails, the **Door Trail** and the **Window Trail,** which are great for stretching the legs. The **Notch Trail** is a more strenuous alternative. Continue north on Highway 240 to return to I-90, and if time allows, visit the **Minuteman Missile National Historic Site,** keeper of the keys of the **Launch Control Facility Delta-01,** a good stop for military history enthusiasts. Otherwise, head west on I-90 and stop at **Wall Drug Cafe** for dinner at the ultimate tourist mecca. The kids will love the backyard dinosaur, and you will love the bookstore, the artwork, and the hot roast beef sandwich. Head back to Rapid City on I-90.

Day 3: Heading South to Hot Springs

It's time to shift your base camp into the hills. Head south on Highway 79 to historic **Hot Springs** (or, if your preference is to stay in one place, note the drive is about an hour from Rapid City). Visit the **Mammoth Site,** drop the kids off at **Evans Plunge,** and treat yourself to a soak at the outdoor mineral waters of **Moccasin Springs Natural Mineral Spa.** Enjoy lunch at **Mornin' Sunshine Coffee House & Boutique.**

Great Outdoor Adventures

The Black Hills offers inspiring experiences for both the wildly adventuresome and the quietly contemplative. Here are some of the best:

RECREATION

- **Go underground at Wind Cave National Park:** The four-hour **Wild Cave Tour** will have you crawling through narrow passages as you learn the basics of safe caving and see the deeper sections of one of the longest caves in the world. Hard hats, kneepads, and lights are provided by the park. Heavy gloves and study boots are required, and old clothes are recommended. Claustrophobics need not apply!

- **Climb a rock at Custer State Park:** Call **Sylvan Rocks Climbing School & Guide Service** and have the adventure of your life. Learn to climb in the Needles of Custer State Park or take the best routes with the most knowledgeable climbers in the hills.

- **Bike the Mickelson Trail:** The Mickelson Trail offers over 100 miles (161 km) of rails-to-trails riding from Edgemont to Deadwood. There are several companies that will shuttle you to and from any trailhead along the way.

- **Backpack the Sage Creek Wilderness:** Bring plenty of water and sunscreen and spend a few days in the remote and otherworldly Badlands National Park. Camping is free at the Sage Creek Campground, but facilities are primitive.

- **Hike the Centennial Trail:** This 111-mile (179-km) trail highlights the diversity of the Black Hills and runs from Bear Butte in the north through Wind Cave in the south. (Many, but not all, sections of the trail are bike accessible, as well.)

- **Challenge your balance:** Visit **Rushmore Tramway Adventures** in Keystone and take to the trees. Think suspended bridges, log ladders, walking on cables, and flying on ziplines. Not recommended for anyone with a fear of heights.

RELAXATION

- **Balloon the Black Hills:** Drift over Custer State Park in the open-air basket of a colorful balloon. Bring a new perspective to your sightseeing as you get a bird's-eye view of herds of bison and pronghorn roaming the park.

rock climbing in Custer State Park

- **Go fly-fishing:** Get out of the car and take some time to fish **Spearfish Canyon** or **Rapid Creek** south of Pactola Reservoir. You can rent equipment and explore on your own or take a guided tour. Streams are stocked with brown, rainbow, and brook trout.

- **Golf:** Play the **Southern Hills Municipal Golf Course** just west of Hot Springs. There are stunning views from every tee of the award-winning front nine.

- **Admire the falls:** Enjoy the sound and sight of cascading water. **Roughlock Falls** has a boardwalk and picnic tables; less visited **Spearfish Falls** is right across the road. See both and finish with a beverage on the deck of the **Latchstring Inn Restaurant.**

- **Kayak, canoe, or pontoon:** Get away from the crowds at one of the remotest lakes in the hills. Consider **Legion Lake** in Custer State Park, check out **Angostura Recreation Area** just southeast of Hot Springs, or rent a pontoon boat on **Pactola Reservoir** in the Central Hills and dive into the water when the sun gets too warm.

- **Bike Rapid City:** The flood of 1976 ravished Rapid City. Instead of rebuilding in a flood zone that was likely to flood again, the city elected to declare all the land around the creek a park. As a result, there are miles of hiking and easy biking trails along the riverbanks of Rapid Creek.

Walk the **Freedom Trail** beside Fall River and enjoy the town's beautiful sandstone architecture. Visit the **Pioneer Museum,** and then head north on U.S. 385 to **Wind Cave National Park** for a cave tour. Return to Hot Springs for the evening. Stay at the **Historic Log Cabins** for a rustic experience or at the **Flatiron Historic Sandstone Inn** for elegance. For dinner, enjoy a full American food menu at **Woolly's Western Grill.**

Day 4: Custer State Park

Head out early today and plan to eat breakfast at the **Blue Bell Lodge** in Custer State Park. To get there, drive north on U.S. 385 and take a right (north) on Highway 87. This will bring you right to Blue Bell Lodge.

After breakfast, backtrack on Highway 87 for a couple of miles to the park's ranger station entrance and enjoy the scenic **Wildlife Loop.** Bring your binoculars and keep an eye out for bison, prairie dogs, pronghorn, and burros. (Stock up on carrots and apples before you go.) Early morning or just around dusk is the best time to travel the loop for wildlife-viewing.

At the end of the loop, head west on U.S. 16A and stop at the **State Game Lodge** just to enjoy lemonade on the porch or a light snack or lunch. Continue west on U.S. 16A through Custer, stopping at **Jewel Cave,** named for its sparkling calcite crystal walls.

Return to Custer for the night. Plan to stay at the hillside cabins of the **Shady Rest Motel** or at the 1950s-themed **Rocket Motel** downtown. Have dinner at the **Sage Creek Grille.**

Day 5: Scenic Drive to Crazy Horse Memorial

After breakfast at **Baker's Bakery,** pack up the car and head back into Custer State Park for the most beautiful drive in the Black Hills. Heading east on U.S. 16A, turn north on Highway 87. (Be careful as it is easy to get turned around in the park.) This will become the **Needles Highway.** This scenic byway loops around towering granite spires and formations,

through a very tight tunnel, and finishes at **Sylvan Lake.**

Avid hikers should note that one of the trailheads to **Black Elk Peak** begins here. For everyone else, a walk around the lake is a nice alternative. Have a casual lakeside lunch, or better yet, walk up to **Sylvan Lake Lodge** for lunch on the deck overlooking the lake and the granite spires of the Needles formation.

After leaving the lake area, continue north on Highway 87 to the junction with U.S. 385. Head south a short distance to **Crazy Horse Memorial.** This is the only large, ongoing mountain carving project in the world. Watch the video featuring the earliest days of the carving as well as admire and learn about Native American art and culture from Native artists and scholars representing tribes from all over the country.

After your visit, return to Custer or turn north on U.S. 385 and head to Hill City, where the boardwalk and dinner await at the **Alpine Inn.** Spend the night at the **Lantern Inn.**

Day 6: Deadwood

Direction north; destination Deadwood, a town steeped in Wild West mythology and mining history. It's known nationally for the TV series that bore its name and locally for gambling and special events.

Start with breakfast at the **Hill City Cafe** and head out of town winding north on U.S. 385. At the edge of Deadwood, stop at **Chubby Chipmunk** to taste some hand-dipped chocolates or truffles. Try your luck at the **Silverado-Franklin** complex downtown and walk the main street to admire the historic architecture.

Stop at **Saloon No. 10** for lunch on the second-story patio of the **Deadwood Social Club.** Visit the **Adams Museum,** one of the oldest museums in the state, and **Mount Moriah Cemetery,** the final resting place of Wild Bill Hickok and Calamity Jane. Visit with **Boot Hill Tours** for deeper historical context.

Hike to the **Mount Roosevelt Friendship Tower,** built by Seth Bullock to honor his friend Theodore Roosevelt, for spectacular views. Plan on dinner at the **Legends Steakhouse** and spend the night at the haunted **Bullock Hotel.**

Day 7: Lead and Spearfish

Eat breakfast in the morning at **Bully's** (in the Bullock Hotel) and head to Lead (pronounced "Leed"). Here, one of the deepest and longest operational gold mines in the West has been converted into a futuristic, underground science lab, and neutrinos are studied almost a mile below the surface of the earth. The exhibits and trolley tour at the **Sanford Lab Homestake Visitor Center** walk you through the conversion. A stop at the hoist room is a must!

Head south out of town on U.S. 85 to U.S. 14A, otherwise known as the **Spearfish Canyon Scenic Byway.** Stretch your legs in Savoy and enjoy the short hikes to **Roughlock Falls** and **Spearfish Falls.** Have lunch at the **Latchstring Inn,** then continue on through the canyon to Spearfish.

Visit the **D.C. Booth Historic National Fish Hatchery** and acclaimed **Termesphere Gallery.** Both are free and fascinating. End your day with dinner at **Killian's Tavern** before spending the night at the **Secret Garden Bed & Breakfast.**

Family Fun

Traveling with children can add a lot of fun to a vacation. With energy to burn, kids encourage us all to take a few more hikes, play minigolf, power a paddleboat, or slide down a mountainside.

Day 1: Reptile Gardens, Mount Rushmore, and Keystone

Leave Rapid City heading south on U.S. 16, also known as Mount Rushmore Road. This is roadtrip heaven for families with children. Stop first at **Reptile Gardens.** Adults will love the grounds and the gardens, and kids will love everything else, including interactive demonstrations with raptors, crocodiles, and snakes. Be sure to visit the Aldabra giant tortoises.

Continue on to **Mount Rushmore National Memorial.** Visit the **Lincoln Borglum Visitor Center,** check out the **Sculptor's Studio** and enjoy the ranger talk, and then hike the **Presidential Trail** around the base of the mountain. Make sure the kids take part in the **Junior Ranger Program!**

Then head to **Keystone,** where there are lots of great family attractions. Stop at **Rushmore Tramway Adventures,** take a ride on the ski lift and zoom down the **Alpine Slide,** or wander out into the trees climbing the ladders and platforms at the **Aerial Adventure Park.** Be sure to

enjoy some creamy gourmet saltwater taffy from the **Rushmore Mountain Taffy Shop.** End the day with a nice dinner at the **Ruby House Restaurant** and spend the night at the **Powder House Lodge.**

Day 2: Needles Highway and Sylvan Lake

After breakfast at the **Powder House Restaurant,** pack your bags and go back in the direction of Mount Rushmore, but take a left before you get to the monument on U.S. 16A, also known as **Iron Mountain Road,** a twisting, turning, tunnel-filled scenic drive that runs toward Custer State Park. (Stay on U.S. 16A; do not head toward Mount Rushmore on Highway 244.) Keep an eye out for County Road 753 (Black Hills Playhouse Rd.). This road will enter **Custer State Park** and join up with Highway 87, which is the **Needles Highway.** These are two of the most scenic byways in the state.

Head north on Needles Highway to **Sylvan Lake.** Hike around the lake and send the kids out in paddleboats. Have a picnic lunch at the lake or treat yourself to lunch at **Sylvan Lake Lodge.** Take Highway 89 South to **Custer.** Spend the night at the **Chief Motel** downtown, where a large pool is available for the kids. Look for

Paha Sapa: Sacred Land

For thousands of years, Native Americans have called Paha Sapa (the Black Hills) their sacred land. Celebrate the history, culture, and ongoing achievement of the people who first called this region home.

- **Sioux History collection at The Journey Museum:** Interactive exhibits and recordings provide an oral history and story-telling approach to the last 200 years of Lakota history.

- **Prairie Edge Trading Company and Galleries:** Find the best in Native American art, crafts, beadwork, and music in this stunning facility.

- **Bear Butte:** Located north and east of Sturgis, this butte is Mato Paha or "Bear Mountain," a place of prayer for the Lakota people. Hiking, boating, and horseback riding are available in the surrounding state park, but be respectful to the land and the people who hold it sacred.

- **Crazy Horse Memorial:** Lakota chief Henry Standing Bear and sculptor Korczak Ziolkowski reached an agreement in June 1948 to carve a monument in the sacred Black Hills to show mainstream America that Native Americans had great leaders, too. Crazy Horse, a Lakota leader who never signed a treaty with Washington DC, was selected for the honor; work on the memorial continues to this day. The complex includes a museum and a cultural center that hosts Native artisans during the summer.

- **Art Galleries:** Look for Native American art at galleries throughout the hills. Visit the Warrior's Work & Ben West Gallery in Hill City and

a Lakota powwow

Red Cloud Heritage Center on the Pine Ridge Reservation.

- **Powwows:** Native American tribes gather from across the country to celebrate their cultural traditions at powwows, held throughout the region all summer long. Guests can enjoy the flash of color and movement that is the grand entry; listen to the drums and witness the fancy, jingle, grass, and traditional dances; and taste the best Indian tacos (Indian fry bread with taco toppings).

dessert at **Bobkat's Purple Pie Place.** Pick up some carrots for tomorrow's adventures.

Day 3: Custer State Park and Hot Springs

Head into Custer State Park for an early breakfast at the **State Game Lodge.** After breakfast, aim for the **Wildlife Loop** just past the State Game Lodge off U.S. 16A. Traveling this road is most rewarding early in the day. Stop to let the kids feed carrots to the wild burros (keeping a watchful eye on their fingers!). At the end of the loop, drive south on Highway 87 to **Wind Cave National Park** for a cave tour. After the tour, continue on to **Hot Springs** via U.S. 385 for lunch at the **Upper Crust Bakery & Café**

Looking for the road less traveled? Enjoy wilderness and solitude? There are hidden places and great campgrounds in every region of the hills.

THE CENTRAL HILLS

- **Horsethief Lake Campground:** The closest campground to Mount Rushmore, this primitive campground is not off the beaten path, but it feels like it. Run by the Black Hills National Forest, it surrounds a 10-acre (4-ha) lake stocked with rainbow trout and perch.

- **Creekside picnic areas:** Black Hills National Forest has 26 beautiful picnic areas, many of them rarely visited. Any place a creek runs is a good spot to enjoy the quiet sounds of moving water, such as at Spring Creek Picnic Area, southwest of Rapid City on Sheridan Lake Road.

THE SOUTHERN HILLS

- **French Creek Natural Area:** This part of Custer State Park has trails marked only by the creek and the boots of other hikers. Expect to see a lot of wildlife. Primitive camping is allowed, but there are no services.

- **Cascade Falls:** About 12 miles (19.3 km) south of Hot Springs, a parking lot with a small sign on the right side of the road marks the spot of this lovely local swimming hole and picnic area. Cross the lot and take the short path down to Cascade Creek. This nearly hidden warm-water, spring-fed pool is a lush spot in the middle of the arid plains.

- **Cold Brook Lake Campground:** This small primitive campground is tucked up next to red sandstone canyon walls in Hot Springs. The nearby lake is great for fishing and swimming. There are picnic tables, and just past the campground is a dog-friendly wilderness area.

Cascade Falls

- **Backcountry Camping, Wind Cave National Park:** Since Wind Cave is most famous for what is underground, the aboveground backcountry of the park is rarely visited. Camping is free; all that's required is a permit. Look for the huge elk herd in the park and avoid run-ins with bison!

THE NORTHERN HILLS

- **Spearfish Canyon 76 Trail:** It's a short, steep hike to the top, but the views are spectacular. If the hike is too rough, contemplate the views from the deck of the Latchstring Inn across the road.

and a stop at **Evans Plunge.** Kids will enjoy the spring-fed pool, as well as the waterslide and the rings. Stay at the **Budget Host Hills Inn** and play minigolf at the Putt-4-Fun next door. In the evening, take a walk down the **Freedom Trail** that winds along Fall River and/or take in a movie at the historic **Hot Springs Theatre.**

Day 4: Mammoth Site and Crazy Horse

Download a self-guided tour from the app, then start the day with a visit to the **Mammoth Site.** (If the kids are interested in digging for mammoth bones, make reservations far in advance for the Junior Paleontologist Program.) Drive north to Custer on U.S. 385. Have lunch in town at **Black Hills Burger & Bun** or **Begging Burro Mexican Bistro** and then continue north on U.S. 385 to enjoy riding horses with **Rockin' R Rides.** Visit **Crazy Horse Memorial,** which is just a couple of miles up the highway from there. Make sure to see the video in the visitor center. Spend the night in **Hill City** at the **Lantern Inn.**

Day 5: 1880 Train to Keystone and Roadside Attractions

After breakfast at the **Hill City Cafe,** it's train time! Head over to the **1880 Train** station for a round-trip ride to Keystone and back. There's plenty of time to relax and enjoy the scenery as the steam train huffs up the hills and through the canyons. Little ones enjoy waving at the folks at the many train crossings. After the ride, visit **The Museum at Black Hills Institute** for a great dinosaur display.

Then it's time to head back in the general direction of Rapid City. Head north on U.S. 385 and then follow the signs to Rapid City on U.S. 16. Consider stopping at **Dairy Twist** for burgers

and ice cream and again at the **Cosmos Mystery Area,** a quick but fun roadside attraction where the rules of gravity are challenged. Continue your journey back to Rapid City and spend the night on the shores of Canyon Lake, staying at the **Canyon Lake Resort,** where the kids can enjoy the heated outdoor pool, paddleboats, or a walk on the path along the lakeshore.

Day 6: Badlands National Park and Wall Drug

Now is the time to visit an entirely different ecological niche. Travel east on Highway 44 from Rapid City until you come to the southern entrance of **Badlands National Park.** Stop at the **Ben Reifel Visitor Center** to get oriented and check the daily activities. Note times and locations for ranger-guided tours and the Junior Ranger Program. Hike the **Door Trail** and the **Window Trail,** and then head north on the Badlands Loop Road. Check to see if there will be a ranger-guided tour at the **Fossil Exhibit Trail.** Continue north on the Loop Road and enjoy the many overlooks. Head out of the park into the town of Wall and visit **Wall Drug**—a must for the kids. Take pictures of them on top of the jackalope, do a little gold panning in the backyard, and enjoy some ice cream. Drive back to Rapid City on I-90.

Day 7: Rapid City

Take it relatively easy today. Choose from **The Journey Museum; Storybook Island,** a charming free attraction for younger kids; or **Dinosaur Park,** where gigantic dinosaurs over look the city. Spend some time at **Pirate's Cove Adventure Golf** and **Prairie Edge Trading Company and Galleries** downtown, and enjoy the dancing waters at **Main Street Square** across the street.

Art, Culture, and History

As you explore the sublime landscape of South Dakota, take the time to steep yourself in history, discover contemporary art, and enjoy some fine shopping while you're at it.

Rapid City

Main Street Square: On a beautiful day, stop by the square, let the kids splash around in the fountain, take your pick of fabulous shops and restaurants, and enjoy a milkshake, a smoothie, or some ice cream at one of the outside tables.

Prairie Edge Trading Company and Galleries: With artwork that is beautiful, eclectic, and fabulously displayed, Prairie Edge is the most attractive gallery and gift shop in the Black Hills. The best Native American artwork, jewelry, and crafts are featured, and artists are frequently on-site.

The Journey Museum: Fossils, dinosaurs, Native American history, the story of the Rapid City flood, the stars, geology, pioneers, and cowboys—this museum has it all.

City of Presidents: Grab a map for the locations of each of the life-size statues of the former U.S. presidents. Each was sculpted by a local artist and designed to portray a distinct character trait. (Notice how short some of them were!) Snap a photo of your favorite president.

Dahl Arts Center: Three galleries contain an ever-changing roster of artists on view and a 360-degree panoramic mural of 200 years of U.S. history. A close view of the work reveals how times have changed . . . and how they have not.

Spearfish

Termesphere Gallery: Named after internationally acclaimed artist Dick Termes, this gallery isn't the easiest place to find, but it's worth

Historic Adams House in Deadwood

D.C. Booth Historic National Fish Hatchery

the search. Termes's three-dimensional paintings on spheres are gorgeous, fascinating, and one of a kind.

D.C. Booth Historic National Fish Hatchery:
A wonderful place to wander and learn the history and purpose of nationally run fish hatcheries, this place is free and fun for everyone. Watch the oversize trout in the see-through tanks, feed the fish in the ponds, and take a tour with the knowledgeable and enthusiastic volunteers.

Latchstring Inn Restaurant:
Location, location, location! Within walking distance of two of the three waterfalls in Spearfish Canyon, this log cabin restaurant has an outdoor patio with unbeatable views. After a short hike to the falls, relax out on the deck with a glass of wine.

Deadwood

Adams Museum: The oldest museum in the Black Hills (built in 1930) includes a display of the first steam train in the hills, artifacts of Wild Bill Hickok and Calamity Jane, and a superb collection of historical photos.

Historic Adams House: After W. E. Adams, a prominent Deadwood citizen, died in 1934, his wife closed up their house and moved to California. It sat, unlived in with contents intact and untouched, for 50 years. Restored and opened to the public, it's a vision of historical Victorian-style living.

Mount Moriah Cemetery: Visit the graves of Wild Bill Hickok and Calamity Jane at the scenic cemetery overlooking town.

Bullock Hotel: When gambling breathed new life into the community, new owners completely restored this historic hotel (built by Seth Bullock 1894-1896), once the finest in the West, to its original Victorian splendor. Fans of paranormal phenomena will be happy to know that Bullock's ghost reportedly continues to supervise the kitchen staff.

Termesphere Gallery

Hill City

Jon Crane Gallery & Framing: Famous for his beautiful and detailed watercolor depictions of historic places and outdoor landscapes, Jon Crane has been perfecting his craft in South Dakota for over 35 years.

Warrior's Work & Ben West Gallery: These two large galleries in one location focusing on contemporary fine arts and Native American arts feature some of the most striking paintings in the hills. They are also notable for the handcrafted leather frames, created by owner Randy Berger.

Prairie Berry Winery: Some of the friendliest and most knowledgeable staff in the hills offer samples of wines created from the fruits, grapes, and honey of the plains. To top it off, the winery features a gourmet restaurant with a lovely outdoor patio. It's just plain fun.

Custer State Park

State Game Lodge: All the lodges in Custer State Park are exceptional, but none beats the State Game Lodge for history and elegance. Built in 1920, this wood and stone lodge was the "Summer White House" for President Calvin Coolidge in 1927. The dining room features the best in South Dakota game including pheasant, trout, and bison. Step back in time and watch as herds of bison freely roam the grounds.

Black Hills Playhouse: The best venue anywhere to enjoy summer-stock theater. Deep in the ponderosa pines of the park, high and low culture combines as ticket holders enjoy hot dogs, ice cream, and classic and contemporary plays.

Hot Springs

Historic sandstone buildings: Walk along North River Street and enjoy the beautiful architecture of the sandstone buildings along the street. The sandstone blocks were carved from a local quarry and dominate, with elegance, the historic district of town.

Pioneer Museum: This nicely curated museum is home to fabulous photos of the carving of Mount Rushmore as well as two floors of artifacts from an earlier time. Ask to see the Flat Earth Poster, otherwise known as the Map of the Square and Stationary Earth by Orlando Ferguson of Hot Springs, South Dakota.

Mount Rushmore and the Central Hills

Mount Rushmore is an enduring testimony to

American exploration, expansion, unity, and preservation. Started in 1927 and completed in 1941, these faces of four presidents—George Washington, Thomas Jefferson, Abraham Lincoln, and Theodore Roosevelt—were created by 400 workers, who toiled to carve them into the hard granite mountain. The creators of the monument picked the location well. Gorgeous lakes, spires, and pine-covered peaks surround Mount Rushmore, offering numerous outdoor activities and winding mountain drives. It's a site not without controversy however, as many Native Americans take issue with this symbolic celebration of manifest destiny and the expansion into what was once their sacred land.

Hill City and Keystone are a few miles from Mount Rushmore, to the

Highlights

Look for ★ to find recommended sights, activities, dining, and lodging.

★ **Lincoln Borglum Visitor Center:** Everything you'd ever want to know about the process of carving **Mount Rushmore,** including the timeline, the artist who designed it, the people who worked on the mountain, and the tools they used, can be found here (page 39).

★ **Presidential Trail:** Winding through the pines at the base of Mount Rushmore, this trail provides the closest views of the monument, potential sightings of rock-climbing mountain goats in their element, and a fabulous view of the plains and hills in the distance (page 40).

★ **1880 Train:** Created by rail enthusiasts who refused to allow steam trains to disappear from the landscape, this train provides a leisurely, nostalgic trip between Hill City (page 57) and Keystone (page 45).

★ **Rushmore Tramway Adventures:** Pick your adrenaline level and choose from activities that range from ziplines and obstacle courses in the trees to a scenic climb up a mountain ridge via chairlift and a thrilling ride back down (page 49).

★ **The Museum at Black Hills Institute:** There are dinosaur bones in South Dakota, and the institute is involved in their discovery—as well as excellent excavation and restoration work (page 59).

★ **Prairie Edge Trading Company and Galleries:** Experience the best in contemporary and historic Native American arts, including exquisite beadwork, star quilts, powwow regalia, ledger art, and music (page 73).

★ **The Journey Museum:** The definitive museum of the Black Hills has great interactive exhibits on Lakota culture, pioneer history, archaeology, geology, and local ecology (page 73).

★ **Storybook Island:** Fairy tales and nursery rhymes come to life at this children's theme park, where kids can meet the Three Little Pigs, the Cat in the Hat, Winnie the Pooh, and over 100 other characters (page 76).

★ **Reptile Gardens:** Meet crocodiles, poisonous snakes, and raptors. Best of all are the free-roaming giant tortoises (page 76).

west and east, respectively. Both communities have seen their share of economic boom-and-bust eras; first it was gold, then mica, then tin, and then a long period of economic recession. When it was time to find a location for the monument, the fact that Keystone had proximity, a road, electricity, and a rail line in place clearly made a positive impression. Mount Rushmore brought life back to both communities, but each has evolved in its own direction. Keystone, closest to the monument, is action central, filled with gift shops, restaurants, and attractions. Hill City has evolved into an interesting mix, a quaint, charming arts center in the hills crossed with the home of Harley-Davidson and the all-terrain vehicles crowd. The result is art galleries, rock shops, fossils, ice cream, pizza, and beer—a little of something for everyone.

As the biggest city in the area, Rapid City is the urban heart of the Black Hills. Initially created to serve as the commercial center for the mining towns of the Northern Hills, Rapid City has evolved into a small city with very big ideas. The rich historic district has much to offer visitors. Cozy pubs, fine dining, art galleries, and boutique shopping are all within easy walking distance. Centrally located, and with the only commercial airport in the region, Rapid City frequently serves as the start and end point of a Black Hills vacation.

PLANNING YOUR TIME

Mount Rushmore and the small communities and tourist industries that grew up around it are filled with sights and activities to delight just about every kind of traveler. It is possible to spend as little as a day here, exploring U.S. history at Mount Rushmore, or a full week or more, experiencing the outdoor recreation opportunities, scenic drives, museums, galleries, restaurants, and attractions of the Black Hills. In order to share in the best that the Central Hills region has to offer, plan to spend a minimum of three days in the area. The Black Hills region in its entirety is compact by Western standards, but the winding mountain roads in the Central Hills can result in a lot of time behind the wheel, so you'll want to map out your time carefully.

There are two basic travel strategies for visiting the Black Hills. You can choose a location to use as a base camp and plot a series of day trips around it or plan a meandering route through all of the regions of the hills, spending one night here, two nights there, as the route and attractions dictate. The ideal itinerary will depend on your overall travel plans and personal preference. The urban center of the hills, Rapid City, offers the most dining, hotel, and shopping options, just 20 minutes from Mount Rushmore, with easy day-trip access to the Northern Hills and the Badlands. Hill City and Keystone have comparable amenities and are within easier reach of the Southern Hills, including Custer State Park.

If you are starting your journey into the hills from Rapid City, the fastest road to Mount Rushmore is U.S. 16, also known as **Mount Rushmore Road.** It is also the best choice if you are driving a large RV. But if you have more time and enjoy a dramatic drive, approach the carving from **Iron Mountain Road** (U.S. 16A). To drive to Mount Rushmore on this scenic byway, travel south from Rapid City on Highway 79. At Hermosa, head west (take a right) on **U.S. 40.** Continue for 13 miles (20.9 km) and take a left onto **Playhouse Road.** At the stop sign (about 4 mi/6.4 km in) take a right on **Iron Mountain Road.** Enjoy the scenery and watch for the faces of Mount Rushmore to appear and disappear across meadows, through the pines, and framed by the tunnels through which the road is carved.

Previous: Mount Rushmore in the pines; Prairie Edge Trading Company and Galleries in Rapid City; mountaintop grill at Rushmore Tramway Adventures.

Mount Rushmore and the Central Hills

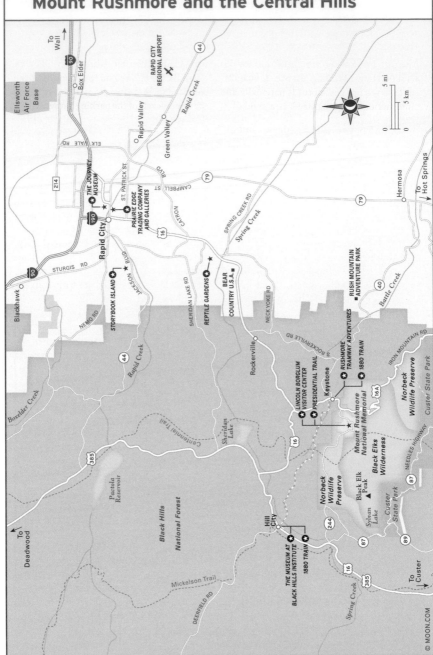

To Wall

Ellsworth Air Force Base

Box Elder

90

RAPID CITY REGIONAL AIRPORT

44

Rapid Creek

Rapid Valley

Green Valley

ELK VALE RD

214

THE JOURNEY MUSEUM

ST. PATRICK ST

PRAIRIE EDGE TRADING COMPANY AND GALLERIES

Rapid City

90

CAMPBELL ST

CATRON BLVD

79

Spring Creek RD

Spring Creek

Hermosa

79

To Hot Springs

5 mi
5 km

STURGIS RD

90

Blackhawk

NEMO RD

JACKSON BLVD

STORYBOOK ISLAND

16

SHERIDAN LAKE RD

REPTILE GARDENS

BEAR COUNTRY U.S.A.

NECK YOKE RD

RUSH MOUNTAIN ADVENTURE PARK

40

Battle Creek

44

Rapid Creek

Boxelder Creek

Rockerville

S ROCKERVILLE RD

LINCOLN BORGLUM VISITOR CENTER

PRESIDENTIAL TRAIL

Keystone

RUSHMORE TRAMWAY ADVENTURES

1880 TRAIN

IRON MOUNTAIN RD

385

Centennial Trail

Sheridan Lake

16

Mount Rushmore National Memorial

16A

Norbeck Wildlife Preserve

Custer State Park

Pactola Reservoir

Black Hills National Forest

Black Elk Peak

Black Elk Wilderness

Norbeck Wildlife Preserve

Sylvan Lake

Custer State Park

87

NEEDLES HIGHWAY

To Deadwood

Hill City

244

87

89

THE MUSEUM AT BLACK HILLS INSTITUTE

1880 TRAIN

16

385

To Custer

Mickelson Trail

DEERFIELD RD

Spring Creek

© MOON.COM

Exploring Mount Rushmore

Mount Rushmore National Memorial (13000 Hwy. 244, Bldg. 31, Ste. 1, 605/574-2523, www.nps.gov/moru) is nationally and internationally recognized as a symbol of the foundation and expansion of the United States.

The memorial is staffed and the buildings are open 364 days of the year, closed only on Christmas Day; **hours vary seasonally.**

Admission to Mount Rushmore is free, but there is a parking charge of $10, or $5 for a car containing any passenger over the age of 62. Active military personnel park for free. The fees are the same for motorcycles and RVs. Pick up a ticket at the entry to the parking garage; the fee may be paid at one of the machines located in the garage, at the memorial entrance, in the gift shop, or in the café. The **parking permit** is good for a full year from the date of purchase. Since this is a use fee and not an admission fee, national park passes (including the America the Beautiful annual, Senior, Military, Access, and Volunteer passes) do not waive the parking fee. **Walk-ins** and **bicyclists** can visit the monument for free. There are bike racks near the entryway, and bicyclists are welcome to wheel their bikes in with them.

The park is **wheelchair accessible** in most areas, with a zone in front of the entryway for unloading passengers and wheelchairs before parking in the lot. Wheelchairs are also available for loan at the Information Center on a first-come, first-served basis. The Presidential Trail is wheelchair accessible from the Lincoln Borglum Visitor Center to the base of the mountain, but not from the base to the Sculptor's Studio. The Sculptor's Studio is accessible to travelers in wheelchairs and other mobility-impaired visitors only through the remote parking lot, which must be arranged with a park ranger at the Information Center inside the park. All other buildings and sites on the grounds are fully wheelchair accessible, when open. **Service animals** are allowed on the grounds of the park, and there are two pet exercise areas near the upper levels of the parking garage. Other than service animals, pets are not allowed.

HISTORY

Mount Rushmore is the physical manifestation of the imaginations of two men: Doane Robinson and Gutzon Borglum.

Doane Robinson moved to South Dakota to practice law and fell in love with the state. A Renaissance man of sorts, Robinson wrote poetry and fiction. He was also fascinated with South Dakota's history. This interest eventually led to his career as the South Dakota state historian. In this capacity, he wrote many

Mount Rushmore

YOUTH EXPLORATION AREA

MOUNT RUSHMORE NATIONAL MEMORIAL ★

LAKOTA, NAKOTA, AND DAKOTA HERITAGE VILLAGE

Presidential Trail

PRESIDENTIAL TRAIL

Amphitheater

LINCOLN BORGLUM VISITOR CENTER

NPS OFFICE

AVENUE OF FLAGS

BORGLUM VIEWING TERRACE

GRAND VIEW TERRACE

COMPRESSOR HOUSE

SCULPTOR'S STUDIO ★

Nature Trail

To Hill City

Gift Shop

CARVERS CAFÉ/ MEMORIAL TEAM ICE CREAM SHOP

AUDIO TOUR BUILDING

INFORMATION CENTER & BOOKSTORE

To Keystone and Rapid City

PARKING P

PARKING P

EXIT   ENTER

SCALE NOT AVAILABLE

© MOON.COM

historical and biographical papers on South Dakota and collected and archived artifacts for the state historical society. An ardent supporter of the state, Robinson believed that South Dakota could boost its tourism income by creating an attraction that would draw visitors from across the country. It was the dawn of the age of the automobile, and Robinson wanted South Dakota to cash in on this new method of traveling across America. After reading about the Stone Mountain project in Georgia, a mountain-carving project under the direction of sculptor Gutzon Borglum, he was inspired. A huge mountain carving seemed the perfect project, and Robinson contacted the sculptor in 1924 to see if he would be interested in such an endeavor. Borglum accepted the challenge, and the Mount Rushmore project began. While Robinson was the man behind the idea of a mountain carving, it was Borglum's vision of a presidential theme that would finally come to fruition.

Gutzon Borglum, born in Idaho in 1867, spent many of his formative years moving with his family. In addition to Idaho, the family lived in Utah, Nebraska, Kansas, and California, where Borglum began his artistic career. Early success allowed him to pursue his studies overseas. He spent two years in Paris, where he was befriended by the famous French sculptor Auguste Rodin. He spent another year in Spain and five years in England, where he continued to experience a level of success most artists only dream of, including an exhibition of some of his pieces for Queen Victoria at Windsor Castle.

Borglum finally returned to the United States in 1901 and brought with him a desire to create a distinctly American art form. Drawn to large surfaces, one of his first projects was a bust of Abraham Lincoln that stood nearly 40 inches tall and weighed about 375 pounds. Lauded by Lincoln's son, the piece received a lot of media attention. (Today, the bust resides in the rotunda of the capitol in Washington DC.) The Lincoln sculpture inspired the United Daughters of the Confederacy to contact Borglum about creating a bust of Robert E. Lee on Stone Mountain in Georgia. Borglum proposed a much more ambitious project, believing that a single bust would be lost on the large mountainside, and his proposal was accepted.

The Stone Mountain project that Borglum envisioned included Robert E. Lee, Stonewall Jackson, and Jefferson Davis, all on horseback, leading a column of Confederate soldiers. Initially, the carving was done with jackhammers and chisels. Later, a visiting engineer showed Borglum how to employ dynamite with precision, and Borglum incorporated this into his work.

Borglum was a controversial character. Larger than life, highly opinionated, and reputedly short-tempered, he was a man not given to compromise. By the time that Robinson contacted him about working at Mount Rushmore, there was trouble brewing at the Stone Mountain project, and, shortly thereafter, Borglum was dismissed. This freed him to accept the Mount Rushmore project. After his departure from Stone Mountain, all evidence of Borglum's work on the mountain was erased with dynamite. Nevertheless, his experience there provided him with the knowledge he needed to tackle the colossal Mount Rushmore. Work began on Mount Rushmore on October 4, 1927, when Borglum was 60 years old.

Originally, Robinson's thought that Borglum could create a veritable parade of sculptures of American heroes, including Native American as well as the founders and explorers of the new country, on the many spires of the Needles formation near Sylvan Lake. After his first visit to the Black Hills, however, Borglum rejected that plan, as he felt that the Needles would be too fragile to withstand the carving process. He began his own search for a good location and selected the granite of Mount Rushmore. The granite wall faced south, which would provide sunshine in the winter months and allow for a longer carving season. Also, granite is extremely hard and would guarantee that the countenances of Mount Rushmore would gaze over

Immortalized in Stone

Gutzon Borglum believed that for a project as monumental as a mountain carving, it would be best to honor individuals with national recognition and respect. He was looking for visionary leaders, and he elected to make his selection from those who had held the position of president of the United States. His first choices were George Washington and Abraham Lincoln. Soon after, the size of the project increased to include Thomas Jefferson and Theodore Roosevelt. These men were key players in the growth of the United States who were known for great leadership.

- **George Washington** was chosen for his role in gaining America's independence from Great Britain and as the first democratic president of the new country.

- **Abraham Lincoln**'s selection elicited some grumbling on the part of the Southern states, but Borglum maintained that Lincoln deserved recognition and the honor of being a part of this great endeavor. (Borglum admired Lincoln's dedication to the preservation of the Union and his firm belief in equality and freedom.)

- **Thomas Jefferson** authored the Declaration of Independence, a document that inspires emerging democracies to this day. He also had an expansive vision of what America could be, engineering the Louisiana Purchase during his tenure.

- **Theodore Roosevelt** was the most contemporary of the presidents selected. He was also the closest to being a local as well as a national character. Roosevelt owned a ranch in Dakota Territory (in what is now North Dakota). Prior to his presidency, he was famous for his service with the Rough Riders in Cuba during the Spanish-American War. After the famous Battle of San Juan Hill, Roosevelt returned home a popular American hero and became president after William McKinley was assassinated in 1901. He was an active conservationist who used his position to protect wildlife and public lands. Under his tenure, Roosevelt safeguarded over 230 million acres (93 million ha) with the creation of national parks, national forests, game preserves, bird sanctuaries, and national monuments. Roosevelt was also known for taking care of the general public. He spearheaded antitrust legislation, created the Food and Drug Administration, and regulated railroads.

the plains for eons to come. In this, Borglum was correct. It is estimated that erosion on the granite face of Mount Rushmore will total 1 inch (2.5 cm) every 10,000 years.

Once Borglum had the appropriate location for his monumental project, he began to contemplate the form it should take. He wanted the monument to be national rather than regional in nature, so he rejected Robinson's idea of carving local heroes. Instead, Borglum opted for a close look at the country's founding fathers and early leaders, choosing from former presidents of the United States.

The presidents were selected, models made, and the carving commenced. Four hundred people toiled for 14 years to create what we see today. Mount Rushmore is huge. It is hard to get a feel for the sheer size of the monument from the various viewing platforms available

at the mountain's base. George Washington's head is six stories tall; the distance from his forehead to his chin is 60 feet (18 m). His eye alone is 11 feet (3.4 m) wide, and his mouth is 18 feet (5.5 m) wide. If his entire body were carved proportionately, he would be around 465 feet (142 m) tall. Add to those dimensions another three heads, making the monument approximately 60 feet (18 m) high and 185 feet (56 m) wide, and you have some insight into the project's size. The tools used to carve the mountain included pneumatic drills, jackhammers, chisels, and dynamite. The workers would hike the 700 stairs to the top of the mountain every morning, climb into sling chairs (called bosun chairs), and be lowered down the face of the mountain to their carving position for the day. The chairs were affixed to the top of the mountain by 3/8-inch

(1-cm) steel cable, and workers were lowered with winches. This was not a job for someone afraid of heights. Dangerous as it was, there were no fatalities and only a few minor injuries incurred at the monument over the 14 years of carving.

Borglum was the designer and director of the project, but he was not always on-site. While he was off in search of additional funding or working on other commissions, he left his assistants, including his son, Lincoln Borglum, in charge. He would return on a regular basis to inspect the progress of the carving and make corrections and changes to the design as needed in order to work with the rock structure of the mountain.

In March 1941, Gutzon Borglum died in Chicago from complications following surgery. He was just a few days shy of his 74th birthday. With the death of the artist, and at a time when the United States was facing involvement in World War II, the decision was made to discontinue work on the monument as the faces of Mount Rushmore were virtually finished. Lincoln Borglum supervised the final touches and cleanup of the monument site, and in October 1941, the monument was declared complete.

SIGHTS
Information Center and Gift Shop

The first stop on your visit to Mount Rushmore is the **Information Center** (8am-9pm daily summer, 8am-5pm daily off-season) immediately to the right as you walk onto the grounds of the monument. Park rangers provide maps and basic guidance for your visit. Schedules for ranger-guided programs are posted, and a park newspaper is stocked at the center. An audio tour ($6) and a multimedia tour ($8) are available at the Information Center during the winter months; in the summer, the tours are available at the **Self-Guided Tour Building** (9am-4pm daily mid-June-Sept.), directly across the walkway from the Information Center. The audio tour is available in English,

Lakota, German, French, and Spanish. The award-winning *Mount Rushmore Audio Tour: Living Memorial* is two hours long. You can listen to the whole recording or at only a few of the stops along the guided tour. The audio includes historic recordings of Gutzon Borglum, Lincoln Borglum, and Mary Borglum Vhay, as well as the words of some of the original workers on the site. The audio provides an informative narration about the people who envisioned and created the monument as well as details about the presidents selected for the carving and histories of the Lakota people and the Black Hills region, including interviews with Native Americans regarding their feelings about the monument. The recording is punctuated by music and sound effects. The multimedia tour is an upgrade to the wand-based audio tour. Visitors receive a smartphone-sized device that includes photos and videos which complement the narrative of the tour. The old photos and videos of the construction and Borglum working on a model of the monument are particularly interesting. In addition, the multimedia tour includes the Junior Ranger Quest game that provides 16 challenges for kids. Upon completion of the challenges, they receive a Junior Ranger badge from the ranger desk in the Information Center or in the Lincoln Borglum Visitor Center.

The **Gift Shop** (9am-10:30pm daily mid-May-mid-Aug., 9am-between 6pm and 8pm off-season) is housed in the first building to your left after the Information Center at the entryway to the monument grounds. The shop is large and well stocked with every kind of branded item you could desire, including photos, T-shirts, sweatshirts, caps, books about the carving and the region, regionally made products, and other items useful to travelers (including sunscreen!).

Avenue of Flags

The **Avenue of Flags** was added to the grounds of Mount Rushmore as part of the celebration of the U.S. Bicentennial in 1976. It was a visitor to the monument who suggested the addition. In 2019 the avenue was renovated to make it more accessible and to better serve visitors. As you enter the park, flags line the pedestrian walkway and form a colorful frame for the majestic presidential faces straight ahead. Fifty-six flags are on display, one for each state, district, commonwealth, and territory of the United States. Beneath the flags are plaques that reveal the date that statehood was attained for each of the corresponding flags displayed. Delaware was the first state of the Union in 1787. South Dakota was the 40th state to be admitted, over 100 years later, in 1889. The states and the District of Columbia account for 51 of the flags on display. The other five include the three U.S. territories (Guam, American Samoa and the Virgin Islands) and two commonwealths (the Commonwealth of Puerto Rico and the Commonwealth of the Northern Mariana Islands). The flags are arranged in alphabetical order, starting at the entrance and moving toward the monument. Keep the kids on the lookout for your home state plaque and flag!

Grand View Terrace

The pedestrian walkway that begins at the entrance to the monument and passes through the Avenue of Flags terminates at the **Grand View Terrace.** Appropriately named, this viewpoint looks straight across at Mount Rushmore and is one of the most popular locations at the memorial for photographs of the monument. Directly in front of the Grand View Terrace, but below the sight line to the monument, is the outdoor **amphitheater** used for evening programs during the summer months. The **Evening Lighting Ceremony** occurs at 9pm from Memorial Day to mid-August and at 8pm from mid August to September. October-March, the sculpture is illuminated at sunset, but there is no ceremony.

★ Lincoln Borglum Visitor Center

The **Lincoln Borglum Visitor Center**

(8am-10pm daily late May-mid Aug., 8am-9pm daily mid-Aug.-Sept., 8am-5pm daily off-season) is the main visitor center at the memorial. It is on the lower level of the Grand View Terrace and accessible by staircases on either side of the terrace or by elevators on the Washington side of the monument. Geared toward interactive education, the exhibits include a timeline of U.S. history, including the Civil War, westward expansion, and the Indian Wars. Here you'll learn about Mount Rushmore's sculptor, Gutzon Borglum, and about the workers who carved a mountain while dangling off the face of a cliff.

Part of the fun of Mount Rushmore is gleaning the facts about what it takes to carve a mountain. Knowing that Washington's nose is 21 feet (6.4 m) long (a foot longer than any of the other presidents' noses!), that all the faces are 60 feet (18 m) tall, and that it took 400 workers more than 14 years to create this icon adds to the experience.

Two small theaters in the museum provide a continuous screening of the film *Mount Rushmore, The Shrine,* about the carving and the artist behind it. It is filled with historical photographs of the work and the time period. The film is narrated by Tom Brokaw and starts every 20 minutes. The bookstore in the visitor center is run by the Mount Rushmore Society. The store features many books about Mount Rushmore and the Black Hills region, as well as those by local writers.

Borglum Viewing Terrace

From the Grand View Terrace, follow the concrete pathway on the Lincoln side of the monument to the **Borglum Viewing Terrace,** the site of the sculptor's first temporary studio, where he worked before a more spacious studio was built closer to the mountain. It is also reachable via the Nature Trail. This feature is not wheelchair accessible.

Just yards away from the Grand View Terrace, the Borglum Viewing Terrace offers a completely different perspective of the monument. More natural in its overall feel, here the view of the presidents is framed by large ponderosa pines—and the faces of Washington and Roosevelt dominate.

The Borglum Viewing Terrace is the only area at the memorial available for weddings. Couples wishing to use the terrace may do so by permit only. With the exception of the period of June 25-July 4 and Christmas Day, weddings are allowed year-round. The cost of using Mount Rushmore as a wedding site is based on the number of rangers assigned to the special event and the length of the ceremony.

Sculptor's Studio

The **Sculptor's Studio** (8am-8pm daily late-May-mid-Aug., 8am-7pm daily mid-Aug.-Sept., check at the information center for hours after Sept.) is at the bottom of the hill just past the Borglum Viewing Terrace. This was Borglum's second studio on-site and contains the working model for Mount Rushmore. The model displayed at the studio is, in fact, the second model for the mountain carving. The first had Jefferson situated to the left of Washington from a viewer's perspective. Much work was carried out on that initial plan until it was discovered that the rock face where Jefferson was originally going to be carved was not stable. Jefferson was dynamited off the face of the mountain, a new model was created, and Jefferson was moved to his current location between Roosevelt and Lincoln.

In addition to the model for the monument, the Sculptor's Studio displays a collection of tools and narrative descriptions of how these tools were used in the carving. There are several early photographs of Mount Rushmore before and after the carving, as well as many photos of the carving in process. A small bookstore is also located in the studio.

The model displayed at the Sculptor's Studio is markedly different from the final project. All the presidents were originally to be carved from head to waist. When Gutzon Borglum died in March 1941, it was determined that with the artist gone and the country facing World War II work on the

monument would not be able to progress. It was decided to leave the monument as it was since the faces were complete and additional carving was deemed unnecessary. Also, because it was Borglum's vision, declaring the monument finished upon his death honored the sculptor. Lincoln Borglum, Gutzon Borglum's son, spent a few more months on the monument after his father's death, supervising the final work on the project and the cleanup of the site.

Ranger talks are given at the studio about the artist's original working model, about the men who carved the mountain, and about the tools and methods used to carve stone. The talks last about 15 minutes and are given throughout the summer. The studio is wheelchair accessible, but getting to it requires making arrangements with the rangers at the Information Center at the monument entrance for close-in parking.

★ Presidential Trail

The **Presidential Trail** is a pleasant 0.5-mile (0.8-km) loop that brings visitors to the closest viewing points for the monument. The trail is wheelchair accessible from the Washington side of the Grand View Terrace to the base of the mountain. It is not accessible from that point on, as there are a total of 450 wooden stairs that climb partially up the mountain and then continue down to the Sculptor's Studio.

It is not uncommon to see mountain goats along this trail—particularly near the beginning at the Grand View Terrace and at the higher locations of the staircase mountainside. These beautiful white animals with contrasting black noses and hooves are not native to the region. In 1924, Canada gave six Rocky Mountain goats to Custer State Park. The goats escaped from their pens and have adapted well to the environment of the hills. There are now estimated to be more than

---

1: Thomas Jefferson's original location on the mountain 2: early model of Mount Rushmore 3: the Avenue of Flags

200 goats in the Black Hills, mainly around Black Elk Peak, Sylvan Lake, Crazy Horse Memorial, and Mount Rushmore.

Lakota, Nakota, and Dakota Heritage Village

Mount Rushmore has always been controversial among the Lakota people. The Black Hills are sacred to them, and the presence of a large sculpture honoring U.S. presidents in the middle of the hills isn't exactly welcomed by all. In recognition of the legitimacy of their sentiments, it was decided that the memorial should also acknowledge the culture of Native peoples at the site.

What is now the **Lakota, Nakota, and Dakota Heritage Village** (10:30am-3pm Tues. and Thurs. early June-mid-Aug.) began with one tipi just off the Presidential Trail. Over the years, the seasonal program has expanded and additional tipis were added. The site was established to highlight the customs and traditions of local American Indian communities. Check with the information desk to verify the schedule for ranger talks at the village on the day of your visit. Take the Presidential Trail from the George Washington side of the monument; the village is located off the trail near the **Youth Exploration Area.**

The Nature Trail

Most visitors enter the park via the wide entryway above the parking lot. However, the **Nature Trail** is a quieter way to approach the monument. As you leave the parking lot, the first structure you encounter is a covered hallway that stretches to the left and right. Continuing straight ahead will bring you to the main entryway. Instead, take a right, follow the hallway, and skirt the edge of the parking lot. (This would be the far right-hand side of the parking lot, closest to the monument as you face the presidents.) The trail is short, not more than 0.25 mile (0.4 km). It is a concrete walkway, but it winds through the sweetly scented ponderosa pines and ends at the scenic Borglum Viewing

Terrace. Before taking the trail, you might want to stop at the Information Center just inside the monument grounds to pick up a map to orient yourself. Alternatively, consider using the trail to return to the parking lot when it's time to leave. This trail is frequently closed during the winter months due to ice.

ACTIVITIES
Ranger-Led Programs

Several ranger-led programs are offered at Mount Rushmore during the summer months. The programs begin near the end of May and cease at the end of summer (the closing date varies from year to year). All of the programs are free. Check with the Information Center or at the Lincoln Borglum Visitor Center on arrival to determine which programs are offered during your visit. Note that many of the programs are suspended during the annual Sturgis Motorcycle Rally held in early August.

Look for the 30-minute **Ranger Walk** that follows the Presidential Trail to the base of the mountain carving. The discussion includes information about the four presidents selected for the monument and about the natural and cultural history of Mount Rushmore and the Black Hills. Other 30-minute talks may include details about the wildlife and plantlife of the region.

A fascinating 15-minute **Sculpture Studio Talk** is presented at the Sculptor's Studio. This program includes a discussion about the tools used to carve the mountain, stories about some of the workers on the mountain, and information about the first model for the sculpture. Samples of the tools are on hand, as is the model for the current sculpture.

The seasonal **Evening Program** (9pm daily Memorial Day-mid-Aug., 8pm daily mid-Aug.-Sept.) is the most popular program in the park. Attended by upward of 2,500 people a night during the summer months, it is an inspirational program lasting 45 minutes about the presidents, patriotism, and our nation's history. A short film entitled *America's Lasting Legacy* is shown, and the program ends with the singing of the national anthem, a flag ceremony honoring military personnel past and present, and the **lighting of the monument.** While the monument is lit from sunset to 9pm from October through the following March, there is no program presentation to accompany the lighting during this period.

Junior Ranger Program

All the informational areas in the park carry free **Junior Ranger Program** activity books. Three booklets are available. One program is designed for children ages 3 5 (Junior Ranger Trainees), one for children ages 5-12 (Junior Ranger), and a third program (Rushmore Ranger) is designed to enhance the Mount Rushmore experience for adults and children ages 13 and older. On completion of the activities, which generally take 30-60 minutes, young participants will receive a Junior Ranger badge and a certificate of completion. Older children and adults also receive a certificate of completion. Another Junior Ranger option is available for those who elect to take the park's multimedia tour. Junior Ranger Quest poses 16 challenges at different spots at the site. With the completion of 12 of the 16 challenges, participants receive a Junior Ranger badge at a ranger desk. The programs include activities designed to educate the participant on the monument's history and ecology.

Youth Exploration Area

This interactive outdoor learning space is aimed primarily at the preteen crowd, giving them a hands-on opportunity to learn about the wildlife, plants, and history of Mount Rushmore. It's located in the first section of the Presidential Trail. Ranger-led presentations may focus on educational games, animal pelts, or state flags. A daily schedule is posted at the Information Center. Activities at this outdoor location take place only during summer months.

FOOD

Carvers Café (9am-5pm daily late June-mid-Aug., 9am-4:30 daily off-season, $13) is near the entrance to the monument grounds on the Lincoln side of the sculpture and provides the only dining facilities on-site. It is a food court-style venue, with selections including hamburgers, pizza, pot roast, chicken, and premade salads. The food is consistently good. The café is the only three-star certified green restaurant in South Dakota. One of its initiatives is to "choose to be straw free" as 500 million straws used daily in the U.S. end up in landfills or littering the landscape. In the high summer season, the café can be busy but service is quick. Keystone and Hill City are two neighboring communities that offer alternative dining options just minutes away.

Memorial Team Ice Cream Shop (11am-9pm daily mid-May-Labor Day) is in the same building as the Carvers Café—the first building on your right past the Information Center as you enter the memorial grounds. The ice cream is great and well worth a small wait. When the ice cream shop is closed between Labor Day and mid-May, you can still get the same delicious ice cream in the Carvers Café.

GETTING THERE AND AROUND

The grounds of Mount Rushmore are relatively compact. Once there, moving from site to site is all by foot. The distances are not great, and there are no shuttles available. The city center of Keystone is just 2.5 miles (4 km) east of Mount Rushmore. Hill City is about 11 miles (17.8 km) north and west of Mount Rushmore. Rapid City is about 24 miles (39 km) northeast from the monument. Any of these cities would serve as a good base location for travel throughout the Central Hills region.

Car

The best way to travel throughout the region is by car. If you fly into Rapid City, which has the only commercial airport in the Black Hills, there are several car rental agencies at the airport, including **Avis** (605/393-0740), **Budget** (605/393-0488), **Hertz/Enterprise** (605/393-0160), and **Alamo/National** (605/393-2664). Mount Rushmore is just 32 miles (52 km) from the Rapid City Airport. **Wheelchair-accessible vans** are available for rental on a per day or per week basis in Rapid City at **Black Hawk Vans** (3156 Haines Ave., 605/342-2104, www.blackhawkvans.com) and **Casey's Auto Rental Service** (1318 5th St., 605/343-2277, www.caseyscorner.com).

Tour Companies

For those who fly into Rapid City and prefer to let someone else take the wheel, there are several tour companies that provide service to Mount Rushmore. Tours are available from several communities in the Black Hills. Each company has a slightly different offering. **Mount Rushmore Tours** (2255 Fort Hayes Dr., Rapid City, 605/343-3113 or 888/343-3113, www.mountrushmoretours.com, mid-May-mid-Oct.) provides two all-day tour itineraries. The first tour package is a full day of activities including a cowboy breakfast, a daylong tour of the hills, and a chuckwagon supper and musical show at Fort Hays, where parts of *Dances with Wolves* was filmed (adult $109, child 12 and under $57). The second tour does not include the chuckwagon supper (adult $90, child $47). Both tours are narrated on a good-size charter bus which visits Mount Rushmore, Custer State Park—including Needles Highway—and Crazy Horse. Both tours begin at the Fort Hays site. The buses do not have lifts for wheelchairs; however, the tour company is happy to make the arrangements for a wheelchair-accessible van rental and private tour of the hills. Call for additional information.

Affordable Adventures (5542 Meteor St., Rapid City, 605/342-7691, www.affordableadventuresbh.com, 7am-9pm daily) has deep family roots in the Black Hills—back to the mining days of the Homestake Mine in Lead! They offer four tours that include Mount Rushmore. A 3-hour tour includes the Evening Lighting Ceremony ($45 pp), a 4-hour tour is spent at Mount Rushmore ($70 pp), and a 6- to 7-hour tour includes Mount Rushmore and Crazy Horse ($125 pp). The longest tour, which lasts 9-10 hours, includes Mount Rushmore, Crazy Horse, and the Custer State Park Wildlife Loop ($145 pp). Riders will be picked up in the Rapid City area and travel in a Lincoln Town Car or a 12- or 14-passenger van depending on the size of the party. Affordable Adventures is also available for several different short or all-day tours in the hills as well as for custom tours.

Helicopter Tours

Black Hills Aerial Adventures (313 Speck Center Rd., Keystone, on the north side of Keystone adjacent to the Baymont Inn & Suites, 605/646-4801, www.coptertours.com, 9am-7pm daily mid-May-Oct., $49-205) has been offering tours throughout the Black Hills for years. The company has three locations in the region: Custer, Keystone, and the Badlands. The six different flights include a short introductory ride; tours featuring Mount Rushmore, Crazy Horse, Black Elk Peak, and Custer State Park; or a longer, 35-mile flight covering most of the central Black Hills. Pick the starting location closest to the sights you wish to go to as flight costs are based on mileage. The Keystone location is the closest to Mount Rushmore offering tours of Mount Rushmore, with prices ranging from $49-110.

Keystone

Minutes from the grounds of Mount Rushmore National Memorial, Keystone is a tourist mecca in the hills. It's a town with a lot of hustle and bustle—a change from the generally quiet pace of the region—and it is *the* place to get souvenirs. Keystone is nestled in a narrow gorge, and many of the shops and activities are along two sections of U.S. 16A, which passes right through the heart of town. The first cluster of shops and restaurants is near the intersection of Highway 40 and the 1880 Train depot. The second cluster of small shops and restaurants is at the Keystone Mall, which is closer to Mount Rushmore, about 1 mile (1.6 km) farther south on U.S. 16A. Finally, look for some interesting shops and historic spots in "old town" Keystone, which is just east of town on Highway 40. Since tourism is the mainstay of the Keystone's economy, there are plenty of lodging options, and the energy level of the community is high during the height of the season. In winter, however, Keystone is extremely quiet. While there are some amenities in town during the winter, they are limited.

Mount Rushmore is open all year, but visitation drops dramatically in the autumn. As a result, many shops, restaurants, and attractions in Keystone begin to close in mid-September, and most are closed by the end of October. Late-season travelers will still be able to find accommodations and a few intriguing shops open. Dining options will be limited. Off-season pricing is always reasonable.

HISTORY

Keystone's story, like that of most of the communities in the hills, is centered on mining. The historic center of town is off the beaten path, just east of the downtown area. Follow Highway 40 east a few blocks to find some of Keystone's more historic buildings. While gold, mica, feldspar, tin, and many rare minerals were a part of Keystone's past, Mount Rushmore ensures its future.

SIGHTS
★ 1880 Train

The main terminal of the Hill City-Keystone **1880 Train** (103 Winter St., 605/574-2222, www.1880train.com, mid-May-mid-Oct., round-trip adult $32, child ages 3-12 $16, one-way adult $27, child ages 3-12 $14) is based in Hill City, but the loop can be made from either terminal. The round-trip narrated ride takes a little more than two hours.

Like many of the attractions in the hills, **operating hours**—and in this case, number of train departures—vary almost weekly as spring leads into the busy summer season and then back into the quieter schedules of fall. Verify departure times before you arrive. Reservations can be made for assigned seating by train car (open-sided cars or enclosed cars with big windows) and are recommended at least two weeks in advance during the busy summer months and during the Sturgis Motorcycle Rally, a 10-day period in August beginning on the first Friday of the month. Passengers select both their departure and return times. **Tickets** are usually available on a walk-in basis the last week in May, the first week of June, and again in late August, as children return to school. Throughout the season, there are four possible departure times for a round-trip ride from the Keystone terminal: 8:45am, 11:15am, 2:30pm, and 5pm. One-way trips are available but the cost and the coordination of the return by another route make it a less appealing option.

If you are a steam aficionado, check with the ticket office or when making your reservation; the train roster includes three steam and two diesel engines. Riding a train is an experience that many people never have the opportunity to enjoy. It's slow-paced and

Keystone

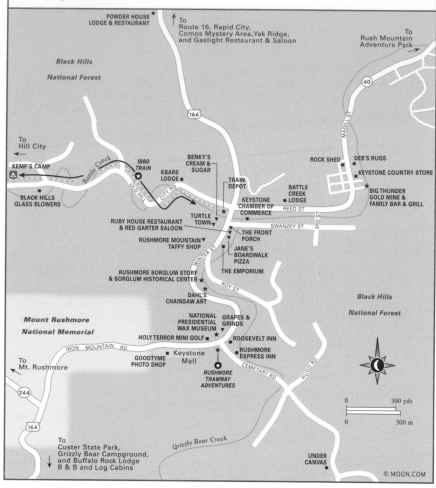

POWDER HOUSE
LODGE & RESTAURANT

To
Route 16, Rapid City,
Comos Mystery Area, Yak Ridge,
and Gaslight Restaurant & Saloon

To
Rush Mountain
Adventure Park

Black Hills

National Forest

16A

40

MADILL ST

To
Hill City

KEMP'S CAMP

Battle Creek

1880
TRAIN

KBARS
LODGE

BENKY'S
CREAM &
SUGAR

ROCK SHED

DEB'S RUGS

KEYSTONE COUNTRY STORE

OLD HILL CITY RD

TRAIN
DEPOT

BLACK HILLS
GLASS BLOWERS

BATTLE
CREEK
LODGE

BIG THUNDER
GOLD MINE &
FAMILY BAR & GRILL

KEYSTONE
CHAMBER OF
COMMERCE

REED ST

3RD ST

RUBY HOUSE RESTAURANT
& RED GARTER SALOON

TURTLE
TOWN

SWANZEY ST

RUSHMORE MOUNTAIN
TAFFY SHOP

THE FRONT
PORCH

WINTER ST

JANE'S
BOARDWALK
PIZZA

RUSHMORE BORGLUM STORY
& BORGLUM HISTORICAL CENTER

THE EMPORIUM

ROY ST

DAHL'S
CHAINSAW ART

Black Hills

National Forest

Mount Rushmore

National Memorial

NATIONAL
PRESIDENTIAL
WAX MUSEUM

GRAPES &
GRINDS

HOLY TERROR MINI GOLF

ROOSEVELT INN

IRON MOUNTAIN RD

To
Mt. Rushmore

GOODTYME
PHOTO SHOP

Keystone
Mall

RUSHMORE
EXPRESS INN

CEMETARY RD

HUGO RD

RUSHMORE
TRAMWAY
ADVENTURES

244

16A

0   300 yds

0   300 m

To
Custer State Park,
Grizzly Bear Campground,
and Buffalo Rock Lodge
B & B and Log Cabins

Grizzly Bear Creek

UNDER
CANVAS

© MOON.COM

relaxing—a good time to sit back and wave at the folks who are waiting at the train crossing for the train to pass by and to enjoy a few peaceful hours gazing at the scenery with someone else at the wheel. Take the morning train from Keystone, shop the Hill City galleries, have lunch on the patio of the Alpine Inn, and return to Keystone for the evening—perhaps for the Evening Lighting Ceremony at Mount Rushmore.

Dahl's Chainsaw Art

Part "site" and part "shop," **Dahl's Chainsaw Art** (121 Roy St., 605/639-0733, www. dahlschainsawart.com, 8:30am-9:30pm May-Sept., call for hours off-season) is a fun place to stop and admire some gigantic wood carvings and sculptures, as well as purchase the carved bears, eagles, and other creations. The site also offers some great photo moments in the form of giant chairs, carved motorcycles, and even a giant Sasquatch. It is a spot that is hard to miss. Heading toward Mount Rushmore on U.S. 16A from the downtown boardwalk area, look for it on the left side of the road.

National Presidential Wax Museum

The **National Presidential Wax Museum** (609 U.S. 16A, 605/666-4455, www.presidentialwaxmuseum.com, 8:30am-8pm daily Memorial Day-Labor Day, 9am-5pm Labor Day-Oct. and early Mar.-Memorial Day, adult $11, senior, active/retired military, and child $9) is a favorite of history buffs. On the self-guided tour, the wax figures of all the presidents to date are portrayed in exhibits that illustrate the key events of their period in office. Visitors are provided with a wand that, at the press of a button, will describe the history behind each display. The timeline of the presidency is a unique way to follow the history of the United States and its development as a country. Before walking through the museum, watch the video about how the wax figures are created. If traveling with children, ask for the scavenger hunt.

Old Town Walking Tour

History buffs interested in walking the older sections of Keystone will enjoy getting a copy of a small brochure and map outlining the **Old Town Walking Tour.** Nineteen storyboards throughout the original downtown include old photos and descriptions of some of the buildings and interesting tidbits about the old mining community. There are an additional 11 plaques through the "new town." Brochures are provided in flip-up boxes around the community, as handouts in many of the retail businesses in town, as well as at the tourist information kiosk at the traffic light at Highway 40 and U.S. 16A.

Big Thunder Gold Mine

The **Big Thunder Gold Mine** (604 Blair, Hwy. 40, 605/666-4847, www.bigthundermine.com, 8am-8pm daily June-Aug., 9am-6pm May and Sept., 9am-5pm Apr. and Oct., adult $12, child ages 6-12 $9), just a few blocks east of U.S. 16A on Highway 40, is a replica of the mine that used to operate on that site. The **mine tour** includes some interesting facts about the history of mining in Keystone as well as access to the adjacent **museum,** which displays a collection of

chainsaw art by Jarrett and Jordan Dahl at Dahl's Chainsaw Art

mining equipment. The last tour of the day goes out one hour before close. In addition to the mine tours, two different options are available for **gold panning**. On-site panning lessons ($10 with the mine tour, $12 without) are the highlight of the mine experience. It seems everyone likes to pan for gold. Staring raptly at the bottom of their gold pans, children and adults alike demonstrate how easy it is to catch gold fever. Claim-panning expeditions (half-day adult $50, child ages 6-16 $40, full-day adult $80, child ages 6-16 $65) are also available. On these excursions, gold seekers drive their own car, following the guide, to a U.S. Forest Service claim site. Reservations are required at least 24 hours in advance for the claim site mining tours. Big Thunder Gold Mine also has a small but nice gift shop and the **Big Thunder Family Bar & Grill** ($15) on-site should the exertion of panning make the family hungry.

Cosmos Mystery Area

Everyone over the age of seven approaches the **Cosmos Mystery Area** (24040 Cosmos Rd., 605/343-9802, www.cosmosmysteryarea.com, 9am-5pm daily Apr.-Oct., adult $12, child ages 5-11 $6, child 4 and under free) with a healthy dose of skepticism. After all, visitors are told that they will change heights, water will run uphill, and a mysterious force will create all sorts of mind-boggling experiences. It's a fun tour (about 40 minutes) where skepticism turns to confusion. Children are confounded and hooked after the first narrated demonstration. Adults take a little longer, but by the time the tour is over, everyone is scratching their heads wondering, "How did they do that?"

In addition to the mystery house tour, the site now has a **geode mine** ($8 or $6 if purchased with the mystery house tour) which offers the opportunity to dig for a geode (finding one is guaranteed) and then cracking it open to be displayed at home. It's fun for kids to see the beauty that can be found inside an ordinary-looking rock.

Cosmos is off of U.S. 16 on Cosmos Road.

Look for the signs. The site, open seasonally, is before the exit to Mount Rushmore if you are headed to the hills from Rapid City. It is about 17 miles (27 km) from Rapid City and minutes away from Keystone.

Rush Mountain Adventure Park

The main attraction at **Rush Mountain Adventure Park** (13622 Hwy. 40, 605/255-4384, www.rushmtn.com, 10am-6pm daily Memorial Day weekend, June-Aug., and Labor Day weekend, 9am-5pm daily May and Sept.-Oct.) is Rushmore Cave, but over time the offerings have grown to include other family activities, including the Gunslinger 7-D Interactive Ride, the Soaring Eagle Zipride, the Mountain Coaster, and a three-story aboveground obstacle course for adults and children. An all-day wristband (adult $60, child ages 5-12 $55, child 4 and under $35, add $5 to ticket price to include a cave tour) allows for unlimited rides but does not include access to the Wingwalker fitness challenge area.

About 5 miles (8 km) east of Keystone on Highway 40 is **Rushmore Cave** (standard cave tour adult $17, child ages 5-12 $11), discovered in 1876 by gold miners digging into the mountain to find a water source to bring to their mine below. The cave was opened to the public in 1927. The standard one-hour fun and informational tour runs continuously throughout the day on a well-maintained and well-lit path through a nice array of stalactites and stalagmites. There are several different cave rooms to see: the "Big Room" is impressively large and filled with interesting formations. Remember that caves remain cool—generally around 58°F (14.4°C) even in the hottest part of summer—so you'll want to bring a sweatshirt to keep warm.

The **Gunslinger 7-D Interactive Ride** ($12) is a three-dimensional gunfight that lasts a quick five minutes for those who find the experience exhilarating and a long five minutes for those who feel the 3-D movement too intensely. Participants are provided with 3-D glasses and a laser gun and strapped into chairs that move with the action on the screen. It's like a roller coaster and 3-D film combined and very realistic. (Folks who find the rushing trains, rivers, and canyon falls too dizzy can unplug themselves). Gunslingers need to be at least 42 inches (107 cm) tall.

The **Soaring Eagle Zipride** ($12) is a short, quick (zippy, as it were) ride down and back up the side of the mountain.

The **Mountain Coaster** (driver $17, passenger $12) is a 3,400-foot (1,036-m) ride that looks like a combination of alpine slide and sled train. It twists and turns down the mountain with good views of the local hills.

The **Wingwalker** and **Sky Tykes** offer above-the-ground physical challenges to adults and children. (Think balance beams and rope walking!) Safety harnesses and backup lines are provided (required), and staff are always on hand to ensure all participant are using the equipment safely. Call for pricing and hours as this is the first activity cut when there are staff shortages or weather issues.

RECREATION
★ **Rushmore Tramway Adventures**
Rushmore Tramway Adventures

(203 Cemetery Rd., 605/666-4478, www.rushmoretramwayadventures.com, 9:30am-6pm daily June-early Aug., 9:30am-5pm daily early Aug.-Labor Day, 10am-4pm Sat.-Sun. May and Labor Day-end of Sept., weather permitting) has a lot to offer for a day of family fun, including the **Scenic Chairlift** and **Alpine Slide** (round-trip chairlift: adult $12, child up to age 5 $8; chairlift up and alpine slide down: adult $16, child up to age 5 with adult $8). The lift is right in Keystone and climbs the ridge of a mountain on a relaxing and quiet ride. On the way up, watch the faces of the folks enjoying the alpine slide, which looks much like a sled on small wheels. There are two tracks on the trip down. One is for the slowpokes, many of whom look terrified as they ride their brakes down the hill; the other is for the racers, who zoom down the hill with a look of sheer manic bliss on their faces. This is a ride for all ages, but not necessarily for the timid.

At the top, there are boardwalk viewing decks, from which there are distant vistas of Mount Rushmore and lofty views of the town of Keystone just below. The rock and flower gardens at the top are beautifully done, and the casual **George's Grill** ($7) serves brats, burgers, and chicken sandwiches. It's a lovely

Rushmore Tramway Adventures

spot with great views surrounded by gardens. Beer is available also, though it would likely not be a good idea to imbibe heavily and then alpine slide down the hill. After enjoying the gardens and the views, slide or ride the chairlift down.

For visitors who enjoy a little adrenaline rush, there are more activities waiting. The **Aerial Adventure Park** (adult $50, child ages 6-9 $45) brings guests into the trees. Eight different courses are geared toward skill sets from beginner to expert climbers. It's an aerial obstacle course with over 100 platforms, rope ladders, suspension bridges, 11 integrated ziplines, and lots of nets. With a ticket comes a 15-minute briefing on harnessing and safety and 90 minutes of free access to all of the aerial courses for adults and five of the courses for children. Those who fear heights and speed should wait it out at the hilltop gardens. Wear closed-toe shoes and comfortable clothing!

Relatively new to the park is the **Tubing Hill** (1 ride $14, 3 rides $19, 5 rides $22). Riders will tube around 400 feet (122 m) down the hill. There are slow courses and fast courses available.

True adrenaline junkies will enjoy the 60-foot (18-m) **Freefall Tower** ($20) and/or the 800-foot (244-m) stand-alone **Zipline** ($25). Riders on this zipline are buckled into a harness, but there is no real seat, no way to hold on, and no hands necessary for the flight.

The **Pinnacle Zip Tour** ($110) is a two-hour narrated adventure, complete with a guide. The tour covers over 1 mile (1.6 km) of mountaintop and features five side-by-side ziplines that reach heights up to 400 feet (122 m). Participants must be at least 48 inches (122 cm) tall. Reservations can be made for this tour (all other attractions at the park are first-come, first-served), but they aren't required.

Miniature Golf

Playing at **Holy Terror Mini Golf** (609 U.S. 16A, 605/666-5170, www.holyterrorminigolf. com, 9:30am-9pm daily mid-May-Sept., weather permitting, adult $10, child ages 6-12

$8, child under 6 free) is a fun way to expend a little energy (especially for the kids) when visiting Keystone. The 18-hole minicourse is nestled into the side of the mountain, and the views from some of the tees are quite pretty, with the lights and hustle-bustle of Keystone down below. Plan on getting a little exercise on this course, as there are more than a couple of steep climbs!

SHOPPING

Keystone has something for every visitor. Kitschy souvenir shops and T-shirt emporiums are right next door to places featuring art and expensive specialty gifts. As is common in most seasonal tourist areas, shops can change from year to year; sometimes the best way to find a treasure is to park the car and go walking. Off-season hours can be fairly whimsical, so it might not be a bad idea to call first if you are planning on visiting a specific place. Look for funky specialty shops in the historic center of Keystone off Highway 40 east of U.S. 16A. Along U.S. 16A (the main road to Mount Rushmore), there are two distinct shopping districts. The first, called "the strip," is a boardwalk near the 1880 Train station at the junction of U.S. 16A and Highway 40. Farther south and closer to Mount Rushmore on U.S. 16A is the Keystone Mall.

In Keystone's old town look for **The Rock Shed** (515 1st St., 605/666-4813 or 866/354-0894, www.therockshed.com, 9am-7pm daily May-Aug., 9am-5pm daily Sept.-Apr., call to confirm hours in winter), one of the enduring shopping spots in Keystone. In business since 1968, and family owned for 37 years, the store specializes in rocks, gemstones, fossils, and minerals. It's a beautiful little shop with bins and bins of sorted rocks and minerals for sale by the pound outside and a clean and organized collection available inside. If you like rock-related products, there are some unique and exquisite items to be found here including jewelry and jewelry-making supplies. They also carry rock tumblers and books on rocks and minerals.

Across the street from The Rock Shed is

Deb's Rugs (510 1st St., 605/666-4679 or 605/381-4400, 10am-5pm daily Memorial Day-Labor Day or by appt., winter hours weather dependent or by appt.), a small shop selling woven rugs, scarves, place mats, baby blankets, and other products such as woven buffalo hide for coasters and table runners. If you enjoy the work of local artisans, check this store out. It's a tiny enterprise run by Deb Lervaag, who works on-site at one of her looms set up in the middle of the shop floor. In Keystone since 2000, Deb is happy to provide custom work.

For fans of everything Victorian, the beautiful dolls residing at **The Emporium** (160 Winter St., 605/666-4836, 10am-6pm daily May, 10am-9pm daily Memorial Day-Labor Day, hours vary Sept.-Oct.) have been a fixture of the Keystone boardwalk since the 1980s. Under the same ownership for the past eight years, the shop features jewelry, nice gifts, and specially themed rooms—one for Christmas items and another for fall and Halloween.

The **Goodtyme Photo Shop** (804 U.S. 16A, 605/666-4619, 10am-7pm Mon.-Wed., 9am-7pm Thurs.-Sun. May-Oct., 10am-5pm Thurs.-Sun. Apr.) is a great place to get something unusual for a souvenir. Take a family photo and bring the Old West home. Photos can be sepia, color highlighted, full color, or black and white. The shop offers 13 different sets, including an Old West bar, a jailhouse, a sod house, a Victorian parlor, a buffalo scene, and a bathtub, all of which are Western or Victorian in nature. And then, just for something different, you can dress like Bonnie and Clyde and pose in front of a 1920s car.

Located just 1 mile (1.6 km) outside of town on the Old Hill City Road, **Black Hills Glass Blowers** (909 Old Hill City Rd., 605/666-4542, www.blackhillsglassblowers.com, 9am-5pm Mon.-Sat., 11am-5pm Sun. mid-May-mid.-Sept., call for hours off-season) is a unique studio and retail shop where beautiful wineglasses, water glasses, plates, vases, and glass figurines are created as you watch. Artisans Peter Hopkins and Gail Damin

have been working together for decades and opened their studio and shop in Keystone in 1991. Each of them is proficient at creating both blown glass (off-hand work) and lamp-worked pieces. While there are no scheduled demonstrations of glasswork, one of them is likely to be at it anytime the shop is open.

FOOD
Casual Dining

One of the coziest spots in town, the ★ **Powder House Restaurant** (24125 U.S. 16A, 605/666-5214 or 800/321-0692, www. powderhouselodge.com, 7am-9pm daily Memorial Day-Labor Day, 7am-11am and 4pm-9pm May and Sept.-mid Oct., breakfast $9-15, lunch $12-15, dinner $17-35) serves up the best breakfast and meals in the area. It's a comfortable restaurant with lots of windows, wood-paneled walls, and booths. The Powder House Lodge serves all the breakfast standards like pancakes, French toast, and egg dishes, with great skillets and specialty items including steak or trout with eggs. Lunch selections range from elk, bison, and beef burgers to salads, club sandwiches, and—the specialty—bison stew. The dinner menu includes the sandwiches offered at lunch but also features pasta, fish, and more vegetarian options. Several varieties of beef cuts and game—including prime rib, bison, and elk—round out the options. Gluten-free items are highlighted on the menu to assist diners with their choices. For the curious, one of the house specialties is a game sampler that includes bison short rib, elk medallion, bison sausage, and a blended game sausage. There is also an excellent selection of wines. The location of the restaurant is the inspiration for its name; it sits on the spot where one of the mining companies in town once stored explosives.

The **Front Porch** (115 Swanzey, 605/666-4041, 7am-9pm daily May-Oct., breakfast $10-14, lunch and dinner $14-25) is the cornerstone of the Keystone boardwalk. With a wraparound deck for outside dining and a light-filled interior, this is a great option for a meal downtown. It's a family operation, and the staff are uniformly courteous and friendly. Breakfast (served until 11am) features several omelets, French toast, hotcakes, and the standard eggs, hash browns, and a choice of meat. Lunch and dinner include a wide variety of burger choices, sandwiches, and wraps. A nice option is that a vegetarian patty may be substituted for any of the various burger creations for an additional charge. Along with several chicken choices, a veggie wrap and a prime rib au jus comprise the sandwich board. The main dinner entrées include salmon, trout, and top sirloin. The trout amandine is absolutely delicious and perfectly cooked.

Most of the restaurants in South Dakota serve standard American fare, but there are some places that provide a uniquely Western feel, which makes even a hamburger taste better. One such place is the **Ruby House Restaurant** (124 Winter St., 605/666-4404, www.rubyhousekeystone.com, 11am-9pm daily Apr.-mid-Oct., lunch $12-18, dinner $17-28) on the strip across the street from the 1880 Train station. Dining is available in the restaurant or outside on the boardwalk deck, where people-watching is the activity of choice. Inside, the decor is classic Victorian red velvet. Lunch features salads, wraps, burgers, chicken, and other sandwiches, and dinner includes bison, prime rib, trout, walleye, and pasta dishes. Adult beverages are provided by the **Red Garter Saloon** (126 Winter St., 605/666-4274, www.redgartersaloon.com, 11am-10:30pm daily Apr.-Oct.), though the Ruby House and Red Garter are two separate entities, so patrons will receive two checks if they dine and consume alcoholic beverages. Otherwise, the two venues flow together seamlessly; you can eat at the bar and drink in the restaurant. While the Ruby House is Western Victorian, the Red Garter is all Western.

In season, look for **Jane's Boardwalk Pizza** (160 Winter St., 605/666-4713, 8am-9pm daily Memorial Day-Labor Day, hours vary May and Sept.-mid-Oct., $10-25) right on the boardwalk, with extremely reasonable prices. The pizza is delicious, and there is beer and ice cream. Aside from pizza, the menu is limited to a few sandwiches (ham, turkey, roast beef, or grilled cheese) and calzones. A major plus: The venue has an open-air deck on the roof.

About 5 miles (8 km) from town, a good place to relax and be hearty (in other words, not worry about making noise) is the **Gaslight Restaurant & Saloon** (13490 Main St., Rockerville, 605/343-9276, www. thegaslightrestaurant.com, restaurant 5pm-8:30pm Wed.-Sun., bar 4pm-close Wed.-Sun., dinner $13-20). Take U.S. 16A North to U.S. 16 and head east toward Rapid City. Look for the exits for Rockerville. Thanks to some interesting highway planning, the town ended up being wedged between U.S. 16 East and U.S. 16 West, which means traffic zooms by at a minimum of 55 miles per hour (89 kph), though once you are inside, you'd never know it. The town has always been a boom-or-bust gold community, but this highway configuration returned the place to near ghost town status, with just the restaurant and bar open all year. Dinner includes steaks, chicken dishes, Mexican food selections, burgers, seafood, salads, and pasta dishes, all reasonably priced (most of the menu items are on the low end of the price range). Soup is homemade daily. It's a favorite spot with local folks. The decor is simple modified country, and it is fun to know you're eating in between the east and west lanes of the highway.

Coffee and Wine

Looking for a good coffee shop or a nice place to taste a few wines? Try **Grapes and Grinds** (609 U.S. 16A, 605/666-5142, www. grapesgrinds.com, 8am-5pm Mon.-Fri., 7am-7pm Sat.-Sun. summer, $4-6). Start the day with a bagel and cream cheese or choose from several varieties of flavored oatmeal to go with your morning coffee. Espressos, lattes, coffee frappes, and even plain brewed coffee are on hand. Choices also include non-coffee frappes, fruit smoothies, and gelato. A little later in the day, take a break with some free wine-tasting. Sample up to five wines at no cost. A glass of any wine offered is $5.95.

Dessert

One of the most popular stops in town is the **Rushmore Mountain Taffy Shop** (203 Winter St., 605/666-4430, www. rushmoremountaintaffy.com, 8am-6pm daily May-Sept., 9am-5pm daily off-season). No vacation-community boardwalk is complete without a taffy shop, and this one makes its taffy fresh daily on-site. I'm not sure what makes the sticky confection so irresistible, but it might be the many choices of exotic flavors. Strawberry cheesecake, peach, and chocolate cherry sound interesting, but jalapeño taffy may be something only a 10-year-old could love. The most popular flavors include cinnamon and huckleberry.

If taffy isn't your brand of sweet, try **TurtleTown** (117 Winter St., 605/666-4675, www.turtletown.com, 8am-10pm daily June-Aug., 10am-4pm daily May and Sept.-Oct.), a fixture on the Keystone strip since 1977. The store owners have expanded the initial offerings from simple fudge to include handmade fine chocolates, ice cream, and a coffee bar. With nine different varieties of fudge alone, plus all kinds of chocolates, truffles, and

caramels, there is something sweet for everyone. Right next door is TurtleTown's sister shop **Benky's Cream & Sugar** (111 Winter St., 605/877-2827, 11am-10pm daily May-Sept. $4-9) offering hot and iced specialty coffees, fruit smoothies, sundaes, malts and shakes. A cool place to be on a hot summer day.

ACCOMMODATIONS

Keystone is the closest town to Mount Rushmore, so demand for rooms is high. Luckily there are many hotels available. Be forewarned that signs that advertise low-rate rooms in town generally refer to early- or late-season rates and are not applicable to the high summer season. On the other hand, there are quite a few charming places tucked away in the region.

Under $150

The ★ **Powder House Lodge** (24125 U.S. 16A, 605/666-4646 or 800/321-0692, www. powderhouselodge.com, mid-May-mid-Oct., $100-150) is just 2 miles (3.2 km) north of Keystone on U.S. 16A, but it is far enough away to recapture the peaceful feel of the Black Hills. The lodge is family owned and operated and beautifully maintained. A number of cabin and motel configurations are available,

ready for breakfast at the Powder House Lodge

sleeping anywhere from 2-13 people (prices quoted cover options for 2-4 visitors, available in both cabin and motel rooms, and are set for the entire season). The rooms are rustic, charming, in-the-pines kinds of places that are tucked into the hillside behind one of the best restaurants in the area. Many of the rooms have outdoor balconies and all have a microwave and minifridge. Other amenities include an outdoor pool, coin-operated laundry facilities, and a playground for the kids. Dogs are allowed, and there's a $15 per dog onetime fee regardless of length of stay.

Close to both Custer State Park and Mount Rushmore, ★ **Buffalo Rock Lodge & Cabins** (24524 Playhouse Rd., 605/666-4781 or 888/564-5634, www.buffalorock.net, mid-Apr.-early Oct.) is a gorgeous, log construction nestled in pine trees. The lodge has two bed-and-breakfast-style rooms ($189 for up to 2 guests, $10 per additional guest), each with a private bath and spa tub. A pool table is available for billiards fans, and the outdoor deck is superb. A massive stone fireplace is another notable feature. Host Marilyn Oakes is extremely knowledgeable about the best activities and dining in the area and also well versed in local history. (Marilyn's grandfather was the contractor for the State Game Lodge in Custer State Park!) A three-night minimum stay is required during peak summer months, unless the only available booking at the time desired is for a shorter period. A Western-style hot breakfast is served every morning, and dessert is served every evening. In 2019, Buffalo Rock added cabins ($119-130 for up to 2 guests, $5 per additional guest), which are nestled in the forest. Cabins sleep from 2-5 people and feature cozy Western decor. They have heating and air-conditioning and are stocked with cookware, a refrigerator, all bedding and towels, and a microwave. Guests have access to the grill in the pavilion but are not provided with breakfast. Each cabin also has a dedicated bathroom in the shower house that is not shared with other guests. A two-night stay is required for the cabins.

Pets are allowed in some of the cabins with no additional fee.

$150-250

In the heart of Keystone, the ★ **Battle Creek Lodge** (404 Reed St./Hwy. 40, 605/666-4800 or 800/670-7914, www.battlecreeklodge.us, $150-215) is a family-run establishment that is a quaint and quiet alternative to the larger hotels. The lodge has nine rooms—split between double queen and kings—free wireless Internet, lovely decks to enjoy the cool evening air, and an outdoor fire pit. The lodge is just a short walk to downtown Keystone shops and restaurants. Guests are served a full continental breakfast, which includes one featured hot item every morning. The owners love the hospitality industry and are friendly and helpful to guests.

For beautiful seclusion, great decks, a gorgeous lobby, views of Mount Rushmore, and a free breakfast featuring delicious waffles, choose the ★ **K Bar S Lodge** (434 Old Hill City Rd., 605/666-4545 or 866/522-7724, www.kbarslodge.com, June-mid-Sept. $155-180, Apr.-May and mid-Sept.-Oct. $90-120, max of 2 pets allowed in specific rooms for $20 per pet per night). Just minutes from Keystone, the lodge has 96 rooms scattered in separate buildings across 45 acres (18 ha) of forested land. It is a holding of Choice Hotels; make reservations early. Amenities include a pool, an outdoor hot tub, and laundry facilities. Large wooden decks welcome guests. In the morning, dine on the included continental breakfast provided between the hours of 6:30am and 9:30am. In addition to pastries, bagels, cereals, and breads, there are scrambled eggs; a fresh oatmeal bar, Greek yogurt bar, and waffle bar; a choice of bacon, sausage, or ham; and fresh fruit, milk, juice, and coffee. For an extra caffeine kick, or for those who sleep late, try **The Coffee Shop** (6:30am-11:30am and 4pm-8pm daily Memorial Day-Labor Day). In the evening, relax at **The Pub** (4pm-8pm Memorial Day-Labor Day daily) and enjoy local beers and a selection of sandwiches and flatbreads. In the distance, you can see the lit profile of

George Washington on Mount Rushmore. Deer and wild turkey are frequent trespassers on lodge grounds. The rooms are clean and spacious, though the beauty of the facility is in the common areas. The lobby has vaulted ceilings and a huge stone fireplace.

The small, family-run **Roosevelt Inn** (206 Cemetery Rd., 605/666-4599 or 800/257-8923, www.rooseveltinnkeystone.com, mid-May-mid Sept. $140-200, mid-Sept.-mid-Nov. $90-150, Mar.-mid-May $70-100) is one of the closest hotels to Mount Rushmore. The inn prides itself on offering reasonably priced, clean, basic rooms. Amenities include microwaves and minifridges in the rooms, self-serve guest laundry, and a pool. The hotel offers accessible rooms and serves a great hot breakfast. Some interesting room layouts include lofts and raised seating alcoves, and many have balconies. One pet is $25 per stay. For more than one pet, check with the hotel.

The **Rushmore Express Inn & Family Suites** (320 Cemetery Rd., 605/666-4483, 800/323-6476, www.rushmoreexpress.com, summer $150-190, spring and fall $80-110, call for winter rates, no pets). Amenities include a pool, fitness room, continental breakfast, refrigerator, and a microwave, along with service from the family that manages the inn. There are several room configurations, some with interesting themes. Because it's situated right across the street from Rushmore Tramway Adventures, views sometimes include people careening across a field (occasionally screaming) harnessed to one of the highest and longest ziplines in the state. It makes for fascinating and sometimes humorous people-watching.

Over $250

A working farmstead with beautifully stocked and warmly decorated cabins, ★ **Yak Ridge** (24041 Cosmos Rd., Rapid City, 605/390-7627, www.yak-ridge.com, May-Oct. $250-375, Nov.-Apr. $195-250) has a Rapid City address but is located just about 15 minutes from Mount Rushmore. It's not your ordinary homestead. A family of Himalayan yaks

live on the property and share the space with free-range chickens and honeybees. The owners also maintain a garden and are dedicated to sustainable agriculture. They provide free tours loaded with information about all aspects of running the homestead. The property is on 10 acres (4 ha) surrounded by forest, and high enough in the hills to provide beautiful and cool starry nights, while still being centrally located. Accommodation options include studios that sleep four and two-bedrooms that sleeps six, with one or two bathrooms. All the luxuries you'd expect in an upscale hotel can be found in the rooms, including sumptuous robes. Additional amenities include a fully stocked full kitchen (including some spices!), outdoor fire pits, grills, and patios. Guests are welcomed with a gift basket when they arrive with fresh farm eggs, cheese, locally roasted coffee, fruit, chocolate, and other snacks. They can also purchase the Yak Ridge honey and eggs during their stay. To keep the whole family entertained, there is a selection of movies, games, and books for both adults and children. There's a minimum stay of 2-4 nights depending on season and holidays.

It's not exactly camping but the "rooms" are **Under Canvas** (24342 Presidio Ranch Rd., 605/787-2865 or 888/496-1148, www.undercanvas.com, early May-late Sept., $199-399, $25 per pet per night). Inspired by an African safari experience and called glamping (as in "glamour camping"), the whole idea is to unplug, relax, and enjoy nature in a beautiful environment, with some luxurious amenities. Based on the power of nature and the importance of connecting to family, some amenities are intentionally left out—like wireless Internet and televisions. The experience here is all about location and services. The tents are nestled in the trees. It's a beautiful location, with Mount Rushmore visible in the distance. Some of the tents allow guests to gaze at the stars from their luxurious king bed. The Safari, Deluxe, and Stargazing tents sleep two. The Suite has a separate bedroom and a living room with a pullout sofa and sleeps six.

All but the Safari have private bathrooms, and all include luxurious linens, woodstoves, and firewood. There are many configurations that can be set up for larger family groups. A "kid's tent" (which contains two twin beds) may be added to any site. Amenities include a limited but lovely breakfast and dinner menu on-site, with to-go lunches available. In addition, there is daily housekeeping and a central dining and socializing tent. At the evening fire pit, kids (and adults) enjoy s'mores and, in the morning, there just might be a yoga class. Several prearranged tours and activities can be explored when you book your site and may include guided hikes or live music. It's quiet, refreshing, and has one-of-a-kind scenic views of Mount Rushmore. Prices vary widely depending on the month you plan to stay and when you book. The best bet with Under Canvas at Mount Rushmore is to book as early as you can; the months of May, June, and September have the lowest rates.

Cabins and Campgrounds
Kemp's Kamp (1022 Old Hill City Rd., 605/666-4654 or 888/466-6282, www. kempskamp.com, mid-May-Oct., tent sites $35-45, RV sites $45-55, sleeping campers $66, sleeper cabins $70, cabins $79-199) is a quiet, well-maintained campground centrally located for all the Black Hills attractions. Amenities include a good-size heated pool, laundry facilities, free Wi-Fi, hot showers, elevated fire pits, and picnic tables, many of which come with large canopies. Cabins have a refrigerator, microwave, air-conditioning, and private bath. Old Hill City Road is the scenic route between Hill City and Keystone, as well as the route that the 1880 Train follows. It's a lovely location. The sleeping camper, a pop-up tent camper, is a fairly novel idea, offered to folks who don't want to haul a camper or sleep on the ground.

Those who love to camp the old-fashioned way can head to the Black Hills National Forest campground called **Grizzly Bear Campground** (605/574-4402 or 877/444-6777, www.recreation.gov, mid-May-Sept.,

tent sites $20, interagency pass discounts available, $2 per pet). It is a primitive site, with no showers, though water and vault toilets are available. Most of the 20 available sites are tent only, but RVs up to 24 feet (7.3 m) are allowed. No towed RVs or equipment are allowed. Most of the sites are first-come, first-served, though a few can be reserved. From Keystone, head up U.S. 16A toward Mount Rushmore and stay on U.S. 16A when it veers left. Locally, U.S. 16A is known as Iron Mountain Road. (If you make it to Mount Rushmore, you missed the turnoff.) About a mile down the road, the campground is on the right. It's a nicely wooded site, and Grizzly Bear Creek runs through the property. There is a picnic pavilion there built by the Civilian Conservation Corp that is still in use today. Campsites have picnic tables and a campfire ring. Trying to save a little money? Alternate a night of camping with a night of motel life (for the hot showers!).

INFORMATION AND SERVICES
The **Keystone Chamber of Commerce** (110 Swanzey Rd., 605/666-4896, www. visitkeystonesd.com, www.keystonechamber. com) is easy to find at the corner of Old Hill City Road and U.S. 16A at the traffic light. Rack cards have information about local events, lodging, and dining, and there is a chamber representative on hand to answer questions. Keep in mind that chamber representatives can't play favorites and represent all members. (If you are looking for opinions, ask shopkeepers or lodging folks.) For campers, basic supplies can be found at the **Keystone Country Store** (408 1st St., 605/666-4912). The Keystone **post office** (605/666-4830) is at 111 Winter Street. The closest hospital is the **Monument Health Rapid City Hospital** (353 Fairmont Blvd., Rapid City, 605/755-1000, www.monument.health). Urgent care can be found at **Monument Health Hill City Clinic** (238 Elm St., Hill City, 605/574-4470, 7:30am-5:30am Mon.-Tues. and Thurs., 7:30am-4pm Wed., 8am-4pm Fri.).

Hill City

The downtown core of Hill City is just a few blocks long and while there isn't *a lot* of anything here, there is a little bit of something for everyone: art galleries, a dinosaur museum, a historic steam train, small-town diners and fine dining, and a great chuckwagon dinner and show a few miles away. For outdoor lovers there is access to trails for hiking, biking, and ATV riding. Two of the larger lakes in the hills are not far from town. There are fine jewelry stores and inexpensive souvenir shops. That's a lot going on for a community with less than 800 permanent residents.

Hill City is just 3 miles (4.8 km) from the ongoing carving of Crazy Horse and 11 miles (17.8 km) from Mount Rushmore. It's the easiest town to reach from the Sylvan Lake area of Custer State Park—so it flourishes during the summer months. Since Harley-Davidson has set up shop in town, it has also become the second-favorite spot for motorcycle enthusiasts during the Sturgis Motorcycle Rally in early August.

While business slows significantly in the off-season, Hill City, less than 30 miles (48 km) from Rapid City and with easy access via U.S. 385/16, remains an enjoyable place to visit throughout the year. Many of the art galleries in town are open year-round, and while dining and lodging options shrink, food and accommodations are still available.

HISTORY

Hill City's mining era was relatively short-lived and not particularly successful. In 1876, placer gold (panned from streams and creeks instead of picked from underground mines) was detected in Spring Creek near town. It wasn't long, however, before reports of richer discoveries sent gold seekers to the Northern Hills. Miners headed back to Hill City when the Harney Peak Tin Mining, Milling, and Manufacturing Company set up headquarters in town in 1883. For about a decade,

the Harney Tin Company, as it was called, paid good wages to many local miners and kept the community bustling. The company bought over 1,100 mining claims in the region. Many of the claims never yielded any tin. Financed mainly by English investors, the company eventually collapsed, apparently under a cloud of scandal. (As an interesting side note, in 1885, a young New York attorney was sent west on the company's behalf to investigate titles to some of the mining claims being purchased. At one point, he asked his guide what was the name of the mountain that they were passing. The mountain didn't have a name on the maps of the time. It does now. The young attorney's name was Charles E. Rushmore. Note the mountain did in fact have a name—the Lakota called it Tunkasila Sakpe Paha, meaning Six Grandfathers.) After the closing of the Harney Tin Company, it was quite some time before Hill City recovered economic ground.

SIGHTS
★ 1880 Train

The original and main depot for the steam-powered **1880 Train** (222 Railroad Ave., 605/574-2222, www.1880train.com, mid-May-mid-Oct., round-trip adult $32, child ages 3-12 $16, one-way adult $27, child ages 3-12 $14) is in Hill City. The train offers a two-hour round-trip rail ride between Hill City and Keystone.

The steam engine locomotive was first brought to the Black Hills in 1879 by the Homestake Mine in Lead. When the first narrow-gauge railroad line was completed in 1881, steam trains carried supplies and people between the mining camps. Most of the standard-gauge track used by the current 1880 Train was built by the Chicago, Burlington and Quincy Railroad during the gold rush and mining boom of the 1890s. By the 1940s, diesel engines were rapidly replacing steam

Hill City

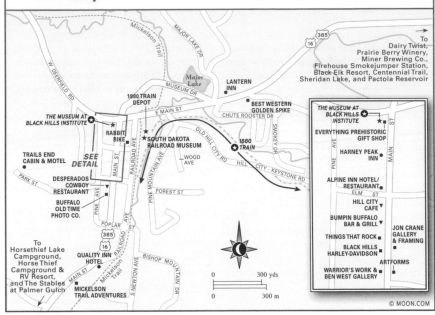

To
Dairy Twist,
Prairie Berry Winery,
Miner Brewing Co.,
Firehouse Smokejumper Station,
Black Elk Resort, Centennial Trail,
Sheridan Lake, and Pactola Reservoir

Major
Lake

LANTERN
INN

1880 TRAIN
DEPOT

E MAIN ST

BEST WESTERN
GOLDEN SPIKE

CHUTE ROOSTER DR

THE MUSEUM AT
BLACK HILLS INSTITUTE

THE MUSEUM AT
BLACK HILLS
INSTITUTE

RABBIT
BIKE

SOUTH DAKOTA
RAILROAD MUSEUM

EVERYTHING PREHISTORIC
GIFT SHOP

HARNEY PEAK
INN

TRAILS END
CABIN & MOTEL

SEE
DETAIL

WOOD
AVE

1880
TRAIN

HILL

ALPINE INN HOTEL/
RESTAURANT

ELM ST

DESPERADOS
COWBOY
RESTAURANT

FOREST ST

HILL CITY
CAFE

BUFFALO
OLD TIME
PHOTO CO.

BUMPIN BUFFALO
BAR & GRILL

JON CRANE
GALLERY
& FRAMING

POPLAR ST

THINGS THAT ROCK

BLACK HILLS
HARLEY-DAVIDSON

To
Horsethief Lake
Campground,
Horse Thief
Campground &
RV Resort,
and The Stables
at Palmer Gulch

QUALITY INN
HOTEL

BISHOP MOUNTAIN DR

ARTFORMS

WARRIOR'S WORK &
BEN WEST GALLERY

MICKELSON
TRAIL ADVENTURES

0   300 yds

0   300 m

© MOON.COM

engines. William B. Heckman, a local businessman and railroad fan, organized a group for the sole purpose of ensuring that "there should be in operation at least one working steam railroad, for boys of all ages who share America's fondness for the rapidly vanishing steam locomotive." The Hill City train depot was built in 1890, but it wasn't until 1957 that the first 1880 Train left the station. All the train cars and engines are historic, with most dating back to the early 1900s; the history of each car is available on the 1880 Train website.

The schedule of departures varies throughout the season. If you prefer a steam to a diesel train, specify that when making reservations. In May and October there are only 1-2 round trip departures daily (11:30am and 2:30pm). During the summer season (June-Aug.) there are four departures (9am, 11:30am, 2:30pm, and 5pm). Some departures provide an "Old West Shoot Out" in the summer months. By September, there are just three standard departures (9am, 11:30am, and 2:30 pm). In the

fall and winter, special weekend trips include a wine express, Octoberfest, Fright Night, and Christmas trains. Check the online schedule or with staff when you've determined the dates you'll be visiting. Patrons can customize their trips; for instance, you can arrange to take the first train out of Hill City, get off in Keystone and spend an hour in town, then catch the next train back to Hill City. In order to know how many seats are available on each ride, custom trips must be arranged at the time of ticket purchase.

On the grounds of the Hill City Train, the **South Dakota Railroad Museum** (222 Railroad Ave., 605/574-9000, www.sdsrm. org, 8am-5pm daily Memorial Day-Labor Day, 10am-5pm daily Labor Day-mid-Oct., adult $7, child 10 and under free, groups of 6 or more $3.50 each) offers a fascinating look at the history of trains in South Dakota. One of the more interesting exhibits is a timeline mural painted on the wall outlining the historical growth of both freight and passenger travel in the state, with comparisons to the history of flight and flight passenger statistics. The curator of the museum, Rick Mills, a true train aficionado from early childhood, is the author of several books on trains, including 125 Years of Black Hills Railroading, published in 2004. Rick can usually be found at the museum and is full of fascinating train information.

★ The Museum at Black Hills Institute

The Museum at Black Hills Institute (117 Main St., 605/574-3919, www.bhigr.com/museum, 10am-6pm Tues.-Sat. Memorial Day-Labor Day, 9:30am-5pm Mon.-Sat. Labor Day-Memorial Day, adult $7.50, senior, active military, and vet $6, child ages 6-15 $4, child 5 and under free) was organized in 1991. Its mission was "to collect, conserve, curate, and display extraordinary geological and natural history specimens that have the power to educate, enlighten, and excite people about the wonders of the natural world." The story of the museum, and of the founders of the related Black Hills Institute of Geological Research, is fascinating. The institute and the museum have been involved in the excavation and preservation of nine T. rex skeletons. The most complete T. rex, Stan, is on display at the museum. Other displays include ammonites, minerals, and fossil remains of many other dinosaurs, including duck-billed dinosaurs and triceratops. The museum is entered through the Everything Prehistoric Gift Shop and is self-guided.

Addicted to the fossil world? The institute has a large catalog of fossil replicas for sale on its website. A replica of Stan's skeleton is $120,000 and a triceratops skeleton would cost around $90,000; but there are lots of items (like a T-rex claw) that cost less than $100. Many of the institute's replicas are purchased by universities for use in classrooms.

Prairie Berry Winery

The **Prairie Berry Winery** (23837 U.S. 385, 877/226-9453, www.prairieberry.com, 10am-8pm daily summer, 10am-6pm Sun.-Thurs. and 10am-7pm Fri.-Sat. fall and spring, 11am-6pm Sun.-Thurs. and 10am-6pm Fri.-Sat. winter) is 3 miles (4.8 km) north of Hill City on U.S. 385/16. The winery is not open for tours, but free wine tastings are available; call for a reservation. Wine-tasting sessions last about 20 minutes, and each person will have the opportunity to taste up to five different wines. While South Dakota seems an unlikely location for grape growing, Prairie Berry has won numerous awards for its wines. South Dakota-grown grapes and honey, as well as raspberries, rhubarb, chokecherries, cranberries, plums, and crab apples, are some of the ingredients used to create the winery's many lines. The wines, packaged with beautiful labels and creatively named, make fabulous gifts from South Dakota. Two favorites include Red Ass Rhubarb and Lawrence Elk. I have never visited the winery without being impressed with the friendly and outgoing staff. Customer service here is consistently excellent, and all the staff members are well educated about the various wines available for tasting. While there, plan on having a snack at the **Prairie Berry Kitchen** ($14) which opens at 11am and closes half an hour before the winery shuts down for the day. The kitchen serves gourmet cheeses, homemade soups, and local salamis and provides a lovely outdoor deck for dining. Most of the food is prepared from locally grown produce, and gluten-free and vegetarian options are available.

RECREATION

TOP EXPERIENCE

Hiking

Every region in the hills has something to offer hikers. About 8 miles (12.9 km) north of Hill City, the **Flume Trail** follows the bed of a water channel built to divert the flow from Spring Creek and carry it to Rockerville. While most flumes are created to carry water for drinking to a growing community, this one was constructed to facilitate the processing of placer gold. The trail is open to foot traffic only and counts as a National Recreation Trail due to its historical significance.

FLUME TRAIL-CALUMET TRAILHEAD TO COON HOLLOW TRAILHEAD

Distance: 11 miles (17.8 km), plus a 3-mile (4.8-km) loop

Duration: 6-7 hours

Elevation Gain: 900 feet (274 m)

Effort: Easy

Trailhead: Calumet Trailhead

Directions: Drive north on U.S. 385 from Hill City. After the intersection with U.S. 16, stay on U.S. 385 for another 1.7 miles (2.7 km) and take a right on Calumet Road. Follow the signs to the Sheridan Lake campground and then to the Calumet (or Flume) Trailhead.

Even though the flume that gives this trail its name is no longer functional, water is still a presence on this hike. The trail starts at Sheridan Lake and crosses Spring Creek five separate times. Interesting features include two tunnels and visible remnants of the old wooden flume. The trail is well marked, and there are interpretive signs posted along the way. It is one of the most popular hikes in the Central Hills outside of the Black Elk Peak area. About 6.5 miles (10.5 km) into the hike, the trail has a spur to the left. This is the beginning of the 2.7-mile (4.3-km) loop portion of the path. If you elect to continue without the loop, follow the trail to the right for 0.5 mile (0.8 km) to the Boulder Hill trailhead. From there, the Boulder Hill overlook is about 1 mile (1.6 km). A fire tower once sat on the top of the hill, and this is the spot that will give the best views of the western Black Hills. Then return to the main trail. From here, it is another 3.8 miles (6.1 km) to the Coon Hollow Trailhead near Rockerville.

Biking

Hill City is a central hub for the **George S. Mickelson Trail** (http://gfp.sd.gov/parks, $4 day-use fee or $15 annual pass), a 109-mile (175-km) biking/hiking trail that runs from Edgemont in the south to Deadwood in the north. This rails-to-trails project is geared toward mountain biking and, as such, has a crushed gravel path.

Two entities in town rent bicycles and provide shuttle service to any of the 14 trailheads. **Mickelson Trail Adventures** (on-site at Trailside Park Resort & Luxury Cabins, 24024 S. U.S 385/16, 605/574-4094 or 605/391-4491, www.mickelsontrailadventures.com, 8am-4pm daily) offers bike rentals for $29 per day, $19.50 per half-day, and $8.75 for one hour plus $5.50 per additional hour. There is four-person minimum for shuttle service. Shuttle rates range from $10-45 per person, depending on the trailhead where riders would like to start their journey. **Rabbit Bike** (175 Walnut Ave., 605/574-4302, www.rabbitbike.com, 8am-5pm Mon.-Sat. and 9am-4pm Sun. summer, 9am-4pm Mon.-Sat. spring) is the only full-service bike shop on the trail. With an extensive inventory of bikes in stock, there are comfort bikes and hardtail bikes, recumbent bikes, electric bikes, as well as bikes for kids. Bicycle gear is available as is a full-service repair shop. Bike rental rates depend on the length of the trip and the bike selected (nonelectric bikes: half-day adult $40-50, child $25, full-day adult $75-85, child $35; electric bikes: half-day adult $75, full-day adult $125). Rentals include tire repair kits (no charge if unused) and helmets. Bikes can also be rented for a week or weeks; call for additional information. Bikers can also rent bike locks, panniers, seat bags, or seat racks. Rabbit offers shuttle service to any trailhead on the Mickelson Trail and will give rides to the Centennial Trail on request. Shuttles from Hill City to any trailhead range $55-115. Rabbit also offer shuttles to Rapid City ($115) from the Hill City location. Shuttle service is also available to folks staying in Deadwood; they will pick up folks in Deadwood and drop them off at any trailhead desired along the trail ($60-195).

Mickelson Trail

MICKELSON TRAIL-HILL CITY TO MYSTIC

Distance: 14.6 miles (23.5 km) one-way

Duration: 4 hours

Elevation Gain: Negligible, and the grade never exceeds 4 percent

Effort: Easy

Trailhead: Burlington Northern Hill City at Tracy Park

Directions: Tracy Park is south of the Hill City Train, near the intersection of Poplar and Railroad Avenues.

The Mickelson Trail was originally the Burlington Northern Railroad line that crossed western South Dakota from Edgemont to the gold mines in Deadwood. The line was abandoned in 1983, and, as part of the state centennial celebration, avid hikers began the project to convert the abandoned rails to trails. Completed in 1998, this 109-mile (175-km) trail has 15 trailheads, one of which is the Tracy Park trailhead located in Hill City. From start to finish, the bed is packed gravel, wide, and well marked. This is a trail you will not get lost on. The segment from Hill City to Mystic is rural. Highlights include riding along Crooked Creek, Newton Lake, the Slate Creek dam and through four railroad tunnels and the historic gold mill town of Mystic. The Mickelson Trail day pass is $4.

CENTENNIAL TRAIL-DAKOTA POINT TRAILHEAD TO PILOT KNOB TRAILHEAD

Distance: 19.6 miles (31.5 km) one-way

Duration: 5-6 hours

Elevation Gain: 1,100 feet (335 m)

Effort: Moderate to strenuous

Trailhead: From Hill City, drive north on U.S. 385 about 10 miles (16.1 km) to Sheridan Lake Road. Take a right on Sheridan Lake Road and continue for 1.6 miles (2.6 km). Take a right on Black Hills National Forest Road 434. The trailhead is in 0.3 mile (0.5 km).

The Centennial Trail is not the easiest trail to navigate. It is officially trail number 89, but the markers are not always easy to find. Be sure to purchase trail maps at one of the Forest Service locations. (It wouldn't hurt to have GPS either!) Also be sure to carry plenty of water. That said, it's an exhilarating ride for

Centennial Trail

Whitewood

BEAR BUTTE LAKE

Sturgis

FT MEADE

To Deadwood

ALKALI CREEK

VANOCKER CANYON RD

Elk Creek

ELK CREEK

Black Hills
National Forest

Centennial Trail

BOULDER FORKS
DALTON
DALTON LAKE

SOUTH BOXELDER CREEK
Nemo

Boxelder Creek

PILOT KNOB

Blackhawk

DEER CREEK

NEMO RD

Rapid City

RAPID CREEK

Pactola
Reservoir

TAMARACK GULCH

Black Hills
National Forest

Rapid Creek

BRUSH CREEK

DAKOTA POINT

Spring Creek

Mickelson Trail
Sheridan Lake

SPRING CREEK

Rockerville

Hill City

FLUME

SAMELIUS

BIG PINE

Keystone

Black Elk Peak
Mount Rushmore
National Memorial

Sylvan Lake

Black Elks
Wilderness
NEEDLES

IRON MOUNTAIN HWY

IRON CREEK

Center Lake

Custer

Stockade Lake

BADGER HOLE

FRENCH CREEK

French Creek

Custer
State Park

WILDLIFE LOOP RD

Centennial Trail

HIGHLAND CREEK

Pringle

Wind Cave
National Park

NORBECK

0   10 mi
0   10 km

ELK MOUNTAIN

To Hot Springs

© MOON.COM

those who want a nice long trip. This section of the trail is hilly, but the hills aren't long. The trail winds through ponderosa pine forest and slate outcroppings and offers good views of Pactola Reservoir.

Boating

Fishing, swimming, and boat rentals are available at two beautiful lakes near Hill City. **Sheridan Lake** ($7 day-use fee) is a 375-acre (152-ha) lake, 10 miles (16.1 km) north of Hill City off U.S. 385. **Sheridan Lake Marina** (16451 Sheridan Lake Rd., 605/574-2169, www.sheridanlakemarina.com, 8am-7pm daily May 1-Sept. 30) has all kinds of boats and recreational gear available to rent for two hours, half a day, or a full day. Pontoons (for 8-14 adults) $195-280 for a half day and $260-350 for a full day. Fishing boats are $75 for a half day and $110 for a full day. Kayaks, canoes, and stand-up paddleboards are available for $35 for two hours, $50 for a half day, or $70 for all day; hydro-bikes, paddled by one person, are available for $20 for two hours, $35 for a half day, and $50 for a full day. Life jackets are provided with all rentals. The marina store also sells bait and South Dakota fishing licenses (one-day resident $8, nonresident $16, $4 agents fee may be charged if not purchased from the state), rents fishing tackle, and provides camping supplies and basic groceries. An apartment that sleeps eight adults (summer $225-265, spring and fall $195-235), overlooking the lake, is available for rental above the marina store.

Pactola Reservoir ($7 day-use fee), at 800 acres (324 ha) and 14 miles (22.5 km) of shoreline, is the largest body of water in the Central Hills. Fifteen miles (24 km) from Hill City and just north of Sheridan Lake off U.S. 385, it is a scenic location for boating or fishing. The marina there, **Pactola Pines** (U.S. 385, 605/343-4283, www.pactolapines.com, 8am-7pm daily Memorial Day-Labor Day, 8am-5pm May and Sept.), has a variety of boats for rent, including several different sizes of pontoons that can accommodate 10-13 passengers as well as fishing boats, kayaks, canoes, and stand-up paddleboards. Boats rent for a half or full day. Pontoons range in price from $195-280 for four hours to $260-350 for a full day. Fishing boats rent for $75 for a half day or $100 for a full day and hold three to four people. Kayaks, stand-up paddleboards, and canoes may be rented for 2 hours ($30), half a day ($50), or a full day ($70). Add a $10 fee per dog to bring your furry friends along. The marina store has a limited menu of breakfast and lunch items prepared for you or wrapped steaks and burgers for cooking on a grill. They will also prepare a "to-go" lunch for on-lake dining if desired.

Both Sheridan Lake and Pactola Reservoir have **camping facilities** (reservations 877/444-6777 or international 518/885-3639, www.recreation.gov, 129 and 83 sites, respectively) that include drinking water and toilets, but no electricity, hookups, or showers. Campsites are $26 per night. The day-use fee of $7 does not apply if visitors are camping in the campgrounds. Pets are allowed in the campgrounds at both locations for a $2 per pet per night fee, charged at check-in.

Horseback Riding

Whether or not you go for the Chuck Wagon Dinner Show at **The Stables at Palmer Gulch** (12620 Hwy. 244, 605/574-3412, www.ridesouthdakota.com, Memorial Day-Labor Day), horseback riding is always an option. Palmer Gulch has a riding permit in the **Norbeck Wildlife Preserve,** and its rides take place in some of the most beautiful country in the hills. There are three rides available offering various experiences, levels of difficulty, and elevation gains. All three take 1.25-1.5 hours at a cost of $50 per rider.

ENTERTAINMENT
Chuckwagon Dinner Show

There is nothing more uniquely Western than a chuckwagon dinner experience. The folks at **The Stables at Palmer Gulch** (12620 Hwy. 244, 605/574-3412, www.ridesouthdakota.com, Memorial Day-Labor Day) present an authentic **Chuck Wagon Dinner Show.**

Choose to ride on a horse (adult $125, child ages 6-12 $100) or in a horse-drawn covered wagon (adult $75, child ages 6-12 $50, child ages 3-5 $25). Trail riders meet at the stables and depart at 4pm. They'll arrive at the Chuck Wagon Camp after a 1.5-hour ride, more than ready for dinner. The wagon riders meet at the stables at 4:30pm and depart promptly at 5pm. Dinner is served at 5:30pm and consists of steak (or hot dogs for kids, if they prefer), baked beans, and Dutch oven fried potatoes with bacon, onion, and bell peppers. Dessert is a Dutch oven peach or pear cobbler. After dinner, the Western music show begins and includes a little dancing, perhaps a little singing. And, as the sun sets, all guests will be returned to the stables via horse-drawn wagons, arriving around 7:30pm.

Brewpubs
Miner Brewing Co. (23845 U.S. 385, 605/574-2886, www.minerbrewing.com, 11am-8pm daily summer, 11am-6pm Wed.-Sun. winter, subject to change!) is part of the Prairie Berry Winery family and located right next door. The facility has a taproom where you can get a signature flight of beer (six 4-oz./118-ml glasses) for $15 or pick your own for $2.50 apiece before you select your beer of choice for the evening. It might be a good idea to split a flight. There are about 14 different brews on tap, with selections varying seasonally. There currently is no food on-site except for intermittent visits from some very excellent food trucks; however, food is available until 7pm from the Prairie Berry Kitchen right next door. Food can be ordered to go. (When staff are available, they might be able to pick up and deliver for you, but there's no guarantee on that service.) In the summer, there's bocce ball in the courtyard, and live concert events are scheduled in the outdoor beer garden. Events are posted on Facebook.

The owners of **Firehouse Smokejumper Station** (23585 U.S. 385, 605/574-2916, www.firehousesmokejumper.com, 11am-8pm daily summer, call for hours off-season) have been brewing longer than any other venture in the hills. The Smokejumper Station hosts both beer and wine-tastings. A six-beer flight of Firehouse beer is $10.50 (it might be a good idea to share!), or try an individual sample for $1.75. Alternatively, try the wines at $5 for six 1-ounce (30-ml) tastes. There's a small but creative menu on-site that includes salads, wraps, sandwiches, burgers, and a daily special. A sample of the creativity? Try the salmon apricot salad (salmon, dried apricots, apples, butter lettuce, almonds, and chevre goat cheese served with a honey-apple vinaigrette). Or a Beyond Burger (veggie) dressed with caramelized onion and smoked gouda on a potato bun. The station is essentially a long rectangular bar, with a modern feel to it. There's a gift shop inside, and outside there's a nice shaded creekside patio, perfect for enjoying a beer or glass of wine on a summer day.

SHOPPING

Hill City's main shopping district spans just a few blocks, but that small space packs in just about everything a shopping vacationer would want to bring home. The atmosphere is festive, with large crowds, a boardwalk, and ice cream cones being enjoyed by many. Hill City looks and feels like summer. As with the lodging and restaurant establishments in town, many of the small shops operate seasonally; hours outside of the peak summer months of June, July, and August can vary with the weather and traffic.

Galleries

Jon Crane Gallery & Framing (256 Main St., 605/574-4440 or 800/288-1948, www.joncranegallery.com, 10am-6pm Mon.-Thurs., 10am-7pm Fri.-Sat. May-Labor Day, 10am-5pm Mon.-Sat. Labor Day-Jan., 10am-5pm Wed.-Sat. Jan.-Apr.) features the work of namesake artist Jon Crane, who is well known for his nostalgic and finely detailed watercolor rural landscapes. Jon's artwork is placed in galleries all over the country. In addition to Jon's work, the beautiful gallery space carries JK Dooley's original Western-themed watercolors, Peggy Detmers's bronze wildlife sculptures, and Joel Bielstein's photographs. There is also locally crafted pottery and beautiful wood furniture. Custom framing on all the pieces in the gallery is available through the shop as well. It's a very beautiful space.

Artforms (280 Main St., 605/574-4894, www.artformsgallery.org, 10am-6pm daily May-Aug., 10am-5pm daily Sept., 10am-5pm Thurs.-Sat. Oct., 10am-5pm Fri.-Sat. Nov.-Dec. and Mar.-Apr., off-season hours may vary) is a local artist co-op, which means that everyone behind the register is one of the artists whose work is represented in the store. Over 20 local and regional artists display their jewelry, painting, sculptures, and other pieces in the gallery.

Across the street, step into **Warrior's Work & Ben West Gallery** (277 Main St., 605/574-4954, www.warriorswork.com, 10am-6pm Mon.-Sat., 11am-4pm Sun. spring-fall, 11am-5pm Wed.-Sat. winter, other hours by appt.). The artwork on the walls is bold and emotionally powerful. Two galleries share the space. The Warrior's Work Gallery features striking pieces by and about Native American people and culture. The Ben West Gallery specializes in contemporary art. Over 25 artists contribute to the pieces displayed at the gallery. The gallery also features sculptures in wood, bronze, glass, and stone. Owner Randy Berger creates custom-designed leather frames that are works of art in themselves. There is a wonderful wardrobe of leather hats, leather jackets, and other fanciful clothing to choose from also.

Gift Shops

Most, but not all, of the great shops in Hill City are in the downtown shopping district. Specialty shops line the boardwalk. Allow yourself a few hours to wander. It's only a few blocks, but you'll be darting in and out of stores.

For a great collection of science-related and educational items (including dinosaur items), visit the **Everything Prehistoric Gift Shop** (117 Main St., 605/574-3919, www.bhigr.com, 10am-6pm Tues.-Sat. Memorial Day-Labor

Day, 9:30am-5:00pm Mon.-Sat. Labor Day-Memorial Day). The store has a great selection of books on archaeology, mineralogy, paleontology, geology, and more; fossils and rocks; and rows and rows of fun and educational toys, as well as local mineral and natural rock jewelry and carved figurines. The gift shop serves as the entryway to The Museum at Black Hills Institute, so tickets for a self-guided museum tour are also available here (adult $7.50 senior, active military, and vet $6, child ages 6-15 $4, child under 5 free).

Things That Rock (257 Main St., 605/574-9096, www.thingsthatrocksd.com, 10am-6pm Mon.-Tues., 10am-7pm Wed.-Sat., 10am-4pm Sun. summer, call for hours off-season) is a beautiful little shop focused on wellness and nature. Crystal, mineral, and stone (polished or raw) jewelry abound. Find books on meditation and geology and gifts ranging from aromatherapy essential oils to wind chimes, beads, stone lamps, and jewelry-making equipment. On occasion, two beautiful dogs are on hand to say hello to visitors.

If you've always dreamed of being a dance hall girl, you can make your dream come true at **Buffalo Old Time Photo Co.** (309 Main St., 605/574-3314, www.buffalophoto.net, 10am-8pm Mon.-Sat. with last session at 7:15pm, 11am-7pm Sun. with last session at 6:15pm Memorial Day-Labor Day). A photograph of the whole family in Western duds and Victorian dresses hanging out at a local saloon may become a favorite souvenir. The family dog can be part of the fun, too.

The Sturgis Motorcycle Rally is one of the biggest events in South Dakota, drawing several hundred thousand bikers to the state each year. That was enough to encourage Harley-Davidson to open a shop in downtown Hill City. Find branded leathers, hats, apparel, mugs, riding gear, and other cool items at **Black Hills Harley-Davidson** (261 Main St., 605/574-3636, www.blackhillshd.com, 9am-5pm Mon.-Sat., 10am-4pm Sun. Memorial Day-Labor Day). Look for longer hours around the Sturgis Motorcycle Rally in early August.

FOOD

Hill City is one of the busiest communities in the Black Hills in the summertime. At prime lunch and dinner times, be prepared to wait a bit for a table. Breakfast isn't generally a problem (so have a substantial one!), and then consider a late lunch or an early dinner to lessen the wait.

Casual Dining

Desperados Cowboy Restaurant (301 Main St., 605/574-2959, 4pm-9pm Mon.-Thurs. and 11am-9pm Fri.-Sun. May-mid-Oct., lunch $11-17, dinner $16-28) is seasonally open and housed in the oldest commercial building in town, a log cabin built in 1885. Don't let the rustic appearance of this building's exterior fool you. Inside the restaurant, the chinked log walls, twinkling lights, wood tables, and chairs and booths with modern cowboy decor make for a cozy dining experience. The upscale Western-themed restaurant features sandwiches, burgers and fries, and salads and soups for lunch; steaks, fish, and pasta are added to the menu for dinner. Billed as "real fine Western food," expect to see add-ons (and meals) including corn bread, fried pickles, country-fried steak, chicken-fried chicken, and chili on the menu. For dessert there's a wide variety of cheesecakes to choose from. It's a family-friendly restaurant, and a children's menu is available.

The **Hill City Cafe** (209 Main St., 605/574-4582, 6am-8pm daily summer, winter hours vary, breakfast and lunch $11-15, dinner $14-35) is the place most likely to be filled with locals. It is a comfort food kind of place and has a bit of a diner feel, but it's friendly, has an extensive menu, and is located right in the middle of the downtown boardwalk shopping district. Breakfast offerings are especially hearty, featuring more than a couple of steak and egg combos. Lunch offers a wide variety of burgers and other sandwiches, and dinner options include beef steaks, bison, chicken, fish, and seafood.

The **Bumpin Buffalo Bar & Grill** (245 Main St., 605/574-2471, www.bumpinbuffalo.

com, 11am-9pm Thurs.-Sat., 11am-7pm Sun. mid-Mar.-mid-Oct., lunch $11-16, dinner $17-32) is a good family choice. The full menu of basic American fare, including steaks, ribs, prime rib, pasta, chicken, fish, and a variety of burgers and sandwiches (and pot roast!), is available for both lunch and dinner. The decor is an interesting mix of beer signs, trains, and antiques, and there is a gorgeous wooden bar back. There was once a model train that circled the room, but every now and again it would derail itself, so for safety's sake, the train no longer moves. If you like views, or outside dining, head for the covered rooftop deck. Overall, with high tin ceilings, it can get a bit noisy inside, but this is still a great place for a beer and a sandwich. There is a kid's menu, as well, just $8 for chicken strips, a small hamburger, or a corn dog.

A local favorite along U.S. 16 just 3.5 miles (5.6 km) from downtown Hill City, **Dairy Twist** (12647 S. U.S. 16, 605/574-2380, http://stayccr.com/dairy-twist, 11am-8pm Mon.-Sat., noon-8pm Sun. Memorial Day-Labor Day, 11am-7pm Mon.-Sat., noon-7pm mid-Apr.-Memorial Day and Labor Day-mid-Oct., $9) is best known for its 22 flavors of milkshakes, malts, and sundaes, as well as inexpensive burgers, fries, and chicken strips. It's counter service only; place your order at one window and shuffle three steps to the right to pick it up at another window. There are picnic tables outside. Locals keep an eye on the Dairy Twist; when it opens, that means summer is almost here.

Fine Dining

★ **Alpine Inn** (133 Main St., 605/574-2749, www.alpineinnhillcity.com, 11am-2:30pm and 5pm-9:30pm Mon.-Thurs., 11am-2:30pm and 5pm-10pm Fri.-Sat. summer, 11am-2:30pm and 5pm-9pm Mon.-Thurs., 11am-2:30pm and 5pm-9:30pm Fri.-Sat. winter, lunch $11-13, dinner $14-16, cash and check only) is always a great place to eat—and if you enjoy outdoor dining and people-watching, it's the best spot in town for lunch, with a spacious deck dining area, although it is first-come, first-served. Inside, dining is scattered throughout various Victorian-style rooms with plenty of old-world charm. The lunch menu is extensive, offering a selection of German plates, creative salad main courses, and a wide variety of sandwiches. In the evening, dinner is perfect for folks who have a hard time making decisions, since there are only two entrées on the menu. The first is either a small or large bacon-wrapped filet mignon, and the second is spaetzle primavera. For dessert ($5-7), the choices are legendary. With over 20 items on the menu, select from apple cheese strudel, raspberry tarts, raspberry white chocolate mousse, ice cream pies, napoleons, turtle waffles, crème brûlée, bread pudding topped with hot caramel, brownies, sundaes, ice cream—well, you get the idea. The inn was built in the late 1880s as the Harney Peak Hotel. The restaurant is on the lower floor of the building and richly decorated in the Victorian style of that era. Have lunch at the Alpine Inn at least once during your time in the hills. It is a victim of its own success, though, so go early to avoid long waits. But even if you are running late, the wait is worth it. Or consider just stopping in for a midafternoon dessert!

The **Prairie Berry Kitchen** (23837 U.S. 385, 605/574-3898, www.prairieberry.com, 11am-7pm daily May-Sept., 11am-between 5:30pm and 6:30pm off-season, $14) is at the Prairie Berry Winery, just 3 miles (4.8 km) north of Hill City on U.S. 385. For those looking for a healthy lunch alternative, it's a wonderful choice. The menu is not extensive but includes gourmet cheeses, artisan breads, and hummus. Soups, flatbreads, and open-faced sandwiches are created daily to complement the wines. Everything is homemade and delicious. Tables are available on the patio (pet-friendly) in summer. In winter, the homemade soups fly out of the kitchen. Prairie Berry offers wine-tastings by reservation only. Taste up to five wines for free. It's great fun, and the

1: 1880 Train 2: ice cream at Dairy Twist 3: Alpine Inn 4: The Museum at Black Hills Institute

staff are very knowledgeable about the wines they serve. Make reservations at 877/226-9453 or online.

ACCOMMODATIONS

As is the case in every community in the hills, the chain hotels are well represented in Hill City. Many are close to the town center and aren't a bad choice. If you are looking for a special experience, however, it's the cabins and smaller hotels that provide the most charm and variety.

Under $150

The ★ **Lantern Inn** (580 E. Main St., 605/574-2582 or 800/456-0520, www. lanterninn.com, June-Aug. $110-120, May and Sept.-mid-Oct. $75-95) has been a locally owned enterprise for many years. This is the perfect road-trippers place to stay. It's basic but within walking distance to groceries and restaurants, with very reasonable rates. The 18 rooms are kept spotlessly clean, and the owner and staff are friendly. Most of the rooms have microwaves and minifridges, as well as hair dryers. All rooms have queen beds, and prices quoted include single and double queen rooms. Flat-screen TVs are in every room, and there is free Wi-Fi. Look for coffee in the office in the morning. Guests who rise earlier than the office staff can request a coffeemaker for their room (given out on a first-come, first-served basis). There is a picnic area and grills for outdoor cooking, plus a small pool and a hot tub on the property. A couple of pet rooms are available for a fee of $10 a night; call in advance to make arrangements.

For location, the **Harney Peak Inn** (125 Main St., 605/574-2544, www.harneypeakinn. com, Memorial Day-Labor Day $139, off-season $89-99, no pets) can't be beat. The rooms have been completely renovated. Each room has a queen bed, high-speed Internet, flat-screen TV, air-conditioning, heat, and a small refrigerator. In the morning, there is a light continental breakfast featuring fruit, muffins, cereal, coffee, and juice. In the

evening, since the property actually holds a beer and wine license, guests can gather on the small private patio or in the small on-site bar and share their days over a glass of beer or wine. Tucked away right off Main Street in the heart of the downtown shopping, this small inn is a downtown bargain. Only five rooms are available, so early reservations are recommended. Smoking is allowed in designated areas only.

Just a few blocks off of Main Street, **Trails End Cabins & Motel** (320 Park St., 605/574-4900, www.hillcitycabin.com, May-Sept., $99-149, two-night minimum, sleeps 2-4) is quiet enough that wildlife wanders through the neighborhood. The property has been owned by the same family for the past eight years. All of the cabins and motel rooms have either a kitchenette with a microwave and refrigerator or a full kitchen stocked with cutlery, dishware, and cookware. Amenities include a hot tub, free firewood, nightly campfires, and patios with grills. Due to the property's close proximity to trails and the downtown Harley-Davidson store, it's a great place for motorcyclists and UTVers, or anyone else looking for a lovely, reasonable place to stay. Cabins are also available for larger groups (up to eight people).

Black Elk Resort (12720 S. U.S. 16, 605/574-9533, www.blackelkresort.com, May-mid-Oct., cabins for 2 $100-119, cabins for 4 $119-149, kitchenette cabins for 6 $159-225, RV camping $49-55, mid-Oct.-Apr. kitchenette cabins $129-175) operates year-round and has eight cabins decorated in rustic country style, with pine paneling and historic Black Hills photographs. All cabins have air-conditioning, a microwave, a minifridge, and a coffeemaker. One of the nicest features is a centralized covered and comfortable picnic area (with nearby grills), where a campfire is lit every evening for guests to enjoy. There is also a family-friendly taproom on-site serving craft beer to adult guests. The grounds are attractively maintained, and amenities include a playground, horseshoes, a laundry facility, and great views. There are also eight 50-foot (15-m) pull-through RV sites that provide full hookups with 30/50 amps, picnic tables, and charcoal grills. Two sites have fire pits. Bathhouses are on-site for RV campers as well.

$150-250

The 87-room **Best Western Golden Spike Inn and Suites** (601 E. Main St., 605/574-2577 or 800/780-7234, www. bestwesterngoldenspike.com, Memorial Day-mid-Oct. $159-229, Apr.-Memorial Day $119-149) is family-owned and operated and a recipient of South Dakota's Great Service Award. A full hot breakfast is included with the room charge. Amenities include an indoor and outdoor pool, a hot tub, a lovely garden area, free wireless Internet, a microwave, a refrigerator, a coffeemaker, business services, and a guest laundry. Pets up to 80 pounds (36 kg) are allowed in standard rooms for an additional rate of $30 per day to a max of $150 for longer stays. Packing for a picnic lunch is easy from this location, as groceries are available just down the street.

Over $250

The **Quality Inn Hotel** (616 Main St., 605/574-2100, www.qualityinnhillcity.com, June-Oct. $228-330, May and Nov. $145-155, no pets) has 55 spacious, smoke-free rooms and is part of the Choice Hotels group. Amenities include free Wi-Fi, a nice breakfast room with small outside deck, indoor heated swimming pool, a whirlpool/hot tub, business services, and a guest laundry. Breakfast is included with the room and can be enjoyed in the breakfast room or taken on the run. Fresh-made waffles, fruit, pastries, coffee, and juice are on offer. The Mickelson Trail runs right behind the hotel, and the hotel provides dedicated bike storage. It's a great location for visiting both Central and Southern Hills sites.

Cabins and Campgrounds

The closest campground to Mount Rushmore is on the Hill City side of the mountain in Black Hills National Forest. The **Horsethief Lake Campground** (605/574-4402 or 877-444-6777, www.recreation.gov, $26 per night plus $8 reservation fee, $2 per pet per night) is 4 miles (6.4 km) southeast of Hill City on Highway 244 and just 2 miles (3.2 km) from Mount Rushmore. Sitting at 4,800 feet (1,463 m), this small, relatively primitive campground has a beautiful location nestled in the trees overlooking nearby Horsethief Lake. The campground does not have electricity or hookups, but there is a campground host, drinking water, and vault toilets. There are only 36 sites, of which 22 are suitable for either tents or RVs, and 14 sites are tent only. Five of the sites are accessible. Reservations are strongly suggested due to the campground's setting near Mount Rushmore. The 10-acre (4-ha) Horsethief Lake is stocked with rainbow trout and perch, and boating is allowed (no powerboats, though). A nice 2.8-mile (4.5-km) hiking trail skirts the water's edge.

With a similar name but entirely different amenities and facilities, there is the ★ **Horse Thief Campground & RV Resort** (24391 Sylvan Lake Rd./Hwy. 87, 605/574-2668, www.horsethief.com, mid-May-Sept., tent sites $30-41, RV sites $46-63 depending on amps and services, sleeping cabins $65-83, cottage $135-145). If there is a *most beautiful* region in the Black Hills, this mountainous, forested, granite-spired area near Sylvan Lake is it. The campground is just 3 miles (4.8 km) south of Sylvan Lake, and sites are tucked into the pines. Services include wireless Internet, picnic tables, a heated pool, a playground, basketball and horseshoe areas, and a camp store with a selection of groceries, camping supplies, and gifts. Bring your own bedding and cooking utensils for the sleeping cabins. Bedding and cooking utensils are included in the cottage. Pets are allowed at campsites but not in cabins. To get there, head south from Hill City on U.S. 385, turn left on Highway 87, and go 2 miles (3.2 km) to the campground

INFORMATION AND SERVICES

For Hill City information, contact the **Hill City Chamber of Commerce** (23935 U.S. 385, 605/574-2368, www.hillcitysd.com).

Campers can find groceries and basic supplies at **Krull's Market** (513 Main St., 605/574-2717). Medical services can be found at the **Monument Health Hill City Clinic** (238 Elm St., 605/574-4470, 7:30am-5:30am Mon.-Tues. and Thurs., 7:30am-4pm Wed., 8am-4pm Fri.). The **post office** is located at 150 E. Main St.

Rapid City

Rapid City rests on the eastern edge of the Black Hills and is the only urban area in the region. While it has the second-largest population in the state after Sioux Falls, Rapid City is a relatively small Midwestern community of about 78,000 residents.

While still a small city by any standards, Rapid City has a fast-growing economy, and it shows in the energy and money being invested in the downtown area. The charming heart of the city has expanded to encompass several more blocks of spruced-up enterprises, including new restaurants and hotels. Spend some time watching families playing in the summer fountain or ice-skating on the rink at Main Street Square. Follow the course of Rapid Creek to enjoy the string of parks and walking/bicycle path that line its banks.

Rapid City is easy to navigate, with four major traffic arteries. **Highway 44** runs east-west and connects the Rapid City Regional Airport to the downtown and western sections of the city. **Highway 79 South** on the east side of town is a four-lane highway that makes travel between the Southern and Central Hills fast and easy. The highway runs along the front range of the hills and as such doesn't involve the winding, twisted roads you find within the hills themselves. **Highway 79 North** cuts through the heart of town and then heads on to Sturgis. **I-90** runs right along the northern fringe of the city and is the primary route used by road-trippers heading to the Black Hills from the east and northwest. **U.S. 16,** otherwise known as **Mount Rushmore Road,** runs south from the downtown area and is the main artery that brings visitors from Rapid City to many of the region's best roadside attractions and to Mount Rushmore.

Lodging in and around the Rapid City core is concentrated in two primary locations: near downtown and along U.S. 16 (Mount Rushmore Rd.) and along I-90. The first is popular because of its quick and direct access to Mount Rushmore and other attractions in the area. The downtown historic district is fairly small, easily traversed on foot, and dotted with galleries, restaurants, and unique shops. The second location along I-90 works for road travelers arriving in Rapid City from either the east or west. Hotels—particularly the large chain hotels—are plentiful around exits 59 and 61. This area provides easy access to the Northern Hills for travelers headed west and to the Badlands (and Wall) for those headed east. Exit 57 is the easiest exit off I-90 to head south to the downtown district and to Mount Rushmore Road. From the airport, Highway 44 heading west will bring travelers right downtown.

To get a feel for the city, its layout, and the location of many important sites, consider taking the one-hour narrated tour provided by **City View Trolley Tours** (333 6th St., 605/394-6631, www.rapidride.org, 10am-5pm Mon.-Fri. June 1-Aug. 31, adult $2, senior and child under 12 $1). The trolley has 15 stops and can be picked up anywhere along the way. Hotel stops include the Rushmore Plaza Holiday Inn on the north end of town and The Rushmore and Alex Johnson hotels downtown. The ticket is good for the entire day. Feel free to get off anywhere, and get back on when you want to resume the tour. The fee for the tour can be paid to the bus driver. The

Rapid City

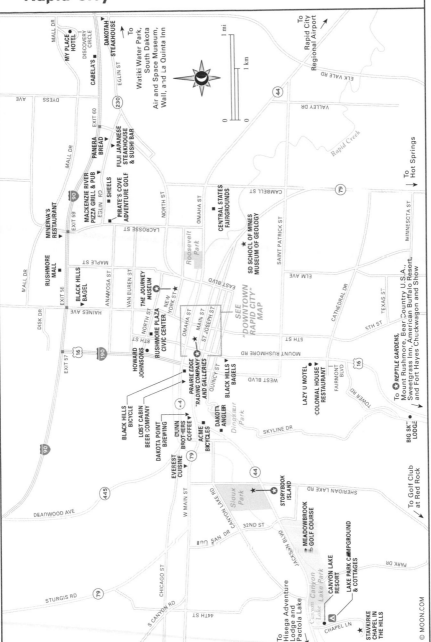

MY PLACE HOTEL
DISCOVERY CIRCLE
MALL DR
CABELA'S
DAKOTAH STEAKHOUSE
EGLIN ST
DYESS AVE
AVE
MALL DR
EXIT 60
230
To Watiki Water Park, South Dakota Air and Space Museum, Wall, and La Quinta Inn
To Rapid City Regional Airport
ELK VALE RD
44
VALLEY DR
Rapid Creek
To Hot Springs
PANERA BREAD
EXIT 59
FUJI JAPANESE STEAKHOUSE & SUSHI BAR
MACKENZIE RIVER PIZZA GRILL & PUB
SHEELS
PIRATE'S COVE ADVENTURE GOLF
EGLIN RD
NORTH ST
OMAHA ST
CAMBELL ST
CENTRAL STATES FAIRGROUNDS
79
MINERVA'S RESTAURANT
EXIT 58
MALL DR
LACROSSE ST
Roosevelt Park
MINNESOTA ST
RUSHMORE MALL
BLACK HILLS BAGEL
MAPLE ST
ANAMOSA ST
VAN BUREN ST
EAST BLVD
SD SCHOOL OF MINES MUSEUM OF GEOLOGY
SAINT PATRICK ST
HAINES AVE
DISK DR
THE JOURNEY MUSEUM
NEW YORK ST
ELM AVE
CATHEDRAL DR
TEXAS ST
5TH ST
RUSHMORE PLAZA CIVIC CENTER
NORTH ST
8TH ST
OMAHA ST
MAIN ST
ST JOSEPH ST
SEE "DOWNTOWN RAPID CITY" MAP
5TH ST
EXIT 57
16
90
HOWARD JOHNSONS
MOUNT RUSHMORE RD
To REPTILE GARDENS, Mount Rushmore, Bear Country U.S.A., Sweetgrass Inn, American Buffalo Resort, and Fort Hayes Chuckwagon and Show
90
PRAIRIE EDGE TRADING COMPANY AND GALLERIES
QUINCY ST
WEST BLVD
LAZY U MOTEL
COLONIAL HOUSE RESTAURANT
FAIRMONT BLVD
16
BLACK HILLS BICYCLE
BLACK HILLS BAGELS
LOST CABIN BEER COMPANY
44
DAKOTA ANGLER
Dinosaur Park
TOWER RD
DUNN BROTHERS COFFEE
DAKOTA POINT BREWING
79
ACME BICYCLES
SKYLINE DR
BIG SKY LODGE
EVEREST CUISINE
445
44
Sioux Park
STORYBOOK ISLAND
To Golf Club at Red Rock
DEADWOOD AVE
W MAIN ST
SHERIDAN LAKE RD
32ND ST
MEADOWBROOK GOLF COURSE
JACKSON BLVD
SAN DR
CANYON LAKE RD
CANYON LAKE RESORT
LAKE PARK CAMPGROUND & COTTAGES
PARK DR
CHICAGO ST
79
STURGIS RD
S CANYON RD
Canyon Lake
Canyon Lake Park
CHAPEL LN
STAVKIRKE CHAPEL IN THE HILLS
44TH ST
To Hisega Adventure Lodge and Pactola Lake

1 mi
1 km

© MOON.COM

Downtown Rapid City

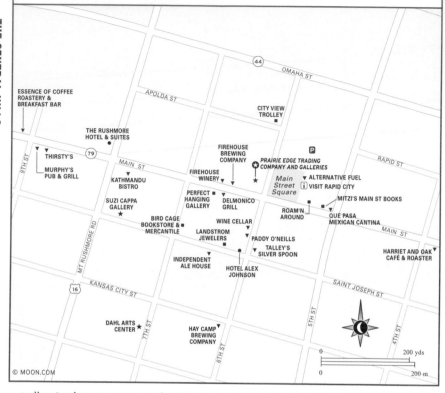

ESSENCE OF COFFEE
ROASTERY &
BREAKFAST BAR

APOLDA ST

OMAHA ST

44

CITY VIEW
TROLLEY

THE RUSHMORE
HOTEL & SUITES

FIREHOUSE
BREWING
COMPANY

PRAIRIE EDGE TRADING
COMPANY AND GALLERIES

THIRSTY'S

79

MAIN ST

9TH ST

MURPHY'S
PUB & GRILL

KATHMANDU
BISTRO

FIREHOUSE
WINERY

Main
Street
Square

RAPID ST

ALTERNATIVE FUEL

VISIT RAPID CITY

PERFECT
HANGING
GALLERY

DELMONICO
GRILL

MITZI'S MAIN ST BOOKS

SUZI CAPPA
GALLERY

ROAM'N
AROUND

QUE PASA
MEXICAN CANTINA

BIRD CAGE
BOOKSTORE &
MERCANTILE

WINE CELLAR

MAIN ST

LANDSTROM
JEWELERS

MT RUSHMORE RD

PADDY O'NEILLS

INDEPENDENT
ALE HOUSE

TALLEY'S
SILVER SPOON

HARRIET AND OAK
CAFÉ & ROASTER

HOTEL ALEX
JOHNSON

SAINT JOSEPH ST

16

KANSAS CITY ST

5TH ST

DAHL ARTS
CENTER

7TH ST

HAY CAMP
BREWING
COMPANY

6TH ST

4TH ST

0   200 yds

© MOON.COM

0   200 m

trolley circulates at approximately 60-minute intervals.

HISTORY

Rapid City, like many of the Black Hills communities, dates back to the late 1800s and the discovery of gold by Custer's expedition in 1874. The original businesses were established to service the mining camps. The community was named after Rapid Creek, which flows through the center of town. Easily accessible from both the south and east, Rapid City also developed as the hub of railroad activity in the hills. As a result, it became a commercial center, not just for mining, but also for the ranching and timber industries that followed. The carving of Mount Rushmore firmly established Rapid City as the center of tourism

for the Black Hills, and the construction of Ellsworth Air Force Base quickly increased the city's population and solidified it as the urban heart of the hills. Rapid City boasts the only commercial airport in the Black Hills region.

In more recent history, a natural disaster contributed to the landscape of Rapid City as it looks today. In June 1972, Rapid City and most of the eastern Black Hills experienced record rainfall. Rapid Creek rose 13 feet (4 m) in five hours and sent a wall of water crashing through town. It was a frightening flood, made more so by its unexpected arrival in the middle of the night. Tragically, 238 people lost their lives, some 1,265 families lost their homes, and another 3,000 homes were damaged. Thirty-six businesses were destroyed, as were 5,000 vehicles. The cost of damage to homes and businesses was estimated to be over $165 million throughout the Black Hills. As devastating as it was, the flood resulted in some positive change for Rapid City. Research into the flood determined that it was likely that a flood of this magnitude could happen again. To prevent future loss of life and property damage, the city decided that rebuilding along Rapid Creek would not be allowed. Instead, the Rapid Creek floodplain is lined with city parks connected by a walking and biking path that parallels the creek all the way through town. It's one of the community's nicest outdoor assets.

SIGHTS
★ Prairie Edge Trading Company and Galleries

In 1972, Ray and Rita Hillenbrand purchased the Triple Seven Ranch, a cattle ranch between the Badlands of South Dakota and Rapid City. In 1985, the Hillenbrands decided to convert the ranch to a more environmentally friendly place and started ranching bison instead of cattle. Bison are much more suited to the plains weather and ecology than cattle. Today, there are over 1,500 head of bison on the ranch.

The Hillenbrands expanded their interest in the plains and plains culture and decided they would also like to honor the heritage of the Northern Plains tribes and present that heritage to the general public. Equally important to them was a mission to create an outlet for the finest in Native American fine arts and crafts. The successful end result is the **Prairie Edge Trading Company and Galleries** (606 Main St., 605/342-3086 or 800/541-2388, www.prairieedge.com, 9am-9pm Mon.-Sat. and 10am-5pm Sun. summer, 9am-7pm Mon.-Sat. and 11am-4pm Sun. spring and fall, 10am-6pm Mon.-Sat. and 11am-5pm Sun. winter). It's not often that a retail establishment qualifies as a sight, but this store presents the best in traditional and contemporary Native American art, as well as work by other local and regional artists. It is not to be missed. From drums to dresses and artifacts to jewelry, beadwork, glassware, pottery, quilts, fine art, clothing, art supplies, books, and unique gift items, this store has it all. The beautiful displays are a pleasure to view, and if you fall in love with something, you can take it home with you.

★ The Journey Museum
The Journey Museum & Learning Center

downtown Rapid City

(222 New York St., 605/394-6923, www. journeymuseum.org, 10am-5pm Wed.-Sat., 1pm-5pm Sun., adult $14, senior and active military $12, student ages 6-17 $9, child under 6 free, admission is good for a two-day consecutive visit) is a great resource for visitors interested in the cultural, historical, and environmental aspects of the Black Hills. Collections include a museum of geology, with exhibits provided by the South Dakota School of Mines and Technology; an archaeology research center that explores the lives of Black Hills inhabitants from ice age hunters through 19th-century miners; a paleontology display outlining the dinosaur history of the area; and a Native American museum that provides visitors with an introduction to the culture and artworks of the various Sioux tribes of the region. Both traditional and contemporary art are on display, and a pioneer museum is dedicated to exploring the lives of mountain men, military expeditions, and miners.

Museums can sometimes feel stagnant and dusty, but not the Journey. It's a dynamic space with many interactive exhibits that visitors can touch, as well as view. In addition to the museum displays, the Journey has a space museum with an exciting digital presentation on the history of the universe. They have added interactive learning labs stocked with puzzles, microscopes, and books inviting visitors to experience some hands-on fun. These labs are highlighted by scheduled talks on various topics that may include Lakota games, dinosaurs, or geology.

The on-site theater continuously runs a series of videos that include an aerial tour of the Black Hills, a view of the universe from the age of dinosaurs through the pioneer era, and a feature on Lakota star knowledge as told through traditional stories and modern technology and science.

The Journey can be overwhelming, so it might be best to pick a couple of collections, give them the full attention they deserve, and call it a day. (Since admission is good for two consecutive days, save your receipt and come back for a second go-round.) The gift shop is marvelous, with a tasteful collection of jewelry, books, science toys, T-shirts, and other items.

Main Street Square Sculptures

Ten granite stones border Rapid City's Main Street Square on the west side. Nine more form a border along the south side. Two 35-foot (11-m) granite-clad spires sit between them. Sculptor Masayuki Nagase was chosen from an international pool of 88 applicants to carve them into representations of the flora, fauna, geology, and cultural and natural history of the Badlands, the Black Hills, and Rapid City. Called *Passage of Wind and Water,* the work began in 2013 and was completed in 2017. The stones were transformed into works of art using Japanese handheld carving tools. The carved stones outline a family-friendly space with tables, umbrellas, and nearby food, shops, and ice cream. Watch children playing in the fountain—or join them!

City of Presidents

The City of Presidents sculpture exhibit is impossible to miss in downtown Rapid City. Life-size bronzes of U.S. presidents adorn many of the street corners. The project began in 2000, with the goal of adding four presidents to the exhibit each year. **Visit Rapid City** (512 Main St., Ste. 240, 605/718-8484 or 800/487-3223, www.visitrapidcity.com, 8am-5pm Mon.-Fri.), located on the second floor of the shops at Main Street Square, is the tourism arm of the community and provides maps of the location of each president. Staff can answer questions about the presidents and the sculptors who created each statue. Maps can also be downloaded from the website along with a walking guide. There's a short scavenger hunt in the guide that's fun for kids and adults too! Statues in public places are usually larger than life-size, which seems to have an impact on our perception and makes these presidential statues look small. Watch as people walk by or stand or sit next to one, and you'll see that they are, indeed, about the size of a normal person. Since the presidents are always lolling about on their assigned corners, the display is viewable all year.

Dahl Arts Center

The **Dahl Arts Center** (713 7th St., 605/394-4101, www.thedahl.org, 10am-5pm Mon. Sat., free, donations welcome) is located in downtown Rapid City. In the mid-1970s, Arthur E. Dahl commissioned artist Bernard Thomas to paint a 180-foot-long (55-m), 360-degree cyclorama depicting 200 years of U.S. history. Dahl was a prominent banker in Rapid City, and his intention was to give the cyclorama and the building it was housed in to the city. Thomas was a Western artist born near Sheridan, Wyoming, in 1918. He was active in mural painting and executed several in the Wyoming region, though the Dahl building is the only art-in-the-round that he created.

The cyclorama was an extremely popular art form in the late 19th century. Painted in a circular space, cycloramas were usually designed to provide a panoramic view of a historic scene, battle, or site. The form eventually fell out of favor, and only a few original cycloramas remain. The Dahl cyclorama is an unusual and interesting return to an expression from an earlier time.

Today, the Dahl has been expanded to encompass three separate art galleries, a children's interactive area, a 250-seat event center, art classrooms, and a gift shop, in addition to the Thomas mural. Exhibitions at the galleries are rotated on a regular basis and eclectic in nature. The event center hosts literary events and concerts including a free Friday night emerging artists programs, where newcomers get to introduce themselves to the community or children learn to perform for an audience.

Museum of Geology

One of the best collections of South Dakota's ancient resources resides at the **Museum of Geology** (501 E. St. Joseph St., 605/394-2467, http://museum.sdsmt.edu, 9am-6pm Mon.-Sat. Memorial Day-Labor Day, 8:30am 4pm Mon.-Sat. winter, free) at the South Dakota School of Mines and Technology. The museum opened in 1885, and today, the collection includes over 350,000 specimens of fossils, rocks, and minerals from the Black Hills' ancient past. Displays include minerals from around the world, including fluorescent ones and local agates, meteorites, and native gold. Several life-size models of dinosaurs are exhibited. A triceratops skull on display at the museum is the official state fossil of South Dakota. Many of the museum's extensive collections are on loan to The Journey Museum. In addition to the museum, there is a small gift shop featuring books on paleontology (study of ancient life) and mineralogy. Guided tours are available for groups; call ahead to schedule.

Note that the museum's website features an "Activity List," which was created for a "Find Your Park" program in 2016. The program is finished, but the list will continue to be posted. It is full of fun and sometimes goofy things to do throughout the Black Hills. Families may find this especially entertaining.

Dinosaur Park

Fun for both kids and adults, **Dinosaur Park** (940 Skyline Dr., 605/343-8687, dawn-dusk daily, free) is one of the odder projects funded by the Works Progress Administration (WPA) in the 1930s. Built in 1936 (WPA project no. 960), the park is on the National Register of Historic Places. For decades, these concrete sculptures—including a T. rex, brontosaurus, stegosaurus, trachodont (reclassified now as an *Edmontosaurus annectens*), and triceratops—have been watching the prairie horizon and welcoming visitors to the Dakota Hogback Ridge upon which they reside. It's a 20-acre (8-ha) park with great views in every direction. The dinosaurs were originally gray but now are painted green and white. They aren't biologically accurate, but they are designed for good climbing. Have a seat on a dinosaur tail and enjoy the view.

The park is located in the **Skyline Wilderness Area,** and several hiking trails originate nearby. Trail maps can be found on Rapid City's Parks and Rec web pages (www. rcgov.org).

The park's **visitor center** (970 Skyline Dr., 605/343-8687, 8am-8pm daily Memorial Day-July, 8am-6pm daily Aug.-Labor Day, 9am-5pm daily May and Sept.) carries a nice collection of dinosaur books and gifts, rocks, and fossils and also has a snack bar with sandwiches and ice cream. Have an ice cream cone and enjoy the back porch picnic tables overlooking downtown Rapid City.

★ Storybook Island

Established in 1959 by the Rapid City Rotary Club, **Storybook Island** (1301 Sheridan Lake Rd., 605/342-6357, www.storybookisland. org, 9am-7pm daily Memorial Day-Labor Day weather permitting, free) is populated by life-size characters from fairy tales and other children's books. Meet the Cat in the Hat, Humpty Dumpty, the Three Little Pigs, Winnie the Pooh, Huck Finn, and more than 100 other stars of children's fiction. Ticketed attractions include a carousel and a small train ($3 each) as well as a bounce house ($2). The park is in a lovely setting next to Rapid Creek and the citywide bike path. There are also a snack bar and a small gift shop on the grounds.

South Dakota Air and Space Museum

Seven miles (11.3 km) east of Rapid City off I-90, the **South Dakota Air and Space Museum** (2890 Rushmore Rd., 605/385-5189, www.sdairandspacemuseum.com, 9am-4pm Tues.-Sat. summer, winter hours vary, free) is just outside the main gate to **Ellsworth Air Force Base.** This is a site for fans of military aviation and history. Over 30 aircraft displays range from WWII bombers to the contemporary B-1B Lancer. The Minuteman II intercontinental ballistic missile and other missiles are also on-site. Some of the planes are inside the hangar, but most are outside on the grounds. Since the museum is outside of the base, a military or other ID is not required for entry.

TOP EXPERIENCE

★ Reptile Gardens

Reptile Gardens (8955 S. Hwy. 16, 605/342-5873 or 800/335-0275, www.reptilegardens. com, 9am-6pm daily Memorial Day-Labor Day, 9am-5pm daily Mar.-Memorial Day and Labor Day-Oct., 9am-4pm daily Nov., rates vary seasonally, adult $12-20, senior $12-18, military $9-18, youth ages 11-15 $8-16, child ages 4-10 $7-14, child under 4 free) is a great family attraction in the hills. Considered one of the largest collections of reptiles in the world, with more species than anywhere else, the grounds of Reptile Gardens also include the Sky Dome; "Rattlesnake Gulch," which includes a 3D safari; a children's playground; gemstone sluicing and other activities; several outdoor exhibit areas, including areas for raptors, crocodiles, prairie dogs, and turtles; and a large gift shop and café. The exhibits are surrounded by beautiful gardens.

Special activities take place on the grounds. The **snake show** features several species, including a mangrove, Burmese python, cottonmouth, cobra, and prairie rattlesnake, which you can see up close while the handler talks about their unique characteristics. At the close of the show, visitors can pet the python! Staff members are always on hand near the **bird habitat** to give visitors an education on the raptors and other birds that live at the gardens. Feeding the alligators is part of the **alligator experience.** In addition, there's a presentation discussing the differences between alligators, crocodiles, and caimans, led by one of their keepers as he's wading among them and demonstrating their strength—and their teeth—when they are fed; check to see if the program is available on the day of your visit. All the activities are highly interactive, humorous, and filled with facts. Also on the grounds during the summer are **Aldabra giant tortoises** from the Seychelles. They are a rare and vulnerable species of gentle giants and a personal favorite.

The **Sky Dome** is landscaped and temperature controlled to create two separate environments: a desert and a tropical jungle. Lizards and frogs hop freely about the lush tropical plants, and finches fly throughout the dome. In the desert zone, cacti and other succulents thrive, and the Safari room of the dome is filled with orchids and more colorful flowers. Large parrots, macaws, and pythons complete the display. Look for the "pet a python" opportunity just outside the dome's entrance. The Sky Dome also houses some of the rarest snakes in the world. Big bugs (in enclosed exhibits) also inhabit the Sky Dome.

Reptile Gardens opened its doors in 1937, the brainchild of the somewhat nutty Earl Brocklesby (who would surprise visitors by removing his hat to display a coiled-up rattlesnake on his head!). Earl passed away in 1993, but the gardens remain family owned and operated to this day.

Bear Country U.S.A.

More than 20 species of animals roam the grounds of **Bear Country U.S.A.** (13820 S. U.S. 16, 605/343-2290, www.bearcountryusa.com, 9am-5pm daily late Apr., 8am-6pm daily May, 8am-7pm daily June-July, 8am-6pm daily Aug.-Labor Day, 8am-5pm daily Sept., 9am-4pm daily Oct., 9am-3pm daily Nov., weather permitting, adult $18, senior and military $16, child ages 5-12 $12, max charge $65 per vehicle) about 8 miles (12.9 km) south of Rapid City off U.S. 16. Motorcycles and convertibles are not allowed to drive through the park, but there are free courtesy vehicles available for use.

The first part of the park is a drive-through wildlife-viewing area. Expect to get an intimate view of the more than 200 bears on-site, as well as elk, reindeer, cougars, deer, bighorn sheep, and other North American mammals on this 3-mile (4.8-km) adventure. The animal habitat is carefully designed to give the animals an environment much like the one they would experience in the wild. It takes

about two hours, with many stops, to travel the loop.

At the end of the drive, stop at the **Wildlife Center** and at **Babyland,** which houses baby animals and smaller animals that would not be visible otherwise. A large gift shop features souvenirs, art prints, mugs, and other items, most of which follow a wildlife theme.

Those fortunate enough to be in the area in late April may be lucky enough to enjoy the annual **"Cub Fest."** The park officially opens during this event, and folks are invited to meet and pet the bear cubs, the next generation of bears for the park.

Chapel in the Hills

Somewhere around AD 1150, a church was erected by Viking longboat builders. The walls were supported with heavy beams. Wooden dowels were used instead of nails, and the only metal was the ornamental iron on the doors and the metal locks. Inside, highly skilled artisans added beautiful wood carving to the structure. That church, the Borgund Stavkirke, still stands today near Laerdal, Norway. Here in Rapid City, you can find an exact replica. The Norway Department of Antiquities generously provided a local builder with the blueprints of the Borgund Stavkirke, and as a result, the **Chapel in the Hills** (3788 Chapel Ln., 605/342-8281, www.chapel-in-the-hills.org, 8am-sunset daily May 1-Sept. 30, free) was born. On the west side of town, the small chapel is a quiet place, where a light breeze usually blows and beautiful gardens bloom—planted and tended by volunteers. The chapel was originally the home of a Lutheran vespers (evening prayer) radio show. The show moved to Minneapolis, and the chapel is now owned by the Evangelical Lutheran Church in America; today, it welcomes thousands of visitors, is the site of many a wedding, and offers vesper services in the summer (30 minutes or so) beginning at 7:30pm. It's a lovely spot, and it is not necessary to be Lutheran to enjoy the history, beauty, and craftsmanship of the pretty chapel. In addition to the church, admire the architecture of

the authentic grass-roofed *stabbur,* or store-house, which was built in Norway and shipped to the United States in pieces and reassembled. Today it serves as the on-site gift shop.

RECREATION
Biking and Hiking

Rapid City has over 13 miles (20.9 km) of municipal biking and walking trails that wind through the city following Rapid Creek. In addition, the **Skyline Wilderness Area** (along Skyline Dr.) on the ridge overlooking downtown and, just north, **Hanson-Larsen Memorial Park** (accessed via Founders Park along W. Omaha St.)—known as "M Hill" to locals—offer miles of hiking and biking trails with great views of the city to the east and of the Black Hills to the west. Contact the **City Parks and Recreation Department** (Recreation Dept., 515 West Blvd., 605/394-4175, www.rcgov.org/parks-and-recreation) for information and maps, or check with local bike shops.

Black Hills Bicycles (1401 W. Omaha St., 605/716-4497, www.blackhillsbicycles.com, 10am-6pm Mon.-Fri., 10am-5pm Sat.) and **Acme Bicycles** (700 Jackson Blvd., 605/343-9534, www.acmebicycles.com, 10am-6pm Mon.-Fri., 10am-4pm Sat.) are happy to share their recommendations for biking in the Central Hills. Both shops offer bike repair and supplies though, for the most part, you need to bring your own bike to Rapid City. That said, if you didn't bring one, check with Acme Bicycles; they sometimes have used bikes available on-site for rental and with advance planning may be able to arrange for bikes to be delivered from an affiliated shop in Hill City.

Fishing

Guided fly-fishing trips can be arranged with **Dakota Angler & Outfitter** (1010 Jackson Blvd., 605/341-2450, www.flyfishsd.com, 9am-6pm Mon.-Fri., 9am-5pm Sat., 10am-3pm Sun., half-day $250 for 1-2 people, $375 for 3 people, $499 for 3 people with 2 guides, full-day $425 for 1-2 people, $599 for 3 people, $850 for 3 people with 2 guides). All trips are catch and release. Note that South Dakota does not allow felt-soled wading boots—only rubber boots are allowed (which can be borrowed from Dakota Angler). The retail shop also carries all kinds of fishing gear, including fly rods, fly reels, waders, boots, flies, and other accessories.

Golf

The Golf Club at Red Rock (6520 Birkdale Dr., 605/718-4710, www.golfclubatredrock.com, 18 holes with cart $95, without cart $70, twilight hours after 3pm $65, 9 holes with cart $45, without cart $40, rental clubs 9 holes $25, 18 holes $40) is ranked as the number one public course in South Dakota by *Golf Week* magazine and has ranked in the top 200 in the country. It is ranked as the most difficult course in the area by local golfers. The 7,000-yard (6,400-m), par-72 course is marked by rolling fairways with dramatic elevation changes and surrounded by prairie grasses and ponderosa pines. **The Rock Bar & Grill** (605/716-3892, bar 8am-10pm Sun.-Thurs., 8am-midnight Fri.-Sat., grill 11am-9pm Mon.-Thurs., 11am-10pm Fri.-Sat., $11-18) on-site offers a full-bar and a great menu of sandwiches and burgers, plus a few chef's specials including steak, chicken, and seafood at reasonable prices.

Hart Ranch Golf Club (23645 Club House Dr., 605/341-5703, www.hartranch.com, 18 holes $59-65 summer, $49 spring and fall, winter with cart $50, 18 holes cart rental $35 for a single rider, $20 pp for 2 riders, 9 holes cart rental $22 for a single rider, $13 pp for 2 riders) is considered one of the best golf courses in South Dakota by *Golf Week* magazine. The 6,841-yard (6,255-m), par-72 course has also been listed as one of the "Places to Play" by *Golf Digest* magazine. In 2021 the course partnered with a local restaurant and opened **Shipwrecks on the Green** (605/399-4336, 8am-8pm Mon.-Thurs.,

1: Dinosaur Park 2: Reptile Gardens 3: Storybook Island 4: Canyon Lake Park

What is Black Hills Gold?

Just about every community in the Black Hills has a shop that sells "Black Hills Gold." Exactly what is that? Legally, all products sold with that label must be manufactured in South Dakota. However, it does not mean that the gold used to create the piece was *mined* in South Dakota. In addition to the legal definition, the Black Hills Gold designation has a traditional meaning. Simply put, traditional Black Hills Gold combines pink, green, and yellow gold in a design that incorporates grapes, grapevines, and grape leaves. The design originated in the gold mining towns of California (hence the grapes), migrated with the jewelers to the gold camps of Montana, and finally, followed the last gold rush in the United States to the Black Hills of South Dakota. The signature colors of traditional Black Hills Gold are created using alloys. To obtain pink gold, 24-karat yellow gold is alloyed with copper. To obtain green gold, 24-karat yellow gold is alloyed with silver.

7:30am-9pm Fri.-Sat., 7:30am-8pm Sun., $11) on-site. The grill menu includes sandwiches and burgers, flatbreads, and nachos. The bar provides a variety of beer and wine offerings.

Closest to town is **Meadowbrook Golf Course** (3625 Jackson Blvd., 605/394-4191, www.golfatmeadowbrook.com, 18 holes $50, cart rental $24 for a single rider, $18 pp for 2 riders, 9 holes $35, cart rental $18 for a single rider, $12 pp for 2 riders), which was voted as "Black Hills Best" golf course via a *Rapid City Journal* readers' choice poll. The course is in western Rapid City near Canyon Lake Park off Jackson Boulevard (Hwy. 44). It is a very pretty course. Nestled into the foothills of the Black Hills, Rapid Creek runs through the property, coming into play on five holes. A **Marco's Pizza** (605/791-4949, 10:30am-10pm Sun.-Thurs., 10:30am-11pm Fri.-Sat., $12-18) is on-site, with a lovely wraparound deck overlooking the course.

Other Recreation

Canyon Lake Park (4181 Jackson Blvd., 605/394-4175) is a municipal park in western Rapid City. Activities at the park include fishing, paddleboating, and biking. Paddleboats can be rented from **Canyon Lake Resort** (2720 Chapel Ln., 605/343-0234, www.canyonlakeresorts.com, 10am-7pm daily summer, weather permitting, 2-seater $8 per half hour, $12 per hour, 4-seater $10 per half hour, $15 per hour, life jackets provided).

Clustered around the hotels off I-90 on the northern side of town are two fun family recreation sites. The best minigolf can be found at **Pirate's Cove Adventure Golf** (1500 La Crosse St., 605/343-8540, www.piratescove.net/rapid-city, 9am-9pm daily Memorial Day-Labor Day, noon-8pm Mon.-Fri., 10am-8pm Sat.-Sun. May and Sept.-mid-Oct., adult $9.50, child ages 4-12 $8.50) off exit 67B from I-90. The course is like a small theme park, and players will find themselves putting into caves, from behind waterfalls, and around other pirate-themed obstacles. It's a charming setting and elevates minigolf to a new level of aesthetics.

The largest water park in a four-state region, the year-round **Watiki Indoor Waterpark Resort** (1314 N. Elk Vale Rd., 605/718-2445, www.watikiwaterpark.com, 8am-10pm Mon.-Sat. and 8am-8pm Sun. Memorial Day-Labor Day, 4pm-9pm Mon.-Thurs., 4pm-10pm Fri., 8am-10pm Sat., 8am-8pm Sun. off-season, summer age 7 and up $30, child ages 3-6 $20, winter $17-20, Spectator Pass $5-10) is off I-90 at exit 61. At 30,000 square feet (2,787 sq m), the park includes an arcade and a small bar and grill serving a limited selection of pizzas, subs, and salads. The park adjoins La Quinta Inn & Suites and Fairfield Inn & Suites.

ENTERTAINMENT
Chuckwagon Dinner Show

A decidedly Western phenomenon, the chuckwagon dinner and show generally feature music, corny jokes, and food served as diners walk through a line, plates in hand. Rapid City's chuckwagon dinner choice is the **Fort Hays Chuck Wagon & Show** (2255 Fort Hayes Dr., 605/343-3113 or 888/343-3113, www.mountrushmoretours.com, opens at 5pm, dinner at 6:30pm, show 7:15pm-8:15pm, daily mid-May-mid-Oct., adult $39, senior $37, child ages 5-12 $22, child 4 and under free) provides traditional chuckwagon food, including sliced barbecue beef or baked chicken with potatoes, beans, and biscuits and honey. The show primarily features a contemporary country music selection of songs and a lot of corny, family-friendly humor. The grounds of the Fort Hays chuckwagon dinner include some of the sets from the movie *Dances with Wolves*. There is also a rope-making shop, a tin plate-making shop, a brickmaker, a blacksmith, and a gift shop.

Tours around the Fort Hays site are available from **Mount Rushmore Tours** (605/343-3113 or 888/343-3113, www.mountrushmoretours.com, mid-May-mid-Oct.). They include breakfast at Fort Hays and an eight-hour narrated tour of many of the major sites of the hills, including Mount Rushmore, Custer State Park, and Crazy Horse Memorial, and return in time for the dinner and show (adult $109 adult, child $57, all you can eat pancake breakfast and chuckwagon dinner included, lunch stop meal not included).

Performing Arts

The **Performing Arts Center of Rapid City** (601 Columbus St., 605/394-6191, box office 605/394-1786, www.performingartsrc.org, box office noon-5pm Mon.-Fri.) lives in the Rapid City High School with other community arts organizations and provides concerts by the Rapid City symphony as well as touring artists, plays, and children's shows. The facility has two theaters available. The historic theater seats 830 patrons, and the intimate studio theater can accommodate 170.

The **Black Hills Symphony Orchestra** (605/348-4676, www.bhsymphony.org, adult $22-32, student $12-22, military $17-27) established in the early 1930s, plays a concert series that runs October-April at the center.

The **Black Hills Shrine of Democracy Chorus** (605/646-3077, www.shrineofdemocracychorus.org) is a chapter of the Barbershop Harmony Society. The group meets on Thursday at a rehearsal room at the center at 6:30-8:30pm and invites others to come and sing with them.

The **Black Hills Community Theater** (605/394-1787, www.bhct.org) also operates out of the center and puts on great performances throughout the year.

Events

Several blocks of downtown Rapid City are closed off to traffic and opened up to pedestrians during the celebration known as **Summer Nights** (www.rapidcitysummernights.com and www.mainstreetsquare.org, 5:30pm-8:30pm Thurs. Memorial Day-Labor Day, free). Music, local artisans, gallery walks, and activities for children and adults are organized. Activities and music for this extremely popular event change every week.

The **Central States Fair** (800 San Francisco St., 605/355-3861, www.central statesfair.com, late Aug.) is a 10-day celebration that features lots of free entertainment, livestock shows, concerts, rodeos, and other events, like a demolition derby and supercross dirt bike races. There are also carnival rides, pig races, food, and hobby and craft competitions. The cost to get into the grounds is free before 3pm and $3 after 3pm for folks without a ticketed event. All concerts are $38, and other events (such as the demolition derby, supercross races, and the PRCA Range Days Rodeo) are $17 for adults and $7 for children. Carnival ride passes for unlimited rides cost $35 per day. Alternatively, tickets can be purchased for individual rides. It's all delightful noise and lights, cheap rides, and junk food—a great way to end the summer.

The **Black Hills Stock Show & Rodeo** (www.blackhillsstockshow.com) is a one-week rodeo and stock show that occurs the last few days of January and the first week of February. It is held at the **Rushmore Plaza Civic Center** (444 N. Mt. Rushmore Rd., 605/394-4115, www.gotmine.com) and at the Central States Fairgrounds. Ticket prices range $10-30. The stock show events include a banquet and ball, livestock shows, horse events, a petting zoo, a Western art show, sheepdog trials, and nightly concerts and rodeo performances. Vendors sell everything from horse trailers to handcrafted jewelry.

Nightlife

The **Independent Ale House** (625 St. Joseph St., 605/718-9492, www.independentalehouse. com, 3pm-close Sun.-Thurs., 11am-close Fri.-Sat.) is the best place for beer selection in Rapid City. For beer tasting at its finest, the alehouse has 40 rotating beers on tap and over 145 different bottle selections. In case you get hungry while here, there is handcrafted pizza available ($10-13 personal size). Brick and wood-paneled walls, a *very* long bar, and lots of wooden tables are the interior features. While beer is their specialty, there is a pretty impressive wine list, too.

Paddy O'Neill's Irish Pub (523 6th St., 605/342-1210, ask for the pub, www. alexjohnson.com, 7am-2am daily) is one of the best-loved pubs in Rapid City. Part of the historic Hotel Alex Johnson, Paddy O'Neill's has a cozy ambience and offers upscale beers and whiskey plus a full-service menu of drinks. There is a pub menu ($11-17) of burgers, sandwiches, and pizza along with a few specialty items like fish-and-chips and Irish steak and mushroom pie. The pub serves breakfast as well. It's another venue that squeezes in local musicians on weekend evenings.

Brewpubs and Wineries

Locally owned and operated **Firehouse Brewing Company** (610 Main St., 605/348-1915, www.firehousebrewing.com, 11am-10pm Sun.-Thurs., 11am-midnight Fri.-Sat, hours vary off-season) is the oldest brewing house in South Dakota and has a state-of-the-art facility in downtown Rapid City. There is

a comfortable bar where patrons can have a glass, and upstairs a dining area—as the brewing company is also a full-service restaurant, patrons can sample on-site crafted beers over meals—overlooking the brewery and bar. Frequently, live entertainment is on hand either in the bar or outside on the patio. The same folks own **Firehouse Winery** (620 Main St., 605/716-9463, www. firehousewinecellars.com, 11am-8pm Sun.-Thurs., 11am-10pm Fri.-Sat.), which offers tours as well as tastings. Six wines may be sampled for just $5. Peruse the gift boutique for interesting items for wine lovers.

At **Hay Camp Brewing Company** (601 Kansas City St., 605/718-1167, www. haycampbrewing.com, 3pm-9pm Mon.-Wed., 3pm-10pm Thurs, noon-10pm Fri.-Sat., noon-6pm Sun.), brewers Sam Papendick and Karl Koth are happy to talk with patrons about the chemistry of beer making. They started brewing beer in Sam's garage and are now in their second location with 3,200 square feet (297 sq m) of serving space due to the popularity of their brews. Sample from a growing roster of beers ($2-3 a sample) and take off with a growler for your home or hotel. Beer aficionados shouldn't miss it. Food is sometimes available from a revolving cast of food trucks. There is a concert space on-site. In addition to concerts, the folks at Hay Camp host some very interesting activities, including a weekly trivia night, so check the calendar of events on their website and Facebook page.

Lost Cabin Beer Company (1401 W. Omaha St., 605/718-5678, www.lostcabinbeer. com, noon-10pm Mon.-Thurs., noon-11pm Fri.-Sat., noon-8pm Sun.) brews small-batch ales and lagers. The decor features walls paneled with pine that has been stained blue by the paths taken by the Black Hills National Forest's nemesis, the pine beetle. Flights are à la carte at $2 per 5-ounce (148-ml) sample. Growlers are also available. The brewpub is small but energized, serious about their brews, and a fun place to sample some distinctive beers, many with a high alcohol content! Food is provided with daily rotating food truck visits. Music is on tap in addition to beer from time to time. A small patio is on the outside parking lot.

Tucked between West Main and Omaha and housed in the remodeled old Landstrom's Jewelry building, **Dakota Point Brewing** (405 Canal St., 605/791-2739, www. dakotapointbrewing.com, noon-8pm Mon.-Thurs., noon-10pm Fri.-Sat., noon-6pm Sun.) has industrial garage-size doors that open out to a patio for great indoor/outdoor beer tasting. Sample a 5-ounce (148-ml) taster for $3. Cask and draft beer are available.

SHOPPING
Downtown Boutiques
The best way to discover unique shops downtown is to put on some walking shoes and roam around. Most of the cute boutiques are in the six-block area bordered by 5th Street, Main Street, Kansas City Road, and Mount Rushmore Road. Many of the shops are run by owners who are more than happy to talk about their products, their businesses, and the best of Rapid City. As in many cities nationwide, there has been an increased focus on energizing the downtown district, and new boutiques are popping up on a regular basis.

The center of downtown activity is a complete city block called **Main Street Square** (512 Main St., Ste. 980, 605/716-7979, www. mainstreetsquare.org). Outdoors, the square sports a dancing water fountain and other water features, along with several rock formations carved into artistic representations of the Black Hills, Rapid City, and the Badlands. Tables, umbrellas, and chairs are available to the public for picnics or just a place to sit for a spell. In the summertime, people are welcome to step into the dancing fountain and enjoy the cool spray. In addition, during the summer months, the square organizers sponsor events almost every weekend, including wine and beer tastings, concerts, free movies under the stars, theatrical performances, and a farmers market. In the winter, the water feature turns into a small ice rink. It's a festive and fun corner downtown.

In addition to the events and the open space, Main Street Square is also home to several small shops. **Mitzi's Main Street Books** (510 Main St., 605/721-2665, www. mitzisbooks.com, 10am-6pm Mon.-Sat., 11am-4pm Sun.) is a great location for folks who support independent bookstores and love paper over screens when it comes to the reading experience. Pick up a book and take advantage of the square's outdoor tables. Right next door is **Roam'n Around** (512 Main St., 605/716-1660, www.roamnaround.com, 10am-6pm Mon.-Sat.), a great little store that carries everything a traveler or outdoor adventurer could want. Look for great outdoor clothing lines, backpacking and climbing gear, maps, helmets, camping accessories, sunglasses, and hats (if it's summer, you should be wearing them). The shop also carries Moon travel guides.

The **Bird Cage Book Store and Mercantile** (524 7th St., 605/431-8231, www. wordcarrier.com, 11am-5pm Wed.-Fri., 11am-6pm Sat., 11am-4pm Sun.) is an independent bookstore and community center. Lakota-owned and operated, the store features Native American, multicultural, and Indigenous literature and nonfiction. The store hosts book clubs, a writer's group, concerts, book signings, and the "Free the Bird Poetry Stage." The mercantile also features handmade quilts and aprons by Lakota women, prairie sage bouquets, journals, skin care products, and other unique gifts items.

Landstrom's Jewelry (620 St. Joseph St., 605/342-6663, 9am-3pm Mon.-Sat.) is the oldest full-service jeweler in Rapid City and carries a significant collection of Black Hills Gold. The friendly shop has a long history in the Black Hills, and the owner knows his business and is more than happy to chat about what the "Black Hills Gold" designation means.

Galleries
The **Prairie Edge Trading Company and Galleries** (606 Main St., 605/342-3086 or 800/541-2388, www.prairieedge.com,

9am-9pm Mon.-Sat. and 10am-5pm Sun. summer, 9am-7pm Mon.-Sat. and 11am-4pm Sun. spring and fall, 10am-6pm Mon.-Sat. and 11am-5pm Sun. winter) is beautiful enough to be listed as a must-see site. The gallery specializes in Lakota works and other contemporary pieces. The bookshop upstairs features works of fiction and nonfiction by and about Indigenous populations. There are beads, quilts, clothing, notecards, and a very eclectic selection of gift items.

The **Perfect Hanging Gallery** (621 Main St., 605/348-7768, www.perfect hanginggallery.com, 10am-5:30pm Tues.-Fri., 10am-4pm Sat.) showcases the works of fine artists from throughout the Black Hills. The gallery has a rotating roster of artists on display. In addition to selling art, the staff at the gallery will help ensure it is perfectly framed. The gallery also carries stationery and interesting gift items, including maps, candles, puzzles, and jewelry.

The **Suzi Cappa Gallery** (722 St. Joseph St., 605/791-3578, www.suziecappaart.com, noon-4pm Mon.-Fri.) is a light, airy space filled with beautiful and creative pieces. A project of Black Hills Works, a nonprofit agency that works for the benefit of adults with disabilities, the gallery demonstrates that everyone has artistic vision. Over 100 artists display their works on a rotating schedule. It is a favorite place to get notecards and prints as many of the artworks are available in those formats.

Sporting Goods Shops

Two sports superstores in Rapid City grapple for your shopping dollars by making a visit to their establishment more of an adventure than a shopping excursion. Both are just off of I-90.

Scheels (1225 Eglin St., 605/342-9033, www.scheels.com, 9am-9pm Mon.-Sat., 11am-6pm Sun.) in Rapid City is part of a 26-state chain that opened in 1902. The store has over 100,000 square feet (9,290 sq m) of merchandise. It's made shopping for equipment a bit of an expedition, with sports simulators, an archery range, and on-site specialists available

to answer questions. Somewhat incongruously, a fudge shop called Gramma Ginna's is at the entrance to the store, so if the thought of hiking leaves you hungry, you can fill up on the likes of amaretto, praline, almond, maple walnut, or any of several other flavors of fudge. In the summer the store rents kayaks and paddleboards. In the winter, snowboards and skis can be rented. The store is off I-90 at exit 60. Head south on East North Street and right on Eglin.

Cabela's (3231 E. Mall Dr., 605/388-5600, www.cabelas.com, 9am-9pm Mon.-Sat. and 9am-7pm Sun.) is most famous for the museum-quality animal displays in its retail outlets. The Rapid City store has more than 80,000 square feet (7,432 sq m) of sports shopping entertainment. In addition to sales, the store is full of events for outdoors enthusiasts. Want to know what your gun is worth or how to prepare for a disaster, buy live bait for fishing, or try your hand at archery? All of these various learning experiences are available at the store. It is off I-90 exit 61; from there, head north (left if you are headed east, right if you are headed west) on Elk Vale Road and take a left on Mall Drive.

FOOD

There are two major centers for food and hotels in and around Rapid City. One area is along the interstate and the other is close to downtown Rapid City including along U.S. 16 heading in the direction of Mount Rushmore. Chains dominate close to the highway. Most local and regional restaurants are closer to downtown. Considering that this is a small community, there are many fine choices.

Downtown
CASUAL DINING

Two side-by-side venues billed as bar and grills both offer great food, a variety of tap and bottled beer (with full bar service), and outside dining areas for customers. It's hard to choose a favorite between these two establishments, but they are different enough that a choice has more to do with mood than preference. ★ **Murphy's Pub & Grill** (510 9th St., 605/791-2244, www.murphyspubandgrill.com, 11am-midnight Mon.-Thurs., 11am-2am Fri.-Sat., 11am-7pm Sun., $11-21) is a little more upscale. It feels more like a contemporary restaurant than a bar and adds a little creativity to its offerings. Start with an "Adult Grilled Cheese" (cheddar, swiss, parmesan, and mozzarella cheese, with tomato and onion), for example, and choose from 10 add-ins like steak, grilled chicken, mushrooms, or peppers. Dinner entrées include grilled salmon, fish-and-chips, and a sirloin with mashed potatoes. Enjoy the outdoor deck and the fire pit in cooler months. **Thirsty's** (819 Main St., 605/343-3104, 11am-9:30pm Mon.-Thurs., 11am-10pm Fri.-Sat., $11-17) is the kind of place where people remember you and it doesn't take long to feel like a regular. Sports fans love it for the local and national sportscasts, and everyone else loves it for the friendly and casual feel. There are 30 beers on tap, including some local and regional craft beer choices and a fairly extensive bar menu including burgers, sandwiches, and wraps with a little bit of Mexico thrown in with a burrito, taco salad, Indian taco, and quesadilla. Thirsty's has one of the nicest patios in town.

On Mount Rushmore Road, the main artery into the Black Hills, the **Colonial House** (2315 Mt. Rushmore Rd., 605/342-4640, www.colonialhousernb.com, 7am-9pm daily, breakfast $12-17, lunch $14-18, dinner $17-28) has long been a local favorite. It's casual, spacious, and features both lots of booths and lots of table. The restaurant specializes in comfort food and is a great choice for any meal. The signature breakfast dish for those with a sweet tooth is caramel nut French toast; for everyone else there is a wide variety of omelets, egg dishes, hotcakes, and waffles. Lunch includes a full range of sandwiches, burgers, pastas, and salads. Dinner includes many of the sandwiches offered for lunch and adds specialties including salmon, shrimp, top sirloin, walleye, and, of course, the comfort foods—chicken-fried steak and Southern fried chicken. The restaurant is also stocked with a full bar.

Firehouse Brewing Company (610 Main St., 605/348-1915, www.firehousebrewing.com, 11am-10pm Sun.-Thurs., 11am-midnight Fri.-Sat., hours vary off-season, $14-26) is not only the first craft beer brewing company in South Dakota but also a restaurant. It's housed in a 100-year-old building that has been renovated and decorated with all kinds of firefighting memorabilia in honor

Firehouse Brewing Company in downtown Rapid City

of the building's history as a fire hall, including great murals, old photos, and a collection of fire marshal badges and firefighting gear. The menu offers such items as sandwiches, burgers, and barbecue (ribs, pork, sausage, and chicken). It's a place for good food, craft-brewed beer, live entertainment, and dining on the outside patio during summer. It's also kid-friendly (children receive fire hats and coloring books). The Firehouse is a very popular local destination.

MEXICAN

Que Pasa Mexican Cantina (502 Main St., 605/716-9800⊠, www.quepasacantina.com, 11am-9pm Sun.-Thurs., 11am-10pm Fri.-Sat., $13-17) has several things going for it: good fajitas, a great tequila bar, and two marvelous outdoor patios. Lit by fire pits and torchlights, dining on either the rooftop or the downstairs patio is a real treat. All the favorites are on the menu; in addition to fajitas, there are enchiladas, tacos, burritos, rellenos, and quesadillas (fish, chicken, shrimp, beef, or steak). A great addition to the menu has been vegetarian options for all of the offerings. Warm, light, and crispy tortilla chips are served with salsa when you're seated and are a delightful introduction to the meal. For tequila lovers, the cantina carries 52 tequila labels—enough to try a new one every week of the year.

SOUTH ASIAN

Two restaurants downtown feature the food of Nepal, India, and Tibet. What these restaurants have in common is they smell delicious from the moment you walk in the door.

Cozy ★ **Kathmandu Bistro** (727 Main St., 605/343-5070, www.kathmandubistro.com, 11am-2:30pm and 5pm-9:30pm daily, $14-25) is nestled in a historic 1886 building. The floors are hardwood, the walls are brick, and the atmosphere is warm and relaxing. There is an extensive vegetarian menu as well as chicken, seafood, lamb, and alligator (yes, alligator) selections. The food is wonderfully enhanced with spice, nuts and/or raisins, curry, chutney, or the familiar onions and garlic.

Everest Cuisine (2328 W. Main St., 605/343-4444, http://theeverestcuisine.com, 11am-2:30pm and 5pm-9:30pm daily, lunch buffet $13, dinner $13-21) serves a wide variety of tandoori, curries, masalas, and kormas, featuring seafood, chicken, lamb, and vegetarian entrées. The buffet varies from day to day and is a great bargain.

FINE DINING

★ **Delmonico Grill** (609 Main St., 605/791-1664, www.delmonicogrill.com, 5pm-9pm Mon.-Sat.) is a beautiful fine dining establishment, with muted chocolate and gray colors, hardwood floors, and cozy booths. They've somehow mastered sound control, too; despite the high ceilings, it's quite comfortable talking at a normal volume. And then there is the food. In addition to specialty entrées ($28-40) and steaks and other grill items ($50-72), the restaurant has many lighter dishes ($12-18). Sandwiches include standard burger options, but look for some creative choices, such as the Kona burger, with an espresso rub, *mosto* (the juice of fresh pressed grapes), and brie. Dinner guests will be offered a wide variety of steak cuts either dry or wet aged. There's also a vegetarian cauliflower steak. Reservations are recommended.

At the **Wine Cellar** (513 6th St., 605/718-2675, www.winecellarrestaurant.com, 3:30pm-9pm Tues.-Thurs., 3:30pm-10pm Fri., 5pm-10pm Sat. summer, winter hours vary, $17-41), dinner is complete only if served with the perfect wine. Housed in a historic building near Hotel Alex Johnson, right in the center of downtown Rapid City, the Wine Cellar sports black tablecloths, hardwood floors, and stamped tin ceilings. Recently renovated by the father-daughter duo, Dave Hirning and Christy Land, the goal is to serve fresh and locally sourced food whenever possible. In the summer, tables are set on the sidewalk for café dining. It's a dog-friendly patio! The chef features seasonal menu offerings every week, in addition to a creative menu of Californian and European choices, such as gourmet pizza, pasta, and traditional pork, chicken, and salmon. Over 20 wines are available by the glass, with 70 wines available by the bottle. This delightful restaurant is cozy and elegant. Reservations are recommended. The kitchen closes 30 minutes before the restaurant closes.

Local favorite **Tally's Silver Spoon** (530 6th St., 605/342-7621, www.tallyssilverspoon. com, 7am-2pm and 4pm-9pm daily, hours vary seasonally, breakfast and lunch $10-20, dinner $16-39) is modern and upscale but still casual and offers tasty, creative meals. Across the street from the Hotel Alex Johnson, it is one of the few sit-down restaurants open for breakfast downtown. And breakfast is a treat here, with offerings including creative pancakes, French toast, crepes, and waffles, and classic comfort foods like chicken-fried steak, omelets, and Benedicts. Vegetarian options exist, and staff are happy to modify meals to exclude meat when asked. Lunch includes a variety of sandwiches, soups, and salads. A happy hour with small plates runs 4pm-6pm daily. Dinner carries forward many of the sandwich options (and prices) from the lunch menu and adds some interesting entrées, including deer, crab, and rib eye. The chef calls the food selections "fine diner" cooking. Reservations are recommended for dinner.

CAFÉS AND COFFEE
Heading for the hills first thing in the morning? Make your first stop ★ **Black Hills Bagels** (913 Mt. Rushmore Rd., 605/399-1277, www.blackhillsbagels.com, 6am-3pm Mon.-Fri., 7am-3pm Sat.-Sun., $9), where the best bagels and cream cheese can be found. Bagel breakfast and lunch sandwiches are also on order with a selection of salads. In the winter the menu is completed with chili and soup. For those folks close to I-90, there is a drive-through **Black Hills Bagels on Haines** (1720 N. Haines Ave.). In both locations, they serve great coffee from Dark Canyon (a local roastery) and specialty espresso coffee drinks.

Located on Main Street Square in the downtown area, **Alternative Fuel** (512 Main St.,

605/7913791, www.alternativefuelcoffeehouse. com, 7am-4pm Mon.-Thurs., 7am-5pm Fri., 8am-5pm Sat., 9am-4pm Sun., $7) is a cozy coffee and pastry shop great for people-watching. The food menu is limited but fun since patrons can design their own sandwiches (from a list of possible ingredients) or just pick from the menu. Menu items include a chicken potpie, a breakfast burrito, soup, and quiches.

The popular **Harriet & Oak Café & Roaster** (329 Main St., 605/791-0396, www. harrietandoak.com 7:00am-3pm daily, $9-12) has a hipster atmosphere, with a VW bus in the dining area. They roast their own coffee on-site and have a full espresso bar. A tasty selection of breakfast and lunch items includes acai bowls, breakfast pasties, creative sandwiches (like a Monte Cristo) and burritos (including one featuring sweet potato), and some nice vegetarian bowls. Beer and wine are available. A favorite of the arts crowd, I've heard it described as rustic/industrial, and that seems about right. With lots of wood and steel and that van, it's a friendly place to hang out.

Essence of Coffee Roastery & Breakfast Bar (908 Main St., 605/342-3559, www.essenceofcoffee.com, 6:30am-3pm Mon.-Fri., 7am-1pm Sat.-Sun., $10-15) is about the coziest roastery in Rapid City, with wood booths and floors, a couple of different rooms, and a small space for open-air dining. The food is good, the coffee excellent, and breakfast is served all day. The breakfast menu has a little bit of everything, including oatmeal, sweet or savory crepes, pancakes, and some interesting egg dishes. Lunch includes some burger choices, sandwiches, and salads (such as balsamic steak and Greek chicken salads).

Dunn Brothers Coffee (405 Canal St., 605/721-0600, www.dunnbrothers.com, 6am-6pm Mon.-Sat., 7am-5pm Sun., $6-10) provides a full menu of hot and cold espresso drinks, pastries, and muffins. Other breakfast options include build-your-own egg sandwiches (grain, meat, vegetable, and cheese choices) or oatmeal. Lunch selections include sandwiches on fresh baked ciabatta, whole-grain wraps, and personal-sized naan pizzas. The location is ideal, with a view of one of Rapid's many parks that follow the course of Rapid Creek. Outdoor and indoor seating are available.

I-90 Corridor

Food options just off the interstate are primarily chains, but some go way beyond the typical burgers and fries. Look to exit 60 off of I-90 and head south (less than a quarter of a mile), then take a right on Eglin Street. It's a busy shopping and dining street that extends for a couple of miles. Exits 59 and 61 also have good dining options just off the interstate.

CASUAL DINING

Regional chain **MacKenzie River Pizza, Grill & Pub** (1205 Eglin St., 605/791-1292, www.mackenzieriverpizza.com, 11am-9pm Thurs.-Mon., $12-25) has both traditional and creative pizzas (with a fabulous crust), pasta, burgers, wraps, and salads served amid rustic river decor. Tall birch trees act as a room divider and a back-lit river photo hangs from the ceiling. A full bar complements the meals. It's good food at reasonable prices in a nice environment.

Off of exit 59, look for the Best Western Ramkota hotel to find **Minerva's Restaurant and Bar** (2111 N. Lacrosse St., 605/394- 9505, www.minervasrestaurants.com, 7am-9pm Mon.-Thurs., 7am-10pm Fri.-Sat., breakfast and lunch $10-18, dinner $18-30) housed inside. The restaurant is spacious and cozy at the same time, with an old-style club feel to it. Dark wood paneling, gold walls, and a beautiful stone fireplace are featured in the main dining area. It's a great place for a comfortable breakfast before setting off for the day. There are extensive offerings of signature dishes, pasta, and sandwiches at reasonable prices. Dinner adds steak entrées. Foods are carefully prepared and complemented with creative touches. It's definitely far and above the kind of menu usually found at a "hotel restaurant."

Panera Bread (1830 Eglin St., 605/646-6084, www.panerabread.com, 6am-9pm daily, $6-12) is a bakery with an extensive selection of bagels and cream cheese, pastries, cookies, muffins, and breads that also happens to be a gourmet fast-food restaurant. Order at the counter, take a number, and it'll be delivered to your table. A variety of egg sandwiches are featured for breakfast. Delicious soups, sandwiches, and flat bread pizzas are featured at lunch.

JAPANESE

The **Fuji Japanese Steakhouse & Sushi Bar** (1731 Eglin St., 605/721-8886, www.fujisteakhouse-sd.com, 11am-2:30pm and 4:30pm-9:30pm Mon.-Thurs., 11am-2:30pm and 4:30pm-10pm Fri., 11am-10pm Sat., 11am-9pm Sun., lunch $11-13, dinner $17-37) is an extremely fun and tasty place to eat. On one side of the restaurant is a light and elegant dining area with table service. On the other side, a circle of guests can enjoy watching entrées cooked on the hibachi grill, with fast knife work and an entertaining chef. Other delicious food options include teriyaki, tempura, and selections from the sushi bar.

FINE DINING

★ **Dakotah Steak House** (1325 N. Elk Vale Rd., 605/791-1800, www.dakotahsteakhouse.com, 4pm-10pm Mon.-Sat., $19-50) is off I-90, exit 61. It's just south of the highway and before the traffic light on the western (right) side of the road. Inside, the restaurant is a combination of casual and elegant and Western in feel, with wood floors, olive walls, and cherry accents. In the winter, there's a roaring fire. It's been rated "the best steakhouse in South Dakota" by *Business Insider*. Several cuts and serving sizes are available; many can be shared by two. Other alternatives include walleye, salmon, chicken, and prime rib. The three sisters soup is delicious as a starter. The menu includes wine suggestions for each entrée. Take a close look at the *Buffalo Sculpture* by Tony Lopez near the entrance to the building. It's superb.

ACCOMMODATIONS

Hotels in the Rapid City area are clustered around exits off I-90 on the north side of town and along Mount Rushmore Road near downtown. In both locations, chain hotels dominate and are easy to find. The western edge of the city, off Highway 44, is closest to the wooded Black Hills, and cabins and campgrounds predominate. For access to the best attractions in the Central and Southern Hills, the best places to stay are near the downtown area or just south of downtown off U.S. 16. Downtown locations provide easy access to boutique shopping, galleries, restaurants, and pubs. Hotels near the I-90 corridor offer quick routes to the Northern Hills and the Badlands. Note that the prices listed below are based on summer season prices (generally Memorial Day-Labor Day) for a typical room, cabin, or space, unless otherwise noted. For venues that only give seasons consider "shoulder season" to be May and September-October and winter to be November-April.

Under $150

As the main route into the Black Hills, traffic-heavy Mount Rushmore Road is lined with chain hotels, but a small motel has managed to hold its own against the competition. **The Lazy U Motel** (2215 Mt. Rushmore Rd., 605/343-4242, summer $89, winter $89-99) offers clean, quiet rooms at reasonable rates year-round. They are "pet-friendly" rooms available with a fee of $20 per night for small pets and $30 per night for larger animals. The original motel, built in 1957, had 16 rooms with the historical beamed ceiling look of the era. Since then, 9 rooms have been added to the mix, and all have queen or double queen accommodations. All rooms have at least a small refrigerator, microwave, and air-conditioning. The rooms are very basic, but this is a great choice for reasonably priced accommodations, close to restaurants and grocery stores, and not far from downtown Rapid City.

On the western side of town, **Canyon Lake Resort** (2720 Chapel Ln., 605/343-0234, www.canyonlakeresortsd.com, Memorial Day-Labor Day motel rooms $119, cabins $119-239, off-season motel rooms $69-99, cabins $119-239, dogs $10 per night) is next to one of Rapid City's prettiest parks. While the rooms are nothing fancy, they are still a good deal. Each motel room has two queen-size beds and a kitchenette. The studio cabin has one queen bed. Two and three bed cabins as well as lodge space for family reunions are available; call for pricing. There is a fire pit outside the rooms, and guests can paddleboat on the lake for free. Sited on two acres, this is a quiet spot, close to the Meadowbrook Golf Course and Canyon Lake Park. There is cable and free Wi-Fi. As a bonus, the City View Trolley stops here at 30-minute intervals. It's a great way to spend a day downtown without having to drive.

$150-250

★ **The Rushmore Hotel and Suites** (445 Mt. Rushmore Rd., 605/348-8300, www.therushmorehotel.com, Memorial Day-Labor Day $190-250, May and Sept. $110-190, Oct.-Apr. $80-145) offers 177 rooms in downtown Rapid City. Floors 6-9 of the hotel are wonderfully unique and provide three styles of rooms, all of which were designed around the concepts of sustainability, incorporating eco-friendly carpeting, energy-efficient lighting, and recycled materials for the room decor wherever possible. Eco-Platinum Rooms are designed with a light and naturalistic feel, while Dakota Rooms are decorated in a bold and eclectic combination of local materials and artwork that results in rooms that are a little retro, a little op art, and all fun. The Presidents Rooms, on a key-access only floor, are distinguished by safes, full refrigerators, and king beds, and are upgraded with more luxurious linens and other amenities. All of the other rooms at the hotel are available with a king or two queens. Deluxe Rooms are fairly standard hotel rooms. Accessible and pet-friendly rooms are included in this category. Amenities include free Wi-Fi, flat-screen TVs, in-room coffeemakers, a free airport shuttle, and a car rental service. The hotel offers three different on-site venues for food and beverages. Enigma (11am-2pm Mon.-Thurs., 11am-10pm Fri., 11am-9pm Sat., lunch $12-15, dinner $18-36) serves fairly standard American fare but provides a more upscale dinner on Friday and Saturday nights. Entrées include filet mignon, pork tenderloin, duck, lamb, and seafood. A second on-site restaurant called Prive (4pm-9pm daily, $12-25) is casual, light, and airy. A full-service bar, the 445 (4pm-11:45pm Thurs.-Sat.), is also on-site and large enough to host live bands.

The Big Sky Lodge (4080 Tower Rd., 605/348-3200, www.bigskylodge.com, Memorial Day-Labor Day $125-175, May and Sept.-Oct. $79-99) is a one-story lodge close to Skyline Drive and Dinosaur Park. The 32-room motel rests on the edge of a ridge overlooking the city. The bulk of the rooms have either a single queen or two full-size beds. There is drive-in parking in front of each room for easy access and unloading. One pet is allowed per room with a fee of $20 per night for small animals and $30 for large animals. The rooms are simple but attractive, with nice quilts, and include a small fridge, microwave, and coffeemaker. Free wireless Internet is also available. There are benches and a hot tub set up on the city view side of the building. In the evening, you can sit in the hot tub and watch the city lights and the stars.

To get to My Place Hotel (1612 Discovery Cir., 605/791-5800 or 855/200-5685, www.myplacehotels.com, mid-May-mid-Aug. $145-155, mid-Aug.-Sept., $99-119, Oct.-mid-May $60-65), off exit 61 from I-90, go north on North Elk Vale Road, take a left on East Mall Drive, and the hotel is on the corner of Discovery Circle and East Mall Drive. Amenities include 24/7 free fresh coffee, free Wi-Fi, 39-inch flat-screen televisions, and a business center. The hotel is pet-friendly, allowing a maximum of two pets weighing up to 80 pounds (36 kg) for a nonrefundable fee of $15 per night. In addition, all rooms have a full refrigerator, microwave, a two-burner stove, toaster, and coffeemaker. Cookware,

dishes, and cutlery are provided on request. There is no pool, and the rooms are not fancy, but if you are looking for really clean rooms at a bargain price, this is the place.

The Sweetgrass Inn Bed & Breakfast (9356 Neck Yoke Rd., 605/343-5351, www.sweetgrassinn.com, summer $150-190, shoulder season $129-159, winter $89-129) is in a great location for exploring all the Black Hills sites. The B&B is about 6 miles (9.7 km) south of central Rapid City off Mount Rushmore Road (U.S. 16), which is the main route to the best Black Hills attractions and Mount Rushmore—and almost directly across the street from Reptile Gardens. The eight rooms feature private entrances and private baths. Check-in is at the Shipwrecks Bar & Grill, the on-site restaurant. Amenities include bicycle parking, a library, barbecue grills in outdoor common areas, separate heat and air controls, free Wi-Fi, and in-room coffeemakers. Rooms are clean, comfortable, and spacious.

Downtown, the 99-room Howard Johnson (950 North St., 605/737-4656, www.hojorapidcity.com, summer $185-205, shoulder season $120-150, winter $85-115) is a modern facility with a nice marble and wood lobby. The pet-friendly hotel features an indoor pool and hot tubs, free Wi-Fi, fitness center, guest laundry, and business services. The nonrefundable fee for adding pets to the equation is $20 per day for a maximum of three dogs that weigh less than 30 pounds (14 kg) each. Complimentary continental or "grab and go" breakfast is included. The standard rooms are spacious and nicely decorated with plenty of lighting. A small desk and a work area are incorporated into each room. The hotel is within walking distance to downtown and the Rapid Creek walking/biking path and parks. In the evening (daily in summer, Mon.-Fri. in winter), the hotel offers a complimentary beer and wine reception to guests.

Over $250

The Hotel Alex Johnson (523 6th St., 605/342-1210, www.alexjohnson.com, mid-May-June $228-274, July- Sept. $266-399, Oct.-mid-May $75-141) is the iconic historic hotel of Rapid City. Construction of the hotel began one day before work started on Mount Rushmore. One year later, in 1928, the hotel opened. Over the course of its history, the hotel has hosted six U.S. presidents. Now on the National Register of Historic Places, the building has been recently renovated. The building's exterior is primarily brick, but the upper floors and roof are in Tudor style, painted white and crossed with dark wood framing. The lobby of the hotel is truly striking, with an interesting mix of Native American decor and German Tudor architecture. The rooms are modern, and fixtures include marble countertops and foyers, luxury bedding, and in-room espresso makers. For visitors staying at the hotel, the **Vertex Bar** (4pm-midnight daily, $14-38) on the top floor of the hotel is an easy spot for dining and drinks. The menu includes burgers, buffalo tenderloin, chicken, pasta, and fish tacos. Open to the hotel, Starbucks is available for coffee and pastries. The world's most delicious truffles, made by Chubby Chipmunk, are sold at a lobby counter. There is lobby access to **Paddy O'Neill's Irish Pub,** considered one of the best nightspots in town and which also serves meals. Note that room rates are extremely variable, with the best deals occurring midweek.

Specialty Lodging

The **Hisega Adventure Lodge** (23101 Triangle Trail, 605/342-8444, http://hisegaadventurelodge.com, May-Oct., call for room and tour pricing) is approximately 10 miles (16.1 km) west of Rapid City off of Highway 44. A historic property that has served tourists since 1908, the lodge has a gorgeous wraparound deck and a fireplace in the common area. There are 10 rooms, all with private baths. Every room opens directly onto the porch or to Rapid Creek, which runs through the property. The lodge has had an interesting history serving visitors for over 100 years. In its latest incarnation, hosts

Tara and Mike Flanery organize and frequently lead adventure tours packages such as off-road motorcycle training, mountain bike adventures for women, and bike racing in the hills. Adventures are added regularly. In keeping with the lodge's history, gourmet healthy breakfasts are included for the adventure participants. Rooms are largely reserved for guests signed up for an adventure tour, though room reservations without a tour are accepted if available. Rooms are likeliest to be available during weeks with no tours scheduled.

Cabins and Campgrounds

★ **Lake Park Campground & Cottages** (2850 Chapel Ln., 605/341-5320 or 800/644-2267, www.lakeparkcampground.com, tent sites $35-50, RV sites with water and electricity $45-55, RV sites with full hookups $75-90, studio and 1-bedroom cabins peak season $155-190, off-peak $130-155) has been family-owned for over 30 years and is a well-maintained property close to Canyon Lake on the west side of Rapid City. The tent sites feature 14-by-14-foot (4.3-by-4.3-m) elevated tent pads on sandy soil, have electricity, and are fully shaded. The RV sites are forested as well. The rates quoted for tent and RV sites are for two people; extra guests incur an additional charge of $2 per person per night. Rates quoted for studio and one bedroom cabins are for two people also and require a minimum three-night stay; extra cabin guests incur an additional charge of $10 per person per night. Pets are allowed for free in tent and RV sites but are not allowed in the cabins. The cabins are fully furnished and simply decorated in lodge style with rustic pine furniture. There are no phones in the cottages, but wireless Internet and cable television are available. Paddleboating and trout fishing are possible on the lake. A fishing license is required and can be purchased online at http://gfp.sd.gov (nonresident 1-day pass $16, 3-day pass $37, youth under 16 free). The Rapid Creek path runs right past the facility for hiking and biking. Bikes can be rented from the campsite office (half day $20, full day $30) and can be reserved in advance of your stay.

American Buffalo Resort (13752 S. U.S. 16, 605/342-5368, www.american buffaloresort.com, May-Sept., tent sites $40-45 plus $10 pp if more than 2 per tent, RV sites with water and electric 30 amp $40-50, RV full hookups with sewer 30/50 amp $55-100, deluxe RV full hookups with concrete pads $85-225, RV sites are for 4 people, additional people are $10 each per night, camper cabins with no bath $80-90, small cabin with bath $125-140 max. 5 people, 1 bedroom kitchenette cabin $140-165 max. 5 people) is nestled in the pines about 9 miles (14.5 km) heading south from Rapid City, just past Bear Country U.S.A. Well-mannered and leashed pets are welcome at tent and RV sites. When making reservations be sure to call and let the managers know how many and what kind of pets you are traveling with. There is no charge for pets at RV sites and tent sites. There is a $20 per pet per night fee in the cabins. The facility is on 38 shady acres and has free limited Wi-Fi, a playground, a 50-foot (15-m) swimming pool, a hot tub, minigolf, basketball court, horseshoe pits, and a beautiful view. Listen to the sounds of howling Bear Country wolves in the evening as local coyotes join in. It's a site that is simultaneously in the middle of everything and very remote. There is a small convenience store and laundry room available. For breakfast, guests have the option of purchasing a $3 all-you-can-eat pancake breakfast, if they aren't in the mood to cook for themselves on available grills.

INFORMATION AND SERVICES

Information

Tourist information is available at **Visit Rapid City** (512 Main St., Ste. 240, 605/718-8484 or 800/487-3223, www.visitrapidcity. com), where special offers and attraction brochures are available. Look to the website for current events and things to do in the area.

Services

For quick access to emergency services, including police or ambulance, call 911. For nonemergency situations, the **police station** is downtown (300 Kansas City St., 605/394-4131). For nonemergency highway assistance, call the **SD Highway Patrol** (605/394-2286).

For medical assistance, **Monument Health Rapid City Hospital** (353 Fairmont Blvd., 605/755-1000, www.monument.health) is south of downtown. To find the hospital, drive south on 5th Street. In addition to the hospital, if you are faced with a nonemergency medical issue while traveling, there are several urgent care locations in Rapid City that serve patients on a walk-in basis. It's like visiting a regular doctor's office. If patients have insurance, the visit is usually subject to insurance only. **Black Hills Urgent Care** (www.bhucare.com) has two locations in Rapid City (1730 Haines Ave., 605/791-7788; 741 Mountain View Rd., 605/791-7777, call for directions). **Monument Health Rapid City Urgent Care** (affiliated with the hospital) also has two locations (2116 Jackson Blvd., 605/755-2273; 1303 N. Lacrosse St., 605/755-2273). For emergency veterinary services call the **Animal Clinic of Rapid City** (1655 S. Valley Dr., emergency number 605/721-0789, general office 605/342-1368) which has a vet on-site 24 hours a day.

The most convenient **post office** for visitors is at 500 East Boulevard.

Small grocery stores are scattered throughout the city. For visitors staying near I-90 on the north end of Rapid City, the most convenient place to stock up is the **Walmart Superstore** (1200 N. Lacrosse St., 605/342-9444), a few blocks south of I-90, exit 59. **Safeway** (2120 U.S. 16, 605/348-5125) can be found on the way to Mount Rushmore from the downtown area. Both **Safeway** and **Family Fare** have stores west of town at the intersection of Mountain View and West Main.

Many campgrounds and hotels provide laundry services for guests, but some do not. For visitors staying on the west side of town near Canyon Lake, the most convenient laundry is the **Dew Drop Laundromat** (3618 Canyon Lake Dr., 605/343-0900). For visitors staying on the north side of town or downtown, the closest laundromat is **Laundry World** (1315 Haines Ave., 605/348-5121), which is south of I-90, exit 58. From downtown, head north on 5th Street, which turns into Haines Avenue.

GETTING THERE AND AROUND
Rapid City Regional Airport
The **Rapid City Regional Airport** (4550 Terminal Rd., www.rapairport.com) is about 11 miles (17.8 km) from downtown, off Highway 44 headed east. Call 605/394-4195 for airport information such as airline info, parking, rental cars and shuttles, the gift shop, airport restaurants, TSA, and lost and found. Shuttle service between the airport and downtown is provided by **Airport Express Shuttle** (605/399-9999 or 800/357-9998, www.rapidshuttle.com, within city limits rates are $25 for 1 person, $35 for 2, and $15 each for 3 or more).

Car Rental
The Black Hills are a driving destination. Car rental companies at the airport include **Alamo/National** (605/393-2664), **Hertz** (605/393-0160), **Avis** (605/393-0740), **Budget** (605/393-0488), and **Enterprise** (605/393-4311). Off-site car rentals can be arranged with **Black Hills Car Rentals** (605/348-3050).

Public Transportation
The **Rapid City Transit System** is based at the **Milo Barber Transportation Center** (333 6th St., 605/394-6631, www.rapidride.org, information available 7am-5:30pm Mon.-Fri., 10am-4:30pm Sat., adult and student $1.50, senior $0.75, youth 18 and under free, exact fare required) and has six major bus routes that carry passengers within the city limits. Downloadable maps of all the routes are available on the website. It's a great transportation deal if you want to spend a morning

downtown or near the I-90 shopping district. Buses run Monday-Friday 6:20am-5:50pm and Saturday 9:50am-4:40pm, leaving the terminal at 35-minute intervals.

Taxi
Taxi services include **Rapid City Taxi** (605/348-8080, www.rapidtaxirc.com, $3 for pickup and $3 per mile) and City **Cab** (605/863-1111, $3 for pickup and $3 per mile). Ride sharing apps **Lyft** (www.lyft.com) and **Uber** (www.uber.com) have been approved for the Rapid City area.

Tour Companies
From half day tours to weeks-long adventures, there are several companies in the area that can provide guided tours to the local attractions and activities. Each has a slightly different offering. Some tour in small groups in vans, and others utilize full buses. Large bus tours are less expensive, while the smaller tours are easily customizable and flexible. The prices are comparable and generally on a per person scale. Almost all of the tour companies (except large bus tours) are happy to work with you if you prefer to design a custom tour. Some tours include snacks and beverages, while some include lunch. Be sure to ask!

Mount Rushmore Tours (605/343-3113 or 888/343-3113, www.mountrushmoretours.com, mid-May-mid-Oct.) utilizes full-size buses for their tours. The company's primary offering is nine hours long, with two options. Option one begins with a cowboy all-you-can-eat breakfast in the morning, makes stops at Mount Rushmore, Custer State Park (including Needles Highway and Sylvan Lake and the State Game Lodge), and Crazy Horse Memorial and finishes with a chuckwagon dinner and show at Fort Hays in the evening (adult $109, child 12 and under $57). Option two is the same tour without meals (adult $90, child $47).

Affordable Adventures (5542 Meteor St., 605/342-7691, www.affordableadventuresbh.com, 7am-9pm daily, $45-185 pp) is a small-group tour company with 7-14 passenger vans.

Visitors may sign up for one of several standard public tours, request private tours, or design customized tours. Tours may have as few as 2 people at a time, or as many as 14. The standard tours range from a four-hour expedition to Mount Rushmore to a wide selection of excursions in the hills lasting up to 10 hours. The company tours leisurely, allowing plenty of time to enjoy the sites of the selected route. This is one of the few tour companies that provides specialty tours of **Devils Tower** ($150) in Wyoming and the Pine Ridge Reservation ($185).

GeoFunTrek (605/923-8386 or 605/430-1531, www.geofuntrek.com, $550 for 2, $100 each additional person, all admissions paid, snacks provided) provides private and customized tours only. The owners of the company, John Esposti and Cynthia Pullen-Esposti, are the guides for every tour. John and Cynthia have worked together in the hospitality industry in the Black Hills for over 35 years. Cynthia's specialties include traditional family tours, art galleries, shopping, and winery tours. John spent three years working for the Black Hills Institute of Geological Research and created a special presentation called "Black Hills Geology and You" for the local Road Scholar program. Not surprisingly, his specialties include local history, geology, paleontology, and natural history, among others. They love working to design tours that match the interests and wishes of their guests. Their website features several "suggested tours," all of which can be modified on request. They like to think of their tours as a blending of art and science, adding geology, paleontology, history, and folklore to their narratives.

Black Hills Adventure Tours (550 Berry Blvd., 605/209-7817, www.blackhillsadventuretours.com, $325 pp, minimum 2 people) provides private sightseeing tours as well as private adventure tours geared toward the active visitor. Sightseeing tours cover the Badlands, Northern Hills, monuments (Mount Rushmore, Crazy Horse, and Custer State Park), and wineries; family tours add in the Reptile Gardens or 1880 Train. Adventures include hiking (in the Badlands and Spearfish Canyon, for example), kayaking (such as in the Pactola Reservoir), biking, climbing, and other action-oriented tours. Custom tours can be arranged as well. Lunch is included as part of the fee for all tours.

Happily, the vehicles at **Open Top Tours** (605/644-6736, cell 605/791-0268, www.blackhillsopentoptours.com, $109-229, discounts available for children 16 and under) are convertible, so they can close up to accommodate the occasionally thunderous and rainy weather of the Black Hills in spring and summer. With an open top there is nothing to impede the view of visitors as they tour Mount Rushmore, Crazy Horse, Custer State Park, Badlands National Park, and the Northern Hills, including Spearfish, Deadwood, and Lead. There are 5- to 6-hour-long tours as well as full-day tours. Lunch is included in all but the shortest tour. Touring options include convertible jeeps and vans. Passengers can be picked up in Rapid City or Keystone, or as arranged.

The Southern Hills

The landscape of the Southern Hills is easy on

the eyes. Soft hills fade into the surrounding plains. The sky is a dominant feature of the landscape. There is a sense of great distance here, and the presence of humans is small. Approaching storms are visible for miles as lightning and rainbows color the vast plains.

For scenic beauty, wildlife-viewing, and outdoor activity, there is no place better in the region than 71,000-acre (28,733-ha) Custer State Park. Hiking trails to lakes and peaks crisscross the park, and bison ramble unfettered throughout. Reminiscent of the great architecture of our national parks, four beautiful lodges provide international dining and accommodations that range from simple cabins to luxury rooms.

The Southern Hills are also home to the monumental

Highlights

Look for ★ to find recommended sights, activities, dining, and lodging.

★ **Crazy Horse Memorial:** The most ambitious mountain carving project in the world demonstrates what a dream and a jackhammer can accomplish (page 99).

★ **Jewel Cave National Monument:** Named after the sparkling calcite crystals of its interior, it's one of the prettiest caves in the Black Hills—and the third-longest in the world (page 102).

★ **Needles Highway:** Scenic byways abound in the Black Hills, but the Needles Highway ranks as number one in my book. It winds and climbs the hills past Cathedral Spires, squeezes through the Needles formation, and ends at peaceful Sylvan Lake (page 115).

★ **Wildlife Loop:** Along this 18-mile (29-km) loop in Custer State Park, bison, pronghorn, prairie dogs, mule deer, white-tailed deer, and wild turkeys graze placidly, undisturbed by their many admirers (page 117).

★ **Black Elk Peak Trail:** Black Elk Peak is the highest point in the Black Hills, and the trail there provides the best hike. It's just the right length and difficulty level to make you feel like you've earned the vast and inspiring views at the top (page 120).

★ **Black Hills Playhouse:** Deep within Custer State Park, the Black Hills Playhouse features wonderful performances in a charming and historic venue, surrounded by scenic beauty (page 126).

★ **Mammoth Site:** It started with one tusk overturned by a bulldozer. Today, the skeletal remains of 61 mammoths, a short-faced bear, and other Pleistocene-era animals are displayed (page 135).

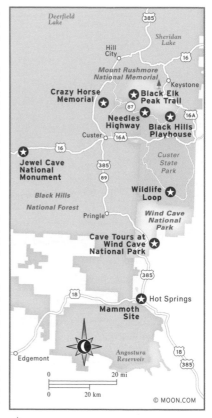

★ **Cave Tours at Wind Cave National Park:** Head below the earth's surface to the seventh-longest cave in the world. There are five tours on offer, including a candlelight tour (page 146).

The Southern Hills

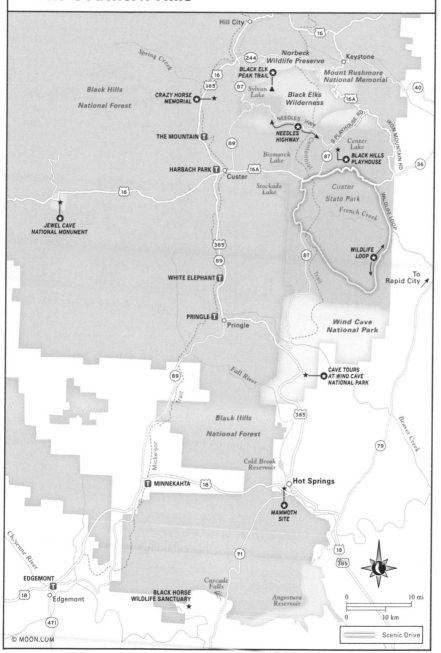

Hill City

Norbeck Wildlife Preserve

Keystone

BLACK ELK PEAK TRAIL

Mount Rushmore National Memorial

Black Elks Wilderness

Black Hills National Forest

Sylvan Lake

CRAZY HORSE MEMORIAL

Spring Creek

NEEDLES HWY

NEEDLES HIGHWAY

THE MOUNTAIN

Bismarck Lake

Center Lake

BLACK HILLS PLAYHOUSE

HARBACH PARK

Custer

Stockade Lake

Custer State Park

French Creek

JEWEL CAVE NATIONAL MONUMENT

WILDLIFE LOOP

To Rapid City

WHITE ELEPHANT

Trail

PRINGLE

Pringle

Wind Cave National Park

Fall River

CAVE TOURS AT WIND CAVE NATIONAL PARK

Black Hills National Forest

Cold Brook Reservoir

Beaver Creek

MINNEKAHTA

Hot Springs

MAMMOTH SITE

Cheyenne River

EDGEMONT

Edgemont

Cascade Falls

BLACK HORSE WILDLIFE SANCTUARY

Angostura Reservoir

0   10 mi
0   10 km

Scenic Drive

© MOON.COM

work-in-progress mountain carving honoring Lakota warrior and leader Crazy Horse. Two of the world's longest caves, the calcite crystal-encrusted Jewel Cave National Monument and Wind Cave (in Wind Cave National Park) offer exciting looks at the world below the surface. The historic town of Hot Springs looks and feels much as it did 100 years ago, with beautiful sandstone buildings, a river walk, and warm, spring-fed "healing waters" that inspired early 20th-century train travelers to come and "take the cure."

PLANNING YOUR TIME

Planning to tour anywhere in the Black Hills involves thinking in circles. And, for the most part, touring involves driving. In order to minimize driving time and maximize fun, plan on at least three days in the Southern Hills. No matter which tour strategy is selected—a base camp with day trips into different regions or a slow meander through the hills—it's good to mix sights and activities into the scenic drives.

Close to both the Southern and Central Hills sights and attractions, the town of Custer and Custer State Park are both great base camp options. Plan on a minimum of two hours for each sight, three hours for each scenic route, a good five hours to hike Black Elk Peak, two hours for cave tours, and an evening for the Black Hills Playhouse. Throw in time for picnics, hiking, biking, golfing, horseback riding, or swimming, and it's easy to see that 3-5 days can happily be spent in this region.

Note that in winter services are largely unavailable in Custer State Park. The main visitor center remains open, but no dining or retail venues are in operation. Lodging is only available at the Creekside Lodge and a limited number of deluxe cabins at the State Game Lodge, and at Game Lodge Campground and French Creek Horse Camp.

Custer

Custer sits on the edge of the Central and Southern Hills and is well situated to serve as a home base for day trips into every region of the hills. There are plenty of lodging and restaurant options in town, and Custer provides easy access to the Mount Rushmore National Memorial, Crazy Horse Memorial, Custer State Park, and Jewel Cave National Monument. Wind Cave is about 30 minutes away, and Hot Springs, the southern gateway to the hills, is just 45 minutes down the highway. Custer's population hovers around 2,000, and a good part of the community's income is generated by tourism.

HISTORY

At one time, the northern Great Plains were highlighted on maps as the "Great American Desert." It took the discovery of gold and the subsequent railroad lines to bring people to the region. The gold rush began when the ore was discovered east of Custer in French Creek. At the time, and by treaty, the land belonged to the Lakota.

The Fort Laramie Treaty of 1868 had delineated a district to be "set apart for the absolute and undisturbed use and occupation" of the Great Sioux Nation, and the land so described included the entire Black Hills region. In 1874, Lieutenant Colonel George Armstrong Custer, in the company of over 1,000 troops, was charged with the mission of exploring the Black Hills of South Dakota, officially to scout out a potential location for a military outpost to control "unsigned" Native Americans. In addition to the troops,

Previous: Needles Highway; bison; State Game Lodge.

however, the expedition included a scientific corps comprising a geologist, a botanist, a zoologist, and two miners. A photographer and several news correspondents also came along.

In July 1874, Horatio Ross, one of the expedition's miners, made the gold discovery near French Creek. In just four days, the news was broadcast to newspapers all over the country. The gold rush was on, and unable to stop the onslaught of miners to the area, the military was eventually charged with protecting them. The Fort Laramie Treaty was broken. By January 1875, just six months after the discovery of gold, an estimated 10,000-15,000 miners had invaded the Black Hills. The U.S. government tried to buy the land, but its offers were rebuffed. The Lakota and other tribes were vehement that the Black Hills were not for sale. The miners couldn't be stopped, however, and the Indian Wars began again in earnest. Custer's population peaked in 1875, and then when richer discoveries of gold occurred in the Northern Hills, it rapidly crashed, as miners rushed to seek their fortunes elsewhere.

★ Crazy Horse Memorial

For 14 years, Native Americans watched the carving of Mount Rushmore, a tribute to the leaders of the U.S. government, in the sacred Black Hills. In 1948, seven years after Mount Rushmore was completed, Chief Henry Standing Bear approached sculptor Korczak Ziolkowski about creating a mountain carving to show the world that Native Americans had great leaders, too. Ziolkowski, who had worked on Mount Rushmore with Gutzon Borglum, agreed, and the plans for the **Crazy Horse Memorial** (12151 Avenue of the Chiefs, Crazy Horse, 605/673-4681, www.crazyhorsememorial.org, 8am until after the laser light show daily summer $15 pp or $35 max per car, $10 pp per motorcycle, bicycle, or walk-in, child 6 and under free, 8am-5pm daily winter $12 pp or $30 max per car, $7 pp per motorcycle, bicycle, or walk-in, child 6 and under free) began to take shape.

Inspired by the stories of Chief Henry

Crazy Horse Memorial

Custer

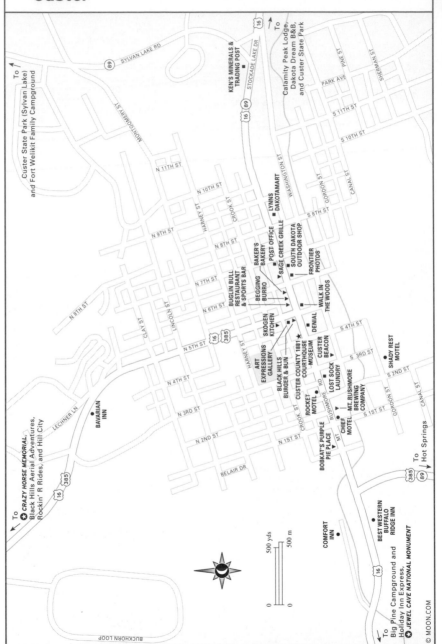

© MOON.COM

The Legacy of Crazy Horse

Sitting Bull, Red Cloud, Spotted Tail, and Crazy Horse were all Native American leaders deserving of recognition, but the choice of Crazy Horse was an easy one for those planning to honor a Lakota leader with a mountain carving.

Crazy Horse was born in the early 1840s near Bear Butte, South Dakota. The Lakota kept no written records, so much of what is known of his youth was carved out of the memories of elders many years after his death.

Crazy Horse lived his entire life under the shadow of outside encroachment on the lands of his people: the central plains of Nebraska, South Dakota, and Wyoming, and the northern plains of eastern Montana, all of which surround the Black Hills. What began as a trickle of outsiders with Lewis and Clark in 1804 turned into a flood. Between 1843 and 1869, it is estimated that somewhere between 300,000 and 500,000 settlers passed though the plains on their way west. With these travelers came the military, the forts, the settlements, and the inevitable skirmishes with Native American tribes trying to preserve their hunting grounds and way of life. Treaties were signed and broken, the most significant of those being the Fort Laramie Treaty signed in 1868. All settlers were banned from the Powder River area of Montana, and the Lakota, Dakota, and Arapahoe were to maintain ownership and hunting rights of the Black Hills and other lands in South Dakota, Wyoming, and Montana. This treaty lasted only until the 1874 discovery of gold.

Crazy Horse, by that time in his thirties, had already distinguished himself as a warrior and as a great hunter. Involved in the victory against the soldiers near Fort Phil Kearney in Nebraska (the "Fetterman Massacre"), Crazy Horse would also be identified as one of the strategic leaders of the 1876 Battle of the Little Bighorn, also known as "Custer's Last Stand," where George Armstrong Custer was killed with all of his troops. From this battle began the relentless military attacks on the Native American tribes in the area.

Constant fighting, a harsh winter, and the scarcity of bison drove the tribes to despair. Crazy Horse could have escaped into Canada alone, but he chose not to abandon his people. In May 1877, Crazy Horse and 900 followers rode into Camp Robinson in northwestern Nebraska and turned over their weapons and horses. Four months later, Crazy Horse was dead, bayoneted by a soldier when he struggled against being locked up in the guardhouse. It was a devastating loss to his community.

A hunter, a warrior, a leader, and a protector, Crazy Horse lived his life in the Lakota way. He was not interested in renown. He did not allow others to photograph him. He did not go to Washington to negotiate. He did not give speeches, and he never signed a treaty. He died trying to maintain his freedom, shortly before all of his people were forced to abandon their way of life and move onto reservation lands. Crazy Horse became a symbol of all that had been lost.

Standing Bear, Ziolkowski imagined a memorial that would include the largest mountain carving in the world, a museum, a university, and a medical center. The carving was to be of Crazy Horse on horseback, pointing to the Black Hills. Ziolkowski, operating alone, started carving in 1948. The work is still underway today, with the third generation of Ziolkowskis still shaping the mountain. When completed, the carving will be 641 feet (195 m) long by 563 feet (172 m) high. No federal funds have been used to finance the project. Today, the carving remains far from complete, and there is no estimated finish date on the memorial. However, it has seen a great deal of progress in the past decade. The face, 87 feet (27 m) high, is virtually complete, and much work has been accomplished on the horse's head. The memorial is not without controversy given that Crazy Horse did not want any images of him to be created, and the mountain into which he's being carved is sacred land to the Lakota. But the carving is a fascinating project, and it provides visitors with a one-of-a-kind opportunity to view an extraordinary piece of artwork in progress.

This is the only ongoing mountain carving in the world.

In addition to the mountain carving, the grounds of the Crazy Horse Memorial include many of the attractions that Ziolkowski originally envisioned. The **Welcome Center** has an information desk, conference facilities, and a small theater. The 20-minute orientation video includes historic film footage following Ziolkowski as he climbs hundreds of stairs to start carving a granite mountain with a jackhammer. It adds a human perspective to the project. Connected to the Welcome Center, the wood-paneled **Indian Museum of North America** is filled with Native American artwork and artifacts, most of which were donated to the facility. In summer, the memorial hosts Native American speakers, artists, musicians, dancers, and craftspeople, who share their special skills with visitors. Other facilities in the Welcome Center complex include the **Ziolkowski Family Life Collection,** where furnishings and the family's personal art and antique collections reflect the time period; Ziolkowski's original **studio,** where some of his other works of art are on display; and a **gift shop.**

At the **Native American Educational and Cultural Center** (9am-8pm daily summer, 9am-4pm or 5pm daily fall), you can meet Native American artists in residence, who spend most of the summer engaging with visitors, discussing their work and culture, heading up workshops, and offering their works for sale. Look for special events by some of the best Native American performing artists. Cultural programs are presented daily in summer. Native American speakers discuss Lakota history and culture. It is a very active and immersive experience.

The **Laughing Water Restaurant** (11am-8pm daily summer, 11am-4pm Mon.-Fri. and 9am-4pm Sat.-Sun. winter, breakfast $9-12, lunch $11-16, dinner $17-25) is a nice spot with a great selection of menu options and equally great views of the mountain. Breakfast offerings include biscuits and gravy, pancakes and waffles, omelets, and country-fried steak. Lunch and dinner entrées include a variety of sandwiches, burgers, and salads. The specialties of the house are traditional Indian tacos and bison stew. Coffee is always free at the memorial.

A bus ($4, 25 minutes round-trip) brings visitors close to the base of the sculpture to get a different perspective on the carving. It runs every 15 minutes or so, depending on weather and the mountain-blasting schedule, and includes a narrative of the history of the carving. It's a short ride, no longer than 0.75 mile (1.2 km), and the bus stops at a parking lot right at the base of the carving where the presentation continues.

In early June and September, hikers are allowed to climb Crazy Horse Mountain during the **Volksmarch.** Admission to the mountain is discounted for hikers ($10 for 1, $15 for 2, $20 for 3 or more per car). The American Volksmarch Association, which organizes the hike, requires a registration fee of $3 per person. Around 10,000 hikers each year climb the mountain and stand on Crazy Horse's outstretched arm—which is getting narrower every year!

During the summer months, a **laser light show** is presented nightly. The spectacle begins as soon as it's dark, so the start time varies with the sunset, generally beginning 9:30pm-10pm Memorial Day-early August, after which the start time shifts earlier as the days begin to shorten.

Crazy Horse Memorial is about 5 miles (8 km) north of Custer off U.S. 16/385.

TOP EXPERIENCE

★ Jewel Cave National Monument

Named for the glittering calcite crystals that line the walls, **Jewel Cave National Monument** was discovered by miners Frank and Albert Michaud in 1900. The brothers filed a mining claim, but it seems clear that their intention was always to create a tourist attraction. Over the next few years, the brothers, with family friend Charles Bush, widened the entrance to the cave with dynamite and constructed a rudimentary trail. They built a lodge on the rim of the nearby Hell Canyon and established the Jewel Cave Dancing Club in 1902. At the time, however, travel was difficult, and the local population was not large enough to provide enough financial support for the cave. Bush was bought out for $300, and after the brothers died, the claim was sold to the government for a nominal amount. While the cave was small, with just 0.5 mile (0.8 km) mapped, and the attempt at tourism wasn't a success, its beauty was well known, and, in 1908, Theodore Roosevelt declared the cave a national monument.

The cave remained virtually unexplored through 1959, by which time the known area of the cave had only increased in size to 2 miles (3.2 km) in length. A local geologist decided to take its exploration more seriously and convinced two avid rock climbers, Herb and Jan Conn, to join him in mapping the cave out. In less than two years, the length of the cave expanded to 15 miles (24 km). This sparked the interest of the National Park Service, and mapping of the cave continued in earnest. Today, the cave is known to be the third-longest cave in the world and growing, currently measuring nearly 210 miles (340 km) in length, honeycombed under just 4 square miles (10.4 sq km) of land. The largest room in the cave is over 570 feet (174 m) long, 180 feet (55 m) at its widest, and 30 feet (9 m) tall. In addition to the sparkling calcite crystals that gave the cave its name, it also features popcorn (small round clusters of calcium carbonate that looks like . . . popcorn), stalactites, and stalagmites.

VISITOR CENTER

The first place to stop at Jewel Cave is the **visitor center** (11149 U.S. 16, 13 mi/20.9 km west of Custer, 605/673-8300, www.nps.gov/jeca, 8am-5pm daily Memorial Day-Labor Day, 8:30am-4:30pm Wed.-Sat. off-season). Information about the available cave tours and ranger-led educational programs can be obtained here. Park rangers offer educational programs during the high summer months that include talks about the ecology and geology of the area, and caving. A sad new addition to the talks is a discussion of white-nose syndrome, a disease that has been devastating bat populations nationwide. In front of the visitor center is a theater that plays a documentary film illustrating the trials and tribulations of what it's like to be a cave explorer in Jewel Cave. It's beautiful and a little frightening to watch. The documentary is shown every half hour. In addition, self-guided hiking tour brochures are available for three hikes of variable length and difficulty near the cave. Depending on staff, guided hikes may be available as well. All cave tours originate at the visitor center. There is no entrance fee for Jewel Cave, but there are fees for cave tours. A small gift shop in the center sells articles of clothing (handy if you need a sweatshirt to enter the chilly cave), books and maps specific to Jewel Cave, as well as books on local and regional flora, fauna, and history.

CAVE TOURS

More than 80,000 people per year enjoy taking the cave tours. If you plan on joining one, remember to bring a sweater. Jewel Cave is one of the colder caves in the hills, with temperatures reaching only 49°F (9.4°C) even during the hottest days of summer. Four tours are available. Leave most of your personal belongings locked up in your car as purses, backpacks, food, pets, and other items are not allowed in the cave. Due to the rough terrain, closed shoes are required; sandals and other types of footwear that are not firmly attached will not be allowed in the cave. Because white-nose syndrome has been spreading to bat populations across the country, visitors who take a tour are not allowed to wear clothing or footwear that they have worn in any other public or private cave in the past. Sadly, evidence of the disease has been discovered in Jewel Cave.

Jewel Cave offers **advance reservations** for the Discovery Tour and the Scenic Tour online at www.recreation.gov. Tickets are also on sale on-site on a first-come first-served basis. Tours frequently sell out by mid-morning during the summer season so be sure to get tickets early. Advance reservations are *required* for the Wild Caving (Spelunking) Tour and processed by Jewel Cave. Please note that tour schedules can change without notice and that tickets can only be purchased with credit or debit cards.

DISCOVERY TOUR

The **Discovery Tour** (reservations at www.recreation.gov, adult $6, senior 62 and over and child ages 6-15 $3, child under 6 free) is an easy tour of about 20 minutes that takes place in one cave room that is wheelchair accessible. The ranger will discuss the history and formations of the cave. Both dogtooth spar and nail head spar, which are the "jewels" of the cave, are visible during the talk. Times and number of tours vary greatly throughout the year. Summer tours typically begin at 9:35am and occur every two hours until 4:35pm. By winter (Nov.-Mar.) the tour is offered only once a day at 9:05am on Saturday and Sunday, weather permitting. Call for times if visiting off-season.

SCENIC TOUR

The very popular **Scenic Tour** (reservations at www.recreation.gov, adult $16, child ages 6-16 $8, child under 6 free) is offered year-round, 15 times per day during the high summer season. The number of tours decreases from summer to shoulder season to winter. By winter (Nov.-Mar.) the tour is only offered three times a day at 10am, 12:40pm, and 2:40pm Saturday and Sunday only. Call to check on the schedule before driving out to the monument. The tour takes about 1.3 hours and is moderately strenuous. There are 734 stairs to climb in a 0.5-mile (0.8-km) loop. The trail is paved, and there is electric lighting along the path. The glittering calcite crystals that gave the cave its name can be viewed in several rooms on this tour. Other cave formations (speleothems) on this tour include knobby calcite formations called popcorn, boxwork, flowstone, stalactites and stalagmites, and cave bacon. (Many formations are named for what they look like.) Most of the formations in Jewel Cave are calcite or gypsum related.

HISTORIC LANTERN TOUR

The **Historic Lantern Tour** (mid-June-Labor Day, adult $16, child ages 8-16 $8, minimum age 8) is designed to replicate the experience of the early cave explorers. Park employees wear historical uniforms, and lighting for the tour is provided only by lanterns carried in by the participants. The tour lasts 1.75 hours and is considered strenuous. It begins at the cave's natural entrance and includes walking up wooden staircases, bending, stooping, duck-walking, and climbing steep ladders. The trail is unpaved, and sturdy shoes with rubber soles and long pants are recommended.

WILD CAVING TOUR

The **Wild Caving (Spelunking) Tour** (mid-June-Aug., adult $45, minimum age 16) is an extremely strenuous, 3- to 4-hour-long tour. Participants must be in good health and physical condition. Tour participants are also required to wear sturdy, leather over-ankle boots, knee and elbow pads, gloves, long pants, and a long-sleeved shirt. (Bring extra clothes, as you will get very dirty.) The tour provides a hard hat and headlamp. This tour is designed for thrill seekers. It will give participants a real feel for what it is like to explore and map a cave in its natural state. Participants will scramble over rough rock, belly crawl through tight passages, rope climb semi-vertical rocks, and chimney between cave walls. Do not even think about this tour if you are even mildly claustrophobic. Before taking the tour, participants must demonstrate that they can fit through a passage 8.5 inches (22 cm) high by 24 inches (61 cm) wide. During the course of the tour, participants will learn about safe caving, caving equipment, and techniques. **Advance reservations** for this tour are required and are processed by Jewel Cave personnel. Call Jewel Cave (605/673-8300, 8am-5pm

Mon.-Fri. summer, reduced hours in winter); the staff will answer any questions and pass your information along to reservation managers, who will contact you to process your reservation.

1881 Custer County Courthouse Museum

The **1881 Custer County Courthouse Museum** (411 Mt. Rushmore Rd., 605/673-2443, www.1881courthousemuseum.com, 10am-5pm Mon.-Sat. Memorial Day-June, 10am-5pm Mon.-Sat., 1pm-4pm Sun. July-Labor Day, adult $6, family $12, student $2, child under 12 free), an original 1881 courthouse and jail, explores the history of the city and county of Custer and of the Black Hills. Museum artifacts include photos of the 1874 Custer Expedition, a hunting gun used by George Armstrong Custer, and some items found at the expedition campsite. Other displays include a Native American room, a mining industry room, weapons of the West, and the original courthouse and judge's quarters. There is also a bookstore in the museum with a collection of books and artwork by local authors and artists. Outbuildings on the grounds of the museum display vehicles from the 1870s to 1920, a forge, a print shop containing equipment from the original town newspaper, and a stage stop cabin.

RECREATION
Ballooning and Helicopter Rides

Custer is the home base for **Black Hills Balloons** (P.O. Box 210, 605/673-2520, www.blackhillsballoons.com, scheduled flights May-Oct., other months by arrangement, adult $375, child ages 4-12 $270, minimum age 4), the longest-running balloon company in the United States. The owners, Damien Mahony and Keely Wade, are both FAA-certified balloonists and intend to keep the perfect safety record of Black Hills Balloons intact. Damien first started working in the commercial balloon business in 1999. Keely received her flight certificate at the age of 13

and has been flying ever since. Potential riders meet at a designated parking lot in Custer at sunrise, where a helium balloon is released to test wind speed and direction. There are no steering wheels on hot-air balloons, so the results of the test determine the best launch site for the day. The most common route includes drifting over the Wildlife Loop in Custer State Park, but the whimsy of the wind currents rule, and each flight is unique. Plan to take three hours for a balloon experience from launch to an end-of-ride champagne celebration. In-air time is usually about an hour. Balloon capacity ranges 2-12 passengers. Specialty flights are available and can be arranged by quote only. Reservations are required for the flights.

Black Hills Aerial Adventures (24564 U.S. 16/385, 605/673-2163, www.coptertours.com, 9am-dusk daily early May-mid-Oct., winter flights by reservation only, $49-255) offers everything from a 6-mile (9.7-km) aerial journey over the Black Hills for those who may have never been in a helicopter before to an all-encompassing 85-mile (137-km) tour of both the Northern and Southern Hills. The company has three different locations: Crazy Horse helipad in Custer, Mount Rushmore helipad in Keystone, and the Badlands helipad in Interior. Choose the helipad closest to your flight destination to save money since the tours are billed by miles and by time. Five different tours are available at the Custer location, from a 6-mile (9.7-km) flight designed for beginners ($49 pp) to the Ultimate Aerial Adventure (call for pricing), which encompasses sections of the Northern, Central, and Southern Hills including flybys of Crazy Horse, Mount Rushmore, over Sheridan, Pactola, and Deerfield Lakes, Cathedral Spires and the Needles, Black Elk Peak and Little Devils Tower. Other shorter flights include the 20-mile (32-km) Black Elk Peak tour ($155 pp), and a 10-mile (16.1-km) flight with a close-up of Crazy Horse ($110 pp). If getting up close and personal with the Crazy Horse Memorial is your goal, this is the right location. To take in some of the most beautiful spots in the Southern Black Hills, enjoy a 35-mile (56-km) flight that covers Sylvan Lake, the Needles Highway, and Mount Rushmore ($255 pp). If you're more interested in Mount Rushmore close-ups, head to the Mount Rushmore helipad for the best price.

Horseback Riding

Rockin' R Rides (24853 Village Ave., 605/673-2999, www.rockingrtrailrides.com, 8am-5pm daily Memorial Day-Sept., 1-hour loop ride adult $50, child $45, 1.5-hour loop ride adult $60, child $55, 2-hour ride adult $80, child $75, Crazy Horse 3.5-hour ride adult $120, child $110) is located at Heritage Village, 3 miles (4.8 km) north of Custer and just 1 mile (1.6 km) south of Crazy Horse on U.S. 385/16. It operates under permit from the U.S. Forest Service. Owners Peggy and Randy have been outfitting riders in the Black Hills since 1998, and their staff are experienced and knowledgeable. It is recommended that reservations be made one or two days in advance, but Rockin' R Rides will accommodate walk-ins if possible. Rides, lasting from one hour to half a day, will bring riders through all kinds of terrain from open fields to forested hillsides. Vistas of the Crazy Horse Memorial, just a mile away, are visible intermittently along the trails.

Other Recreation

A visit to **South Dakota Outdoor Shop** (632 Mt. Rushmore Rd., 605/673-2240, www.southdakotaoutdoorshop.com, 7:30am-6pm daily summer) will supply you with everything needed to enjoy the outdoors in the Black Hills. It rents equipment including bicycles, bike trailers, stand-up paddleboards, kayaks, and coolers (think picnic lunch!). Staff at the store fit bicycles—including hardtail mountain bikes (3 hours $35, calendar day $50, 24 hours $60), upright cruisers (3 hours $35, calendar day $50, 24 hours $60), and e-bikes (3 hours $60, calendar day $100)—by height. All bicycle rentals include helmets, an extra tube, a pump, and tool kits. Bike trailers can also be rented (3 hours $20, calendar

day $35, 24 hours $45). For water lovers, kayaks (calendar day $50 day, 24 hours $60) and stand-up paddleboards (calendar day $50, 24 hours $60) can be rented as well. The shop also sells outdoor gear for just about any adventure.

ENTERTAINMENT

The Custer Beacon (351 Washington St., 605/673-3800, www.custerbeacon.com, Wed.-Thurs. 4pm-9pm, Fri.-Sat. 4pm-10pm) presents a regular lineup of bands and is also a great restaurant (kitchen hours 4pm-8:30pm Wed.-Sat.) and bar, even on nights without music. It's an attractive facility with a large stage and space enough for 650 or more folks to spend an evening enjoying live music, sipping on beer, and partaking of very good food. There is an outside dining area with in-and-out access to the concert room. The menu is not typical of a music venue; while there are the usual chips and salsa, a burger, a burrito, and chicken wings, offerings also include grain bowls (with a base of toasted quinoa), panini with a twist (ham, brie, green apple, and arugula), and artisan flatbreads.

Denial (430 Mt. Rushmore Rd., 605/673-2264, noon-6:30pm Thurs.-Sun. Memorial Day-mid-Oct.) is a lovely place with friendly owners that offers a local wine- and beer-tasting experience in a soothingly decorated environment with silvery blues and grays and wood. A flight of beer includes your selection of four six-ounce beers ($10). Local wine flights are available as well. On offer are several wines from Firehouse Wine Cellars, affiliated with Firehouse Brewing Company in Rapid City. A sampling of five wines is $12, and with the flight comes a gift glass that says "I make pour decisions - Denial South Dakota." Lunch at Denial is a daily special ($10-12), homemade by the owner. There is no real menu per se. For folks who like to share, there are artisan meat and cheese boards that serve 2-4 people ($24-36). Out back there's a large pet-friendly patio for sitting and sipping

1: Jewel Cave **2:** Bobkat's Purple Pie Place

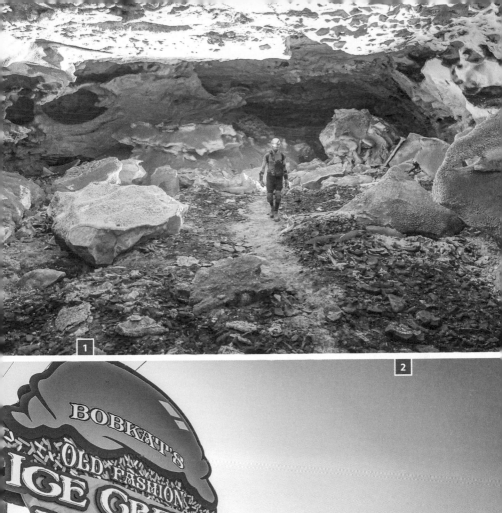

or listening to acoustic music, which occurs in the afternoon or early evening most Friday and Saturday nights.

SHOPPING

Custer is a small town, and most of the shopping is clustered downtown, along U.S. 16/385 (Mt. Rushmore Rd.). Many of the shops are open year-round, but in winter, hours depend on weather and foot traffic; call ahead.

A Walk in the Woods (506 Mt. Rushmore Rd., 605/673-6400, 10am-5pm daily) features country-style home decor, gifts, clothing, and the work of local and regional artists. It's a two-story shop just crammed full of gift ideas.

Over 30 artists are shown at the **Art Expressions Gallery** (17 N. 5th St., 605/673-3467, 10am-5pm daily mid.-Mar.-Dec.), just half a block off the main street in Custer. You'll usually find one of the artists behind the counter, prices are reasonable, and the artwork is quite varied, including jewelry, paintings, pottery, and photography.

Stop by **Frontier Photos** (604 Mt. Rushmore Rd., 605/673-4660, 9:30am-9pm Mon.-Sat., 9:30am-8pm Sun. Memorial Day-Labor Day) for souvenirs or to create your own memory with an old-time photo shoot ($37 for 2 people, $6 per additional person). The shop has a wide variety of costumes and props on hand, and since it is a full-service photography studio, it can handle large groups. Scenes include a saloon, jail, log cabin, and formal setting. An 8x10 and two 5x7s come with the sitting. Additional charges apply for reprints and additional photos.

Love rocks and minerals? **Ken's Minerals and Trading Post** (12372 U.S. 16A, 605/673-4935, 9am-6pm daily May-mid-Oct., 10am-4pm mid-late Apr. and mid-late Oct.) hosts a treasure trove of gorgeous rocks, minerals, fossils, and jewelry. Open since 1936 and in this location since 1954, the shop is now run by the third and fourth generations of the Spring family.

South Dakota Outdoor Shop (632 Mt. Rushmore Rd., 605/673-2240, www. southdakotaoutdoorshop.com, 7:30am-6pm daily summer) sells camping supplies, footwear, clothing, climbing equipment, and hiking gear for just about any adventure, as well as rents equipment for bicycling and paddling.

FOOD
Casual Dining

The seasonally open ★ **Baker's Bakery** (541 Mt. Rushmore Rd., 605/673-2253, www. bakersbakerycafe.com, 6:30am-3:30pm Mon.-Fri., 6:30am-4pm Sat.-Sun. June-Oct., call for Apr.-May hours, $9-13) in downtown Custer is a favorite for breakfast and lunch. The small but choice breakfast menu includes omelets, pancakes, biscuits and gravy, and egg dishes; the specialties of the house include homemade bread and caramel rolls, great coffee, and pastries. The restaurant is a cozy, friendly place to start the day. Wall murals mirror the restaurant's theme: "You'll love our buns!" Breakfast is served until 11am. Sandwiches and burgers, wraps, and salads comprise the lunch menu. Vegetarians will be able to find a few choices on both the breakfast and lunch menus, including omelets and veggie burgers.

Mt. Rushmore Brewing Company (140 Mt. Rushmore Rd., 605/673-4200, www. mtrushmorebrewingcompany.com, taproom 11am-9pm daily mid-May-Sept., upstairs restaurant 11am-4pm and 4pm-9pm daily mid-May-Sept.) brews 13 different beers, 5 of which are seasonal. With Scottish-style ales, porters, IPAs, lagers, pilsners, and stouts, there is a beer for every preference. In addition to the brews, there is a **Taproom Kitchen** ($11-23), with a menu described as "pub fare" but offering a variety of other choices. There is pizza, fish-and-chips, and nachos, but there is also a beef stew bread bowl, corn fritters, and stuffed mushrooms. Patrons can build their own burgers (beef, bison, elk, chicken, or veggie) and pizzas. The taproom is a lovely room that opens to an outside deck where people and leashed pets are welcome. On the second floor above the taproom, **Pounding Father's** (lunch $10-20, dinner $20-30) has a similar menu to the taproom for lunch but with a few additional creative appetizers like lager mussels, steak tips, and buffalo meatballs. Dinner adds steaks, pasta dishes, pork chops, walleye, salmon, and other specialties. Like the pub and kitchen below, the upstairs restaurant has a wonderful open deck as well as indoor dining. Overall, it's a great addition to Custer dining.

The **Buglin' Bull Restaurant and Sports Bar** (511 Mt. Rushmore Rd., 605/673-4477, www.buglinbull.com, 11am-8pm Mon. and Wed.-Thurs., 11am-9pm Fri.-Sun. summer, 11am-8pm Thurs.-Mon. winter, $13-25) is situated in a beautifully remodeled historic building and can be counted on to be open year-round. The restaurant and bar are cozy, sporting old brick walls, wood tables, and tin ceilings. A sweet bonus is the rooftop deck that overlooks the main business district. Look for a wide variety of lunch items, including sandwiches, salads, and a selection of steak and bison meals. The bulk of the lunch menu burgers and sandwiches are included in the dinner menu, although dinner has a larger selection of entrées (such as wild boar).

The **Begging Burro Mexican Bistro & Tequila Bar** (529 Mt. Rushmore Rd., 605/673-3300, 11am-9pm daily summer, lunch $13-16, dinner $16-30) has been decorated with color and charm. With a great menu of Mexican plates, over 40 different tequila offerings, and great service, this is a restaurant not to be missed.

One of the busiest places in town, **Black Hills Burger & Bun** (441 Mt. Rushmore Rd., 605/673-3411, www.blackhillsburgerandbun.com, 11am-2:30pm Tues.-Wed., 11am-2:30pm and 5pm-7:30pm Thurs.-Sat. summer, 11am-2:30pm Tues.-Sat. winter, $12) has some of the most creative and tasty burgers to be found. Try the Hot Granny (bacon, cream cheese, fresh jalapeños, and sweet spicy jalapeño sauce) or Black Hills Blues (blue cheese crumbles, bacon, garlic aioli, and caramelized onion). There is also chicken, fish, and some vegetarian selections. Their beef is ground every morning and the buns baked from scratch daily, the butter and cream come from a local dairy, and yes, desserts are made every day, as well. There's always a wait, but most people walk out happy.

Fine Dining

Contemporary and casual, the ★ **Sage Creek Grille** (611 Mt. Rushmore Rd., 605/673-2424, www.sagecreekgrille.com, 11:30am-2:30pm and 5pm-8pm Tues.-Sat. summer, winter hours vary, lunch $10-15, dinner $14-30) has a light and airy feel, with hard wood floors and light oak tables. The high ceilings can sometimes make the room a bit noisy—but it's the chatter of happy customers. The menu changes weekly, offering more than the standard South Dakota fare; some past examples include the almond and panko walleye, Jamaican jerk pork, and Bourbon Street Cajun Fettuccine. Enjoy a glass of wine in the bar, complemented by a cheese plate. The lunch menu features a variety of salads, soups, and sandwiches. The soup, dressings, and desserts are all homemade. Even the sandwiches are, for the most part, not standard fare (look for the beef pot roast sandwich, for example). All of the sandwiches are offered on both the lunch and dinner menu for the same price. Reservations are not required.

The innovative **Skogen Kitchen** (29 N. 5th St., 605/673-2241, www.skogenkitchen.com, 5pm-8pm Tues.-Sat., $28-40) is a chef-centered addition to the Custer restaurant scene. It's small and elegant, with outdoor dining available. The menu may change any time the chef's creative juices kick in! Dinner offerings might include artfully and tastefully prepared lamb, duck, scallops, halibut, salmon, or steak. Reservations are required. Check on the night's offerings when you call!

Dessert

Painted with the bright purple and white stripes that give the restaurant its name, **Bobkat's Purple Pie Place** (19 Mt. Rushmore Rd., 605/673-4070, www.purplepieplace.com, 11am-8pm daily mid-Apr.-Oct., slice of pie $5, whole pie $24) is hard to miss! Pie isn't the only sweetness on order though. There are milkshakes and ice cream cones and sundaes to tempt as well. And while dessert is the sweet specialty of the house, lunch ($7-12) is also served. There are sandwiches, panini, and two specialties of the house: homemade mac and cheese and chicken potpie—comfort food at a very affordable price. Start with dessert first! The local favorite, bumbleberry pie, is made from rhubarb, apples, strawberries, blueberries, and raspberries.

ACCOMMODATIONS

Custer is full of hotels, motels, cabins, and campgrounds. Many of the chains are present, and there are several nice family-run hotels as well. Custer has the closest access to Custer State Park at a lower cost. As a result, advance reservations are always recommended.

Under $150

The ★ **Shady Rest Motel** (238 Gordon St., 605/673-4478, www.shady-rest-motel.com, Memorial Day-Labor Day $85-140, May and Sept. $80-110 with a 10 percent discount for stays longer than three days, $10 per dog per night) is actually a collection of charming cabins that date back to the 1930s. The original owners believed that since the establishment was nestled up against the hill and away from the main street of Custer, they needed to be brightly colored to be seen. To this day, many of the cabins remain the same historic colors of bright yellow with red trim that they were painted when they were first opened. Inside, the cabins are all pine and very cozy. There are 13 available, Wi-Fi is free, and each has a full or partial kitchen and a deck or covered porch. Cookware is supplied to guests. Views from the cabins extend to the Cathedral Spires of Custer State Park, and the backyard is national forest. There is a hot tub, a city park across the street, and access to the Custer City Pool is prepaid for all guests. For bicyclists, the Mickelson Trail is one block away. Restaurants and downtown activities are just a few blocks away as well. Outgoing and friendly owners complete the experience.

The **Chief Motel** (120 Mt. Rushmore Rd., 605/673-2318, www.chiefmotel.com, May-mid Oct., $85-125, no pets) has been operated by the same family since 1995. The rooms are clean and comfortable, and there are several configurations available for families. Amenities include Wi-Fi, a microwave and refrigerator in every room, a very large swimming pool, and a hot tub and sauna. Some special weekends and holidays may require stays of a minimum number of nights.

The **Calamity Peak Lodge** (12557 U.S. 16, 605/673-2357, www.calamitypeaklodge. com, mid-May-mid-Oct., $75-130, $15 per pet per night) is an older but well-kept property 2 miles (3.2 km) east of downtown Custer on U.S. 16A. Just minutes from the west entrance to Custer State Park, the views are great, the rooms are clean, and the price is right. The rooms are pine-paneled and cozy and evoke feelings of summer camp. About half of the rooms have full kitchens, and all have a microwave, satellite TV, and free Internet. The rooms do not, however, have air-conditioning. French Creek, where gold was first discovered in the Black Hills, winds through the property.

$150-250

The 1950s and the automobile road trip go together like peanut butter and marshmallow fluff. That is why it's fun to spend some time in a 1950s historic motel or cabin. Family-owned since 1950 and open year-round, the ★ **Rocket Motel** (211 Mt. Rushmore Rd., 605/673-4401, www.rocketmotel.com, May-Oct. $149-199, winter $89-129) fits the bill. It is a AAA-rated hotel with 27 clean rooms, free wireless Internet, refrigerators, microwaves, and really friendly service. The owners have gone out of their way to keep the rooms authentic to the era, with furniture and lamp fixtures from the 1950s and black-, gray-, and white-checked 1950s-style carpet. At the high end of the rate range are several two-bedroom options designed especially for families. It's a great way to enjoy a family vacation that leaves mom and dad with a little privacy. If you are passing through the area off-season, call and check to see if they have a room available.

Midrange hotel rooms are primarily chains. The 88-room **Best Western Buffalo Ridge Inn** (310 W. Mt. Rushmore Rd., 605/673-2275, www.bestwestern.com, May-Sept., $139-239, $25 per pet per night) provides spacious and clean rooms. Hotel amenities include a free continental breakfast, an indoor heated pool, a hot tub, a business center, and free high-speed Internet access. A microwave and refrigerator are provided in the majority of the rooms. Many of the rooms have drive-up access, which is a nice feature when you have a lot of luggage and equipment to unload.

The **Dakota Dream Bed & Breakfast & Horse Hotel** (12350 Moss Rd., 701/690-4801, www.dakotadreambandb.com, May-Dec. $159-185, 2-night minimum stay, Jan.-Apr. $119-139, no pets) is a secluded, lovely log cabin-style establishment with two rooms available for guests. The rooms are accessed through the common guest area, which provides seating, a table for dining, a TV, and a refrigerator with complimentary beverages. Wi-Fi is available throughout the facility, and shampoo and hair dryers are provided in each room, which also have private baths. Horse people are welcome to stable their horses in the three-stable barn on the property for $25 a night. Riders must provide for all of their horses' needs and clean the stalls daily. The B&B also has a 500-square foot (46.5-sq-m) one-bedroom log cabin, which sleeps five, available for $195 over the course of the spring and summer with a three-night minimum stay. It easily sleeps four with a queen bed in one room and a queen-size sleeper sofa in the main room. It's a lovely cabin with a beautiful front deck, kitchenette, a gas grill, and lots of privacy.

The **Bavarian Inn** (855 N. 5th, U.S. 16/385 N., 605/961-0203, www.bavarianinnsd.com, June-Aug. $209-269, Apr.-May and Sept.-Oct. $169-209, $25 per pet per night) is a beautiful chalet-style property 1 mile (1.6 km) north of Custer on U.S. 16/385. The rooms sport varying creative decor and come with many amenities. Every room has a microwave and refrigerator. There is free Wi-Fi, and a guest laundry. The grounds include a heated pool inside and a heated pool outside. A hot tub is next to the indoor pool. The property also has two playgrounds, a tennis court, and an 0.75-mile (1.2-km) fitness trail. Tennis racquets, croquet games, basketballs, and soccer balls can be checked out at the front desk. The **Feel Good Café** is on-site and open for breakfast and will even deliver to rooms. A bonus to Tesla drivers—Tesla chargers are available here.

The **Comfort Inn** (339 W. Mt. Rushmore Rd., 605/673-3221 or 800/424-6423, www.choicehotels.com, May-mid-Oct., summer $144-205, spring and fall $110-144, no pets, smoke-free) has 83 spacious rooms which were remodeled in 2018. Overall, the feel is somewhat spare and elegant with light wood furnishings throughout. Hotel amenities include an indoor pool and hot tub, free high-speed Internet, free local calls, newspapers in the lobby, a guest laundry, a small exercise room, and a hot breakfast with grab-and-go choices as well. A small business center has been set up with a couple of computers and printers. Hair dryers, coffeemakers, microwaves, and refrigerators can be found in all the rooms.

The **Holiday Inn Express** (433 W. Mt. Rushmore Rd., 605/673-2500 or 888/465-4329, www.ihg.com, mid-Apr.-Oct., $185-250) is an attractive stone and wood property equipped with a fitness center, pool, and hot tub. This hotel is completely nonsmoking. All rooms include a microwave and coffeemaker. A breakfast buffet is included in the room rate, as is high-speed Internet access. An interesting feature of the hotel is a nice outdoor patio where guests can enjoy the beautiful landscaping.

Cabins and Campgrounds

Close to Custer State Park, the ★ **Fort Welikit Family Campground** (24992 Sylvan Lake Rd./Hwy. 89, 605/673-3600, www.fortwelikit.com, May-mid-Oct., rates based on two-person occupancy: basic tent sites $25, tents with electricity $35, pull-in 30/50 amp full hookup RV sites $46-55, 30 amp electric-only RV sites $45, tipis $33, covered wagons $25, fully equipped cabins $155-165, camping kegs $45-65, pets allowed except in camping kegs, $10 per pet per night charged in the cabins, 2 pets maximum) has location, location, location going for it. Nestled in ponderosa pines, the campground is just minutes from Sylvan Lake in Custer State Park. Showers, horseshoes, badminton, and basketball are available as well as a replica of an Old West fort in the children's playground. Tents sites may come with 12-by-12-foot (13.4-sq-m) shelters. Covered wagons are narrow and best for children, but they might be a great way for parents to carve out a little privacy and provide fun for the kids. The camping kegs are an unusual form of the standard camping cabin with a queen bed (no bedding); they come with and without electricity. The cabins have full kitchens and baths and are furnished with bedding, towels, and dishes. The site has showers and laundry facilities for guests as well. A special bonus is the fenced-in dog park for safe romping for the furry loved ones. There is a camp store on-site where snacks, camping supplies, beer, and wine can be purchased. Propane tanks can be refilled here, and there is a full-service dump station.

The **Big Pine Campground** (12084 Big Pine Rd., 605/673-4054, www.bigpinecampground.com, mid-May-mid-Oct., tent sites with no hookups $25, tent/pop-up sites with water and electricity $40, RV sites $45-50, camper cabins $75, based on two adults, two children) is a large campground with 90 wooded sites nestled into the hillside. The sites are well spaced and large enough for any size RV, with plenty of roof clearance. The camper cabins have two queen beds with no bedding, water, or bathrooms; however, they do have a microwave, a small refrigerator, and an outdoor propane grill. Pets are not allowed in the camper cabins but are permitted elsewhere in the campground. Two large, well-maintained restroom facilities,

shower houses, laundry facilities, and dump site are on-site. Amenities include DSL cable, Internet service, free Wi-Fi, a playground, a volleyball court, hiking trails, horseshoe pits, a recreation room with video games, and a grocery and gift shop, which also provides RV supplies and firewood. The campground is 2 miles (3.2 km) west of the downtown area of Custer.

INFORMATION AND SERVICES

Many of the campgrounds and bed-and-breakfasts in the Custer area provide accommodations for travelers bringing horses to the region. Contact your veterinarian to obtain the necessary certificates and tests required for livestock being transported across state lines.

Custer comes complete with basic services. Picnic supplies and groceries can be found at **Lynn's Dakota Mart** (800 Mt. Rushmore Rd., 605/673-4463), a regional grocery chain. The **post office** is at 634 Mount Rushmore Road, and laundry facilities are provided at **The Lost Sock** (242 Mt. Rushmore Rd., 605/673-2932). Custer also has health care providers available at **Monument Health Custer** (1220 Montgomery St., 605/673-9400), where a hospital and urgent care services are available.

For more information about the city of Custer, including vacation guides to Custer and the Southern Hills, contact the **Custer Visitor Center** (615 Washington St., 605/673-2244 or 800/992-9818, www.visitcuster.com, 8am-5pm Mon.-Fri., 9am-5pm Sat., 10am-4pm Sun. Memorial Day-Labor Day).

GETTING THERE AND AROUND

Dave's World Tours (Custer, 605/673-1130, www.blackhillsvantours.com, 8am-10pm daily, all tour prices negotiated by phone) specializes in private family and friends van tours in the hills. It's the only company that will pick up patrons in Hot Springs and Custer as well as Keystone and Hill City. Tours can be for a full or half day. They have two suggested (but flexible) tours on offer but also have a long list of sites that folks can choose to put together for their own custom tour. They are friendly folks making touring a little easier for visitors staying in the Southern Hills.

Custer State Park

Some of the most beautiful locations in all of the Black Hills can be found in **Custer State Park** (13329 U.S. 16A, headquarters 605/255-4515, SD Game, Fish, and Parks customer service 605/223-7660, http://gfp. sd.gov/parks, seven-day pass $20 per vehicle, $36 annual). Encompassing 71,000 acres (28,733 ha), Custer State Park is one of the largest state parks in the United States and offers much in the way of scenic diversity and outdoor activities. In the southernmost areas of the park, the landscape is all soft rolling hills, with fields of prairie grasses and small stands of ponderosa pine scattered throughout. Vast views and big skies dominate. It is here that grassland wildlife abounds. Bison, pronghorn, deer, and prairie dog populations are common sights. Traveling north, the elevation rises, and the scattered stands of ponderosa pine turn into dense forest. The rolling low hills turn into craggy peaks with steep canyon walls and sheer granite outcroppings. The deer remain, but the bison are scarce in the northern sections of the park. Instead, look for Rocky Mountain sheep and mountain goats.

The park is accessible year-round, although most of the park facilities are closed mid-October-May. During the winter months, fees are collected on the honor system, with envelopes and deposit boxes located at several park entrances. Onetime admission fees are good for seven days from the date of purchase in any South Dakota state park. There are access roads to the park from every direction. Highway 87 runs north-south through the park from Wind Cave just north of Hot Springs to just south of Hill City. Scenic U.S. 16A circles through the park and has exit/ entry points near the city of Custer and in the northeasternmost corner of the park. Highway 36 enters the park from the east, as well. Highway 79 runs north-south along the front range of the Black Hills, and many of the gravel county roads and Forest Service roads, including Forest Road 16 and County Roads 14 and 12 heading west, will bring you into the park.

Custer State Park provides some of the best lodging, dining, and outdoor recreation opportunities (including hiking, biking, horseback riding, rock climbing, fishing, and boating) in the Black Hills. Add exceptional wildlife-viewing opportunities, a summer playhouse, a chuckwagon dinner, and many scenic drives and it is understandable why Custer State Park is a must-see for any visitor to the Black Hills.

There are **four major lodging and campground areas** within the confines of the park boundaries, each with a distinctly different feel (resort reservations 888/875-0001, www.custerresorts.com, campground reservations 800/710-2267, http://reservations. gooutdoorssouthdakota.com). If you are planning to stay at the park, one of the four regions is likely to suit your personal preferences: The Western feel of the Blue Bell Resort with its hayrides, horseback riding, and chuckwagon dinners; the elegant State Game Lodge, the center of many of the park's activities; the casual fishing-, boating-, and swimming-centered Legion Lake area; or the majestic beauty and high peaks near Sylvan Lake Lodge. Whether you are staying in the park or in the nearby communities of Hot Springs or Custer, plan to spend a minimum of three days in the park.

Custer State Park

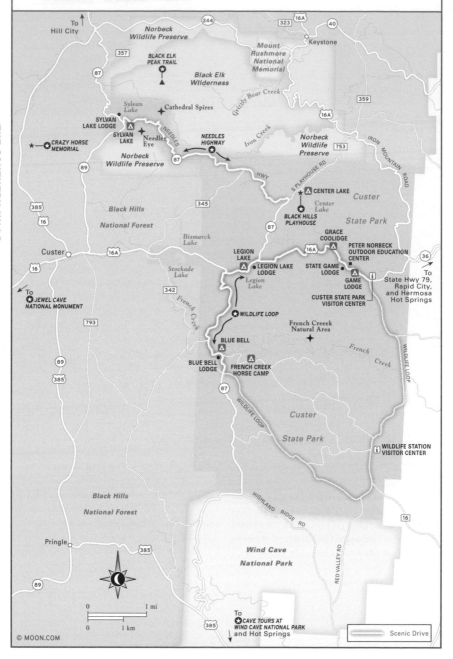

To Hill City

Norbeck Wildlife Preserve

244

323 16A

40

Mount Rushmore National Memorial

Keystone

357

87

BLACK ELK PEAK TRAIL

Black Elk Wilderness

359

Sylvan Lake

Cathedral Spires

16A

Grizzly Bear Creek

SYLVAN LAKE LODGE

SYLVAN LAKE

Needles Eye

NEEDLES HIGHWAY

Iron Creek

Norbeck Wildlife Preserve

753

IRON MOUNTAIN ROAD

CRAZY HORSE MEMORIAL

87

Norbeck Wildlife Preserve

89

HWY

S PLAYHOUSE RD

CENTER LAKE

Custer

385

Black Hills National Forest

345

87

Center Lake

BLACK HILLS PLAYHOUSE

State Park

16

Bismarck Lake

GRACE COOLIDGE

PETER NORBECK OUTDOOR EDUCATION CENTER

36

Custer

16A

16A

Stockade Lake

LEGION LAKE

LEGION LAKE LODGE

STATE GAME LODGE

To State Hwy 79, Rapid City, and Hermosa Hot Springs

16

342

French Creek

Legion Lake

GAME LODGE

To JEWEL CAVE NATIONAL MONUMENT

CUSTER STATE PARK VISITOR CENTER

793

WILDLIFE LOOP

French Creek Natural Area

BLUE BELL

89

385

BLUE BELL LODGE

FRENCH CREEK HORSE CAMP

French Creek

87

WILDLIFE LOOP

Custer

WILDLIFE LOOP

State Park

WILDLIFE STATION VISITOR CENTER

Black Hills National Forest

Pringle

385

HIGHLAND RIDGE RD

16

89

Wind Cave National Park

RED VALLEY RD

0   1 mi

0   1 km

To CAVE TOURS AT WIND CAVE NATIONAL PARK and Hot Springs

385

Scenic Drive

© MOON.COM

VISITOR CENTERS

Custer State Park Visitor Center

The **Custer State Park Visitor Center** (U.S. 16A and the junction of the Wildlife Loop Road, 8am-8pm daily Memorial Day-Labor Day, 8am-6pm daily Labor Day-Sept., 9am-4pm daily Oct.-Memorial Day, closed Thanksgiving, Christmas) is a good stopping point to learn something about the park. Inside are interpretive exhibits and displays about the history, geology, and ecology of the park, in addition to park maps and information about the timing and content of ranger-led programs and activities. Originally the location of the now defunct Custer State Park Zoo, the site is the main information center in the park and also the park location for all lost and found items. Pick up some trail maps, take a break, and enjoy a 20-minute movie about the park in the small theater on-site. The movie runs every half hour.

Wildlife Station Visitor Center

The **Wildlife Station Visitor Center** (8am-8pm daily Memorial Day-Labor Day, 8am-6pm daily Sept.) is a beautiful building constructed out of stone and wood about midway through the Wildlife Loop on the southeastern corner of the park. Park rangers at the Wildlife Station have information about the current location of the park's bison herd and can answer any questions visitors might have about the flora and fauna they view along the loop. Restrooms are available at the station, as well.

Bison Center

The **Bison Center,** projected to open in 2022, will be located near the corral complex off of the Wildlife Loop. It focuses on the history and other facts about the bison herd at Custer State Park. The park plays an important part in the conservation of the species; the herd at the park numbers about 1,400 bison.

SIGHTS

Peter Norbeck, the governor of South Dakota in the early 1900s, was enamored with western South Dakota. It was his conservationist vision that led to the creation of Custer State Forest, which was converted to Custer State Park in 1919. The **Peter Norbeck Scenic Byway,** named in his honor, winds 68 miles (109 km) through the Black Hills. Segments of that byway, including the Needles Highway and Iron Mountain Road, traverse sections of Custer State Park. The byway is not long in terms of mileage, and the entire scenic route can be driven in about four hours—but the road is narrow and winding, and it is more comfortable and relaxing to drive it in short stretches, taking time to stop and enjoy the wildlife and other scenic attributes along the way.

TOP EXPERIENCE

★ Needles Highway

Peter Norbeck wanted to simultaneously preserve and provide access to some of the most beautiful regions of the Black Hills. In 1919, he designed the route for the Needles Highway, a road that many engineers deemed impossible to build. Two years and 150,000 pounds of dynamite later, the route was opened to automobiles. The most dramatic way to travel the Needles Highway is from south to north. Begin in Custer State Park at the junction of U.S. 16A and Highway 87. Highway 87 North turns into the scenic highway. The 14-mile (22.5-km) road slowly climbs in elevation as it winds through narrow tunnels and weaves its way past towering granite spires and ponderosa pine forests. The road is named for the many towering, pointed rock columns that look like needles of rock piercing the sky.

Several turnouts along the way allow viewing some spectacular formations. **Cathedral Spires** is a collection of massive granite towers. The **Eye of the Needle** is a narrow spire over 30 feet (9 m) tall; time, wind, and water have eroded it to create a 3-foot-wide (0.9-m) slit in the top of the formation that looks like the eye in a sewing needle. There is parking at the base of the Eye. The tunnel leading to the formation is so narrow (8 ft./2.4 m by 9 in./23

Peter Norbeck Scenic Byway

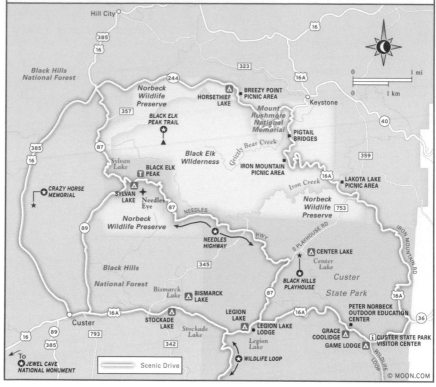

cm wide by 10 ft./3 m by 10 in./25 cm high) that buses driving the route have less than 2 inches (5 cm) of clearance on each side.

Initially, this region was suggested for the location for massive stone carvings in South Dakota. Doane Robinson, considered to be the father of Mount Rushmore, visualized a series of heroic characters carved into the spires. His vision included both Native American and U.S. leaders. When sculptor Gutzon Borglum came to investigate the area, he rejected the Needles due to the fragility of the towering spires. Borglum selected nearby Mount Rushmore instead.

The Needles Highway ends at **Sylvan Lake,** the most northern and western spur of the park. Sylvan Lake is not a natural lake. It was created in the 1930s when a dam was constructed by the Civilian Conservation Corps. This high-elevation reservoir is surrounded by towering granite peaks and ponderosa pine. It is one of the jewels of the park.

The Needles Highway is the only road in the park that is closed with a locked gate in the wintertime. Officially, the road is closed November-April, but the actual time depends on the weather. Once the gate is closed, the road remains that way until spring.

Iron Mountain Road

Peter Norbeck worked closely with Gutzon Borglum, the man who carved Mount Rushmore, to design Iron Mountain Road. The result of their combined efforts is a road with several pigtail bridges and three tunnels, each of which frames the Mount Rushmore monument as you drive through them. At 17 miles (27 km) in length, Iron Mountain Road connects the northeastern corner of Custer State Park to Mount Rushmore. It's not the fastest route, but it is certainly the most scenic and dramatic approach to the memorial. There are two picnic areas and many scenic overlooks along the way.

TOP EXPERIENCE

★ Wildlife Loop

The Wildlife Loop, at 18 miles (29 km) long, is the longest of the three byways in the park. On the north side of the park, the Wildlife Loop begins just east of the State Game Lodge off U.S. 16A. The southwestern entrance to the loop is off Highway 87, just about one mile south of the Blue Bell Lodge area. It doesn't matter which end of the loop you start from, but what does matter is the time of day. Wildlife is most active and visible early in the morning or near dusk. Pronghorn, bison, white-tailed deer, mule deer, and prairie dogs are common along the route. On lucky occasions, the elusive elk herd will make an appearance, or a coyote will slink into the underbrush. Even the endangered black-footed ferret may be sighted as it has been reintroduced in the park. The Wildlife Loop runs through the rolling prairie regions of the park, so visibility is exceptionally good.

Bring carrots on this drive. The park's small herd of burros is usually found somewhere along the way. While the burros are not wild animals, these burros have lived in the wild for decades. They are used to visitors and are generally friendly, but keep an eye out for overly aggressive behavior and watch your children. In their enthusiasm to grab carrots, especially early in the spring and summer when visitors come by less frequently, burros could knock over a child. The park discourages feeding wildlife but the burros are not, strictly speaking, in that category.

There are turnouts along the route to allow for photographs and wildlife-viewing. Expect "traffic jams" when bison herds decide to

cross the road. Keep in mind that bison are wild, dangerous animals quite capable of turning on a dime and of reaching speeds of up to 45 miles per hour (72 kph) in a matter of seconds. You cannot outrun them if they choose to charge, so keep your distance—over 100 yards (91 m) is about right.

RECREATION

Custer State Park programs can vary on a daily basis. Be sure to check with either of the visitor centers or with park staff to receive information as to the times, locations, and topics of talks and activities occurring during your visit.

Peter Norbeck Outdoor Education Center

The **Peter Norbeck Outdoor Education Center** (U.S. 16 just past the State Game Lodge from the east entrance to the park, 605/255-4464, 9am-5pm daily Memorial Day-Sept.) was the visitor center for many years but was recommissioned after the new, expanded center was opened. The building was constructed by the Civilian Conservation Corps in 1934-1935 and is a beautiful stone and log structure. It now serves as the host location for activities for kids of all ages. During the **Junior Naturalist Program** (children ages 7-12), children interact with park staff and participate in hands-on activities focused on wildlife, habitat, and other conservation topics. Native American history in the region is discussed as well. The **Pups Program** (children ages 4-6) is also interactive and hands-on as the kids are encouraged to be fascinated with the natural environment and the creatures with whom we share the earth. In addition to the programs, there is an outdoor play area for children. Outside on the patio, adults and children both can enjoy naturalist talks, before or after which the whole family can enjoy guided hikes along Creekside Trail, which is stroller and wheelchair accessible. Other programs at the education center may include archery lessons, rock climbing, rotating art-based activities and/or full moon

The Pronghorn

pronghorn

Antilocapra americana means "American goat-antelope," but the pronghorn is unrelated to goats or antelopes. Native only to North America, this beautiful animal has been roaming the plains since the days of saber-toothed tigers. If our enemies make us what we are, the predatory cat may well have made the pronghorn we know today.

A skittish animal, the pronghorn can detect motion up to 4 miles (6.4 km) away. If startled, it can attain speeds of 55 miles per hour (89 kph) in a quick sprint, with a stride that can exceed 20 feet (6 m). It is the second-fastest land mammal in the world, second only to the cheetah. While a cheetah could outrun a pronghorn, it could not outlast it. At half its top speed, the pronghorn can run for hours and travel vast distances. As nimble as this beautiful animal is, the pronghorn will generally not leap over fences, preferring instead to crawl under them.

Pronghorn stand about 3 feet (0.9 m) tall at the shoulder. The males are distinguished by black patches on the lower jaw below the eye and by a black mask from the nose back. Both the male and female of the species have horns, though only the male horns grow large enough to split. They are the only animals that shed their horns, which they do annually. They will live 9-10 years in the wild.

hikes. (Note: Preregistration at the center is required for the archery and rock-climbing programs.) There is no charge to the public for any of the activities at the center.

Ranger-Led Programs

There's nothing like an expert to make any experience more rewarding. The park offers several ranger programs for visitors May-September. All the programs are provided free of charge. Presentations include the **evening programs** led by naturalists on a rotating basis at four of the campgrounds in the park (Blue Bell, Center Lake, Game Lodge, and Stockade Lake North). Topics vary but generally include information about the wildlife, plants, geology, astronomy, fire ecology, park history, or outdoor recreation activities in the park. Naturalist talks also occur at the visitor centers and at other locations throughout the park.

Park naturalists also provide hands-on tips for trout fishing in the Black Hills through the **Hook 'Em & Cook 'Em fishing program**

(Center Lake, U.S. 16A, June-Labor Day), during which participants get to try their hand at catching a fish. If successful, participants will learn to clean their fish as well. A South Dakota fishing license is not required for this program. Participants may bring their own equipment or borrow from the park. Keep in mind, however, that the program is very popular and the number of participants in the fishing program is limited. Space and equipment are provided on a first-come, first-served basis. Meet at the boat ramp.

A **paddling program** is on the roster of park offerings and provides instruction in the basics of canoeing, including discussion of paddling techniques, parts of the canoe, and water safety. The presentations are at Center Lake (meet at the boat ramp) several days a week. Children must be at least 7 years old and accompanied by an adult.

Look for the **Speaker Series** (7pm Mon., Game Lodge Campground, Tatanka Barn Theater, free), which features presentations on topics like the Custer Expedition, caves in the Black Hills, and historical biographies and expands to include musical performances, storytellers, and actors portraying characters from Western history.

Tours

The **Buffalo Safari Jeep Tour** (605/255-4388 or 888/875-0001, 1.5-2 hours, departures 8am-6pm daily, adult $60, child 11 and under $50, reservations recommended) takes participants off-road to places where only park employees can drive. Learn about the history of the park and the wildlife on a scenic tour of the park's backcountry. Check-in is at the Creekside Lodge, on the State Game Lodge property. The jeep tour is available year-round, weather permitting, blankets are provided to participants for the ride. In season, it is possible to combine with the Chuck Wagon Cookout for an additional cost.

Opting for the jeep tour with the **Chuck Wagon Cookout** (605/255-4541, May-Oct., adult $93, child 11 and under $86, child 3 and under free, reservations required by 2pm)

at the **Blue Bell Lodge** creates a full day of touring, entertainment, and dining. The three-year-old and younger crowd must sit on a parent's lap for the jeep tour and eat off a parent's plate at the chuckwagon dinner in order to be served for free. These tours depart from the State Game Lodge and join the Chuck Wagon Cookout when the jeep tour is complete (departure times vary; confirm the time when making your reservation). Participants return to the jeeps for their trip back from the Blue Bell Lodge to the State Game Lodge after the dinner and evening entertainment.

Note that you can also enjoy the cookout dinner without the jeep tour. On the **Hayride and Chuck Wagon Cookout** (604/255-4531, May-Oct., adult $58, child 11 and under $51, child 3 and under free), instead of the jeep tour, participants enjoy a 45-minute hayride, wildlife tour, and folk song sing-along with a guitar-playing guide. Reservations are required by 2pm but walk-ons are allowed if there is room. Participants should check at the time of reservation when they must be at the Blue Bell Lodge to board the hay wagons; departure times vary between 4:30pm and 5pm. The hayride ends at the meadow where the Chuck Wagon Cookout dinner is served, and returns participants to the Blue Bell Lodge after dinner and entertainment close out the evening.

There is no time like early morning to appreciate the beauty of the park. Early risers will appreciate the **Needles Highway Sunrise Jeep Tour** (605/255-4541, May-Oct., 1.5-2 hours, adult $60, child 11 and under $50, reservations required), which departs at 6am only from the Creekside Lodge. Taking the tour allows all members of your party to sit back and enjoy the beauty of the ride.

Hiking

Over 63 miles (101 km) of marked trails in the park range in difficulty from wheelchair accessible to strenuous. Hiking off designated trails is allowed and, as a matter of fact, hiking is permitted anywhere in the park. Trail maps are available at the visitor centers. On various days (currently Tuesdays at 8:30am) park naturalists lead **Adventure Hikes** which visit different trails in the park including the popular but somewhat strenuous Sunday Gulch Trail and the Lover's Leap Trail.

Bring water with you as no water is available along the trails. Do not drink from any of the streams. Remember to keep your distance from buffalo and other wildlife, and be careful of poison ivy along the trail. Camping is allowed only in the campgrounds, and open fires are not allowed along the trails, except in designated picnic areas. (Check at one of the visitor centers or look for signs that broadcast the fire danger level. In case of high danger, fires are not allowed anywhere.) Remember that afternoon thundershowers are not uncommon in the summer, so bring light rain gear. Watch where you step, as prairie rattlesnakes live in the Black Hills. They are not aggressive snakes, but will strike if threatened. Finally, the only predator in the Black Hills is the mountain lion. They are shy of people and have never attacked anyone, but if you do see a lion, do not run. Maintain eye contact, make yourself as large as possible, and throw rocks and sticks. Keep children close. Do not allow them to run too far ahead or lag too far behind the group.

TOP EXPERIENCE

★ BLACK ELK PEAK TRAIL

Distance: 6.6 miles (10.6 km) round-trip
Duration: 4-5 hours
Elevation Gain: 1,100 feet (335 m)
Effort: Moderate to strenuous
Trailhead: Sylvan Lake, north of Highway 87 (Needles Hwy.)
Directions: To find the trailhead from the entrance gate, drive past the park store at Sylvan Lake off Highway 87 and take your first left. (This would be a right onto the road if you are traveling Needles Highway and are entering the lake area from the south.) There is a parking lot at the end of this short road. Park there and cross the footbridge leading to the swimming area. To your right is a trail information board and the start of the trail.

The hike to Black Elk Peak from the Sylvan Lake trailhead (Trail #9) is one of the best in the park. Moderate in difficulty, it is a 6-mile (9.7-km) round-trip that provides spectacular views of both the plains and the hills. The peak elevation is 7,242 feet (2,207 m), the highest point in South Dakota and, for that matter, one of the highest points between the Rocky Mountains and the Eastern Seaboard.

Trail #9 is marked by blue diamonds. The trail is well traveled and wide enough at the start for two to hike side by side. The trail was closed late in 2009 for a short time to allow removal of a large number of trees with pine beetle infestation. The tree removal is still noticeable, but it doesn't affect the overall scenic impact of the hike. The trail begins in Custer State Park but crosses into the Black Elk Wilderness Area. The elevation climb is constant but not steep in the earlier sections of the trail, and small forest meadows and marshes glitter in the sunlight that filters through the pine and spruce trees in the area. Small streams of water cross the path and, as the trail progresses, large rock formations loom to the left and right. As the elevation increases, more and more granite outcroppings become evident, and the sky opens up. By the time you reach the Black Elk Wilderness Area, the trees are thinner and the views encompass great distances.

When you reach the peak, what you see is a 360-degree panorama. The views extend past the Black Hills into Wyoming to the west, and as far as the eye can see over the plains to the east. Black Elk Peak is crowned with a fire tower that was built entirely of stone by the Civilian Conservation Corps in the 1930s. The tower is open for exploration, though it is no longer staffed.

SYLVAN LAKE SHORE TRAIL

Distance: 1-mile (1.6-km) loop
Duration: 30 minutes
Elevation Gain: Negligible
Effort: Easy
Trailhead: Pick up the trail at any point near the shore of Sylvan Lake. The trail is a loop around the lake.

Directions: Sylvan Lake is north of Highway 87 (Needles Hwy.) in the park, near the intersection of Highways 87 and 89.

If there isn't enough time to hike to Black Elk Peak, the Sylvan Lake Shore Trail is a relaxing alternative. This is an easy but scenic 1-mile (1.6-km) loop trail around the water. A level path for the most part, there is a moderately strenuous section behind the dam with a short but steep climb on a stone staircase. Views from the trail are primarily of the granite-circled lake, though on the top of the rocks near the dam side of the trail, some of the spires of the Needles formation can be seen, as well.

SUNDAY GULCH TRAIL

Distance: 2.8-mile (4.5-km) loop
Duration: 2 hours
Elevation Gain: 500 feet (152 m)
Effort: Strenuous
Trailhead: Between the swimming area and the dam at Sylvan Lake

Directions: The trail begins and ends at Sylvan Lake, though there are two trailheads. One is just behind the dam to the left (with the lake behind you). The other is between the dam and the swimming area of the lake. The left-side trailhead starts easier and ends strenuous, and the right-side trailhead starts with a steep descent into the gulch.

The Sunday Gulch Trail passes through some of the greatest diversity of plants, trees, and scenery in the park and was designated a National Recreation Trail in 1971. National Recreation Trails are designated by the secretary of the interior or the secretary of agriculture to recognize trails of local and regional significance. For dramatic impact, begin the trail at the northwest trailhead and hike counterclockwise. The first part of the trail descends steeply and requires some scrambling over huge granite boulders. It's just 0.25 mile (0.4 km) to the bottom of the gulch, but take the trail with caution. It can be slippery here as overflow from Sylvan Lake cascades down the rocks. The Park Service has carved stone steps into the boulders and provided handrails. This trail is closed in winter due to the likelihood of extremely icy conditions. Once the bottom of Sunday Gulch is reached, the trail meanders through the valley surrounded by towering granite cliffs and crosses the streambed many times. In addition to the ponderosa pines that dominate the hills, you will find birch, aspen, and spruce in this region. The last 0.5 mile (0.8 km) or so of the loop is a little too close to roads and power lines, but overall, it's a spectacular hike.

LOVER'S LEAP TRAIL

Distance: 3-mile (4.8-km) loop
Duration: 3-3.5 hours
Elevation Gain: 500 feet (152 m)
Effort: Moderate to strenuous
Trailhead: South side of U.S. 16A, across the street from the Peter Norbeck Outdoor Education Center
Directions: In the State Game Lodge area in the northeastern quadrant of the park, the Lover's Leap Trail begins behind the schoolhouse, across the street from the Peter Norbeck Outdoor Education Center.

The Lover's Leap Trail starts with a very steep climb to the top of a ridge. Hiking along the ridge provides beautiful views of the Cathedral Spires rock formation and of Black Elk Peak in the distance. The hardest part of the hike comes early, so don't be discouraged. At the top of the first ridge, about 45 minutes into the hike, there is a sign marking the spot where legend has it two lovers leapt to their deaths. The summit of this hike is near 4,800 feet (1,463 m), and the views are spectacular. The trail descends to Galena Creek. There are several creek crossings here and no bridges, so be prepared to get wet. The trail ends back at the road, a short walk from the schoolhouse where the hike begins.

CREEKSIDE TRAIL

Distance: 4 miles (6.4 km) round-trip
Duration: 1.5 hours
Elevation Gain: None
Effort: Easy (wheelchair accessible)
Trailhead: The trail runs from the State Game Lodge to Grace Coolidge Campground and can be accessed at many points along U.S. 16A.

The wheelchair-accessible Creekside Trail

runs parallel to U.S. 16A near the Game Lodge Campground. The hard-surfaced trail follows Grace Coolidge Creek and connects the Game Lodge Campground and the Grace Coolidge Campground. The trail covers about 2 miles (3.2 km) and passes by the State Game Lodge, the Peter Norbeck Outdoor Education Center, the Coolidge General Store, and the park office. It is not uncommon to see bison along this trail.

TOP EXPERIENCE

Mountain Biking

Mountain biking is allowed on all the trails in the park unless they are closed for maintenance or restoration. Check at the visitor center for any closures. Mountain bikes are not available in the park. The trails described here are multipurpose, but due to their length or location, they are great for biking. Bikers must yield to both horseback riders and hikers.

The **Centennial Trail,** Trail #89, is a 111-mile (179-km) trail that runs from just south of Bear Butte in the Northern Hills to Wind Cave National Park in the south. Almost 22 miles (35 km) of the trail runs through Custer State Park. Three trailheads in the park (Iron Creek, Badger Hole, and French Creek) provide access to the Centennial Trail. The trail is marked by brown fiberglass posts and gray diamonds. The trail enters the park in the northwest corner of the main section of the park off Highway 87 and ends near the spot where Highway 87 enters Wind Cave National Park.

IRON CREEK TRAILHEAD

Distance: 7.3 miles (11.7 km) to Badger Hole Trailhead
Duration: 5 hours
Elevation Gain: 600 feet (183 m)
Effort: Strenuous
Directions: North of Highway 87 (Needles Hwy.) on Camp Remington Road

This segment of the Centennial Trail begins at the northern end of Custer State Park and ends near a historic cabin once lived in by Badger Clark, South Dakota's first poet laureate, just south of Legion Lake. The trail rises and falls with the gently rolling hills of the area. There are several small stream crossings. About 6 miles (9.7 km) in, the trail climbs steeply and enters an area that was burned in the 1988 Galena fire, a lightning strike fire that burned over 17,000 acres (6,880 ha) of the park. The trail continues on to the Badger Hole, the nickname for the cabin once occupied by Badger Clark.

BADGER HOLE TRAILHEAD

Distance: 4.2 miles (6.8 km) to French Creek Trailhead
Duration: 3 hours
Elevation Gain: 700 feet (213 m)
Effort: Strenuous
Directions: This trailhead is located 1 mile (1.6 km) off U.S. 16A on CSP Road 9, near Legion Lake.

The distance between the Badger Hole Trailhead and the final trailhead at French Creek is only 4.2 miles (6.8 km), but it is the most difficult segment of the Centennial Trail in the park. The trail winds near CSP Road 9 for about a mile and then heads south and begins to climb up a steep, rocky hill. The entire park can be seen from the summit. The trail then descends into the French Creek Natural Area. The path is very steep and rocky as it descends and can be muddy at the bottom. The trail follows French Creek, crossing the creek several times.

FRENCH CREEK TRAILHEAD

Distance: 10.3 miles (16.6 km) to the border of Wind Cave National Park Highland Creek Trailhead
Duration: 3.5 hours
Elevation Gain: 750 feet (229 m)
Effort: Moderate
Directions: This trailhead is 3 miles (4.8 km) from the Blue Bell Stables on CSP Road 4. Follow the signs to the horse camp/Centennial Trail. You will pass through the camp to reach the trailhead.

This section of the trail crosses the Wildlife Loop and enters the open grasslands of the park. Pronghorn and prairie dogs will be frequent companions. There are large herds of bison in this region, so try to keep a good distance from any you spot. Bison are especially protective in the spring, when the calves are born, and aggressive in late August, when the rut season begins. You cannot outrun or outride them, so maintain at least 100 yards (91 m) between you and them. The trail passes through a gate and then ends at the border of Wind Cave National Park. Wind Cave does not allow mountain biking; only hikers are permitted south of this point.

GRACE COOLIDGE WALK-IN FISHING AREA TRAIL
Distance: 6 miles (9.7 km) round-trip
Duration: 1.5 hours
Elevation Gain: Negligible
Effort: Moderate
Trailheads: Center Lake or Grace Coolidge Campground
Directions: The trail can be accessed from the north near the Center Lake swimming beach shower house or from the south from the parking lot located across U.S. 16A from the Grace Coolidge Campground.

Bring a bathing suit or a fishing pole and ride the Grace Coolidge Walk-In Fishing Area Trail. The trail runs between the Grace Coolidge Campground and the Center Lake Campground, a distance of 2.8 miles (4.5 km), and follows Grace Coolidge Creek the entire distance. From the south, the trail parallels the creek, with several crossings along the way. Be careful as the crossings can be challenging, especially in the spring when stream flow is high. This is also a popular creek for trout fishing, so try not to create too much mud when splashing through the water. As you near Center Lake, the trail begins to climb sharply. From the top of the hill, you can see the lake nestled in the pines. The descent is steep and will bring you to the swimming beach near the shower house at the lake.

Horseback Riding

Horseback riding is allowed in most areas of the park, with the exception of the Sylvan Lake watershed and the Grace Coolidge Walk In Fishing Area. Guided trail rides are available at **Blue Bell Stables** (13389 Lame Johnny Rd., 605/255-4700, mid-May-Sept., one-hour ride $50, two-hour ride $90, half-day $190 pp, full-day $275 pp, half-day and full-day rides include lunch, reservations required). The Blue Bell area is nicely forested. Pretty French Creek meanders through the trees. All rides provide a little of every kind of terrain. Arrive early to fill out insurance-related paperwork. Children must be able to ride alone and meet minimum safety requirements.

Rock Climbing

Rock climbing is not a park-sponsored activity, but climbing is allowed. Most climbing takes place in the northern spur of the park and includes routes near Sylvan Lake, the Needles rock formations, and Cathedral Spires. The **Sylvan Rocks Climbing School & Guide Service** (605/484-7585, www.sylvanrocks.com) has permits with Custer State Park to teach and guide climbers in the park. The school offers classes for every level of climber, including beginners, and provides all equipment for the climbs. For many, a climb with Sylvan Rocks is a vacation highlight. Per person price is based on group size. Cost for beginners is $100 per person with a minimum of two persons per class, or $150 for a single-person class. Expect the class to last 3-4 hours. They also offer several other options for a personalized day of climbing both for beginners and advanced climbers, with a guide for an individual or group. Climbers meet with the Sylvan Rocks guides at their designated hour at **South Dakota Outdoor Shop** (632 Mt. Rushmore Rd., Custer, 605/673-2240, www.southdakotaoutdoorshop.com). Sylvan Rocks is an American Mountain Guides Association-accredited climbing school.

Water Sports

With the exception of the area around Blue Bell Resort in the southwestern corner of the park, there is a lake or pond near each of the major lodging areas in the park. **Swimming** is allowed at all locations, but be aware that there are no lifeguards on hand. The park admission fee includes use of all the beaches.

Fishing is permitted in all the park waters with a valid South Dakota fishing license, which can be obtained at convenience stores near any of the four resort areas in the park. A one-day license costs $8 for state residents and $16 for nonresidents. A three-day nonresident pass is available for $37. An annual pass is $28 for residents and $67 for nonresidents. The three-day nonresident pass and the annual pass for both residents and nonresidents are also subject to a $25 additional charge for the "Habitat Stamp," which is used by the parks department to improve wildlife habitat. Finally, vendors are allowed to charge a fee of $4 for selling the license. Bottom line, pretax, the one-day pass for residents is $12 and the annual license is $57. For nonresidents, the one-day pass is $20, the three-day pass is $66, and the annual license costs $96. In some locations the $4 fee is not charged. Note that when purchasing the one-day pass, you must specify the day you intend to use it. Keep in mind that the pass is valid from midnight to midnight, so if purchased at 4pm, it is valid from 4pm to midnight the same day. For the three-day pass, specify the first day you want to start fishing.

Boat and other water sport rentals are provided at Legion Lake (605/255-4521) and Sylvan Lake (605/574-256) and may include paddleboats, paddleboards, kayaks, or canoes. Hourly rates for rentals are per person and are $14 for a half hour, $24 for an hour. There is a family rate of $50 for one boat for one hour for 4-6 people. Fees are the same for all locations in the park. Life jackets are included with the rental fees.

Sylvan Lake is in the high-elevation area near Black Elk Peak in the northwesternmost spur of the park. From the town of Custer, head east on Mount Rushmore Road and then turn left (north) onto Highway 89 and follow the signs. From Hill City, head south about 3 miles (4.8 km) on U.S. 385 and turn left on Highway 87. From within the park, the lake is the end point of the Needles Highway, Highway 87 headed north. It is a small lake but the prettiest in the park, with wonderful views of the surrounding granite formations. Large boulders line the lake. An easy, 1-mile (1.6-km) walking trail meanders around the water, and trailheads for hikes to Black Elk Peak, the Little Devils Tower, and the Sunday Gulch are found here. There is a small beach for swimming and ducks to watch. Mountain goats are frequently visible on the high granite outcroppings nearby. Paddleboats, canoes, kayaks, and rowboats are available for rental.

The **Sylvan Lake general store** (605/574-2561, 7am-9pm daily May-Oct.) sells bait and fishing licenses in addition to souvenirs, gifts, and fast food. Brook and rainbow trout are the most likely catches here. Boats with small electric motors are allowed on the lake, but as small as the lake is, it seems more suited to rowboats.

Stockade Lake on the park's far west boundary is the biggest lake in the park. The town of Custer is just down the road (Mt. Rushmore Rd./U.S. 16A). Stockade Lake also offers the best fishing in the park. In addition to the rainbow, brown, and brook trout found everywhere in the park, it is not uncommon for anglers to catch northern pike, bass, perch, crappie, and bullhead here. This is the only lake in Custer State Park that allows gas-powered engines on boats, and there is a boat ramp. This is still a very small lake, however, so don't expect to go waterskiing. There are camping facilities near the lake and a small sandy beach for swimming.

Legion Lake runs along U.S. 16A in the northern third of the park. There is a restaurant on-site, as well as a gift shop that sells bait and other fishing supplies during the summer. Cabins are available for rent. Paddleboats, paddleboards, and kayaks rentals are right next to the lodge. A nice swimming beach is tucked back from the lodge and away from view of the road, which makes it feel secluded. Look to catch rainbow and brook trout. Boats with electric motors are allowed.

Center Lake is the remotest lake in the

1: Black Hills Playhouse **2:** Sylvan Lake **3:** creek on the way to Center Lake Campground **4:** wild burros in Custer State Park

park. A 3-mile (4.8-km) hike from the Grace Coolidge Campground parking lot, just past the park office on U.S. 16A, will bring you to the lake. Drive-in access to the lake is also available. From U.S. 16A in the park, take Highway 87 north to the intersection with County Road 753 and follow signs for the Black Hills Playhouse. Go past the turnoff to the playhouse and take your next right on Center Lake Road. This will bring you straight to the lake. There is a picnic area and swimming beach on the north end of the lake. Only slow, non-wake boating is allowed. This is one of the quietest areas in the park. Rainbow, brown, and brook trout are the most common catches.

ENTERTAINMENT AND EVENTS
★ Black Hills Playhouse

The **Black Hills Playhouse** (24834 S. Playhouse Rd., 605/255-4141, www.blackhills playhouse.com, box office 9:30am-noon, 1pm-4pm, and 1 hour before shows Tues.-Sat., 1pm-4pm Sun., evening performances 7:30pm Wed.-Sat., matinees 2pm Tues., Wed., and Sun., adult $35, senior and military $33, college student $26, child ages 16 and under $16) has been entertaining visitors in Custer State Park for over 75 years. Located off the beaten track in the north end of the park, the theater can be reached from the State Game Lodge by taking U.S. 16A west to the junction of Highway 87. Take Highway 87 north to County Road 753 and follow the signs to the playhouse. Advance reservations are suggested!

In addition to the indoor theater, the playhouse opened an outdoor venue in 2021 which should allow for a variety of new creative endeavors in the future. When making reservations, call to determine which venue will be in use at the time of your visit.

The theater originated in 1946, when Dr. Warren Lee, director of the University of South Dakota theater program, brought a traveling troupe of actors to the Black Hills. The troupe lodged at the old Civilian Conservation Corps (CCC) facility, built in the park in 1933, while it presented plays in other theaters in the hills. In 1947, the University of South Dakota became actively involved in the theater, and performances began to be held in the park. The first venue was a 50-seat theater that served as the dining hall when the CCC camp was active. By 1955, the current facility had been built, and in recent years, air-conditioning and heating capabilities were added. Now with seating for over 300 patrons, the theater remains an intimate, warm performance venue with low balconies and beautiful wood beams throughout. There isn't a bad seat in the house. Tickets can be purchased at any of the resort lodges in the park, online, or at the ticket booth located next to the theater.

There is something special about the Black Hills Playhouse. Set on a dead-end road in the middle of the forest, the remote location adds to the mystique of the experience. While theater is high culture, there's nothing formal about an evening here. The air smells like pine instead of perfume. The snack bar serves brats, hot dogs, cookies, and ice cream before the performance. Shorts and jeans are as comfortable as dresses and diamonds. The quality of the performances is generally high, and set design is consistently delightful. The theater has tackled many a Broadway play, and musical productions have included *Sherwood: The Adventures of Robin Hood, Mama Mia!, The 25th Putnam County Spelling Bee,* and many other fabulous productions. After the performance, drive slowly and carefully through the park. Be alert for shining eyes in the dark; bison and elk will be wandering the roads.

Annual Buffalo Roundup

Custer State Park winds down the summer season with a task that started as bison herd management and is now an event that attracts thousands of people. Between the third and fourth week of September, the bison are herded into corrals for vaccinations, tests, branding, and sorting. Most bison are returned to the park, but many will be auctioned off. Park management noticed early on that the sight of 1,300 bison being rounded up was fairly impressive and elected to open the process to the public.

Roundup festivities begin with the **Arts Festival.** Thursday through Saturday, hundreds of artists and craftspeople set up booths across from the Peter Norbeck Outdoor Education Center in the park. The **Chili Cookoff** (in which buffalo meat must be included in the recipe) is a festival highlight; there's also a pancake breakfast. Entertainment is scheduled throughout the day. Dancing, music, and a buffalo chip toss are other festival favorites.

Friday morning brings the roundup itself. The Wildlife Loop provides access to the viewing areas from either end, though the south viewing area has more extended bison views. Park staff direct visitors to parking areas. Go early as the crowds start to arrive at 6:30am. Breakfast, for a fee, is served at both the south and north viewing areas. Bring coffee and snacks since bison aren't always amenable to being herded and the wait can be unpredictable. The bison are guided to the corrals by men and women on horseback, a dangerous task for both horse and rider. Behind the horses are pickup trucks and ATVs, which take away from the ambience of the event but add to its expediency and safety.

Artists in Residence

During the summer, the park hosts artists in residence at the Game Lodge. Check with park staff as to artists at other locations in the park. The rotating roster of artists work on-site and answer questions from visitors. Recently featured artists have included photographers, painters, watercolorists, potters, and sculptors.

FOOD

The **State Game Lodge Dining Room** (13389 U.S. 16A, 605/255-4541, www.custerresorts.com, 7am-9pm daily Memorial Day Sept., 7am-8pm daily May, breakfast: buffet $13, menu items $8-12, lunch: buffet $14, menu items $10-16, dinner: entrées $16-39, sandwich selections $10-16, reservations suggested) is a casual place for breakfast and lunch. Dinner carries with it a more elegant and formal atmosphere. The Game Lodge offers a breakfast buffet that includes an assortment of eggs with a selection of meats and potatoes, fruit, blintzes, pastries, biscuits and gravy, a waffle station, omelets, juices, and coffee. Non-buffet menu items include pancakes, an omelet, eggs and potatoes and toast, or eggs, meat, potatoes, and toast. When coffee is added to the tab, the buffet is definitely the deal. The lunch buffet features an array of soups, salads, hot dishes, vegetables, and dessert. Other menu items include the standard sandwiches and burgers plus lunch entrées with a gourmet touch. Specialties include beer-battered chicken and honey-smoked salmon pasta. At night, the lodge seems to gleam. The lobby's hardwood floors shine with rich polish, the dining room tables are covered with white tablecloths, and tables are spaced well, giving each party a sense of privacy and intimacy. The dinner menu is extensive. Highlights include local game such as bison, pheasant, elk, and trout, as well as a wide variety of salads and pasta. The restaurant has an extensive wine list, and wine recommendations are included with every entrée listing. There is also a full bar.

The **Blue Bell Lodge Dining Room** (25453 Hwy. 87, 605/255-4531, www.custerresorts.com, 8am-8pm daily late Apr.-mid-Oct., breakfast $10, lunch $10-16, dinner $12-30) is casual and keeps with the very Western theme of the Blue Bell Resort. The lodge, a dark brown and cream log cabin structure, is set back from the road, surrounded by tall pines. The inside is all Western, with chinked log walls, wooden tables, and trophy animals displayed on the walls. There is a lovely patio for outside dining, if desired. The menu looks saddle stitched, and food selections have Western-style titles. Appetizers become "Bits & Spurs," and you are invited to "Saddle Up" for salads. Any of the sandwiches can be requested to go for a box lunch in the

A Taste of the West

The **Blue Bell Lodge**'s **Hayride and Chuck Wagon Cookout** (page 119) is an experience to be had for those seeking a sampler of the West. A hayride brings you out to a nearby meadow where long lines of picnic tables await patrons, who can choose to dine on either an 8-ounce (227-g) sirloin steak or a half-pound (227-g) hamburger (a vegetarian option is available) with cowboy beans, corn bread and honey, potato salad, coleslaw, watermelon, cookies, coffee, and lemonade. After dinner, a sing-along country/folk band entertains throughout the evening. Participants meet at the Blue Bell Lodge to load the wagons. Check the departure time with the lodge. Generally, the ride, dinner, and show run 5pm-8pm.

Even better, kick off your day with a horseback ride with **Blue Bell Stables** (page 123), just across the street).

park. Supper features a large number of steak dishes, pasta, and a variety of bison and fish entrées. "Wet Your Whistle" with wine, beer, or cocktails. Look for the locally brewed Crow Peak beers.

The **Legion Lake Lodge Dockside Grill** (12967 U.S. 16A, 605/255-4521, www.custer resorts.com, 8am-8pm daily May-early Oct., $10-12) is the most casual dining facility in the park. Breakfast ranges from the standard two eggs any style to breakfast burritos and chicken-fried steak. Lunch and dinner are primarily sandwiches, salads, and burgers. Dine inside or out on the deck overlooking the lake and enjoy the views. The lodge will also prepare picnic lunches for 4-8 people to pick up and go. Choose from the picnic menu ($24 feeds 4, $36 feeds 6, $52 feeds 8) or build your own. Meat selections include broasted chicken, barbecue pulled pork, or St. Louis ribs, sold by the rack or by the pound. Biscuits, coleslaw, potato salad, potato wedges, and/or baked beans comprise the side dishes.

The **Sylvan Lake Lodge Dining Room** (24572 Hwy. 87, 605/574-2561, www.custer resorts.com, 7am-8pm daily late Apr.-mid-May, 7am-9pm daily mid-May-Sept., 7am-11am and 4pm-8pm daily Oct. with no lunch served, breakfast $8-11, lunch $10-22, dinner includes lunch items plus dinner entrées $22-36) is lined with windows, and the furnishings are light wood. The best feature, though, is right outside. Perched high above the lake,

Black Elk Peak is clearly in view from every spot. Dine outside on the veranda and you are in paradise. The breakfast menu is fairly limited, with just a few standard entrées, including eggs, pancakes, French toast, and country-fried bison steak and eggs. Lunch includes a variety of soups, salads, burgers, and sandwiches; the staff can pack you a lunch to go so that you can enjoy an outdoor picnic in the park. Many of the lunch sandwiches are also on the dinner menu; dinner entrées include quite a few wild game dishes like elk, bison, and pheasant in addition to better steak cuts. Fish is also popular on the menu with both walleye and trout served.

ACCOMMODATIONS

Accommodations in the park include four lodge and campground communities in different regions of the park. Each area has a different feel, and each location is somewhat self-contained with dining, convenience stores, and other amenities provided close by. Pick a place that suits your personal style. They are all beautiful, and while the prices vary, they are comparable. Each has a variety of cabins. Sleeping cabins do not have a kitchen (except at Blue Bell Lodge), while housekeeping cabins do, though they have limited eating and cooking equipment. All cabins have coffeepots, microwaves, small refrigerators, TVs, heat, and air-conditioning. Note that access to the Internet is sketchy in the park and for the most part only available in the lobby of the lodge buildings. Rates provided here are for 1-6 people per cabin, or a double for lodge and motel rooms. Pets will incur additional charges of $10 per pet per night and are only allowed in select cabins. Pets must be on a leash at all times and, except service animals, are not allowed on designated swimming beaches or in most park buildings including camping cabins, lodge and hotel rooms, and comfort stations.

Most accommodations in the park close seasonally, but it is possible to find lodging at Custer State Park year-round at Creekside Lodge and in a limited number of deluxe cabins at the State Game Lodge. In addition, the Game Lodge Campground and French Creek Horse Camp (horses required!) are open year-round, though camping cabins are only available at the former in the off-season. Facilities available at both campgrounds include drinking water, vault toilets, tables, and fire grates. Electricity is available but there is no water or sewer hook-ups for campsites.

There are also several large group hospitality cabins available at the park.

Information and reservations for lodges and cabins with modern facilities are managed by **Custer State Park Resort** (www. custerresorts.com) while campgrounds are run by the **Game, Fish, and Parks department of the State of South Dakota** (http://reservations.gooutdoorssouthdakota. com). All properties managed by the state are classified in the Campgrounds section below.

State Game Lodge

The **State Game Lodge** (13389 U.S. 16A, 605/255-4541 or 888/875-0001, www.custer resorts.com, May-Oct.) is a beautiful granite and frame structure reminiscent of the style of early national parks. Built in 1922, the lodge is now on the National Register of Historic Places. Nicknamed the "Summer White House" after President Coolidge spent the season at the lodge in 1927, the lodge is set next to Grace Coolidge Creek and surrounded by ponderosa pine forest. The property features

historic lodge rooms ($140-350), hotel rooms ($195-210), sleeping cabins ($190-195), and housekeeping cabins ($225-275). There are also deluxe two-bedroom cabins (from $380) which, unlike the lodge's other options, are available year-round. Pets are allowed only in select cabins at an additional charge of $10 per pet per night. A gorgeous dark wood and stone porch runs along the front of the lodge, and inside, the lobby has hardwood floors, wood-beamed ceilings, a stone fireplace, leather furnishings, and fine art prints on the walls. The rooms are painted in soft colors and decorated with wildlife prints and scenic prints of the Black Hills. All the rooms have television and air-conditioning, and free wireless Internet is available on request. (It is possible to reserve President Coolidge's room.)

The **Creekside Lodge** (summer $235-295, winter $144-150) is the only lodge in the park that is open year-round. The lodge features large rooms with either two queens or one king bed and has a more contemporary feel than its neighbor. Since there are no restaurants open in the park during the winter season (Nov.-Apr.), all Creekside Lodge rooms come with a two-burner hot plate, refrigerator, microwave, coffeepot, dining table, and basic cookware and cutlery.

The State Game Lodge offers its own elegant restaurant. The Peter Norbeck Outdoor Education Center is across the street from the lodge. The Coolidge General Store and Gift Shop is also here and offers groceries, deli items, fishing licenses, gasoline, camping supplies, and souvenirs. Nondenominational services are held at the State Game Lodge Chapel every Sunday June-August.

Legion Lake Lodge

Legion Lake Lodge (12967 U.S. 16A, 605/255-4521 or 888/875-0001, www.custer resorts.com, May-Oct., sleeping cabins $209, housekeeping cabins $245-295, $10 per pet per night) is the most casual of the park's lodges. The lodge is situated next to Legion Lake, which got its name from the American Legion, which leased the land for years. Built in 1913, the lodge predates the region's status as a state park. At the time it was constructed, the area around the lodge was a game preserve situated within what was then Custer State Forest. Custer State Forest became Custer State Park in 1919. Close to Needles Highway and the park exit to the town of Custer, Legion Lake Lodge is a quiet area where family picnics, swimming, and fishing are the activities of choice. Sleeping and housekeeping cabins are nestled into the side of the hill behind the lodge, tucked away from sight of the road. The housekeeping cabins have limited cooking and dining supplies. It's very secluded and feels like a summer camp. All the rooms have air-conditioning. Paddleboats, paddleboards, kayaks, canoes, a casual café providing indoor and outdoor dining overlooking the lake, and a small gift shop are on-site.

Blue Bell Lodge

Blue Bell Lodge (25453 Hwy. 87, 605/255-4531 or 888/875-0001, www.custerresorts.com, late Apr.-mid-Oct., summer sleeping cabins $257, housekeeping cabins $190-216, $10 per pet per night) is the southernmost lodge in the park; its theme is decidedly Western. The main lodge holds the dining room and lounge, but there are no lodge rooms. Sleeping and housekeeping cabins are sited along French Creek, nestled into the ponderosa pine forest. All cabins have a kitchen or kitchenette with pots, pans, dishes, and utensils, in addition to coffeepots, and flat-screen TVs. The lodge was built in the early 1920s by an executive of Bell Telephone, and the logo for the phone company, a blue bell, inspired the resort's name. The only horseback riding stable in the park is here. Chuckwagon dinners and hayrides are offered nightly. A dining room and lounge, general store, and gift shop are located near the cabins. There are fire grates at every cabin. The Blue Bell Lodge is close to the southern entrance of the Wildlife Loop and not far from Wind Cave National Park.

Sylvan Lake Lodge

Perched on the top of a hill with a fabulous view of Black Elk Peak, **Sylvan Lake Lodge** (24572 Hwy. 87, 605/574-2561 or 888/875-0001, www.custerresorts.com, May-Oct.) is within reach of some of the best hiking, rock climbing, and mountain scenery in the hills. The lodge interior has the feel of a woodland hunting lodge, with high cross-beamed ceilings and hunting trophies displayed on the walls. There are 35 rooms in the lodge ($170-255), as well as sleeping cabins ($225-230) and housekeeping cabins ($210-270) on the property. Sylvan Lake Lodge is also the closest location to Hill City, Keystone, and Mount Rushmore. Today's lodge was not the original lodge in this area. The first Sylvan Lake Lodge was built in 1895 right on the shoreline. Unfortunately, the original lodge burned down in 1935. The current lodge opened in 1937 about a 0.25-mile (0.4-km) walk to the shores of Sylvan Lake, and that short distance ensures an air of peaceful relaxation on the lodge grounds. There is a beautiful, outdoor stone patio behind the lodge, and a dining room and lounge are on-site. At the lake, a general store and gift shop provide casual dining, groceries, fishing licenses, and souvenirs. Paddleboats, paddleboards, and kayaks are available for rental.

Campgrounds

Custer State Park has **nine campgrounds** (800/710-2267 or http://reservations.gooutdoorssouthdakota.com for reservations, international reservations 714/602-4453, $2 phone reservation fee, $7.70 nonresident fee) located near the four major lodge areas or near the lakes in the park. The prices shown are for the base campsite cost. If the reservation is made over the phone, there is an additional $2 fee, plus a $7.70 fee for nonresidents and taxes. The campgrounds are run by the South Dakota Department of Game, Fish, and Parks. Most of the campsites are gravel or paved and have electricity, a fire grate, and a picnic table. All but the Center Lake Campground have at least one wheelchair-accessible site. It is highly recommended that reservations be made as early as possible as these sites are among the most popular in the region. Reservations can be made up to a year in advance. Center Lake Campground, however, follows a same-day reservation policy, which means open sites can be reserved beginning at 6am Mountain Time on the day the campsite will be used. Folks staying more than one day at Center Lake must call before 6am to extend their stay. All of the campgrounds are well maintained and surrounded by the beauty of the park.

Blue Bell Campground (campsites May-mid-Oct. $15-30, late Apr.-Oct. camping cabins $55) is set in the ponderosa forest close to the Blue Bell Lodge. It offers 31 campsites, ranging from tent-only sites to accommodations for larger RVs, as well as 23 camping cabins. One site is wheelchair accessible. There is a campground host on-site. Evening ranger-led programs are on a rotating schedule with other campgrounds. Nearby amenities include a full-service restaurant, laundromat, convenience store and gift shop, and fuel pumps. Nearby activities include hayrides and chuckwagon cookouts, horseback riding, and fishing.

Center Lake Campground (May-Sept., $19) is a primitive wooded campground on the shores of Center Lake, with 71 sites available on a same-day reservation policy. There is no electricity and the only facilities are vault toilets and showers. The campsites can accommodate smaller RVs. There is a boat dock on the lake (no-wake only), and activities include swimming and fishing. According to park employees, camping here is almost always available, with the exception of Sturgis Motorcycle Rally week and July 4th weekend. The campground is also close to the Needles Highway, Iron Mountain Road, and the Black Hills Playhouse. The closest services are 5 miles (8 km) south at Legion Lake Lodge, where a casual restaurant and convenience store are located.

The **French Creek Horse Camp** (May-Oct. full facilities and electricity, Nov.-Apr. basic camping services, camping cabins close Nov. 1, campsites $40, camping cabins $55) was designed for campers with horses. Each campsite is assigned two corrals. This campground has 29 large back-in RV/tent campsites with electricity, and three camping cabins with electricity. There is a campground host on-site, and amenities include a dump station, flush toilets and showers, drinking water, vault toilets. Water for the horses is provided by the creek. Check with park personnel regarding the paperwork required for the horses.

The **Game Lodge Campground** (year-round, campsites $26-30, camping cabins $55) has 59 sites, two of which are accessible. Some of the sites are tent only. Large RVs can be accommodated here. It also has 11 camping cabins, which include electricity, heat, and air-conditioning, and come with a porch, bunk bed, double bed, table, and benches, but no bedding is provided and no cooking is allowed in the cabins. Activities include swimming, fishing, hiking, and evening programs narrated by park rangers. There's also a playground. The State Game Lodge is just 0.25 mile (0.4 km) away and has a restaurant and lounge. The park store and gift shop, with fuel, is within a mile, as are laundry facilities. Activities near the State Game Lodge include the Buffalo Safari Jeep Tour and nature programs at the Peter Norbeck Outdoor Education Center.

Located on both sides of Grace Coolidge Creek, the **Grace Coolidge Campground** (mid-May-mid-Oct., $15-30) has 6 tent-only nonelectric sites on the north side of U.S. 16A, and 21 sites suitable for larger trailers and tents on the south side of the road. One of the sites is accessible. There is a campground host on-site. Amenities include flush toilets and showers for the sites with electric service and vault toilets in the tent camping area. Fishing is allowed in the creek. The Coolidge General Store is 1 mile (1.6 km) east of the campground, with a laundromat as well as convenience store and gift shop with fishing licenses and fuel available. The State Game Lodge is 1.5 miles (2.4 km) east of the campground, with a full-service elegant restaurant, jeep tours, and a great little gift shop.

At the **Legion Lake Campground** (May-mid-Oct., $15-30), activities center around the water. A swimming beach is available strictly for campers, and there are hiking trails that run through the campground, which has 23 sites. A campground host is on-site. The campsites can accommodate large RVs and tents. There is one accessible site. The nearby Legion Lake Lodge offers a casual dining facility and gift shop. Outside of the lodge, canoes, kayaks, and paddleboats are available for rent.

The **Stockade North** (mid-May-early Oct., $26-30) and **Stockade South Campgrounds** (mid-May-early Oct., campsites $15-30, camping cabins $55) are located on the western side of the park, tucked into the shores of Stockade Lake just 4 miles (6.4 km) east of the town of Custer and about 4 miles west of the Legion Lake Lodge. This is one of the larger lakes affiliated with the park. The north campground has 42 sites and can accommodate all sizes and types of camping units with a campground host on-site. The south campground has 23 sites, including both tent-only sites with no electricity and sites for midsize RVs, as well as 13 camping cabins. Evening programs are held at Stockade North, and there is a playground there as well. Both campgrounds have showers, flush toilets, and vault toilets.

The **Sylvan Lake Campground** (mid-May-Sept., $15-30) is close to one of the most popular locations in the park. There are several hiking trailheads near Sylvan Lake, including the Black Elk Peak Trail, which concludes at the top of the highest peak in the hills. The campground itself has 39 sites and sits at 6,200 feet (1,890 m). Fishing, swimming, and boat rentals (paddleboats, canoes, and kayaks) are available at the lake. Also lakeside is a limited-menu restaurant that serves sandwiches, burgers, and fries and has an attached convenience store and gift shop. The Sylvan Lake Lodge, where a full-service restaurant and lounge await, is about a mile from the campground.

Intrepid campers who love the wilderness experience may appreciate the **French Creek Natural Area** ($7 pp), accessible year-round via a 12-mile (19.3-km) trail that follows the creek in a completely undeveloped area of the park. Be sure to wear good waterproof footgear as there are over 40 creek crossings. Backpackers must register at the east or west trailhead. There are no reservations required and no amenities except for the abundance of wildlife.

The **Bismarck Lake Campground** (reservations 877/444-6777 or www.recreation. gov, $26) is not part of Custer State Park but is just across U.S. 16A from Stockade Lake, 5 miles (8 km) east of the town of Custer, and it's accessed through the park's west entrance. The campground is managed by Black Hills National Forest (www.fs.usda.gov/main/ blackhills/home). There are 23 sites (of which five are accessible) near the lake for tent camping only. Day use of the area includes picnic tables, potable water, and toilets. Canoeing and fishing are allowed. It is a no-wake lake.

INFORMATION AND SERVICES

Information

Park headquarters are at 13329 U.S. 16A, 1 mile (1.6 km) west of the State Game Lodge and can be reached at 605/255-4515. The **park website** is www.custerstatepark. info, which redirects to the South Dakota Department of Game, Fish, and Parks website. **Campground reservations** can be made by calling 800/710-2267 or accessing http:// reservations.gooutdoorssouthdakota.com. **Lodge reservations,** managed by a private company, can be made at 888/875-0001 or online at www.custerresorts.com.

Services

Laundry facilities are located at the State Game Lodge Campground. **Fuel** is available at the **Coolidge General Store and Gift Shop** (8am-8pm daily) and at the **park**

store (8am-8pm daily) across from the Blue Bell Lodge. Three **convenience stores** carry limited grocery, deli, and snack items, as well as gifts, souvenirs, and camping supplies at the State Game Lodge, at Sylvan Lake, and across the street from the Blue Bell Restaurant. **Restrooms** are available at the visitor centers, park headquarters, lodges, and campgrounds. Three **nondenominational chapels** provide Sunday services. These are near the State Game Lodge, the Sylvan Lake Lodge, and the Blue Bell Lodge Dining Room.

Hot Springs

Hot Springs, perched on the southern edge of the Black Hills, is one of the prettiest towns in the region. With steep red canyon walls, a warm-water river meandering through town, pine-covered hills, and an aura of history wrapped around its sandstone buildings, it will never be one of those prairie towns that flourish for a bit and then fade away, abandoned by its residents for greener pastures. The history of the community lives on in the beautiful architecture. In 2009, Hot Springs was named by the National Trust for Historic Preservation as a Distinctive Destination. For those seeking a sense of another era and a quiet respite from the hectic pace and crowds surrounding Mount Rushmore, Hot Springs is a great place to visit.

Hot Springs is a bit dusty and its edges are still a little rough, but it is a special community. It follows a "boom and bust" economic cycle of new and closing retail establishments. The shops are usually the dreams of their owners, which make them unique and fun to explore. The town is always, according to its residents "on the cusp" of growth and development. This time they could be right. Look for exciting new developments as the past becomes present once again. One of the new developments will be improving access and amenities along Fall River. In 2023, the main road through Hot Springs, U.S. 385, will be under construction due to this river project and improvements to the roadway; travelers should expect some detours and traffic through town and possible construction noise if staying at accommodations along the road.

HISTORY

While many Black Hills communities were founded as a result of the 1874 gold rush, the establishment of Hot Springs was different. No gold was ever discovered there. By 1875, when a second geologic expedition was exploring the region, reports began to surface of warm springs in the Fall River Valley. The healing powers of warm mineral springs had long been in the prescription bags of medical doctors at the time, but the area where the springs were discovered was virtually uninhabited and unreachable. The rush of miners to the Black Hills brought the railroads, the ranchers, and other support industries. Transportation and population created an environment in which development of a spa resort became possible.

In 1879, one of the members of the expedition that found the warm waters of Hot Springs decided to return, and this time he brought a young reporter from Deadwood with him. The reporter wrote an article about the warm springs and published it in the Deadwood newspaper, which attracted the notice of a local physician named Jennings, but it would be another year before Jennings would venture south to investigate.

The springs were tracked down, claimed, and sold for nominal sums two or three times before Dr. Jennings finally revisited the area in 1881. He formed a stock company with Fred Evans, E. Dudley, and L. Graves, then bought the springs and set out to make improvements. During the next few years, word got out about the warm waters of the region, and a slow but steady stream of visitors began

Hot Springs

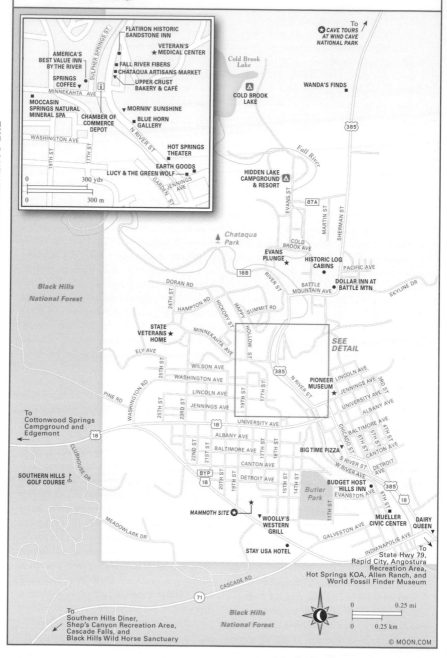

To
CAVE TOURS
AT WIND CAVE
NATIONAL PARK

DETAIL MAP:

FLATIRON HISTORIC
SANDSTONE INN

VETERAN'S
★ MEDICAL CENTER

AMERICA'S
BEST VALUE INN
BY THE RIVER

FALL RIVER FIBERS
CHATAQUA ARTISANS MARKET

SPRINGS
COFFEE

UPPER CRUST
BAKERY & CAFÉ

MINNEKAHTA AVE

MOCCASIN
SPRINGS NATURAL
MINERAL SPA

MORNIN' SUNSHINE

CHAMBER OF
COMMERCE
DEPOT

BLUE HORN
GALLERY

WASHINGTON AVE

N RIVER ST

HOT SPRINGS
THEATER

EARTH GOODS
LUCY & THE GREEN WOLF

JENNINGS
AVE

GARDEN
ST

0   300 yds

0   300 m

SULPHER SPRINGS ST

Cold Brook
Lake

WANDA'S FINDS

COLD BROOK
LAKE

385

Fall River

HIDDEN LAKE
CAMPGROUND
& RESORT

EVANS
ST

87A

MARTIN ST

SHERMAN ST

Chataqua
Park

COLD
BROOK AVE

EVANS
PLUNGE

HISTORIC LOG
CABINS

PACIFIC AVE

18B

RIVER ST

DOLLAR INN AT
BATTLE MTN

SKYLINE DR

DORAN RD

BATTLE
MOUNTAIN AVE

24TH ST

HAMPTON AVE

HICKORY ST

HAPPY
HOLLOW ST

SUMMIT RD

STATE
VETERANS
HOME

MINNEKAHTA
AVE

SEE
DETAIL

ELY AVE

25TH ST

WILSON AVE

WASHINGTON AVE

385

N RIVER ST

PIONEER
MUSEUM

LINCOLN AVE

JENNINGS AVE

3RD ST

PINE RD

LINCOLN AVE

17TH ST

19TH ST

UNIVERSITY AVE

ALBANY AVE

Black Hills
National Forest

WASHINGTON RD

JENNINGS AVE

CHICAGO AVE

BALTIMORE AVE

4TH ST

6TH ST

25TH ST

23RD ST

UNIVERSITY AVE

18

ALBANY AVE

CANTON AVE

DETROIT
AVE

To
Cottonwood Springs
Campground and
Edgemont

22ND ST

21ST ST

17TH ST

16TH ST

BIG TIME PIZZA

S RIVER AVE

W RIVER AVE

BALTIMORE AVE

CLUBHOUSE DR

BYP

18

CANTON AVE

20TH ST

19TH ST

DETROIT AVE

15TH ST

14TH ST

Butler
Park

BUDGET HOST
HILLS INN

EVANSTON AVE

385

18

SOUTHERN HILLS
GOLF COURSE

MAMMOTH SITE ★

WOOLLY'S
WESTERN
GRILL

17TH ST

MUELLER
CIVIC CENTER

DAIRY
QUEEN

MEADOWLARK DR

GALVESTON AVE

STAY USA HOTEL

INDIANAPOLIS AVE

To
State Hwy 79,
Rapid City, Angostura
Recreation Area,
Hot Springs KOA, Allen Ranch, and
World Fossil Finder Museum

CASCADE RD

71

Black Hills
National Forest

To
Southern Hills Diner,
Shep's Canyon Recreation Area,
Cascade Falls, and
Black Hills Wild Horse Sanctuary

0   0.25 mi

0   0.25 km

© MOON.COM

to come to the area with the goal of improving their health. By this time, those who were going to be lucky enough to strike it rich in the Northern Hills had already done so, and many of those individuals were looking for new opportunities. The idea of a pleasure resort resonated with many of them, and a lot of the historic founders of Hot Springs arrived here after spending some years in Deadwood first.

Most of the buildings that exist in the historic district today were built in a period of rapid growth between 1890 and 1910. Many of the first buildings were hotels, erected to house those seeking the cure from the warm mineral waters of the community. The elegant Evans Hotel was completed by 1886. All the sandstone used in construction was quarried locally. In 1888, Hot Springs became the seat of Fall River County (and remains so to this day). Hot Springs was also selected as the site for the Soldiers' Home and the Battle Mountain Sanitarium due to the common belief in the healthy environment of the community's air and water. By 1890, the railroad came to town, a defining moment and a requirement for growth for any prairie town. By 1891, the Evans Plunge had been built. It remains a cornerstone of Hot Springs tourism.

SIGHTS
★ Mammoth Site

The fascinating **Mammoth Site** (1800 Hwy. 18, 605/745-6017, www.mammothsite.org, 8am-8pm daily mid-May-mid-Aug., 8am-6pm daily mid-Aug.-Labor Day, 9am-5pm daily Labor Day-Oct. and Mar.-mid-May, 9am-3:30pm Mon.-Sat. and 11am-3:30pm Sun. Nov.-Feb., adult $12, senior $10, active and retired military and child ages 4-12 $9, child under 4 free) is a must on any vacation to the Black Hills. The first mammoth tusk discovered at the site was overturned by accident. Early in 1974, a bulldozer, working to level out the hill for a planned real estate development, exposed the item. Thankfully, the owner of the property was willing to halt development until the site could be evaluated. Since then, the skeletal remains of 61 mammoths have

been found and are displayed where they were uncovered. In addition to the mammoths, 85 other species of animals, plants, and several unidentified insects dating back 26,000 years to the Pleistocene era have been archived.

Mammoth Site tours are currently self-guided. Visitors may elect to download the Mammoth Site tour app or alternatively pick up a printed copy of the self-guided tour to the Mammoth Site upon arrival at the **Sink Hole and Dig Site.** Mammoth Site staff will get the tour started by guiding visitors to the learning center theater, where a seven-minute high-definition video about the bone bed is shown. At the completion of the video, participants will be guided to the bone bed, where they begin their own tours with the help of the app or the printed guide. Visitors are free to wander the site as long as they please and to explore the **Ice Age Exhibit Hall** adjacent to the dig site. The hall features replicas of many of the animals found at the dig, a mammoth bone hut, and a collection of some of the oldest North American arrowheads. Skeletons of now-extinct carnivores like the short-faced bear and the American lion are on display, along with the mummified remains of some baby mammoths recovered from the ice of Siberia.

The Mammoth Site offers a **Junior Paleontologist Excavation Program** for children ages 4-12 (10am, noon, 1pm, and 2pm daily June-mid-Aug., $12) and an **Advanced Paleontology Program** for children 10 and older (11am daily June mid-Aug., $12). Program schedules may change without notice. Fees are in addition to the site admission fee. The Junior Paleontologist will dig at a simulated excavation site with the same tools used at the real dig. The program takes about one hour and includes lessons on ice age animals and specimen identification. Children will get dirty during the dig, so spare clothing is recommended. The Advanced Paleontology Program is a two-hour session that teaches participants bone identification and excavation techniques, including how to map and jacket a bone. Both programs are very popular, and it is a good idea to make advance reservations long before arrival in South Dakota! Reservations can be made as early as January of the year plans are being made to visit the site.

Folks interested in joining the **Ice Age Explorers** program and participating in the excavation can call 605/745-6017 or write to news@mammothsite.org for more information. Excavation occurs for four weeks in the summer, Monday-Friday, generally in the month of June. Only 10 explorers work at the site each week. Weekends are free for program participants to explore the Black Hills. It's fascinating to watch the dedicated volunteers at work with tiny tools that look much like dental equipment.

Evans Plunge

One of the favorite family spots in town is the **Evans Plunge Indoor Pool and Mineral Spa** (1145 N. River St., 605/745-5165, www. evansplunge.com, 6am-7pm Mon and Thurs.-Fri., 10am-6pm Sat.-Sun., adult $14, child ages 3-15 $10, child under 2 free, admission includes health club access, sauna, hot tubs, and steam room). Evans Plunge, a 50-by-150-foot (696.8-sq-m) gravel-bottomed mineral pool, came into being at a time when mineral springs were believed to have great medicinal value. Doctors recommended that patients drink mineral water to cure all kinds of internal ailments and prescribed soaking in it to ease joint problems. The warm mineral springs cure has been with us almost as long as recorded history. That all changed with the creation of synthetic drugs in the 1930s. Why travel uncomfortably for hundreds of miles when a solution is waiting in your bathroom medicine cabinet? So began the slow decline in medical tourism.

There are whispers that old-fashioned pools like the Evans Plunge have no future in the highly competitive water-park market of the 21st century. But that would be unfortunate. The inside of the Evans Plunge today looks much as it did 100 years ago. The water is crystal clear since the spring-fed pool has

a complete change of water 16 times a day. Very little chlorine is needed because of the constant water change, so there is no chlorine smell and no burning red eyes. The Evans Plunge has two waterslides, a set of rings to swing out over the pool, basketball hoops, rafts to float on, and a children's shallow pool. The gravel bottom is a refreshing change from the bright aqua color of most standard swimming facilities. Lifeguards are on duty at all times. The pool is big enough for the kids to have a great time and small enough to keep an eye on them. In the summertime, there is also an outdoor pool available (in the winter it's sometimes used for a polar plunge!).

The first amenity at the site where the Evans Plunge now stands was a bathtub-like structure picked out of the rock about 3 feet (0.9 m) wide by 3 feet (0.9 m) deep and 8 feet (2.4 m) long. Guests generally brought their own towels, and accommodations included a tent by the side of the spring. The original soaking site was outdoors. In 1891, Fred T. Evans, one of the original founders of Hot Springs, opened the luxurious Evans Plunge complex. Unlike most bathhouses of the time, which were somewhat serious institutions of healing, Evans built the plunge with slides and rafts for guests to enjoy. Over time, the original wood-frame building had to be replaced as the damp and warped rafters surrendered to the wet environment; today, the exterior of the plunge is a rather uninteresting concrete block (but with a nice new mural!). Inside, the slides, the rafts, and the fun remain.

Pioneer Museum

In 2011, the Library of Congress accepted a copy of the "Square Earth Map" created by Professor Orlando Ferguson of Hot Springs, South Dakota, thinking it was the only one in the world. They were wrong. You can view the map and all kinds of items of historical interest at the **Pioneer Museum** (300 N. River St./U.S. 385, 605/745-5147, www. fallriverpioneermuseum.wordpress.com, 9am-5pm Mon.-Sat. mid-May-early Oct., adult $6, senior $5, child 11 and under free if accompanied by an adult, family pass $15). The museum is housed in a beautiful historic building constructed in 1893 of pink sandstone from the local Burke Quarry. The building was active as a school until 1961. Three floors of exhibits include artifacts from pioneer and town life from the 1880s through the 1970s; it's an eclectic collection representing life in everyday Fall River County. The museum has an extensive collection of turn-of-the-20th-century artifacts, including furniture, glassware, farm implements, photographs, and clothing. Three rooms of the museum include re-creations of life in a schoolroom, kitchen, and parlor. There is also a fully stocked general store and post office. Not surprisingly, the museum has a collection of medical equipment, too, including an iron lung and an early 1900s dentist's office. The Pioneer Museum also owns one of the early sculptures created by Gutzon Borglum, the artist behind the carving of Mount Rushmore. The museum is family-friendly, with special activities just for children. Kids especially enjoy participating in the museum's scavenger hunt and ringing the schoolroom bell.

World Fossil Finder Museum

A relative newcomer to Hot Springs, the **World Fossil Finder Museum** (719 Jensen Hwy., 605/745-5007, www.worldfossilfinder museum.com, 9am-5pm daily summer, call for hours off-season, adult $10, senior $8, military and child ages 6-12 $5) provides a guided tour of the small museum. Guides are well educated, full of information, and will answer any questions. Frank Garcia, the co-founder of the museum, is a self-taught paleontologist who is well known in the world of fossil collectors. The museum is stocked with his fossil collections from around the world, including the largest Tylosaurus (a fierce ancient sea predator over 45 ft/13.7 m long!) discovered in South Dakota.

RECREATION
The Springs
One of the most frequently asked questions

in Hot Springs is, "Is there somewhere outdoors that I can go and sit in the hot springs?" And the answer is a qualified no; most of the springs here are warm, not hot. But it is publicly accessible and free to take a dip in them along the **Freedom Trail,** a paved pathway about a mile long that follows the **Fall River** from the corner of North River Street and Minnekahta Road down to the Mueller Civic Center. Fall River is fed by over 100 warm springs and maintains an average temperature of 87°F (30.6°C) year-round. Wading is allowed anywhere along the river, although the best spot is behind the Brookside Apartments (201 S. River St.). There are picnic tables and a safe, fun spot to let the kids get wet. On hot days, if you start at the northern end and head south, you can reward yourself with a Dairy Queen ice cream cone. Otherwise, outdoor access to "hot springs" (where the natural springs are heated) can be found at the **Moccasin Springs Natural Mineral Spa,** a private venue.

Another spot favored by locals is **Cascade Falls,** about 12 miles (19.3 km) south of town off Highway 71. From the road, it looks like an ordinary roadside rest stop. Walk to the western edge of the area, though, and look down to see a good-size pond and a fast-flowing shallow stream cascading over the rocks. The falls aren't big, but there is something appealing about this hidden stream. There are no lifeguards or services other than picnic tables and restrooms, and there is no fee. Be careful walking through the tall grasses that line the stream above and below the small falls and pond; these are not roads well-traveled, so keep an eye and an ear out for snakes.

Spa
The **Moccasin Springs Natural Mineral Spa** (1829 Minnekahta Ave., 605/745-7625, www.moccasinsprings.com, 8am-5pm Wed.-Sun. May-Dec., 11am-5pm Fri.-Sun. Feb.-Apr., closed Jan., drop-in soak $20, all-day pass $25) is built on the location of the original 1889 Minnekahta Baths, a historic mineral water spa that closed in 1963. The buildings

were torn down, and all that remained were the foundational walls. Like the phoenix rising from the ashes, Kara Hagen, the current owner, built her pools within those old foundations. There are four outdoor, spring-fed pools at the spa, with temperatures ranging 88-102°F (31.1-38.9°C). In addition to the mineral waters, the spa offers an extensive list of therapeutic treatments, including yoga sessions ($12) and massages (30 minutes $55-70, 60 minutes $100-125, 90 minutes $145-160), along with other spa offerings such as a sauna, healing touch therapy, and hot stone therapy. It's a beautiful and relaxing facility. The on-site restaurant, **Buffalo Dreamer** (605/745-6100, www.buffalodreamer.com, 11am-2pm and 5pm-9pm Wed.-Sun. summer, hours vary in winter, closed Jan., lunch $13, dinner $30-40), specializes in farm-to-table cuisine. It's a small and intimate spot, and reservations are highly recommended.

Angostura and Sheps Canyon Recreation Areas

For those who love serious boating, fishing, and swimming, there is the **Angostura Recreation Area** (13157 N. Angostura Rd., 605/745-6996, http://gfp.sd.gov/parks, camping reservations 800/710-2267 or http://reservations.gooutdoorssouthdakota.com, day-use fee $8 per vehicle, annual pass $36, campsites $22, with electricity $26, camping cabins $55). Just 10 miles (16.1 km) southeast of Hot Springs off U.S. 385/18, Angostura is part of the South Dakota State Park system and requires a park pass for entrance. If an annual or seven-day pass was purchased at Custer State Park, it will be valid for usage at Angostura as long as a visit is within the seven-day period. With 36 miles (58 km) of shoreline, Angostura is the largest reservoir in western South Dakota. Single and double kayaks, canoes, and paddleboards are available for rental at the northern entrance to the area. A three-hour rental is $15; daily $30. Four campgrounds at the lake have a total of 169 sites and 12 cabins, with showers, water, and dump stations. **Angostura Resorts**

(605/745-6665 or 800/364-8831), operating with a special permit with the park, runs three marinas at the lake, with a beach club, convenience store, and pizza shop near the beach and six rental cabins. Two of the cabins have three bedrooms (sleeps 8, $332) and four cabins have two bedrooms (sleeps 6, $275). Four 22-foot (6.7-m) pontoon boats are available for daily rental at the marina ($320-375).

On the other side of the reservoir, a newer campground is located in **Sheps Canyon Recreation Area** (28150 S. Boat Ramp Rd., http://gfp.sd.gov/parks, camping reservations 800/710-2267 or http://reservations.gooutdoorssouthdakota.com, day-use fee $8 per vehicle, annual pass $36, campsites $22, with electricity $26, camping cabins $55). It adds 22 campsites, 11 horse campsites, and one camping cabin to the roster of rustic lodging on the lake. The cozy size of the campground and the access to a horse trail system and horse camp differentiates it from the much larger Angostura Recreation Area. Single and double kayaks, canoes, and paddleboards are available for rental. A three-hour rental is $15; daily $30.

Golf

If swinging a club sounds more satisfying than swimming, try golf at the **Southern Hills Municipal Golf Course** (W. U.S. 18, 605/745-6400, www.hotspringssdgolf.com). This beautiful par-70 course was cited by *Golf Week* as one of the "2009 Best You Can Play" golf courses and given 4.5 stars by *Golf Digest*. The Seven Sisters range is just east of the course, prairie views are to the south, and ponderosa pines and scenic hills are to the north. Greens fees are $32 for 9 holes, $49 for 18 holes. Cart rentals range from $14 per person for 9 holes to $21 per person for 18 holes.

ENTERTAINMENT AND EVENTS

With a completely historic front and a completely modern digital interior, enjoy a night at the movies at the historic **Hot Springs Theatre** (241 N. River St., 605/745-4169, adult

$8, senior and youth 15-18 $7, child 14 and under $5, cash only). Enjoy a contemporary movie and appreciate the 1920s art deco design. The rows are widely spaced with plenty of leg room, and the heat works! (Before 2017, moviegoers in Hot Springs brought blankets, coats, and hats to enjoy films in the chilly winter months.)

For something completely different, check to see if the **Edgemont Theatre** (918 2nd Ave., Edgemont, 605/662-6275, one block past the city park, 7pm dinner and show $40, 8pm show only adult $8, senior and child 12 and under $7, cash only) is presenting one of its summer dinner and melodrama nights. The shows are usually for a weekend or two in June and July and provide a great deal of fun. It's an audience participation event: You are required to sigh when the beautiful heroine appears, hiss at the villain, cheer the handsome hero, and groan at the corniest of the dialogue. (At one time peanuts were thrown at the actors when a really corny line was uttered, but the audience proved too enthusiastic and actors were worried about suffering injuries!) Dinner consists of steak, baked potato, a lettuce wedge, and angel food cake and is served by the cast. Reservations are required for dinner. General admission tickets can be bought at the theater on the night of the performance. Edgemont is about a half hour from Hot Springs, heading west on U.S. 16.

A beautiful event to watch is the annual **Fall River Hot Air Balloon Festival** (605/745-4140, www.fallriverballoonfest.com, free), which is held in late August. Thirty or more hot-air balloons launch into the air from the Hot Springs Municipal Airport. It's a sunrise sensation.

SHOPPING

It is along U.S. 385, which cuts through the middle of Hot Springs, that most retail venues are found. All stores with addresses on River Street, Jennings Avenue, and Chicago Street are on U.S. 385. Hot Springs has a special kind of beauty that appeals to artists. Many jewelers, painters, and musicians live in the community, but it isn't always easy to find them. Galleries tend to have unpredictable hours, so keep an eye out for "Open" signs.

Wanda's Finds (27237 Wind Cave Rd./U.S. 385 N., 605/745-4040, www.wandasfinds.com, 9am-4pm Tues.-Sat.) is just about 1 mile (1.6 km) north of town on U.S. 385. This is one of the larger stores in the area, with over 12,000 square feet (1,115 sq m) of fascinating new and used merchandise including jewelry, clothing, antiques and collectibles, and furniture. The space is jam-packed, and it's one of those places where there is always something special to find if you take the time to explore.

Fiber fanatics should check out **Fall River Fibers** (631 N. River St., 605/890-2750, www.fallriverfibers.com, 9:30am-5:30pm Tues.-Sat.) for spinning, weaving, knitting, crochet supplies, and instructional books. Shop for looms or spinning wheels, take lessons, discover books on dyeing, felting, knitting, weaving, and other fiber arts. Owner Terry Slagel creates handwoven home decor and other gift items, some of which are also featured right next door at **Chautauqua Artisans Market** (629 N. River St., 605/745-4684, www.chautauquacraftsmen.org, 9:30am-5:30pm Tues.-Sat., 10:30am-2:30pm Sun. summer, call for winter hours), which carries the works of over 30 local artists, including stained-glass pieces, pottery, dyed silk, paintings, jewelry, photography.

Housed in a beautifully restored sandstone building, the **Blue Horn Gallery** (407 N. River St., 605/745-3717, 11am-4.30pm Tues.-Sat. Apr.-Sept., other hours by appointment) features beautiful Native American star quilts, Pendleton blankets, moccasins, gift items, jewelry, and more!

Lucy and the Green Wolf (740 Jennings Ave./U.S. 385, 605/745-3415, www.lucyandthegreenwolf.com, 11am-6pm Mon.-Fri., 11am-4:30pm Sat.) is a colorful place with a focus on sustainable, environmentally friendly, reusable, fair-trade, and handmade items. There are one-of-a-kind hand-dyed shirts, printed in the U.S., and upcycled goods—beautiful items crafted with salvaged wood or creatively repurposed discarded materials. Think organic cotton, biodegradable laundry soap, woven baskets, jewelry, and handmade candles. These imaginative items that remind us that "Whatever you do, consider the next seven generations." Next door, find **Earth Goods** (738 Jennings Ave./U.S. 385, 605/745-7715, 9am-5pm Mon., Wed., and Fri., 9am-6pm Tues., 10am-4pm Sat.), which specializes in organic foods and quality supplements, as well as some lovely gift items. It's been an institution in Hot Springs since 1996. New owners have recently purchased the business and plan to carry on the healthy traditions of the past.

FOOD

South Dakota is not famous for creative dining. It's a land of comfort food where beef, chicken, meat loaf, pork chops, and the occasional salmon are the main fare. Portions are generous, prices are low, and salad bars frequently feature iceberg lettuce, ambrosia, and potato salad. However, most every restaurant has something special to offer, and the culinary arts are making a lot of inroads in the state.

Casual Dining

Good coffee, a beautiful brick-walled interior, and friendly staff make the ★ **Mornin' Sunshine Coffee House & Boutique** (509 N. River St., 605/745-5550, 7am-3pm Mon.-Thurs., 7am-5pm Fri.-Sat., 7am-1pm Sun., $8-15) a great place to bring a friend. Grab a cup of coffee, a smoothie, and a pastry, or have a meal. Breakfast offerings include corned beef hash, steak and eggs, as well as other choices. Lunch has a small but sweet menu with a Reuben sandwich, club wrap, honey chicken sandwich, and chipotle BLT among the offerings. It's a café with both a warm and friendly environment and staff. It also serves as a venue for local musicians from time to time.

One of the prettiest restaurants in town, **Woolly's Western Grill** (1648 U.S. 18 truck bypass near the Mammoth Site, 605/745-6414, www.woollys.com, 4pm-9pm daily summer,

$18-30) specializes in steak, seafood, and ribs, with a daily burger special. A portabella mushroom "steak" is also available as a vegetarian option. All entrées come with a trip through the salad bar and the sides bar.

Visit the **Upper Crust Bakery & Café** (627 N. River St., 605/745-4144, 6am-2pm Sun.-Fri., $10) for breakfast or lunch and enjoy a hearty serving of some American comfort food. Breakfast includes pancakes, omelets, burritos, and eggs cooked your way. Lunch offerings include greens, chicken, steak, and taco salads. Look for chicken-fried steak, hot beef, hot turkey, or hot burger sandwiches with brown gravy. There is also the blue buffalo or patty melt. Finally, a wide selection of cold sandwiches and lots of side dishes round out the menu. Diane, the owner, has been providing breakfast and lunch for the Edgemont/Hot Springs crowd for years. It's not a fancy place, but it's open early enough to get visitors off to a good start.

There's some great breakfast and brunch items hiding at **Springs Coffee** (602 N. River St., 605/745-5553, www.springscoffeesd.com, 5:30am-2pm daily summer, hours vary off-season, $5-10), located next to the Americas Best Value Inn by the River. Also known locally as the Hot Springs coffee kiosk, the owners were the chefs at Woolly's Western Grill for many years. It's a place where breakfast burritos, scrambled egg casseroles, and biscuits and gravy can be carted to a nearby picnic table (or hotel room) for dining. After 11am, there are tostadas, quesadillas, burritos, burrito bowls, and a variety of chicken salads or wraps available to go.

Angostura-bound travelers should look for the **Southern Hills Diner & Bakery** (12572 Shep's Canyon Rd., 605/745-7203, 8am-8pm daily summer, 9am-3pm Thurs.-Mon. winter, $10-15) for breakfast, lunch, or dinner. It features lots of homemade food, created with fresh ingredients and including some scrumptious homemade pies. Breakfast specialties

---

1: Hidden Lake Campground & Resort **2:** the Mammoth Site

range from steak and eggs to buttermilk pancakes; lunch features sandwiches and burgers; and the dinner menu includes comfort food like spaghetti, macaroni and cheese, and country-fried steak but, in summer, adds shrimp creole, top round steak, and grilled salmon.

Never to be counted out in any small town, **Dairy Queen** (901 Jensen Hwy., 605/745-7777, www.dairyqueen.com, 10:30am-10pm daily summer, call for winter hours, $12) is a "go-to" place any day of the week. Order burgers and other grilled sandwiches with Orange Julius on the side and all kinds of soft ice cream desserts. This location is independently owned and operated by longtime Hot Springs locals.

Fine Dining

Buffalo Dreamer (1829 Minnekahta, 605/745-6100, www.buffalodreamer.com, 11am-2pm and 5pm-9pm Wed.-Sun. summer, hours vary in winter, closed in Jan., lunch $13, dinner $30-40, reservations recommended), located on the grounds of Moccasin Springs Natural Mineral Spa is the Hot Springs hot spot for fine dining. It's a small venue with a chef that loves to turn simple ingredients into irresistible meals.

ACCOMMODATIONS

There's something about Hot Springs that attracts the creative and independent entrepreneur. While chain hotels and motels are represented, there are plenty of family-run establishments as well. Chain lodgings include **Econo Lodge** (541 Indianapolis Ave., 605/745-6666), **Super 8** (800 Mammoth St., 605/745-3888), and the **Baymont** (737 S. 6th, 605/745-7378). All rates reflected below are for summer season, double occupancy or as noted.

★ **Americas Best Value Inn by the River** (602 Sulphur Springs St., 605/745-4292, www.redlion.com/hotel-search, Apr.-Oct. hotel rooms $100-140, cabins $160, Nov.-Mar. hotel rooms $50-80, $10 per pet) is a pretty property with a great central location near the historic district of town. Remodeled in 2021, the hotel is open year-round and located close to the Freedom Trail, which meanders along Fall River. Room amenities include cable TV, Wi-Fi, hair dryers, microwaves, and mini-fridges. An on-site coffee shop/café kiosk is extremely convenient with great-tasting offerings. Guests receive a 20 percent discount at the kiosk. Cabins sleep six, have log exteriors and wood-paneled interiors that are light and lovely, and come with full kitchens. The inn is also walking distance to the Moccasin Springs Natural Mineral Spa.

The **Flatiron Historic Sandstone Inn** (745 N. River St./U.S. 385, 605/890-0641, www.flatiron.us, Apr.-Dec., guest rooms w/ shared bath $40-70, studio and 1-bedroom suites $90-105, large suites $155-195, no pets) was built in 1911 as the Gibson hotel. Over the years it has hosted many enterprises, including a JCPenney outlet and a café/coffee shop. In recent years the hotel has returned to its origins. There are six suites with full kitchens and baths and three beautiful rooms that share a bathroom. All of the suites and rooms are attractively decorated and have a contemporary feel. The fabrics used for the curtains, bedspreads, and linens are plush. Fine-quality wood furnishings, light fixtures, ceiling fans, beautiful kitchen tiles, countertops, and tile and hardwood flooring throughout create a luxurious feel. There is a nicely stocked library and beautiful courtyard for guests to enjoy as well.

The **Budget Host Hills Inn** (640 S. 6th St., 605/745-3130 or 800/283-4678, www. hotspringshillsinn.com, mid-Apr.-mid-Oct., summer $100-110, shoulder season $70-80, pets allowed) has been family owned and operated since 1995. It is located on the south end of Hot Springs, close to the Freedom Trail that runs along Fall River. Remodeled with new room furnishings in 2017, the 35-room facility has a small outdoor pool, free Internet, coffeemakers, hair dryers, microwaves and refrigerators, free cold continental breakfast, and a guest laundry. The rooms are not fancy, but they are clean and the price is right. The hotel has limited designated pet rooms (no fee); accommodations may be offered in non-pet rooms where a cleaning fee would apply. Park right in front of your room with drive-in parking. **Putt-4-Fun,** a nice, little minigolf course right next door, is run by the hotel and is free to guests. This inn has nice people, is in a great location, and is a bargain all rolled in to one.

Stay USA Hotel (1401 U.S. 16 bypass, 605/745-4411, www.stayusahotel.com, summer $104-130, shoulder season $84-104, winter $64-74, pet fee $20 per stay) is across the street from the Mammoth Site and not far from the golf course. Built originally as a Holiday Inn Express, the 81-room hotel is now locally owned. Room amenities include free Wi-Fi, a microwave and small fridge, a desk and lamp, and cable TV. The property sports a nice courtyard, an indoor pool and whirlpool, a fitness center, and a guest laundry. A hot breakfast comes with the room.

If you are looking for an authentic log cabin experience, check out **Historic Log Cabins** (500 Pacific Ave., 605/745-5166, www.historiclogcabinsinc.com, from $129). Perched on a hilltop on the northern edge of town, just off U.S. 385, the cabins were built in the late 1920s and have many configurations, with some including kitchenettes. The smallest cabins are single queen and are very cozy. The largest cabin has four beds. To this day, the cabins retain a rustic charm, with several nice decks overlooking the VA hospital campus and the community. All rooms have free wireless Internet access and a coffeemaker, microwave, and refrigerator. A continental breakfast is available during the summer months. There are picnic tables, gas grills, and viewing decks. All of the rooms are themed and for the most part country-style, but football fans . . . there are a couple of cabins just for you.

Campgrounds

★ **Hidden Lake Campground & Resort** (27291 Evans St., 605/745-4042, www.campathiddenlake.com, tent sites $30, RV sites $45,

one-bedroom cabin with kitchenette $62-72, with full kitchen $79-89, king cabin $105-125, two-bedroom cabin with kitchen $150-170, minimum stay 2 nights, $15 per pet per night) is a hidden gem with a private lake and beautifully maintained grounds. It feels remote and peaceful yet is located just a few minutes from town. RV sites have full hookups, a picnic table, and a fire pit. Campground amenities include a small store, private beach, guest laundry, shower house, and playground. For those who want to go out on the lake, canoes and kayaks can be rented for the day at a rate of $20 and $15, respectively. Fishing is allowed at the lake, and a camp fishing license can be purchased for $10 for 1-4 days.

The **Hot Springs KOA** (27585 Hwy. 79, 605/745-6449 or 800/562-0803, www.koa.com, Mar.-Nov., basic tent sites $29, tent sites with electricity $35, RV sites $50-73 in summer and $40-64 in spring and fall, camping cabins $71 in summer and $55 in spring and fall, deluxe cabins with full bath $112-157) is beautifully maintained and has a lot to offer. In a wooded location, the campground amenities include showers, restrooms, guest laundry, free Wi-Fi, and a dog park. On-site activities include volleyball and basketball, and there is a beautiful heated outdoor pool, community fire pit, and playground for the kids. The camping cabins do not have a kitchen or linens, but linens can be provided for an extra charge. From Memorial Day to Labor Day there is a small café on-site that serves breakfast (7am-10am), including all-you-can-eat pancakes, scrambled eggs, and a few other options. Have evening munchies? Call the office and purchase a pizza. The hosts will deliver them to your site, hot and ready to eat.

In the mood to float down a river? **Allen Ranch** (13065 Fall River Rd., 605/745-1890, www.allenranchcampground.com, tents $30, RV sites $40, tipis $70) encourages folks to do just that. Several tent sites and back-in RV sites are nestled into the cottonwoods that line Fall River. (It's a small river but great for keeping cool on a hot summer day.) Large pull-through RV sites are located close by. RV sites have water and electricity, and a dumping station is nearby. A shower house and restrooms are also on-site. This is a working ranch, and the sounds of bleating sheep may well be your morning wake-up call. Don't forget your tubes and "floaties."

The Army Corps of Engineers is responsible for two tucked-away, lovely, primitive campgrounds in the Southern Hills. **Cold Brook Lake Campground** (27279 Larive Lake Rd., 605/745-5476, www.recreation.gov, May 15-Sept. 15, $10, pets allowed) is just 1 mile (1.6 km) north of Hot Springs. There are 13 sites, a boat ramp, a beach area, and the lake is stocked with trout. While the feeling is remote, the grounds are only 10 minutes from town. There are no showers or electricity; however, there are vault toilets and drinking water is available at the site. To find the campground, follow North River Street past Evans Plunge. Take your first right after Evans Plunge on Cold Brook Road, then take the second left on Evans Road and follow the signs to the lake. **Cottonwood Springs Campground** (Picnic Area Rd., 605/745-5476, www.recreation.gov, May 15-Sept. 15, $10, pets allowed) is located 5 miles (8 km) west of Hot Springs via U.S. 18. Look for signs on the north side of the road directing you to Cottonwood Springs Lake. There are 17 sites available for various sizes of RVs ranging 38-69 feet (11.6-21 m). Each site allows a maximum of eight occupants and two vehicles. Tents are welcome also. There are flush toilets and drinking water is available, but there are no hookups or showers. There is a playground near the lake, which is a mile drive from the campground. There is a steep boat ramp at the lake for small boats, but no gas motors are allowed. There are picnic shelters, and grills lakeside as well.

INFORMATION AND SERVICES

The **Hot Springs Chamber of Commerce** (801 S. 6th St., 605/745-4140, www.hotsprings -sd.com) is inside the Mueller Civic Center. In the summer (Memorial Day-Labor Day), the chamber also operates a **visitor center** on North River Street at the old train depot. Campers can find laundry facilities at **Quality Cleaners Laundromat** (1605 University Ave., 605/745-6201, self-service 6:30am-9pm daily) and groceries at **Sonny's Superfoods** (801 Jensen Hwy., 605/745-5979) or **Lynn's Dakota Mart** (505 S. 6th, 605/745-3203). The **post office** is at the corner of Chicago Street and Jennings Avenue (146 N. Chicago St./U.S. 385, 800/275-8777). There are two hospitals in the community. The **VA Medical Center** (500 N. 5th St., 605/745-2000, www.blackhills. va.gov) is available for veterans. The other is **Fall River Hospital** (1201 Hwy. 71, 605/745-8910, www.frhssd.org). **Fall River Rural Health Clinic** (1201 Hwy. 71 S., 605/745-8928) is located in the same building. The clinic accepts walk-ins seven days a week. Animal care and pet boarding can be found at **Fall River Veterinary Clinic** (27618 Scenic Rd., 605/745-3786, 8am-5pm Mon.-Tues. and Thurs.-Sat., 8am-8pm Wed.).

Wind Cave National Park

TOP EXPERIENCE

On the surface, Wind Cave National Park, at more than 33,000 acres (13,355 ha), boasts over 30 miles (48 km) of hiking trails. The mixed-grass prairie ecosystem supports abundant wildlife, including bison, mule deer, white-tailed deer, prairie dogs, pronghorn, wild turkeys, and elk. The topography of the park is vastly different from that of the Northern Hills. Lower-elevation and eroded round hills provide scenic viewing as far as the human eye can see. It is a place where east meets west, where the Great Plains prairie meets the ponderosa pine forest. It's a wonderful area to watch the not infrequent summer thunder-storms cross the plains.

Below the surface, under just 1 square mile (2.6 sq km) of the park, lies over 156 miles (260 km) of explored cave passages. Wind Cave is the third-longest cave in the United States and the seventh-longest cave in the world. It may move up in the standings, however, as it is estimated that only 10 percent of it has been explored and mapped.

Wind Cave is famous for its boxwork, an unusual type of speleothem (cave formation). Most cave formations are created when dripping or seeping water deposits calcium on the cave walls and ceilings, forming the stalactites (which hang from the ceiling like icicles) and stalagmites (built up from the floor) most visitors expect to see. Since Wind Cave is relatively dry, the formations are subtler. Boxwork is made of thin slices of calcite that project from the cave walls and intersect with each other in a honeycomb-like fashion. The pattern looks like a collection of diamond and rectangular boxes protruding from the walls and ceilings. It is suspected that the boxwork formation results from the uniform seepage of water, literally through the pores of the rock, instead of from larger cracks and crevices. Other common formations found in the cave include popcorn (knobby deposits of calcite) and frostwork (thin needles of calcite crystals in patterns that resemble a three-dimensional version of frost on a window).

The latest addition to Wind Cave is the discovery of a new cave on the park grounds, announced in the summer of 2015. **Persistence Cave** was named as a tribute to its discoverer, who spent years looking for a new cave on the property. The cave is currently not open to the public. Its entry is full of sediment rich in ice age fossils dating back 11,000 years. Wind Cave has partnered with the Mammoth Site in Hot Springs to study the fossils as they are unearthed. As the sediment, full of thousands of small bones, is removed, the cave entry will be enlarged and exploration will begin in earnest to see if it leads to larger passages. Persistence

Cave is less than a mile from Wind Cave, and they may well be connected.

HISTORY

Wind Cave has been considered sacred by Native Americans for hundreds of years. It wasn't until 1881, however, that the cave was discovered by Europeans. Two brothers, Jesse and Tom Bingham, heard a loud whistling noise while passing through the region. Upon investigation, they found a small hole in the ground from which a strong gust of wind was emanating. This small hole is the only natural entrance to the cave that has ever been uncovered.

After the cave's discovery, several mining claims were established in the area. J. D. McDonald managed one of those claims for the South Dakota Mining Company. Mining operations at Wind Cave turned out to be an unsuccessful venture, but McDonald and his family found that they could make money by giving cave tours and selling cave formations. In 1891, the McDonalds teamed up with John Stabler and formed the Wonderful Wind Cave Improvement Company. The company widened the entrance to the cave, built a wooden staircase, erected a hotel nearby, and started offering stagecoach rides from Hot Springs.

In 1893, there were stirrings of trouble between the Stabler and McDonald families. J. D. and Alvin McDonald headed off to an exposition in Chicago to promote the cave. Alvin got typhoid fever on the trip and died shortly thereafter. Arguments then broke out between the families about how profits were being split, and the fight ended up in court. After years of courtroom battles, the Department of the Interior decided that since there was no mining and no homestead activity involved, neither party held any ownership in the cave; in 1901, it withdrew the property from availability as a homestead. In 1903, Theodore Roosevelt, a frequent visitor and supporter of conservation, signed a bill creating Wind Cave National Park.

Wind Cave was designated a national park in 1903 and was the first site to be set aside to preserve a cave. In 2011, the National Park Service increased the size of the park with the purchase of an additional 5,555 acres (2,248 ha) adjacent to the original boundaries. The acquisition, originally the Sanson Ranch, includes a thousand-year-old buffalo jump and a historic homestead. There is limited access to the newer area while the park develops a land management plan for it. Check at the information desk when you arrive to see if new hiking or interpretive activities have been developed. Wind Cave National Park is just 11 miles (17.8 km) north of Hot Springs on U.S. 385.

VISITOR CENTER

The first place to stop is the **Wind Cave Visitor Center** (26611 U.S. 385, 605/745-4600, www.nps.gov/wica, 8am-6pm daily summer, 8am-4:30pm daily winter). From the north, the visitor center is on the right just past the junction of U.S. 385 and Highway 87. From the south, the road to the visitor center is a left off U.S. 385 and clearly marked with park signage. It is here that you can find maps, arrange your cave tour, obtain free backcountry camping permits, or purchase National Parks and Federal Recreation Lands Passes. A nice bookstore is on-site. There are no dining facilities.

Rangers at the visitor center can provide you with information about activities going on at the time of your visit and answer any questions you may have about the park and its environment. They are usually aware of where the bison herd has roamed and will provide updates if seeing the herd is also on your agenda.

There is no entrance fee; hiking and backcountry camping are free. Cave tours and camping at the campground are fee-based services.

★ CAVE TOURS

Cave tours are available year-round, though in the summer, there is a wider variety in difficulty and in price. Note the tour schedules may change at any time. The temperature in the cave hovers around 53°F (11.7°C), so bring a sweatshirt or sweater.

Due to the popularity of the tours, Wind Cave offers **reservations** up to 90 days in advance through www.recreation.gov. Tickets may still be purchased on-site on a first-come, first-served basis.

Accessibility cave tours (adult $6, child 6-16 and senior over 61 $3) are available for visitors with special needs. The accessibility tour is 30 minutes long and takes place in one of the cave rooms that can be entered via elevator. Hearing-impaired visitors will be provided with written scripts of the cave tours on request. Park staff may also be able to arrange to have sign-language interpreters available for any of the tours. Call the park in advance to set these up.

America the Beautiful National Parks and Federal Recreational Lands Passes do not receive discounts on cave tours, but most are half price for adults 62 years of age and over.

NATURAL ENTRANCE TOUR

The **Natural Entrance Tour** (Apr.-mid-Sept. tours every 20 minutes, winter 2-3 tours alternating with the Garden of Eden Tour, adult $16, senior $8, child ages 6-16 $8, child under 6 free) is a 1.25-hour moderately strenuous trip, requiring about 0.5 mile (0.8 km) of hiking. There are 300 stairs along the route, most of which are downward climbs. (Exit from the cave is via elevator.) This tour brings visitors to the only natural entrance to the cave to discover how the cave got its name. Entry is via an artificially constructed entrance, and the tour takes visitors to the middle level of the cave, where the boxwork formations for which the cave is famous are abundant.

GARDEN OF EDEN TOUR

The year-round **Garden of Eden Tour** (tours every two hours beginning at 10:40am, adult $14, senior $7, child ages 6-16 $7, child under 6 free) is the shortest and least strenuous of all the cave tours, with just 150 stairs to navigate.

1: elk at Wind Cave National Park **2:** Wind Cave tour

The tour takes about one hour and requires about 0.25 mile (0.4 km) of walking. Entry and exit to the cave is by elevator. Small amounts of popcorn, boxwork, and frostwork are seen along the trail.

FAIRGROUNDS TOUR

The **Fairgrounds Tour** (daily mid-June-Labor Day, tours every two hours beginning at 9:40am, last tour at 2:20pm, adult $16, senior and child ages 6-16 $8, child under 6 free) takes about 1.5 hours to complete and requires about 0.5 mile (0.8 km) of hiking. This tour is the most strenuous of the walking tours, as there are over 450 stairs to climb, including a single staircase of more than 90 stairs. The tour visits the upper and middle levels of the cave. Boxwork is abundant in the middle section, and the upper level of the cave features large rooms in which popcorn and frostwork are common.

HISTORIC CANDLELIGHT TOUR

The **Historic Candlelight Tour** (Memorial Day-Labor Day, adult $16) is a two-hour tour that requires about 1 mile (1.6 km) of hiking. Call the visitor center to check the status of the tour for the anticipated date of your visit. Advance reservations are recommended. This is a strenuous excursion that takes place in a less-developed area of the cave along a fairly rugged trail. Participation is limited to 10 people per tour, and the minimum age is eight. Participants are required to wear shoes with nonslip soles, so no sandals are permitted. During this tour, visitors explore Wind Cave the way that early cavers did, without benefit of electricity. Each participant carries a candle bucket, which is the only lighting for the tour. Cave walls loom into the light and shadows dance along the walls, heightening the sensation of visiting another world below the surface of our day-to-day lives.

WILD CAVE TOUR

For the adventurous soul, the **Wild Cave Tour** (Memorial Day-Labor Day, one tour daily, $45) is the best choice. Be prepared to get dirty, as this tour requires crawling through some very narrow spaces while learning the basics of safe caving. Wear old clothes. Long pants, long sleeves, and sturdy, lace-up boots or shoes with nonslip soles are required. The park will provide kneepads, hard hats, and lights. Note that participants must be at least 16 years old, and that young adults ages 16-17 must have a signed parental consent form to participate. This tour takes about four hours and covers about 0.5 mile (0.8 km), much of it spent crawling. This is not a tour for people with claustrophobia! Advance reservations are required.

RANGER-LED PROGRAMS

Several ranger-led programs are available during the summer. Times and hours vary, so check with the visitor center to determine the what, where, and when during your visit. Most of the programs begin at the campground amphitheater. Ranger-led programs typically include the following.

Evening **campfire programs** take place at the Elk Mountain Campground amphitheater. Rangers and interpreters present 45-minute programs that range in topic from wildlife to plants, cave exploration, history, geology, or astronomy.

The **Prairie Hike** is a 2-mile (3.2-km) walk. Bring water and wear hiking boots or sturdy shoes. During the course of the hike, you'll learn about the varied habitats of the park and about the plants and animals that inhabit them. In July, the **Evening Hike** is sometimes added to the campfire program schedule. It is an interesting nighttime visit to a prairie dog town. The hope is that participants will get to see the endangered black-footed ferret. Hikers meet at the amphitheater in the Elk Mountain Campground and then drive to a nearby site. Bring a **flashlight** and wear **hiking boots.**

Children up to age 12 may enjoy participating in the **Junior Ranger Program.** Junior Ranger booklets are available at the park bookstore and contain activities designed to help kids understand the park's ecosystem, the cave, and local animals. Participants who complete the activities receive a Junior Ranger badge.

HIKING

The over 30 miles (48 km) of marked hiking trails in the park range from easy to strenuous. Options include three self-guided nature hikes and eight backcountry hikes. Visitors are also welcome to leave the trails and wander the park at will. Topographic maps can be purchased at the visitor center, but visibility at the park is good, and it is not a difficult place to navigate.

Remember that bison can be found in most areas of the park. Do not approach them. They are wild animals, and though their size may give the impression that they are slow reactors, they aren't. Weighing in at around a ton, bison can reach speeds of up to 35 miles per hour (56 kph) in just a few strides. Keep at least 100 yards (91 m) between you and a bison!

For a short hiking excursion, try one of the three **nature trails** in the park. The trails are marked with interpretive signage and displays, and each is about 1 mile (1.6 km) long. The Elk Mountain Trail begins at the end of the Elk Mountain Campground road and circles up through the forest near the park's boundary. This trail highlights the intertwined ecologies of the meeting of prairie grasslands with the forest habitat. The Prairie Vista Trail begins at the visitor center, and the interpretive signage focuses on information about the prairie grasses. The Rankin Ridge Trail is off Highway 87 in the northwestern corner of the park. The hike begins and ends at the parking lot of the Rankin Ridge Lookout Tower. The ridge provides beautiful views in all directions—open prairie to the east and the Black Hills to the west.

Lookout Point-Centennial Trail Loop
Distance: 4.5-mile (7.2-km) loop
Duration: 3 hours

Elevation Gain: Minimal
Effort: Moderately strenuous
Trailhead: Southern trailhead of the Centennial Trail
Directions: From the visitor center, head north on U.S. 385 and take an almost immediate right on Highway 87. The trailhead is 0.7 mile (1.1 km) down on the east (right) side of the road.

This nice loop trail exposes the hiker to all of the diversity of the park. From the trailhead, the hike begins in a stand of ridgetop pines and then descends rapidly to the valley floor. From there, it meanders along Beaver Creek, winding between the low hills of the park. About 2 miles (3.2 km) in, the Centennial Trail takes a fairly sharp left. Continue straight at this point, and you will be on a short stretch of the Highland Creek Trail. This trail will loop around to join up with the Lookout Point Trail. Where the Highland Creek Trail veers south, continue west along the Lookout Point Trail; it will return you to the Centennial Trail trailhead. Throughout the hike, you will traverse a streambed, pass through prairie grasslands and rolling hills, and climb into some of the pine forests of Wind Cave National Park.

Wind Cave Canyon
Distance: 3.6 miles (5.8 km) round-trip
Duration: 1.5 hours
Elevation Gain: None
Effort: Easy
Trailhead: The trailhead is on the east side of the road 1 mile (1.6 km) north of the junction of the southern entrance to the Wind Cave Visitor Center and U.S. 385.

This easy hike follows what used to be a service road in the park and trails Wind Cave Canyon to the park's boundary fence. It is one of the best places in the park for bird-watching, as it winds along limestone cliffs filled with cliff swallows and great horned owls. Dead stands of trees make great nesting places for several varieties of woodpeckers.

BIKING AND HORSEBACK RIDING

Biking is allowed in the park but is limited to established park roads. U.S. 385 is a wide, broad-shouldered road and comfortable for biking. State Road 87 is a winding and narrow road which requires much more caution on the part of bikes and cars.

Horseback riding is allowed in the park. Free permits are available at the visitor center. Riding permits are for day use only, and no feed is allowed in the park. Riders are required to avoid water sources, maintained hiking trails, and park roadways.

CAMPING

The only accommodations available in Wind Cave National Park are in the **Elk Mountain Campground.** One mile (1.6 km) north of the visitor center, the campground has 62 sites available on a first-come, first-served basis. Each can accommodate two vehicles and up to eight people. There are two wheelchair-accessible sites. Facilities include restrooms with flush toilets and cold running water. There are no showers and no hookups for RVs, although there are some pull-through sites available for RV use. In the summer, fees are $24 per site per night. In the winter, once the water is turned off, fees drop to $12 per night. Visitors holding a Senior or Access Pass, or a Golden Age or Golden Access Pass, pay half price a night per site any time of the year. Pets must be kept on a leash but are allowed in the campground.

Backcountry camping is permitted in the northwestern part of the park. Campers must have a permit, which is free and can be obtained at the visitor center. Pets are not allowed in the backcountry. If you elect to go hiking or camping in the backcountry section of the park, bring water with you or carry equipment to boil and purify or filter water found in local streams.

The city of Hot Springs 11 miles (17.8 km) south of the park has many hotels and other accommodations for park visitors.

The Northern Hills

Life seems more adventurous, wilder, and flashier in the Northern Hills. From the tattoos, leather, and roaring bikes of the Sturgis Motorcycle Rally in August to the year-round ringing bells and flashing casino lights in Deadwood, the high-energy, late-night crowd has a home here.

Gambling keeps the energy level up and the hours long; its legalization in 1989 breathed new life into an area that was starting to fall into disrepair. The funds generated from the gambling industry allowed the area to revitalize its historic buildings. The entire town of Deadwood is now a registered National Historic Landmark, and it embraces its Wild West past with daily gunfights and historical reenactments. Check out the local museums (and cemetery!) for information about some of

Highlights

Look for ★ to find recommended sights, activities, dining, and lodging.

★ **D.C. Booth Historic National Fish Hatchery:** Thousands of trout wait to be fed at this surprisingly delightful site in Spearfish, which features an underground viewing window, a fish railcar, and even a fish rescue boat (page 156).

★ **Termesphere Gallery:** Dick Termes is an internationally acclaimed artist who has chosen an unusual canvas: spheres of all sizes. The tiny painted worlds in this one-of-a-kind gallery are captivating (page 158).

★ **Spearfish Canyon Scenic Byway:** Waterfalls, wildlife, and recreation abound on this beautiful drive connecting Spearfish and Lead (page 167).

★ **Sanford Lab Homestake Visitor Center:** The center provides a surface tour of the Homestake Mine, the richest mine in the region in terms of production and longevity (page 176).

★ **Adams Museum:** See early mining artifacts, the first steam locomotive in the hills, and memorabilia from Deadwood's most infamous characters, including Wild Bill Hickok and Calamity Jane (page 184).

★ **Saloon No. 10:** Billed as the only museum with a bar, Saloon No. 10 reenacts the killing of Wild Bill Hickok nearly every day during the summer. Downstairs, it's bars, beers, and rock and roll, while upstairs, it's all fine dining and martinis in the **Deadwood Social Club** (page 192).

The Northern Hills

Belle Fourche

212

34

85

To
Devil's Tower, WY

90

SEE
"SPEARFISH"
MAP

34

79

North
Spearfish

Spearfish

D.C. BOOTH
HISTORIC NATIONAL
FISH HATCHERY

14A

Crow
Peak

TERMESPHERE
GALLERY

Whitewood

85

Spearfish Creek

Spearfish
Peak

SPEARFISH CANYON
SCENIC BYWAY

Bridal Veil Falls

Little Crow Peak

ADAMS MUSEUM

SALOON NO. 10

BEAR BUTTE LAKE

14A

Sturgis

FT MEADE

Deadwood

SANFORD LAB
HOMESTAKE
VISITOR CENTER

Lead

DEADWOOD

ALKALI
CREEK

Savoy

Spearfish
Falls

LEAD

KIRK

222

Roughlock
Falls

SUGARLOAF

14A

Terry Peak

VANOCKER CANYON RD

Elk Creek

85

CHEYENNE
CROSSING

14A

795

ELK CREEK

To
Rapid City

ENGLEWOOD

Black Hills
National Forest

Centennial Trail

SEE
"SPEARFISH
CANYON"
MAP

205

DALTON

DUMONT

To
Newcastle, WY

BOULDER
FORKS

SOUTH BOXELDER
CREEK

Mickelson Trail

Boxelder Creek

0   10 mi

0   10 km

Scenic Drive

ROCHFORD RD

385

ROCHFORD

To
Hill City

© MOON.COM

South Dakota's most famous and infamous characters who at one time called Deadwood home.

Sister mining community Lead (pronounced "Leed"), just 3 miles (4.8 km) down the road from Deadwood, was once home to the largest and deepest gold mine in North America. Closed in 2002, the mine has been reborn as the Sanford Underground Research Facility. A guided tour of the grounds reminds visitors of what inspired people to trespass on Native American land, break the law, and risk their lives in the hope of finding great wealth.

Diversity is the watchword of the Northern Hills, as adventure extends to the great outdoors. Black Elk Peak, the highest peak in the hills, is in the Central Hills region, but there are several peaks in the Northern Hills that reach heights of 6,900 feet (2,103 m) and above. Here you can explore some of the best rock climbing, hiking, and biking trails in the state. Tired of trying your luck at the blackjack table? Head to Spearfish Canyon and try your hand at fly-fishing in Spearfish Creek instead. The Spearfish Canyon Scenic Byway cuts dramatically through steep canyon walls, drops more than 2,000 feet (610 m) in elevation, and winds along the creek to connect the historic mining town of Lead to the historic ranching community of Spearfish.

PLANNING YOUR TIME

Offering history, gaming, and scenic byways, the Northern Hills attracts a diverse audience. For those seeking the excitement of the casinos and Wild West shows, Deadwood is just 45 minutes from Rapid City and makes for an easy day trip if time is limited. But to enjoy the historical and scenic beauty of the region, you'll want to spend at least one night and two days. Start in Spearfish, drive the scenic byway, spend a night in Lead, visit the mining museums, and then spend the rest of the day in Deadwood.

The town of Sturgis is situated on the edge of the northern Black Hills. Every year during 10 days in August (beginning on the first Friday of the month) somewhere in the vicinity of half a million motorcyclists come to the hills for the **Sturgis Motorcycle Rally.** It's a happy, high-energy crowd of visitors. With their arrival, however, comes a lot of noise (roaring Harleys dominate), packed campgrounds, restaurants, bars, and attractions, and high room rates. (Rooms remain reasonably priced in Rapid City—though its rates go up there as well.) Drive carefully, these riders can be hard to see!

Spearfish

At the mouth of Spearfish Canyon, Spearfish is surrounded on three sides by Black Hills National Forest. Spearfish Creek, a premier trout-fishing creek, winds through the heart of the city. With easy access off I-90, coffee shops, great dining, lots of students and their energy, and easy access to the canyon, it's a great spot for outdoor fishing, hiking, and biking.

HISTORY

Spearfish, staked out and founded in 1876, sprang into existence because of the 1874 gold rush. Thousands of people streamed east from California and west across the plains in search of that precious metal. The founders of this community, however, saw their gold in the form of timber, crops, cattle, horses, and other livestock. Gold camps needed food and

Previous: Roughlock Falls in Spearfish Canyon; Black Hills Mining Museum in Lead; entering Deadwood.

Spearfish

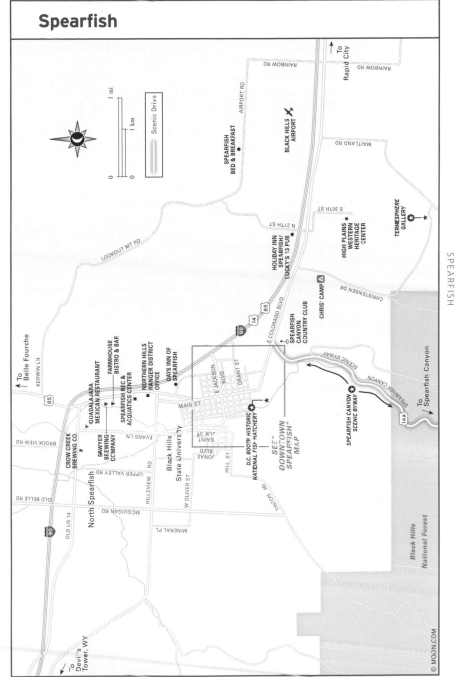

supplies, after all, and life aboveground was more enticing to many than digging below the surface. Unlike many of the gold rush towns, growth for this community was comparatively slow.

Calling itself the Queen City (a popular choice out west) due to the crown of mountains to the south and west of the town proper, Spearfish was one of the first Black Hills communities to host a post-high school educational institution. In 1883, this small community was funded by the state legislature to start the Spearfish Normal School, which would eventually become Black Hills State University. Later, the railroad brought a new kind of commerce. When the Grand Island and Wyoming Central Railroad completed a spur between Spearfish and Deadwood through Spearfish Canyon in 1893, the transport of timber and tourists flourished. (A note for train aficionados: Shortly after the completion of this amazing railroad highway, the spur was sold to the Chicago, Burlington, and Quincy Line.)

Only one train per day traveled through the canyon between the gold camp of Deadwood and the city of Spearfish. It was a spectacular ride filled with tight turns, steep elevation gains and descents, and a number of breathtaking creek crossings. The train conductor was more than happy to stop and let people on and off the train at various points throughout the canyon. Passengers would disembark for a day of creekside picnicking and fishing. One of the favorite stops was atop a trestle that crossed over Spearfish Falls. Passengers would step off the train to feel the shaking of the tracks as the waterfall thundered below them.

By 1899, a national fish hatchery was opened in Spearfish. The creek and other Black Hills lakes were stocked with trout, and fish were shipped all over the country. Frank Lloyd Wright visited the area and declared Spearfish Canyon to be as majestic as the Grand Canyon. Unfortunately, in 1933, two miles of track washed out. By then, the expense of rebuilding far outweighed the need for train transportation for supplies. Outdoor lovers continued to visit the canyon, however, and eventually, the canyon would be paved. The road, Spearfish Canyon U.S. 14A, was declared a National Forest Scenic Byway and a South Dakota Scenic Byway in 1989.

SIGHTS
★ D.C. Booth Historic National Fish Hatchery

The **D.C. Booth Historic National Fish Hatchery** (423 Hatchery Circle, 605/642-7730, www.dcboothfishhatchery.org, grounds dawn-dusk daily year-round; Pond Shop, museum, railcar, and Booth House 9am-6pm daily May-Sept., free) is a surprisingly delightful experience. Opened in 1896, and functioning as a hatchery until 1989, the facility was originally called the Spearfish National Fish Hatchery. Its mission was to propagate, stock, and establish trout populations in the Black Hills of South Dakota and Wyoming. Today the facility continues to work with the U.S Fish & Wildlife Service to rear rainbow trout for South Dakota streams. While trout are not native to the region, the fast-flowing, cold springwater of the region is a perfect environment for them.

The hatchery is situated on 10 acres (4 ha) of land a few blocks from downtown Spearfish and adjacent to Spearfish City Park. Beautiful landscaping—including ponds, wooden bridges, rock walls, and flower gardens—complement the historic superintendent's residence, the 1905 **Booth House,** and the attractive **Von Bayer Museum of Fish Culture.** All the ponds are stocked with trout; fish food is available from dispensers located near the ponds, and small bags of food can be purchased from the gift shop on-site called the **Pond Shop.** Near the entryway to the park, a below-surface walkway allows visitors to watch some very large trout swimming about in the stock pond. Feeding the trout is a fun and inexpensive source of entertainment for both kids and adults.

Thoughtfully designed displays and interpretive signs are scattered throughout the grounds, including a **Yellowstone Boat** and

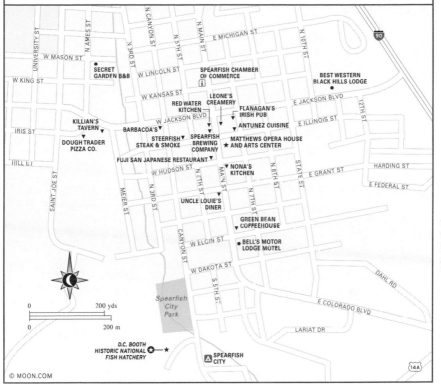

Downtown Spearfish

a replica of a **Fish Car**. The Yellowstone Boat on display is a Great Lakes-style cabin cruiser. It was used at Yellowstone Lake to collect fish eggs. The boat was originally designed to rescue fish stranded by receding floodwaters when the Mississippi River flooded. These boats were selected for the Yellowstone project because they were sturdy enough to withstand the heavy waves on Yellowstone Lake. The Fish Car is a replica of the railcars that were used to transport fish ready for stocking in the days before refrigeration. Volunteers walk visitors through the replica, explaining how fish were kept alive and how the cars evolved at a time when the only way to keep the fish cool was with ice and the only way to keep the water aerated was with hand pumps. Today, fish are transported from hatcheries in specially designed tanker trucks that are filled with refrigerated, aerated, and constantly circulated water. In the 1880s, that was not yet an option. Over 72 billion fish were transported by fish railcars between 1873 and 1947.

The **Von Bayer Museum of Fish Culture** houses a collection of more than 185,000 artifacts related to the fisheries industry. Guided tours of the museum and the 1905 Booth House, which served as the superintendent's residence, are possible daily in season subject to the availability of volunteers. The tours start whenever visitors are interested in taking one and last as long as the visitors like. And even after the tour begins, anyone can tag along. Guides provide information about the history of fisheries in the United States, as well as the D.C. Booth Historic Site, and explain what many of the artifacts in the museum were used for.

★ Termesphere Gallery

Dick Termes is an internationally acclaimed and award-winning artist whose three-dimensional paintings on spheres make for a stunning artistic display. Lauded for his work from San Francisco to Paris, Termes acknowledges M. C. Escher and Buckminster Fuller as early influences. His work is on display at the **Termesphere Gallery** (1920 Christensen Dr., 605/642-4805 or 888/642-4805, www.termespheres.com, 9am-5pm daily summer, call for hours off-season). Colorful spheres, ranging in size from a small Christmas ornament to 24 inches (61 cm) in diameter, hang from the ceiling of the gallery and quietly spin, the result of a small electric motor, giving the visitor a 360-degree view of a hand-painted scene created by Termes. His work has included depictions of the Globe Theater in London, the Pantheon in Rome, and St. Mark's Square in Venice. Termes continues to experiment, using mirrors and painting scenes from the inside of the sphere out. Some are brightly colored scenes and some are intricate graphical designs. It's hard to begin to explain the six-point perspective approach that Termes uses to create his spherical masterpieces, but the results are absorbing. Housed in a geodesic dome built by the Termes family, the hanging and spinning spheres are available for sale. When he isn't on the road doing shows or giving lectures, Termes can be found on-site, happy to chat about his work. The gallery space is located in his home, as is his studio.

Matthews Opera House and Arts Center

The **Matthews Opera House and Arts Center** (612 N. Main St., 605/642-7973, www.matthewsopera.com, Arts Center 10am-5pm Mon.-Sat. June-July, 10am-5pm Tues.-Sat. Aug.-May, self-guided tours during gallery hours, concerts $20-25, community theater $15, national theater $25) share a building in downtown Spearfish. The Matthews Opera House holds concerts, community theater events, and film presentations. The box office opens 90 minutes before any ticketed event; otherwise tickets can be purchased in the Arts Center. Opened in 1906, the Opera House was built on the second floor of a sandstone building owned by Wyoming rancher Thomas Matthews. The theater featured colorful prefab murals, tin columns painted a rich cream color and accented in gold, incandescent lighting, hardwood floors, box seats, a balcony, and paintings of several playwrights, including Shakespeare. The Opera House was used for stage productions and traveling shows through the 1920s. The next decade saw a rapid decline in live performances as the general public became enamored with "moving pictures." For about a decade, the Opera House was used as a movie house, but it was abandoned when the owner moved the screenings into a new and larger facility down the street. Hard times continued to plague the small Opera House after the theater department of Black Hills State University built a venue that could seat twice as many patrons. Many small arts groups made efforts to revive the Opera House over the years, but it required more work than they could afford. The community came together in 1985 to start restoring the Opera House and completed the historic restoration of the little jewel of a theater in time for its centennial in 2006. The restoration added air-conditioning, dressing rooms, and gallery space on the first floor, which now houses the Spearfish Arts Center. Concerts at the Opera House have included everything from jazz to folk music events. The gallery features paintings and photographs by local Spearfish and regional Black Hills artists and hosts artists receptions on a regular basis.

High Plains Western Heritage Center

The **High Plains Western Heritage Center** (825 Heritage Dr., 605/642-9378, www.westernheritagecenter.com, 9am-4pm Mon.-Sat., 1pm-4pm Sun. May.-Oct., 9am-4pm

Tues.-Sat. Nov.-Apr., adult $10, child ages 6-16 $3, child under 6 free, family $22) opened in 1989. The mission of the museum is to preserve the history of the early pioneers in the five states of South Dakota, North Dakota, Wyoming, Montana, and Nebraska. Displays in the museum include frontier fashions, a pioneer kitchen, a blacksmith shop, and cowboy gear, as well as on the ranching, agriculture, and timber industries. Artifacts include one of the original Cheyenne-Deadwood stagecoaches, photographs and memorabilia from early rodeos in the region along with explanations of rodeo events. When the facility was built, a 200-seat theater complex was included. Several times a year, concerts and other special programs are presented at the center. In addition, the local historical society or traveling shows give lectures and workshops at the facility. (Ticket prices vary from free admission to $40 per ticket, depending on the program.) Summer programs include a chuckwagon dinner and cowboy show. Call for information about lectures, workshops, and concert performances occurring during the time of your visit.

RECREATION

Some of the best outdoor recreation in the Black Hills is concentrated along the Spearfish Canyon Scenic Byway, which runs south from Spearfish to Lead. Drinking in the beauty of the canyon, hiking, rock climbing, and fly-fishing are all activities enjoyed within the bounds of the canyon walls. The canyon road was designed to allow safe biking. The shoulders on both sides are about 4 feet (1.2 m) wide. It's a wonderful 20-mile (32-km) trek. The fastest access to the byway is to take exit 14 off I-90, and then stay on U.S. 14, which parallels I-90 headed west. Just past the Spearfish Canyon Golf Club, take a left (heading south) on U.S. 14A—this highway is the **Spearfish Canyon Scenic Byway.**

Hiking

There are several scenic hiking and biking trails southwest of Spearfish in the Black Hills National Forest. And there are several peaks that afford spectacular views. The Crow Peak Trail is one of the best and, not surprisingly, one of the most popular hikes in the region.

CROW PEAK TRAIL
Distance: 7 miles (11.3 km) round-trip
Duration: 6 hours
Elevation Gain: 1,600 feet (488 m)
Effort: Strenuous
Trailhead: Crow Peak Trailhead
Directions: From Spearfish, take Forest Road 214 (Higgins Gulch Rd.) about 7 miles (11.3 km) south of town. The trailhead is in a good-size parking lot on the right.

The trail starts off winding west though ponderosa pine, aspen, and birch trees. The path quickly turns steep, ascending the mountain through a series of tight switchbacks. At higher elevations, the trees thin and the trail becomes rocky. At the summit, the views encompass several peaks including Terry Peak (second only in elevation to Black Elk Peak in the Central Hills), Cement Ridge, Spearfish Peak, and Bear Butte in the distance to the east. The name Crow Peak comes from the Lakota name Paha Karitukateyapi, which means "the hills where the Crow were killed," a reference to a battle between Crow and Lakota warriors.

OLD BALDY TRAIL
Distance: 5.7-mile (9.2-km) loop
Duration: 4 hours
Elevation Gain: 300 feet (91 m)
Effort: Moderately strenuous
Trailhead: Old Baldy Trailhead
Directions: The trailhead is 13 miles (20.9 km) south of Spearfish off Forest Road 134.

Do not let the modest elevation gain of just 300 feet (91 m) fool you. The entire hike takes place above 5,800 feet (1,768 m); high-elevation hiking can be wearying. Add 0.7 mile (1.1 km) for the spur to the summit of Old Baldy Mountain. The trail loop winds through quaking aspen, ponderosa pine, and paper birch. From the top, there is a stunning panoramic view of Crow Peak to the north,

Terry Peak to the east, and the stone tower of the Cement Ridge fire lookout tower in Wyoming to the west.

Biking and Cross-Country Skiing

The Big Hill Trails present a great selection for bicyclists of all skill levels and for cross-country skiers. Five interconnected loops allow for an easy family ski trip in the winter or an all-day difficult bike ride covering more than 13 miles (20.9 km) for mountain bikers in the summer season.

BIG HILL TRAILS

Distance: A loop plus A1 loop 3.3 miles (5.3 km) round-trip; A-C-D outer loop 10.9 miles (17.5 km); B loop 3.6 miles (5.8 km); Loop C 6.9 miles (11.1 km); Loop D 4.5 miles (7.2 km); 7.5 miles (12.1 km) total from trailhead

Duration: Varies from 2 hours to a full day of combining interconnecting loops

Elevation Gain: 400 feet (122 m)

Effort: Easy to moderately strenuous

Trailhead: Big Hill Trailhead

Distance: From Spearfish, take exit 10 off I-90 and head toward town on North Main Street. Just past the Forest Service office (2014 N. Main), take a right on Utah Street. Continue to a four-way stop. Drive south 0.5 mile (0.8 km) on the gravel road until the intersection with Forest Road 134. Drive south on Forest Road 134 for 7.8 miles (12.6 km) to the trailhead.

These trails range in difficulty from easy to strenuous. During the winter, some portions of the trails are groomed for cross-country skiing and cross-country ski racing. Loops A (2.8 mi/4.5 km, easy to moderate) and A-1 (0.5 mi/0.8 km, easy) are fairly level, groomed in the winter, and meander through stands of quaking aspen and birch trees. Loop B (3.6 mi/5.8 km, difficult) starts out on Loop A (head right on Loop A) and then veers off about 0.5 mile (0.8 km) into the trail. At that point, the trail earns its difficult rating as it gets fairly steep in spots. Loop B is not groomed in winter and is a more challenging trail popular with mountain bikers. Loop C (6.9 mi/11.1 km, difficult) also starts out on Loop A (head left on Loop A from the

trailhead) and is another groomed trail that extends past the aspens into the ponderosa pines. The longest trail here is Loop D, which runs for 7.5 miles (12.1 km) of groomed trail with a 0.2-mile (0.3-km) ungroomed spur that offers a scenic overlook of Spearfish Canyon and Spearfish Mountain. This trail is rated as moderately strenuous and winds through extensive ponderosa pine forests. Hikers will enjoy Loop D best for its views. Novice mountain bikers will enjoy Loops A and A1. All the other loops are fine for intermediate riders.

Fly-Fishing

Spearfish Creek is a fast-moving creek with fly-fishing access year-round. The river is stocked with rainbow, brown, and brook trout. Perfectly good fish can be caught right in the heart of Spearfish. A fishing license is required and can be obtained in Spearfish from Walmart (2825 1st Ave.) and High Mountain Outfitters (313 W. Jackson Blvd.) or at the Spearfish Canyon Lodge (10619 Roughlock Falls Rd.) in Savoy. A one-day license is $8 for state residents and $16 for nonresidents. A three-day consecutive fishing license is available to nonresidents for $37. With a three-day consecutive license, a habitat stamp must also be purchased ($25). Note that retailers are allowed to charge up to $4 for selling licenses. Licenses can also be bought online at http://gfp.sd.gov.

Golf

Spearfish Canyon Golf Club (120 Spearfish Canyon Rd., 605/717-4653, www.spearfishcanyoncountryclub.com, Mon.-Thurs. 9 holes $29 walking/$41 with cart, 18 holes $53 walking/$74 with cart, Fri.-Sun. 9 holes $31 walking/$43 with cart, 18 holes $58 walking/$79 with cart) is the only 18-hole golf course (6,744 yd/6,167 m, par 72) in the Northern Hills. Established in 1921, the club is one of the oldest in South Dakota. Relatively recent upgrades to the facility include a driving range and a short game area. This semi-private club is open to the public with the exception of Wednesday 10am-4pm, when the course is open for members only. Amenities include a full-service bar and grill and a pro shop. The pro shop carries a full line of apparel and equipment and can arrange for golf instructions or golf club rentals.

Water Park and Fitness

The **Spearfish Rec and Aquatic Center** (122 Recreation Ln., 605/722-1430, www.spearfishreccenter.com, rec center 5:30am-9pm Mon.-Fri., 8am-7pm Sat., 11:30am-7pm Sun., adult day pass $5, youth ages 4-17 $3; water park 1pm-7pm daily Memorial Day-Labor Day, $9 for child over 48 in./122 cm tall, $7 for child under 48 in./122 cm, $3 spectators) opened in 2008 and is a state-of-the-art facility. The rec center offerings include cardio equipment, weight training, fitness classes, cycling, a walking track, and a standard swimming pool. In addition, visitors may attend any of the many classes offered. The real fun for families, though, is the water park. If the kids are restless, it's a good place to burn off some energy. There are three large waterslides, a climbing wall, and an adventure walk. Snacks are available at the concession stand. Remember, though, no one under 48 inches (122 cm) tall is allowed to use the slides.

NIGHTLIFE

Bar

Flanagan's Irish Pub (729 N. 7th St., 605/722-3526, 4pm-midnight Mon.-Thurs., 4pm-2am Fri.-Sat.) is exactly the kind of place its name suggests: fun and friendly, with good beer on tap and a loyal crowd. Enjoy live music, open mics, sing-alongs, trivia nights, games, and a lot of green. There's also outdoor seating. It's a great place to spend an evening. Eat dinner before you go, though, as there are only snack foods on hand!

Brewpubs

Sawyer Brewing Company (2537 Yukon Place, 605/569-2676, www.sawyerbrewingco.com, 11am-10pm Mon.-Sat, 11am-9pm Sun.) is a relatively new brewpub in Spearfish. The specialty of the house is creative tap beer and handcrafted pizzas ($14-19). There are lots of IPAs available, as well as a couple of ales and stouts. Favorites include the American Style Stout, with hints of coffee and chocolate. There are some one-of-a-kind beers here, including Key Lime Tart IPA and Strawberry Whip. Not sure what to get? Sample a few at the 5-ounce (158-ml) level ($2) before selecting your beverage of choice (10 oz./296 ml $4, 16 oz./473 ml $5.50-6.50). Situated adjacent to Spearfish Creek, the pub is all hewn wood and steel, with a great little deck looking down at the creek. It's a very comfortable spot. Dogs are welcome on the deck.

Right downtown, the **Spearfish Brewing Company** (741 N. Main St., #130, 605/717-6999, www.spearfishbrewing.com, 11am-11pm Mon.-Sat., 11am-9pm Sun.) has a rotating collection of 16 beers on tap. Specialties include Belgian and German beers as well as pilsners, ales, tangy summer citrusy beers, stouts, and lagers. Beer is offered in a 4-ounce (118-ml) sample size ($2.50), 9-ounce (266-ml) light-drinker size, and 16-ounce (473-ml) beer-lover size ($5-8). The pub opens into the **Red Water Kitchen,** which provides it with snack foods like fries, cheese curds, and pretzel bites and a selection of comfort foods including mac and cheese, chicken tenders, and pulled pork sandwiches. The tap wall is colorful, modern, light, and cheery. Chairs and tables are wood with light blonde being the color of choice.

The **Crow Peak Brewing Company** (125 W. Old U.S. 14, 605/717-0006, www.crowpeakbrewing.com, noon-10pm Mon.-Thurs., noon-midnight Fri.-Sat., 11am-9pm Sun.) was the first Spearfish brewpub and will please the palate of any beer drinker. Its beverages, ranging from pale ales to pitch-black porters, have built a successful fan base and are now distributed throughout South Dakota. It's located in a beautiful barnlike building with second-story decks and outdoor tables. The barroom itself has wooden tables and stone decor.

FOOD
Casual Dining

Healthy eaters may want to fire up their energy with a delicious lunch at ★ **Green Bean Coffee House** (304 Main St., 605/717-3636, 6am-4:30pm Mon.-Fri., 7am-4pm Sat.-Sun., $10), where a full array of great coffee and espresso drinks is served with an assortment of wraps, sandwiches, panini, and soups. The Green Bean is inside a spacious, homey old house with many rooms, interesting decor, and a nice front porch. Free Wi-Fi is available.

It must have something to do with the student population in town. Many of the best restaurants are also some of the best bars. ★ **Killian's Tavern** (539 W. Jackson Blvd., 605/717-1255, www.killiansfoodanddrink. com, 11am-10pm Sun.-Thurs., 11am-11pm Fri.- Sat., lunch $12-15, dinner $15-25) is not a typical Irish bar, though it does serve corned beef and cabbage. Creative and inclusive, the menu offers gluten-free and vegetarian options and serves organic foods wherever possible. Don't worry though, a lot of comfort foods are available, too (think hand-cut fries topped with white cheddar cheese curds, chicken-fried steak, and brown gravy). Bottom line is that the focus is on offering options to every taste. The decor features hanging bicycles, rough-cut wood, and old photos of the Black Hills. An especially nice touch are the 17 craft beers on tap.

Plan to come hungry to **Steerfish Steak and Smoke** (701 N. 5th St., 605/717-2485, www.steerfish.com, 11am-late Mon.-Sat., 11am-10pm Sun., lunch $10-17, dinner $15-35). The extensive menu of smokehouse ribs, brisket, barbecue, and burgers features top-quality hand-cut Angus beef. And it doesn't stop there: walleye, trout, salmon, and chicken can be smoked, sautéed, fried, grilled, or served in pasta dishes. There is an attractive and full bar with multiple taps of great beer. The charming old sandstone building interior features themes from the West and from the river, decorated with a lot of wood and art focused on rodeos and fishing.

Uncle Louie's Diner (447 N. Main, 605/559-0366, www.unclelouiesdiner.com, 8am-8pm Wed.-Sat. 8am-2pm Sun., $6-13) is the go-to place for breakfast in town, serving egg dishes, omelets, breakfast burritos, pancakes, and French toast, all for reasonable prices. Lunch and dinner share the menu and include burgers, sandwiches, a soup and salad bar, and a limited selection of Mexican food. It's good food with outrageous portions and great prices.

Fine Dining

★ **The Farmhouse Bistro & Bar** (2525 Yukon Place, 605/559-0196, www. thefarmhousespearfish.com, 11am-8pm Tues.-Thurs., 11am-9pm Fri.-Sat., 9am-2pm Sun., lunch $12-20, dinner $18-35) is a relative newcomer to Spearfish dining. Opened in 2019, the Farmhouse brings the taste and presentation of food to a fine art. With a lot of wood and large windows, the decor is softened with soothing greys and blues. The restaurant overlooks Spearfish Creek. The lunch menu includes creative burgers, wraps, and a variety of mac-and-cheese choices (including shrimp and scallops with mac and cheese). Dinner entrées include grilled or fried chicken, pork flat iron, steak, shrimp, scallops, walleye, ahi tuna, and fish-and-chips. All meals look sumptuous.

The **Red Water Kitchen** (741 N. Main, 605/717-2404, www.redwaterkitchen.co, 11am-9pm Mon.-Fri., 8am-9pm Sat.-Sun., brunch $9-17, lunch and dinner $12-30) takes a farm-to-fork approach. The food is made from scratch, and no processed foods are used. A full bar is available for drinks. And if good craft beer is on your wish list, right next door and sharing the same address and ownership is the **Spearfish Brewing Company,** which features 16 taps of classic American lagers and craft ales.

Italian

Nonna's Kitchen (544 N. Main St.,

1: Spearfish Brewing Company 2: Bridal Veil Falls
3: visitor at the Termesphere Gallery

605/607-1345, www.nonnaskitchensd.com, 11am-10pm Wed.-Sun., $14-26), located in a beautiful sandstone building downtown, serves authentic Italian food including Bolognese, scampi, fettuccine, spaghetti and meatballs, and lasagna. Enjoy a nice glass of wine or a locally crafted beer while dining. There is a child's menu as well. On Sunday, the menu is all about brunch. Enjoy stuffed French toast, a frittata, or eggs with a polenta cake. Mimosas are served here!

Dough Trader Pizza Co. (543 W. Jackson Blvd., 605/642-2175, www.doughtraderpizza.com, 11am-9pm Wed.-Mon., $15-19, cash only) specializes in handcrafted designer stone-oven pizzas and beer. It's not easy to find but worth the hunt. The address is West Jackson Boulevard, but to get there, you need to head up the hill on North Arena Street. Inside the unassuming building is a charming and romantic interior, with low lighting, textured walls, and a long faux marble bar. It's no credit cards, cash only; but there's an ATM inside.

Mexican

★ **Antunez Cuisine** (117 E. Illinois, 605/722-8226, www.antunezcuisine.com, 11am-8pm Tues.-Thurs., 11am-9pm Fri.-Sat., all-day fare $14-16, dinner $26-40) serves Mexican, Spanish, and South American cuisine. Look for flavorful carnitas, enchiladas, tostadas, and steak. Vegetarian and gluten-free items are included on the menu. All of the favorites of Latin cuisine are on the menu, plus items like a roasted cauliflower or green chili quesadilla with scallops. It's a menu that encourages many repeat visits. It's small but cozy, with an old-world charm.

Family-run **Guadalajara Mexican Restaurant** (83 Old U.S. 14, 605/642-4765, www.guadalajaraspearfish.com, 11am-10pm daily, $10-15) is the most colorful and cheerful restaurant in town. The high wooden booths are carved with brightly colored sun motifs and festive flags hang from the ceiling. All the food is made from scratch, with favorites like tostadas, fajitas, burritos, enchiladas,

featuring chicken, pork, seafood, and beef. Generous portions and reasonable prices are the order of the day here.

Barbacoa's Burritos & Wraps (305 W. Jackson Blvd., 605/722-1774, 10am-10pm Mon.-Fri., 8am-10pm Sat.-Sun., $8-12) serves delicious monster burritos, as well as wraps and salads. Breakfast burritos are available on the weekends. Order at the counter and dine inside—or get takeout and picnic at the Spearfish City Park, just down the road (recommended!). They even have a drive-through window.

Japanese

Fuji San Japanese Restaurant (126 W. Hudson, 605/642-2268, 3:30pm-8pm Tues., 11am-8pm Wed.-Sat., noon-7pm Sun., $11-18) has a beautiful and calming atmosphere, with warm colors, wood tables, and beautiful prints on the wall. It feels cozy and elegant at the same time. The lovely sushi bar has a full menu of rolls. Other meal options include poke bowls, sashimi, chicken teriyaki, sesame chicken, and shrimp and vegetable tempura.

Ice Cream

There's nothing better than ice cream on a hot summer day. ★ **Leones' Creamery** (722½ Main St., 605/644-6461, http://leonescreamery.com, noon-10pm Wed.-Mon. summer, noon-9pm Fri.-Sun. winter, $2-6) fits the bill. It serves an ever-changing selection of eight homemade, small-batch flavors, some traditional and some truly unique. The treat is enhanced with the lightest, sweetest in-house handmade daily waffle cones. Fall in love with a flavor and you can buy it by the pint or quart!

ACCOMMODATIONS

Lodging options in Spearfish are dominated by chain hotels. Most of the chains use pricing based on availability of rooms. As a result, the earlier reservations are booked, the better. Many smaller cabins and bed-and-breakfasts post their rates for the season and do not fluctuate. Pet policies are noted, but be forewarned—one bad experience and the acceptance of pets may be curtailed. Rates noted do not include holiday weekends or the Sturgis Motorcycle Rally (the rally begins the first Friday in August and lasts 10 days).

Under $150

The ★ **Spearfish Bed & Breakfast** (4220 Airport Rd., 605/642-2485, www. spearfishbedandbreakfast.com, summer $100-125, winter $85-100), was once the Swenson family ranch. It was renovated into a four-room bed-and-breakfast and is now run by terrific hosts, one of whom grew up in the house. Acres of land surround the ranch, with great views of the ridge of peaks that ring Spearfish. One of the rooms is ADA approved. No pets are allowed, and there is no smoking in the rooms, though it is allowed outside. Queen beds, a private bath, and minifridges are featured in every room. A six-person sheltered hot tub is on the grounds, and a fire pit is available for guests to share their stories on-site as well. The generous breakfast served here varies daily, and the hosts are known to go out of their way for their guests.

Bell's Motor Lodge Motel (230 N. Main St., 605/642-3812 or 800/880-2095, www. bellsmotorlodgemotel.com, May-Sept., $69-119, no pets) harkens back to another era and provides basic accommodations in a family-run motel. Thirty rooms are available; some have microwaves and small refrigerators. There are two kitchenettes. Coffeemakers, hair dryers, and irons can be checked out at the office if desired. The outdoor pool is very small, but the property is close to town, safe, and offers free high-speed Internet access and cable TV. It is located within walking distance of downtown restaurants and shops.

$150-250

The **Secret Garden Bed & Breakfast** (938 N. Ames St., 605/642-4859, www. secretgardenbandbspa.com, guest rooms $145-185, carriage house $209) is a large, historic Victorian-style home built in 1892 that has three guest rooms and a carriage house (with a full kitchen) available. The year-round B&B is owned and managed by a local family (three sisters and their mom!). All of the rooms are beautiful and have a minifridge, cable television, and a private bath. Water glasses and wineglasses and a microwave are available in the beautiful common area. Behind the house, guests can relax in the garden/patio area or enjoy a soak in the outdoor hot tub. Guests are free to borrow a bicycle for an easy (and healthy) way to explore the town. A gourmet breakfast (farm-to-table as available) is served in the dining room or in the outside garden patio.

Days Inn of Spearfish (240 Ryan Rd., 605/642-7101 or 800/225-3297, www. wyndhamhotels.com, June-Aug. $134-219, Sept.-May $69-134, $10 per pet per night) is open year-round, has easy access to the interstate, and is close to the Spearfish recreation center. It's just a few blocks to the center of town, where all the restaurants reside. Room amenities include free Wi-Fi, microwaves, small fridges, coffeemakers, and hair dryers. Breakfast is included with the room charge. There is an attractive breakfast room, a guest laundry, and a fitness center. The rooms are pretty standard mid-level hotel fare but spacious and clean. The staff have been consistently cited for their friendly and helpful service to guests.

The 50-room **Best Western Black Hills Lodge** (540 E. Jackson Blvd., 605/642-7795, www.bestwestern.com/blackhillslodge, summer $165-280, shoulder season $119-140, winter $84-104) is an outdoor-themed hotel off I-90 at exit 12. Amenities include an outdoor heated pool, free continental breakfast, a microwave and refrigerator in every room, coffeemakers, and hair dryers. The rooms are extra-large and have either a small dining table or desk. There is free Wi-Fi, and the hotel is smoke-free. Children under the age of 17 are free with an adult reservation. Up to two dogs are allowed for a cleaning fee of $20 per day to a maximum of $100 per week. (Other animals are allowed at the hotel's discretion.)

Holiday Inn Spearfish (305 N. 27th St., 605/642-4683 or 800/465-4329, www.ihg.com, summer $160-240, shoulder season $161-185, winter $135-150) offers a large heated pool, a whirlpool, and a fitness center. There is a small video game room to entertain the kids. Pets are allowed with a onetime $25 cleaning fee for your entire stay. The clean and comfortable rooms are nice, fairly standard accommodations with free wireless Internet. The hotel provides a shuttle ($5) to Deadwood. A full-service family restaurant and bar, **Lucky's 13 Pub** (Sun.-Thurs. 7am-9pm, Fri.-Sat. 7am-10pm), is a local hangout on-site. It's all wood and rich green in decor and a comfortable spot to dine.

Campgrounds

★ **Spearfish City Campground** (404 S. Canyon St., 605/642-1340, www.cityofspearfish.com, May-Sept. tent sites $25, RV hookups $45, RV no hookups $30, Oct.-Apr. $20) is a beautiful site not far from the town center and across the street from the city park and the D.C. Booth Historic National Fish Hatchery. Spearfish Creek runs through the grounds, and since the campground is at the end of a dead-end street, there is no traffic in the area except for fellow campers. Reservations are recommended for the sites with hookups. The primitive sites are on a first-come, first-served basis. Amenities include Wi-Fi, picnic tables, restrooms, showers, grills, and lots of trees. Pets are allowed but must be leashed. Off-season camping (Oct.-Apr.) is allowed for a fee paid on arrival (although the office is not open in the off-season, self-registration envelopes are available on-site). Amenities off-season are minimal; electricity and sewer are available but there is no access to bathrooms or showers. This is a super spot for folks who love to fish for trout.

Another nice spot is **Chris' Camp** (701 Christensen Dr., 605/642-2239 or 800/350-2239, www.chriscampground.com, May 1-Oct. 15, tent sites $27-33, primitive sites vans/trailers $29, water and electric hookups $43, full hookups $48-53, camping cabins, electricity, no bedding $75), which has been family owned and operated for over 40 years and two generations. Amenities include three heated pools, a recreation room, guest laundry, a playground, a campground store, free wireless Internet, and a petting zoo. Pets are welcome at the campground. There's lots of shade for those hot summer days, and the grounds and facilities are nicely maintained.

INFORMATION AND SERVICES

The **Spearfish Visitor Information Center** (603 N. Main St., 605/717-9294 or 800/344-6181, www.visitspearfish.com, 8am-5pm Mon.-Fri., 10am-2pm Sat.-Sun. Memorial Day-Labor Day, 8am-5pm Mon.-Fri. off-season) has information available on Spearfish and the Black Hills for visitors to the region. The **Spearfish Chamber of Commerce** (106 W. Kansas St., 605/642-2626 or 800/626-8013, www.spearfishchamber.org, 8am-5pm Mon.-Fri.) is downtown and oriented to businesses and folks looking to relocate. For maps and information on hiking, biking, and camping in the Black Hills National Forest, contact the **Northern Hills Ranger District Headquarters** (2014 N. Main St., 605/642-4622, 8am-4:30pm Mon.-Fri.). There are no emergency animal care centers in Spearfish, though **Belle Fourche Veterinary Clinic** (406 Summit St., Belle Fourche, 605/892-2618) does provide 24/7 emergency services and is just 20 minutes away on U.S. 85 heading north.

Groceries can be found at **Leuders Food Centers** (620 7th St.) or at **Safeway Stores** (1606 N. Ave.). The **post office** is located at 120 Yankee Street. Transportation services are provided by **Canyon Cab** (605/717-9997). For walk-in medical services look for **Black Hills Urgent Care** (120 E. Michigan, 605/722-7777, 8am-6pm Mon.-Sat.) or **Monument Health Spearfish Urgent Care** (1420 N. 10th St., 605/717-8595, 8am-7pm Mon.-Thurs., 8am-5pm Fri., 9am-3pm Sun.). For emergency health care services, **Monument Health Spearfish Hospital** (1440 N. Main St.,

605/644-4000) is located right next to their urgent care facility.

★ SPEARFISH CANYON SCENIC BYWAY

Spearfish Canyon Scenic Byway is a state and national forest scenic byway that winds for about 20 miles (32 km) along Spearfish Creek between the communities of Spearfish and Lead. The byway is U.S. 14A, which is also a commercial highway, so be sure to pull well off the road when stopping to view the scenery. All the views are straight up the canyon walls to heights of over 1,000 feet (305 m), but don't forget to keep an eye on the road, as many bicyclists and hikers may be riding or walking along the shoulders.

Over two billion years ago, the area that is now the Black Hills was covered by an inland sea. Over time, as the sea receded and returned and receded again, layers of sediment were deposited on the seabed. As these strata hardened, different sedimentary layers were created. Around 65 million years ago, a dome-shaped uplift in the earth's crust formed the Black Hills. In the Northern Hills, crevasses within the limestone layer, created by the uplift, filled with magma. These magma flows, called intrusions, cooled, forming igneous rocks. Limestone and other sedimentary layers erode faster than the harder igneous rock, so while the sea receded, the overlying sedimentary layers were eroded, exposing the igneous intrusions. Crow Peak, Spearfish Mountain, and Terry Peak in the Spearfish area are all igneous intrusions, as is Bear Butte, the easternmost igneous peak in the region.

About five million years ago, the erosion of the limestone layer near Spearfish was accelerated by the power of water. Many of the streams that flow out of the hills begin as springs within the limestone plateau on the western side of the hills. Spearfish Creek is one of those streams. Today, the streambed of

Spearfish Canyon is more than 1,000 feet (305 m) below the highest canyon walls.

The river runs south-north and passes through four different plant communities on its way. The Northern Coniferous Forest, featuring white spruce trees, merges into the dominant biome of the region, the Rocky Mountain Pine Forest, which includes the ponderosa pine and covers 85 percent of the Black Hills region. Next, the Eastern Deciduous Forest makes inroads into the hills with stands of quaking aspen and birch. As the creek spills into the Spearfish River Valley, the Northern Great Plains habitat of oak, cottonwood, and prairie grasses appears. Of the 1,585 plant species found in the state of South Dakota, 1,260 are found in the Black Hills, and most of these have a foothold in Spearfish Canyon.

When the communities of Spearfish and Lead were founded in 1876, the canyon between the two was impassable, even on horseback. It wasn't until 1893 that the Grand Island and Wyoming Central Railroad built a direct rail line through the canyon, which made the area accessible for day trips. Visitors to the canyon could ride the train to any point they wished, and the train would stop and pick them up on the return trip.

Driving from Spearfish: Take exit 10 or exit 14 off I-90 and follow the signs to the Spearfish Canyon Highway. At the intersection of U.S. 14 and U.S. 14A (the scenic byway), head south.

Natural Features

Spearfish Canyon is beautiful from start to end, but you'll want to keep an eye out for some special features. Starting from the Spearfish side of the canyon, **Bridal Veil Falls** is about 6 miles (9.7 km) in, just south of the **Botany Bay Picnic Area.** The falls are on the left side of the canyon. There is a pullout on the right-hand side, across from the falls, for safe parking. In the spring, water cascades over the canyon wall (look up!), but by late summer, the stream of water slows to a trickle. The rock over which Bridal Veil Falls cascades

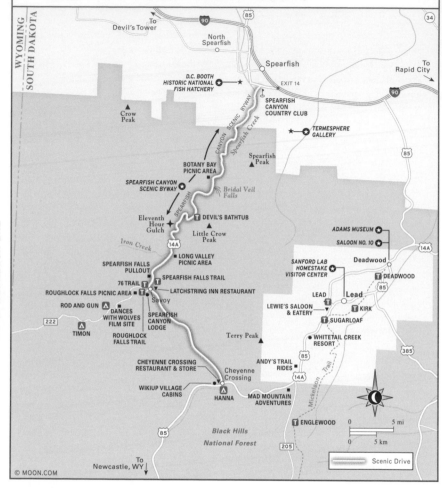

Spearfish Canyon Scenic Byway

is part of the igneous intrusions that occurred during the uplift of the hills. At one time, Spearfish Creek ran level with the falls, but as erosion ate away at the softer limestone formations, the streambed burrowed deeper and deeper, creating the canyon. Continue south along the byway, and at about 3.3 miles (5.3 km) past Bridal Veil Falls, **Eleventh Hour Gulch** meets Spearfish Canyon. The canyon rims of Eleventh Hour Gulch are so close together the canyon floor receives just one hour

of daylight per day and the sun doesn't enter the canyon until at least 11am. The narrow canyon and high rim walls of the gulch present a striking formation. The gulch isn't easy to spot. Look for large rock cubes in the middle of Spearfish Creek. The entrance to the gulch is across the roadway.

In addition to Bridal Veil Falls, there are two other waterfalls in the canyon. Both are near the small community of Savoy. The trail to **Spearfish Falls** is at the north corner of the **Latchstring Inn Restaurant.** **Roughlock Falls** is on the other side of U.S. 14A. There is a gravel road just before the **Spearfish Canyon Lodge.** Take the road near the lodge and drive until you reach a picnic area. Just a few short feet away are the cascading falls of Little Spearfish Creek. If you prefer, there is a lovely trail that starts just behind the lodge and winds next to the creek for about a mile before arriving at the falls. It's an easy, level, and shaded trail.

Hiking

There are several beautiful hiking, biking, and horseback riding trails along Spearfish Canyon Scenic Byway. Remember to carry water and wear sunscreen and a hat. Keep an eye on the sky for thundershower activity, as lightning storms are not uncommon during the summer season. If a storm does arise, head down the trail as fast as you can. Please respect private landowner's property wherever you hike, and make sure to leave no trace. Pack it in and pack it out!

Near Savoy, about 13 miles (20.9 km) south of Spearfish on the scenic byway, there are three great trails. There are two different waterfalls to visit in this area, and since both are short and easy hikes, it's worthwhile to do

them both. There is also a hike to the canyon rim that provides the best views to be found within the canyon proper.

DEVIL'S BATHTUB TRAIL
Distance: 0.75 mile (1.2 km)
Duration: 1-1.5 hours
Elevation Gain: None
Effort: Moderate
Trailhead: From Spearfish, take U.S. 14A south; go about 2 miles (3.2 km) south of Bridal Veil Falls and look for signage. The parking lot is on the left side of the road.

This is a great hike for interesting geology and water features. It is a popular hike but not an official one. The hike follows Cleopatra Creek, and there are several stream crossings. Be prepared to get wet. It is a moderate, relatively flat hike that ends at two pools of blue-green water carved into the rock. The trail is hard-packed dirt, well-worn, and easy to follow. At one time, it was possible to slide down the stream right into the pool, but a large boulder fell into the chute, blocking the slide. The pool is still a nice place to dangle your feet for a bit—but just a short bit, because the water is very cold. Note that due to overuse and trespass on private land, a new trailhead and parking lot was created; there

black-headed grosbeak in Spearfish Canyon

is signage for the parking lot, which is located on the left side of the road.

SPEARFISH CANYON FALLS

Distance: 1.5 miles (2.4 km) round-trip
Duration: 1 hour
Elevation Gain: 400 feet (122 m)
Effort: Easy to moderate
Trailhead: The trailhead is on the north side off the Latchstring Inn Restaurant parking lot in Savoy.

The hike to Spearfish Canyon Falls is a backward one. You will travel down first, and then climb back up the slope when you return. As you walk down the gently sloping trail, keep a watchful eye out for *Oreo helix,* a miniature snail. There are thousands of these near Spearfish Canyon Falls. As the trail descends, the vegetation changes first to the ponderosa pine forest that blankets most of the hills, then to the aspen and birch of the Eastern Deciduous Forest. Since birds are particular about the environmental niches they occupy, a wide variety make their home in the multifaceted habitat here, including mountain bluebirds, grosbeaks, warblers, goldfinches, and even golden eagles.

At the bottom of the trail, continue over the bridge that crosses Spearfish Creek to the point at which Little Spearfish Creek cascades into Spearfish Creek. From a nearby clearing, you'll see the falls from the bottom. The trail begins to climb here, 400 feet (122 m) up to a beautiful bridge that crosses a 120-foot (37-m) gorge over Spearfish Creek. On the other side of the gorge, the trail winds another 400 feet (122 m) to an arched bridge crossing Little Spearfish Creek. You have arrived at the top of Spearfish Canyon Falls. At this point, you can continue along the trail to finish a strenuous loop that winds back to the Latchstring Inn Restaurant via a steep incline or return the way you came. Just about all the plant communities in the hills meet here. At the rim, 80 feet (24 m) above the creekbed, look for the towering spruce trees of the Northern Coniferous Forest, some of which are over 120 feet (37 m) tall.

ROUGHLOCK FALLS TRAIL

Distance: 2 miles (3.2 km) round-trip
Duration: 1.5 hours
Elevation Gain: None
Effort: Easy
Trailhead: Behind the Spearfish Canyon Lodge at Savoy at the far end of the parking lot.

This is a wheelchair-accessible trail that follows Little Spearfish Creek. The packed-dirt trail starts off in a forested area paralleling the creek. In this region, ponderosa pine, spruce, aspen, and oak trees line the path. There are several wooden benches tucked along the trail for rest stops. Soon the path clears, with views overlooking a marshlike area with willows and high grasses. Look for blue heron in this area. At the end of the trail, wooden bridges allow close access to the falls. Little Spearfish Creek cascades over large boulders on its way to join Spearfish Creek a couple of miles down the canyon. At the end of the trail, a wooden bridge crosses over the stream and inclines slowly to a parking lot and picnic area. Walk down the road back to the lodge or turn around and return along the trail.

76 TRAIL

Distance: 1.5 miles (2.4 km) round-trip
Duration: 1.5-2 hours
Elevation Gain: 1,000 feet (305 m)
Effort: Strenuous
Trailhead: Across the gravel road from Spearfish Canyon Lodge at Savoy

The 76 Trail is the only formal hiking trail to climb to the top of the rim of Spearfish Canyon. The trail is short, but it rises more than 1,000 feet (305 m) from start to finish. Benches are tucked into the side of the path for catching your breath. The panoramic view from the ridge at the top of the canyon makes the effort well worthwhile. Be careful and attentive while hiking as many spots are slippery with pine needles and loose soil.

Biking

The Spearfish Canyon Scenic Byway sports 4-foot-wide (1.2-m) shoulders specifically to allow bikers safe use. From Spearfish to

Lead, the byway is about 20 miles (32 km) and a beautiful biking road trip. The canyon road can get very busy in the summer however, so spring and fall make the best times to ride the shoulders of the byway. Bridal Veil Falls is visible from the roadway, and near Savoy (about 13 mi/20.9 km into the canyon) and at the Spearfish Canyon Lodge, there is 1-mile-long (1.6-km) road to Roughlock Falls passable by both road and mountain bikes, which makes a nice side trip. Both e-bikes and fat-tire bikes can be rented at **Spearfish Canyon Lodge** (10619 Roughlock Falls Rd., Savoy, 605/584-3435 or 877/975-6343, www. spfcanyon.com, full-day fat-tire bike $35, full-day e-bike $70).

Mountain biking is also a good way to go in Spearfish Canyon.

LITTLE SPEARFISH TRAIL (TRAIL #80)
Distance: 7.8 mile (12.6 km) loop
Duration: 1.5-2 hours
Elevation Gain: 850 feet (259 m)
Effort: Easy to moderate
Trailhead: From Savoy, head west on Forest Service Road 222 (the gravel road to the right of Spearfish Canyon Lodge when facing the lodge) for 4.7 miles (7.6 km).

This is a trail good for just about every experience level. It meanders through ponderosa pines, aspens, and birch trees. It's a good ride for enjoying wildflowers and bird-watching.

Rock Climbing
Spearfish Canyon has started to develop a reputation for climbing and has been featured in many rock-climbing magazines. With more than 300 routes up the limestone walls, there is suitable climbing for all skill levels. Climbing in the canyon is accessible year-round and courses and guides, if needed, can be arranged with **Buck Wild Climbing Guides** (307/281-1630, www.buckwildclimbing.com, from $125 pp). Will Buckman and his group have partial day learning sessions for first-timers and half-day tours for subsequent climbs, and they are happy to design full-day custom tours as well. Permitted to guide in Spearfish Canyon by Black Hills National Forest, Will grew up climbing in the Black Hills and has over 16 years of experience climbing and teaching at sites around the country.

Fly-Fishing
Spearfish Creek provides some of the best trout fishing in the Black Hills. A fast-moving creek with fly-fishing access year-round, the river is stocked with rainbow, brown, and brook trout. A fishing license is required and can be obtained from at the Spearfish Canyon Lodge in Savoy. A one-day license is $8 for state residents and $16 for nonresidents, which includes an agent's fee. Visitors wishing to try their luck for more than one day can get a three-day fishing license for $37. Sales outlets are allowed to charge up to a $4 service charge on the license.

ATV/UTV Riding and Snowmobiling
There are 350 miles (565 km) of groomed trails in the Black Hills used for snowmobiling in winter and ATV/UTV riding in summer. Within Spearfish Canyon, the most accessible is Trail #4, just west of **Spearfish Canyon Lodge** (10619 Roughlock Falls Rd., Savoy, 605/584-3435 or 877/975-6343, www.spfcanyon.com), where snowmobiles and ATVs can be rented. It is a beautiful site, tucked inside Spearfish Canyon in the town of Savoy, located within walking distance to Roughlock Falls and Spearfish Falls. **Snowmobiles** can be rented for a full day (8am-4pm daily mid-Dec.-Mar. weather permitting, single passenger $205, double passenger $225) or half day (8am-4pm Mon.-Thurs. mid-Dec.-Mar. weather permitting, single passenger $170, double passenger $185). On weekends, rentals are available for full days only. For those who have their own machines, a registration fee must be paid if the owner is not licensed in another state. The fee is $40 for a five-day permit. These can also be purchased at the lodge. Snowmobiles that are licensed in another state can be operated in

South Dakota without the permit. All snow-mobilers must have proof of insurance on public trails.

ATV/UTV rentals (May-Oct.) are available for half-day ($290-350) or full-day use ($350-425) and are equipped with two, three, four, or six passenger seats. Licensing information for ATVs can be found by calling 605/343-1567 in the Rapid City area or 605/673-9200 in Custer. Other equipment rentals include **snowshoes** ($25 per day) and **fat-tire bikes** (from $35 per day). Fat bikes are available year-round.

Weather in the Black Hills can be unpredictable, especially in the Northern Hills in winter, where the wind comes whipping across Wyoming! Be sure to wear plenty of layers and keep at least a minimal amount of food and water on hand. Check for trail conditions and closures with the Black Hills National Forest (www.fs.usda.gov).

Picnic Areas

There are three picnic areas along the scenic byway. Traveling from Spearfish to Lead, the first, **Botany Bay Picnic Area,** is 5-6 miles (8-9.7 km) from the intersection of U.S. 14A and U.S. 14, inside the mouth of the canyon. This picnic area is named for the wide variety of unusual and rare plant species (including ancient ferns) that can be found there. The **Long Valley Picnic Area** is another 5.2 miles (8.4 km) past Botany Bay and has tables right next to the creek. **Roughlock Falls Picnic Area** is near the Spearfish Canyon Lodge in Savoy. Take a right just north of the lodge and follow the road 1 mile (1.6 km) back. From the parking lot there, a short walk will take you to picnic tables and the cascading Roughlock Falls.

Food and Accommodations

Spearfish Canyon is all about scenic beauty, but there are a couple of places to dine along the byway. Look for the town of Savoy. It isn't big, but you'll find food and lodging there, about 13 miles (20.9 km) into the canyon measured from the intersection of U.S. 14 and U.S. 14A in Spearfish, or about 5.5 miles (8.9

km) into the canyon from the intersection of U.S.14A and U.S. 85 in the south.

★ **Spearfish Canyon Lodge** (10619 Roughlock Falls Rd., Savoy, 605/584-3435 or 877/975-6343, www.spfcanyon.com, mid-May-mid-Oct. $179-209, mid-Oct.-mid-May $119-149, $25 per pet per night) has it all in terms of beauty and location for those seeking a quiet place near the best scenery, hiking, and biking in the region. The facility features large log construction and a light and airy lobby with a huge stone fireplace. The large log motif is carried into the full-service lounge. Amenities include microwaves, minifridges, coffeemakers, hair dryers. and outdoor hot tubs. Several trailheads are within walking distance of this site, including the Roughlock Falls Trail, Spearfish Falls Trail, and 76 Trail. Guests can take advantage of bike rentals, arrange for fly-fishing packages, obtain fishing equipment and licenses, and rent UTVs and snowmobiling equipment. The lodge also has conference facilities.

The ★ **Latchstring Inn Restaurant** (10619 Roughlock Falls Rd., Savoy, 605/584-3333, www.spfcanyon.com/latchstring-restaurant, 7am-9pm daily May-Oct., 7am-8pm daily Nov.-Apr., breakfast $8-15, lunch $9-17, dinner $17-40) is a beautiful log cabin with high ceilings, a fireplace, large windows, and simple wood tables. The restaurant is run by the same folks who operate the Spearfish Canyon Lodge across the street. In the summer, dining is available outside on the wooden deck overlooking the canyon, as well as in the dining room. The breakfast menu includes omelets, pancakes, eggs, and specialties including trout and country-fried steak. Lunch features a variety of salads, soups, sandwiches, and buffalo stew. Dinner entrées range from trout, walleye, a variety of burgers, and shrimp to buffalo rib eye, beef rib eye, country-fried steak, and pasta. The establishment has a beer and wine license.

Just barely on the edge of the scenic byway at the intersection of U.S. 14A and U.S. 85, look for **Cheyenne Crossing Stage Stop Café** (21415 U.S. 14A, Lead,

605/584-3510, www.cheyennecrossing.org, 7:30am-4pm Mon.-Tues. and 7:30am-8pm Wed.-Sun. summer, 7:30am-8pm Thurs.-Sun. winter, breakfast and lunch $9-16, dinner $13-25), which has the best breakfast around, served in the summer until 3pm. Choose from sourdough pancakes, buttermilk biscuits, buffalo sausage, and steak tips and eggs, among other items. Lunch and dinner are great, as well. The house specialty is Indian tacos, served at lunch and dinner, which start with a homemade base of Wooden Knife Indian Fry Bread (a family recipe from Interior, South Dakota) and add traditional taco toppings (ground beef, lettuce, red onions, tomato, olives, cheese, picante sauce, and sour cream). The rest of the lunch menu includes a wide variety of hot and cold sandwiches. The dinner menu includes salmon, cod, top sirloin and rib eye steaks, and shrimp. On the lighter side, choose from chicken dishes, fish, and beef sandwiches. It's a real country-style kind of restaurant—cozy and warm with delicious food. There's a nice little gift shop on-site and conveniently located above the café is the **Upstairs Lodge.** Three lovely pine-themed rooms can be rented in any configuration, when available (one bedroom $125, two bedrooms $150, three bedrooms $175). The space is rented to just one individual, family, or group of friends traveling together, so the space is not shared with folks not in your group.

Campgrounds

There are two campgrounds in **Black Hills National Forest** (www.fs.usda.gov/blackhills) that are accessible from within the canyon. Both campgrounds are primitive. Drinking water and restrooms are available. No reservations are required for these campgrounds. The maximum length of stay 14 nights. The **Rod and Gun Campground** (May-Dec. weather permitting, $18) is just 3 miles (4.8 km) from the junction of U.S. 14A and Forest Service Road 222 near the Spearfish Canyon Lodge at Savoy. There are seven sites available. It's a pretty location with shady sites sitting near Little Spearfish Creek. This is a high-elevation campground sitting at about 5,500 feet (1,676 m) above sea level. It is close to where the winter scenes in *Dances with Wolves* were filmed. The **Timon Campground** (May-Dec. weather permitting, $18) is another 1.5 miles (2.4 km) past the Rod and Gun Campground. It also has seven sites right beside Little Spearfish Creek

Latchstring Inn Restaurant

and is at an elevation of more than 5,600 feet (1,707 m).

The **Hanna Campground** (May-Sept., $18) is off U.S. 85 just south of the U.S. 14A junction at Cheyenne Crossing. Look for the sign and turn left. The campground is about 2.2 miles (3.5 km) in and has 13 sites, about half of which are next to East Spearfish Creek. It is also a primitive campground with drinking water and restrooms.

Lead

The town of Lead (pronounced "Leed") has an alpine feel to it, with houses carved into the hills and the streets built on precariously steep inclines. It's hard to imagine driving these streets in winter without visualizing cars sliding out of control down the perilous slopes and through intersections. There is little room for expansion here, but there is room for improvement, and improvements have been constant. The town is a quaint and historic host for visitors. The rooms are inexpensive, Spearfish Canyon is nearby, and in keeping with current trends, a brewpub has opened in town. It's a small town with an optimistic population of about 3,000 people.

While the town's past was steeped in mining, the future is in science—specifically the Sanford Underground Research Facility, which is engaged in the search for subatomic particles called neutrinos (associated with dark matter).

HISTORY

Like many Black Hills communities, Lead traces its founding back to the discovery of gold. In February 1876, Thomas Carey found placer gold in Gold Run Gulch. As was always the case with gold, as soon as word got out, other prospectors rushed to the gulch. By July 1876, the residents had laid out the town between the north and south forks of Gold Run Creek. The town was named after the large number of ore outcroppings (called "leads") in the area. The gold rush lasted about two years in the Deadwood/Lead area. However, the uncovering of gold at the Homestake Mine would have an impact on the community for several decades.

The Homestake Mine was originally claimed by brothers Moses and Fred Manuel and a partner, Hank Harney, in April 1876. In June 1877, George Hearst purchased the claim from the brothers for $70,000. The mine went on to produce approximately 40 million ounces (1.13 kt) of gold; before it closed, it was the oldest, largest, and deepest mine in the Western Hemisphere, reaching more than 8,000 feet (2,438 m) below the town of Lead.

By the time Hearst invested in Homestake, mining was second nature to him. A graduate of the Franklin County School of Mining in Missouri, he already had interests in mines in Missouri, California, Montana, Nevada, and Utah. Hearst headed the company Hearst, Haggin, Tevis and Co., which became the largest private mining company in the United States. Hearst and his wife, Phoebe, were the parents of William Randolph Hearst, who elected not to operate his father's mining interests and instead took over the *San Francisco Examiner,* which was to become the foundation of the Hearst publishing empire.

George Hearst died in 1891 and left Phoebe Hearst as his sole heir. Phoebe took over his business investments, including the controlling interest in the Homestake Mine. Though she didn't spend all that much time in Lead after George's death, she became one of its biggest benefactors. In 1894, Hearst gave the city a library with over 8,000 books and public documents, which she maintained at her personal expense until she died (and which she endowed through 1925 in her will). In 1900, she endowed and then continued to support the Hearst Kindergarten. In 1914, the Homestake Opera House and Recreation

Lead

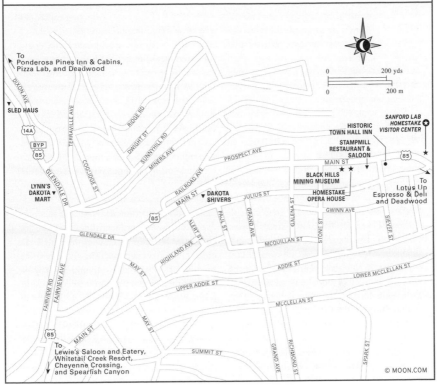

Building was a gift to the town from the Homestake Mine. It housed an opera house, bowling alley, swimming pool, library, social rooms, and billiards and pool tables; with the exception of the opera house, all were free to the public. The Homestake Mine also provided free medical care to employees and their families at the Homestake Hospital. Phoebe Hearst died in 1919.

By 1910, Lead had become one of the largest cities in South Dakota, weighing in with a population of over 8,000 people, most of whom were affiliated with the Homestake Mine. Even through the Great Depression of the 1930s, miners did well at Homestake. Eventually, however, the rich deposits of ore were mined out and what was left was not economical to extract, and so, in 2002, the mine closed.

The same year that the mine officially closed, Dr. Ray Davis was awarded the Nobel Prize for a neutrino detector that he had installed 4,850 feet (1,478 m) below the surface at Homestake Mine. An experiment that spanned decades of collaboration between the mine and Davis made the mine famous in the world of science. When the mine was closed, a proposal to convert it into an underground laboratory quickly spread. By July 2007, Homestake Mine had been chosen for the new location of an underground laboratory where experiments would take place deep below the earth's surface—a place where cosmic rays can't affect their outcome. In 2010, the lab—at that time known as the

Deep Underground Science and Engineering Laboratory (DUSEL)—was abandoned by the National Science Foundation, but funding was picked up by the U.S. Department of Energy. Today, the Homestake Mine, the deepest, oldest mine in the West, has been transformed into the Sanford Underground Research Facility, which plans to conduct experiments in the areas of particle physics, astrophysics, biology, geosciences, and engineering.

SIGHTS
★ Sanford Lab Homestake Visitor Center

The **Sanford Lab Homestake Visitor Center** (160 W. Main St., 605/584-3110, www.sanfordlabhomestake.com, 9am-5pm daily, free) sits on the edge of a huge gouge in the surface of the hillside. Known as the "Open Cut," the gouge was created by miners hauling tons of rock from the Homestake Mine. During 1875-2001, the mine reached depths of more than 8,000 feet (2,438 m) below the town and pulled 39.65 million ounces (1.12 kt) of gold out of the hills. By comparison, the entire Black Hills region in that period produced a total of 46.5 million ounces (1.3 kt) of gold.

Today, the visitor center features both the mine's fascinating history and its current reincarnation as an underground lab focused on unlocking the secrets of dark matter. The center is full of photographs and touch screen video presentations about the building of the lab and science. The most fascinating display is a three-dimensional map of the mine, from the top to the bottom 8,000 feet (2,438 m) below. Mining artifacts share the history of the site.

The most popular offering at the center is the one-hour **guided tour** (10am, 11:30am, 1pm, 2:30pm, and 3:30pm daily May-Sept., adult $15, senior and student $10, child under 5 free) of Lead and of the surface operations of the Sanford Underground Research Facility. The tour starts at the Open Cut behind the visitor center, where a presentation is given about the open pit mine. After the presentation, the group boards a trolley. As the trolley travels through town, the guide provides information about the historic buildings, the history of the town, and the geology of the region. A stop at the Yates Hoisting Room and the surface area of the mine/lab includes a discussion of mining processes, such as the hoisting, crushing, and milling of the ore. It's a fascinating transition from extraction of ore to scientific exploration. One tidbit of interest: From the viewing deck at the visitor center, onlookers can make out small round holes at every level of the Open Cut below. Those tiny round holes are exposed mine shafts, 8 feet (2.4 m) high by 8 feet (2.4 m) wide. This little bit of knowledge adds perspective to the actual size of this gouge in the side of the mountain.

The tour also covers the problem of subsidence in Lead. At one time, there was so much excavation under the town that parts of the community began to sink into the earth as old mine shafts collapsed. The entire eastern portion of the town moved west as parts of the community started to sink as much as 35 feet (11 m).

Black Hills Mining Museum

The **Black Hills Mining Museum** (323 W. Main St., 605/584-1605, www.blackhillsminingmuseum.com, 9am-5pm Mon.-Sat. May-Oct., museum and mine tour adult $12, senior and military $10, child ages 13-17 $6, child 12 and under free, museum-only admission $6) was established to preserve the mining heritage of the Black Hills. The upstairs area of the museum contains a collection of old photographs, maps, displays of equipment, and informational exhibits of mining techniques. The museum also has a mining document archive of records spanning 1876-1940. Gold panning instruction ($13 per gold pan) is provided upstairs. Elect to try your hand at gold panning here, and the discovery of some placer gold is guaranteed. A small theater presents a 20-minute mining video continuously.

Mine tours begin below the museum, running every hour beginning at 9am; the last tour starts by 4pm. The tour begins as visitors take 17 steps down into the lower levels of the building. The building disappears into a simulated underground mine, where the equipment used to dynamite and mine the rock is explained. The 45- to 60-minute guided tour is an education in the evolution of mining technology, from the earliest days of mining in the 1870s to the present. The underground mine was created by 140 miners working together to provide an accurate rendition of the environment of a mining operation. The information is fascinating. Did you know that the temperature at the lowest levels of the Homestake Mine was 138°F (58.9°C)? Knowledgeable guides add to the experience.

Homestake Opera House

The **Homestake Opera House** (313 W. Main St., 605/584 2067, www.homestake operahouse.com, 9am-5pm Mon.-Fri., guided tours May-mid-Sept. on the hour 10am-2pm, adult $10, child under 18 $5, wheelchair accessible) has come a long way since it was gutted by fire in 1984. Construction of the original opera house was orchestrated by Phoebe Hearst, the widow of mining magnate George Hearst. Completed in 1914 and given as a gift to the city, the complex included the opera house and an attached recreation center. The opera house was called the "Jewel of the Black Hills," and no expense was spared in building the beautiful hall. The 1,016-seat opera house had eight private boxes and a balcony in addition to the floor seating. The box seats were high-backed chairs upholstered in black leather. The floor seating featured mahogany wood upholstered in dark green velvet. Hand stenciling and hand-painted murals decorated the ceilings, ornate plaster columns adorned the walls, and glass chandeliers hung from the ceilings. The recreation facility included a bowling alley, swimming pool, library, and billiards room.

For 70 years, the opera house served as the community center. Everything from vaudeville shows and silent movies to musical concerts and boxing competitions were presented. When the fire struck in 1984, the town voted to save the structure, but it sat empty for 20 years until serious restoration began in 2004. Slowly but surely, the community has returned the opera house to its former splendor with thousands of volunteer hours. While restoration work continues, much has been completed, and today the opera house now hosts plays, melodramas, concerts, movies, weddings, and other events year-round.

RECREATION
Horseback Riding

One of the best horseback riding locations in the hills is **Andy's Trail Rides** (11264 U.S. 14A, 605/645-2211, www.andystrailrides.com, custom trail rides $47 pp per hour, reservation only), where Andy and his staff go out of their way to make your ride a personal experience and a memory to savor. Rides can be customized. Rides may take in the vistas of Terry Peak or follow the historic railroad beds. Arrange for a breakfast ride to the Cheyenne Crossing Café or a sunset honeymoon ride by the creek. If you're comfortable on the horse, feel free to trot or gallop. The pace is not fixed, depending on the skill level of the riders. In one case, a couple of families traveling together designed their own trip. They all rode to Spearfish Creek carrying fishing poles. The men were dropped off and the women continued to ride. On the way back, they stopped to gather up the men, and everyone had a great day. Also available are 1-, 4-, 8-, and 14-hour rides. Weather permitting, rides are available year-round. In the winter there are also sleigh rides.

TOP EXPERIENCE

Mountain Biking

The **George S. Mickelson Trail** is a 109 mile (175 km) biking, hiking, and horseback riding trail that was once a "rails-to-trails" project. The route travels between Deadwood in the north and Edgemont in the south. There is a daily usage fee of $4, or an annual fee of $15, payable by drop-off envelope at any trailhead. There are three trailheads near Lead.

THE NORTHERN HILLS
LEAD

The **Kirk Trailhead** is 0.5 mile (0.8 km) south of Lead on U.S. 85; the **Lead Trailhead** is a 0.8-mile (1.3-km) spur that starts in town off Hearst Avenue (across from the high school); and the **Sugarloaf Trailhead** is 1 mile (1.6 km) southwest of Lead on U.S. 85. All the trailheads are well marked, and the paths are packed gravel, great for mountain bikes. Seasonal bike rentals are available at the trailhead in Deadwood.

UTV Riding and Snowmobiling

More than 350 miles (565 km) of groomed trails are dedicated to snowmobiles and UTVs and ATVS in the summer in the Northern Hills. Snow season generally runs mid-December-March. Two trails (Trail #7 and Trail #5) are easily accessible from Lead. To get to Trail #5 from Lead, drive 4 miles (6.4 km) southwest on U.S. 85 to Rochford Road. Take a left onto Rochford Road and continue for half a mile. The parking lot for Trail #5 will be on your right. Continue south on Rochford Road for another 5.5 miles (8.9 km) and you'll be at the Dumont parking lot at the trailhead for Trail #7.

Snowmobiles can be rented at **Mad Mountain Adventures** (Recreational Springs Resort, 11201 U.S. 14A, 605/578-1878, www.madmountainadventure.com, 8:30am-4:30am daily). Single-person (full day $180, half day $140) and double-passenger (full day $200, half day $175) snowmobile rentals are available. For summer fun (mid-May.-Oct.), UTV vehicles can also be rented here, including two-seaters (full day $325, half day $275) and four-seaters (full day $375, half day $325). All rentals are Polaris UTVs, and the rental includes a helmet, goggles, and a map.

Skiing and Snowboarding

Terry Peak Ski Resort (21120 Stewart Slope Rd., 605/584-2165, www.terrypeak.com, Dec.-Mar., lifts 9am-4pm daily, Ski School 8am-4pm daily, guest services 8am-4:30pm daily, lift tickets adult $66 full day, $50 half day, $34 beginner slope, child ages 6-12 $50 full day, $38 half day, $25 beginner slope, senior 70 and over $10 flat rate, child under age 5 free, prices may vary depending on snow conditions and number of trails open) is the place to go for downhill skiing and snowboarding in the Black Hills. Trails are available for all ability levels, with 6 beginner, 11 intermediate, and 13 advanced black diamond trails. Elevations range 5,900-7,000 feet (1,798-2,134 m). Check the website when planning your visit to confirm snow and trails conditions. Looking to learn? Call the resort and ask for the Ski School to find out about the wide variety of ski and snowboard lesson packages available on-site. Ski rentals are also available (ages 13 and over $35 full day, $25 half day, ages 6-12 $28 full day, $20 half day) as are snowboards ($33) and helmets ($10). Tired and hungry skiers can enjoy food and drink at two day-use lodges on-site.

BREWPUB

Even a town as small as Lead can host a delightful brewpub. **Dakota Shivers Brewing** (717 W. Main St., 605/580-7403, www.dakotashiversbrewing.com, 2pm-8pm Tues.-Sat) is a rustic, comfortable place to enjoy one eight handcrafted beers on tap. It's a friendly place with the support of locals. Dog-friendly too!

FOOD

The best burgers in town are at ★ **Lewie's Saloon & Eatery** (711 S. Main St., 605/584-1324, www.lewiesburgers.com, 11am-11pm Wed.-Sun., $12), just south of Lead on U.S. 85. The rustic bar is decorated with antiques, old motorcycles, old signs, and all kinds of interesting artifacts hanging from the walls and rafters. It's famous for the 38 televisions (at last count) that cater to local sports enthusiasts in addition to the high quality of its burgers. In summer, enjoy dining on the great outdoor deck. Trivia competitions are held on Friday nights during the winter (Oct.-Apr.).

If you're looking for breakfast or a light

1: Sanford Lab Homestake Visitor Center
2: Homestake Mine 3: Dakota Shivers Brewing
4: Stampmill Restaurant & Saloon

lunch, search out the **Lotus Up Espresso & Deli** (95 E. Main St., 605/722-4670, www.lotusuplead.com, 6am-2pm Mon.-Sat., 8am-2pm Sun., $9). Enjoy a wide variety of baked goods, panini, and wraps with a specialty coffee or smoothie. The second story deck is perfect for sipping on a mocha mudslide and watching the sunrise.

Housed in a beautifully restored historic building, the **Stampmill Restaurant & Saloon** (305 W. Main St., 605/717-0554, 11am-8pm Thurs.-Mon. summer, 11am-8pm Fri.-Mon. winter, $11-19) is a charming place for lunch or dinner. The menu of sandwiches, burgers, and dinner entrées is limited, but the service is great, the food is good, and the environment is delightful, with brick walls, high-backed wooden booths, high ceilings, and a fireplace. There are great local and regional brews on tap and a lot of locals at the bar happy to visit with travelers.

The Sled Haus (209 Glendale Dr., 605/639-5322, 5pm-9pm Tues., noon-8pm Wed.-Sat., $15-20, cash only) serves sandwiches, burgers, and a varying menu of German food platters to a crowd that loves to have fun. Tuesday night is pizza night. The building is unassuming, but the boisterous, happy crowd and the great food sell the place. Craft beer from local breweries add to experience. The motto of the restaurant is "Gourmet Grub, beer and wine," and they live up to that billing.

Families will be pleased to find **Pizza Lab** (124 U.S. 14A, Central City, 605/578-9933, www.thepizzalab.com, 11am-7:30pm Tues.-Sat., $15-22), which has all the standard pizzas and some interesting specialty combinations. There are vegetarian pizzas, a Thai chicken pizza with peanut sauce, a bacon cheeseburger pizza, and a barbecue chicken club pizza. There is also a select menu of salads, chicken wings, and ribs. The restaurant serves wine and beer, and seating is available for up to 150 people. Pizza Lab will deliver for a fee, or you can call ahead and carry out. Dessert comes in the form of 17 different flavors of hand-scooped hard ice cream. If that isn't enough,

there are a couple of pool tables on hand ($1 per game) and a wall full of arcade games for the everyone to enjoy.

ACCOMMODATIONS

The **Whitetail Creek Resort** (11295 U.S. 14A, 605/584-9085, www.whitetailcreekresort.com, Jan.-Mar. and May-Oct.) is 2 miles (3.2 km) west of Lead on U.S. 14A/U.S. 85 and has a variety of accommodations. Motel rooms (summer $119-179, winter $59-99) and cabins (summer $119-159) are furnished with a microwave, coffeemaker, air-conditioning, and either a full kitchen or a minifridge. Free Wi-Fi is available to all guests. In addition, guests can enjoy a sauna and hammocks or swing chairs set alongside Whitetail Creek, or meet with other guests at the large beam-framed pavilion and enjoy a glass of wine or a beer from the taproom (aka, the **Buck Snort Beer Patio**). Picnics tables and grills are dispersed throughout the property and are also features of the cabins. Camping cabins ($49-79) come with built-in beds (twin, full, or queen) and mattresses. For an extra $10, guests can add sheets, blankets, and towels. Some of the camper cabins have electricity, but none have plumbing. A shower house is on-site. RV sites ($55) are all 30 amp with full hookups. There are also yurts ($89-99). Cabins, RV sites, and yurts are only open Memorial Day-September. Pets are not allowed in the motel but are allowed elsewhere for a fee of $10 per pet per night (dogs only). Located near groomed trail #5W and the Mickelson Trail, the resort is a haven for UTV and snowmobilers, hikers, bicyclists, and travelers with horses.

Ponderosa Pines Inn & Cabins (705 Glendale Dr., 605/584-3321, www.blackhillsponderosapines.com, June-Aug. excluding Sturgis $199-249, Sept.-May $99-139) is a beautifully maintained and attractive property with nine log cabins and five lodge rooms nestled in the pines. The cabins have beautiful decks and cozy rooms and range in size from one to three bedrooms. Amenities include microwave ovens, refrigerators, and an outside pavilion and fire pit. Dishes are provided in the cabins. A limited number of rooms are pet-friendly for a fee of $10-15 per pet per night.

Wickiup Village (21381 U.S. 85, 605/584-3382, www.spearfishcreekcabins.com, mid-May-early Oct., $120-160, $15-35 per pet per night depending on weight) is a quiet spot providing beautiful log cabin lodgings. The property has cabins that will sleep up to six; prices quoted are for cabins that sleep 2-4. Situated right on Spearfish Creek, activities nearby include fishing, tubing (tubes are available for rent by guests), off-roading, and hiking canyon trails. The cabins have light knotty pine interiors and lots of windows. Many of the cabins have kitchenettes with a full refrigerator and stovetop. Some have a minifridge, microwave, and stovetop. All have heat and coffeemakers. Located close to what's called "icebox canyon," they do not have air-conditioning, but fans are available. There is a playground for the kids, a community campfire in the evening, and a picnic pavilion.

A beautiful hotel, the **Historic Town Hall Inn** (215 W. Main St., 605/584-1112 or 866/285-4872, www.townhallinn.com, summer $105-150, shoulder season $85-125, winter $65-99) was constructed in 1912 and has 12 large rooms with private baths available. A light continental breakfast is offered in the morning. Amenities include microwave ovens, refrigerators, coffeemakers, and free Wi-Fi. The entire inn features beautiful woodwork, Victorian-style furniture, and lots of light. Guests can enjoy several Belgian beers on tap in the **Jailhouse Taps** room, along with a Biere de Garde (French aged/mature beer) and a beer from a parti-gyle method of brewing (several beers from the same mash). Located right in downtown Lead, the inn is within walking distance of shopping and restaurants.

INFORMATION AND SERVICES

Visit the **Lead Chamber of Commerce** (160 W. Main St., 605/584-1100, www.leadmethere.org, 8am-4pm Mon.-Fri.) and the **Sanford Lab Homestake Visitor Center** (160 W. Main St., 605/584-3110, www.sanfordlabhomestake.com, 9am-5pm daily) at the same address. The main **post office** is at 329 West Main Street. Groceries can be found at **Lynn's Dakota Mart** (145 Glendale Dr., 605/584-2905). The taxi service in town is **Dakota Taxi** (605/920-2020, www.dakotataxinow.com), which services most areas in the Northern Hills and offers shuttles to the Rapid City Airport. Medical needs can be met at the **Monument Health Lead-Deadwood** (61 Charles St., Deadwood, 605/717-6000)

Deadwood

Gold was first discovered in the Black Hills in the town of Custer in 1874 by two members of the Custer Expedition. As prospectors flocked to the region, claims were paying off all over the hills, but the richest claims and longest-running mines were to be found in Deadwood and its sister city of Lead, just 3 miles (4.8 km) away. Life was wild in all the gold camps, but Deadwood managed to attract the most colorful characters, including James Butler, "Wild Bill" Hickok, and Calamity Jane.

To this day, Deadwood remains one of the edgiest and most dynamic towns in the hills. The entire town was designated a National Historic Landmark in 1976, yet it wasn't until 1980 that the last four brothels in town were closed. Refusing to be tamed, the community legalized small stakes gambling in 1989, and the stakes were upped in 2000. The entire town is also on the National Register of Historic Places and feels much as it did in the late 1800s with, of course, the addition of a lot of flashing lights and ringing bells.

Deadwood Gulch is a fairly narrow canyon, and most of the town is squeezed in along just a few main streets. In 1879, fire (the plague of many a rickety wooden mining community) roared through the narrow gorge and destroyed 300 buildings in an area just 0.5 mile (0.8 km) by 0.25 mile (0.4 km). Over 2,000 people were left homeless. The town was quickly rebuilt upon the ashes, but this time, most of the buildings were of solid brick and sandstone construction. The historic district of the town looks much as it did after the fire, as most of the existing buildings trace their construction to post-fire rebuilding. Today, Deadwood is a center for historic reenactments (including the daily shooting of Wild Bill Hickok), fine dining, rodeos, special events, and gambling.

HISTORY

A big part of Deadwood's history has to do with the characters who migrated here. It's hard to tell how much of **Wild Bill Hickok**'s past was hype and how much was true, but by the time he reached Deadwood in 1876, his reputation as a gambler, womanizer, and gunfighter preceded him. Just 39 years old at the time, he was already suffering from too much time spent in saloons. He continued that pattern in Deadwood. Most of his days there were occupied drinking and gambling. The story is told that one day a man named Jack McCall, playing poker at Wild Bill Hickok's table, lost a lot of money. According to legend, Hickok gave him back enough to get something to eat and warned him against gambling if he didn't have enough to cover his losses. The next day, Wild Bill was playing poker at the same table, with his back to the door, a seat he would rarely agree to accept. McCall, drinking heavily at the bar, came up behind him and shot Hickok in the back of the head. As he died, Wild Bill spilled his poker hand on the table—a pair of aces and a pair of eights—a hand that has since that day been called the "dead man's hand."

Calamity Jane, born Martha Canary in Missouri in 1862, was another famous character that made her way to Deadwood. After both her parents died within a year of each other, Calamity Jane found herself, at the age of 15, the head of a household that included five younger siblings. To support the family, Jane took whatever work she could find, including cook, nurse, dance hall girl, waitress, ox-team driver, and prostitute. In 1870, she joined Lieutenant Colonel George Armstrong Custer as a scout; this is when she first began dressing as a man, a habit she maintained throughout her life. By the time she joined Custer, she was known as a fearless rider and formidable shot. Calamity Jane stayed with the Western cavalry, fighting Native Americans for several years.

In 1876, Calamity Jane was ordered to the Black Hills with General Crook. Once there, she became severely ill and spent two weeks in the hospital at Fort Fetterman. After her recovery, she headed to Laramie, Wyoming, and met up with Charles Utter's wagon train headed to Deadwood. With Utter was Wild Bill Hickok. Both heavy drinkers and prone to great exaggeration, it seems Calamity Jane and Hickok hit it off. While there are stories that they were romantically linked, there are also stories that this was just wishful thinking on her part. (The latter is the most currently accepted theory; the romance was in her head.) At any rate, she stayed with the wagon train to Deadwood. Calamity Jane took a job with the Pony Express when she arrived, delivering mail between Custer and Deadwood.

At the age of 52, Calamity Jane died a natural death—at least as "natural" as a death that is caused by the ravages of alcohol can be. This fearless rider, champion cusser, deadly shot of a woman was another character of the West loved by dime-store novelists. As she died, she had one last request—to be buried next to Wild Bill Hickok. She got her wish. Both are interred in Mount Moriah Cemetery in Deadwood.

Deadwood

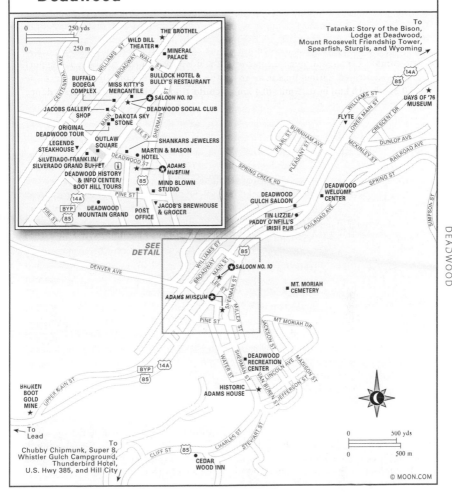

SIGHTS

Deadwood Welcome Center

The **Deadwood Welcome Center** (501 Main St., 605/578-1876, www.deadwood. com, 9am-5pm daily) provides visitors with information on local attractions and points of interest along with exhibits that highlight things to do in Deadwood and the northern Black Hills. This is essentially the visitor center for the community. One of the big benefits of hitting this establishment first is that the plentiful parking is free, there are public restrooms, and, for a dollar, the city trolley will pick up passengers and drop them off anywhere along the main strip downtown.

Deadwood History and Information Center

Tucked into a building that was constructed in 1897 as a railroad depot, the **Deadwood History and Information Center** (3 Siever

St., 605/578-2507, 9am-5pm daily) has some great displays and multimedia exhibits about the history of the town. Visitors can purchase trolley tickets here and learn about the current events and activities going on in Deadwood on any particular day. Deadwood is a town of many festivals and events. It's surprising how many things there are to do that do not involve casinos! There are several 20-minute free parking spaces here for quick answers to questions; otherwise the parking is fee-based.

★ Adams Museum

William Emery Adams was born in 1854 and moved to Deadwood at the age of 23 with his brother. Like most, Adams went looking for gold, but eventually teamed up with his brother to run the Banner grocery store. The store was destroyed, along with 299 other buildings, in a fire in 1879. Undaunted, The Adamses rebuilt and remained successful. William Emery Adams served as mayor for several terms over the course of his residency in Deadwood. He married Alice Burnham, from the nearby community of Fountain City, in 1880. Their daughter Lucile was born in 1884, and daughter Helen followed in 1892. Lucile died of typhoid in 1912. In 1925, Alice went to Pasadena, California, to assist Helen,

who was about to give birth to their first grandchild. Alice, who had recently been diagnosed with cancer, died unexpectedly while she was there. Distraught, Helen went into early labor and died the next day. The baby lived only a few hours. In the course of just 48 hours, Adams lost his entire family. He was grief-stricken.

Adams was to find happiness again, however. In 1927, he married his second wife, Mary Mastrovich Vicich. He was 73, and she was just 29. It was also in 1927 that a group of businesspeople decided that a museum was needed to preserve the history of Deadwood. It was Mary who encouraged Adams to contribute to the project in honor of his first wife and his daughters. He donated over $75,000 to construct the **Adams Museum** (54 Sherman St., 605/578-1714, www.deadwoodhistory. com, 9am-5pm daily May-Sept., 10am-4pm Tues.-Sat. Oct.-Apr., suggested donation adult $5, child $2). It was completed in 1930 and is considered to be the oldest museum in the Black Hills. The museum has three floors of pioneer, mining, and Lakota artifacts; artwork; old photos; maps; and cultural items outlining Deadwood's wild and diverse history. There are also artifacts left by some of the local town characters. Look for Wild Bill

Adams Museum

Hickok's gun collection and N. C. Wyeth pencil sketches of Hickok. A highlight on the main floor of the museum is the first steam train ever used in the Black Hills. Weighing in at about five tons, it makes for an impressive display. The controversial Thoen Stone claiming a gold strike in the Black Hills 40 years before the Custer Expedition (is it real or a hoax?) is also on display at the museum. It's a fascinating museum, with great displays.

Historic Adams House

Sister site to the Adams Museum, the **Historic Adams House** (22 Van Buren St., 605/578-3724, www.deadwoodhistory.com, 9am-5pm daily May-Sept., 10am-4pm Tues.-Sat. Apr. and Oct., adult $10, child ages 6-12 $5) is shown by guided tour only. Tours are on a first-come, first-served basis, but it wouldn't hurt to call ahead to see if there are folks waiting.

The house was built in 1892 and is one of the finest examples of a Queen Anne-style home in Deadwood. W. E. Adams bought the house in 1920 with his first wife Alice. It was closed in 1936 by his second wife, Mary Mastrovich Vicich, after W. E. Adams died in 1934 at the age of 80. For 50 years, the house remained empty and fully stocked. For a brief period, 1987-1992, it was opened and used as a bed-and-breakfast. In 1992, the house was sold to the city for preservation, carefully restored, and reopened to the public in 2000.

Today, guided tours give visitors a peek into the wealthier side of Deadwood's early days. Imagine entering a home where virtually nothing has changed since the late 1920s. The original silverware, found in a safe, is on display, as are all the furnishings, knickknacks, artwork, and other personal possessions all relatively undisturbed to this day. It's a fully authentic walk through another era.

Mount Moriah Cemetery

While W. E. Adams represented the more refined side of Deadwood, a large part of the town's historical appeal can be attributed to the shady characters that were drawn there. The **Mount Moriah Cemetery** (10 Mount Moriah Dr., 605/722-0837, www.cityofdeadwood.com, 9am-6pm daily, $2), on the hillside above Sherman Street in the southeast corner of town, is the resting place of many of Deadwood's famous and infamous characters. During the summer, admission is collected at a ticket booth on-site, where a brochure of the layout of the cemetery is available to visitors. Directly across the street from the ticket booth is the Mount Moriah Cemetery Visitor Center, which houses a gift shop and where a 15-minute interpretive video can be viewed. It is possible to access the cemetery after hours. A donation box is set up near the entry gate for contributions to be made on the honor system.

James Butler "Wild Bill" Hickok and Calamity Jane are two of the famous residents of the cemetery. Mount Moriah is actually the second resting spot for Wild Bill. Originally interred in the Whitewood Gulch Cemetery, he was moved to Mount Moriah with the rest of the Whitewood Gulch inhabitants when the town fathers decided that the relatively flat land of Whitewood was better suited for buildings than for graves.

It is actually quite pretty in the cemetery. A short walk to the top of the hill provides nice views of Deadwood and makes a great spot for photographs.

Days of '76 Museum

The **Days of '76 Museum** (18 76th Dr., 605/578-1657, www.daysof76.com, 9am-5pm daily May-Sept., 10am-4pm Tues.-Sat. Oct.-Apr., adult $8, child ages 6-12 $3) is an offshoot of the Days of '76 Rodeo and Parade that started in 1923 to honor the memory of the wild days of the gold rush and the founding of Deadwood in 1876. The museum started out housing many of the horse-drawn carriages and stages that were in the original rodeo parade, including one of the original Deadwood Stages, and has continued to add to that collection. Photographs and artifacts from more than 80 years of the Days of '76 Rodeo comprise another of the museum's

The Thoen Stone

In 1887, brothers Louis and Ivan Thoen were hauling building stone from the base of a mountain near Spearfish when they found a sandstone slab inscribed with a message. On one side of the stone was carved:

Came to these hills in 1833
seven of us
DeLacompt
Ezra Kind
G. W. Wood
T. Brown
R. Kent
Wm. King
Indian Crow
all dead but me Ezra Kind
killed by Ind beyond the high hill got our
gold June 1834

On the reverse:

Got all the gold we could carry
our ponies all got by Indians
I have lost my gun and nothing to eat
and Indians hunting me.

There is no controversy surrounding the idea that gold might have been found by someone before Custer announced its discovery in 1874. But the stone's authenticity is questionable. After all, if you were weaponless, hungry, and being hunted, would you stop and carve a relatively long message into stone? And the men who found the carved message were, coincidentally, stoneworkers, who very well might think about inscribing a message in stone.

Researchers have been trying to determine if the Thoen Stone is a hoax or real ever since its discovery. To date, it has been determined that many of the men named on the stone did, in fact, head west in the 1830s and were never heard from again. And, apparently, it is possible to carve wet sandstone fairly easily with just a knife. So perhaps this was the equivalent of a desperate miner's last words. Or . . . perhaps not. See the stone at the **Adams Museum** in Deadwood and decide for yourself.

major collections. The crown jewel of the displays, however, is the Clowser collection. Don Clowser first came to Deadwood in 1926 when he was just 12 years old. Clowser became an avid collector of historic artifacts and Native American art, and eventually ran the Deadwood Trading Post. He personally amassed thousands of pioneer, mining, and Native American artifacts. A member of the Days of '76 committee for 35 years, Clowser asked if the organization would be interested in housing his collection. The response was an enthusiastic yes. Some of the artifacts are priceless and some are just interesting, but all of them contribute to the preservation of the history and culture of the region.

Tatanka: Story of the Bison

Tatanka: Story of the Bison (100 Tatanka Dr., 1 mi/1.6 km north of Deadwood, 605/584-5678, www.storyofthebison.com, 9am-5pm daily mid-May-Sept, adult $12, child ages 6-12 $6) is a facility dedicated to the history of the bison and the Native culture built around it. The facility includes a dramatic sculpture by local artist Peggy Detmers of 14 life-size bison pursued by three Native Americans on horseback, an interactive interpretive center, a gift shop featuring the arts and crafts of Native American and other regional artists, and a snack bar. Start a visit at the center by viewing the 20-minute DVD that runs throughout the day in a small theater; it covers the creation of the sculpture and the mission of the center. Created by actor Kevin Costner to serve as an education center, the Tatanka story is an interesting approach to learning about the culture and social history of a people. Presentation times start on the hour at 10am, 11am, 1pm, 2pm, 3pm, and 4pm and last 30-45 minutes. On the simplest level, just about everything you'd ever want to know about the bison is explained. But beyond that, interpreters and displays demonstrate how Native Americans depended on the bison for food, clothing, and housing and how the near extinction of the bison affected their culture. Artifacts including tipis, sinew, and clothing are displayed to support the discussion, and Native American interpreters are on hand to answer any questions.

Mount Roosevelt Friendship Tower

It's a short walk through the woods to the **Mount Roosevelt Friendship Tower** (free), built by Seth Bullock, the famed sheriff of Deadwood, as a memorial to his lifelong friend Theodore Roosevelt. A climb up the narrow stairs of the winding staircase inside the tower can be a bit dizzying, but the view from the top is beautiful. Crow Peak can be seen in the southwest quadrant. It's a peaceful break from the noise and glitter of the Deadwood casinos. To reach the tower from downtown Deadwood, head back toward Sturgis on U.S. 14A and take a left on U.S. 85 just on the outskirts of town. Drive about 1.5 miles (2.4 km) to Mt. Roosevelt Road (Forest Service Rd. 133) and continue through the pines for about 2 miles (3.2 km) to the parking lot. It's a short hike to the tower.

Broken Boot Gold Mine

It wouldn't be right to visit a famous gold mining town without venturing into an old gold mine. The **Broken Boot Gold Mine** (Upper Main St., U.S. 14A, 605/578-9997, www.brokenbootgoldmine.com, 8am-6pm daily Memorial Day-Labor Day, adult $8, senior and military $7, student ages 6-17 $6), established in 1878, was a mine that made its owners more money selling fool's gold than the real thing, but about 15,000 ounces (425 kg) of gold were extracted from what was originally known as Seim's Mine. Tours leave every 30 minutes and take about 30 minutes. The guides are knowledgeable and demonstrate how some of the mining equipment, including dynamite, was used in the mine. The history of the Broken Boot Gold Mine is presented, as is a general history of mining in the Deadwood area. At the end of the tour, participants can pan for gold ($10 pp). Every visitor receives a replica of a stock certificate in the mine at the completion of the tour as a souvenir. A special tour at 5:30pm called the Candlelight Ghost Tour ($10 pp) requires that participants be over the age of 12. The tour is a little longer than the daytime tours, and participants literally carry candles and listen to ghost stories as they walk through the mine. If the wind blows too hard, it could get pretty dark in there.

The Brothel Deadwood

The newest site in Deadwood is focused on the oldest profession. **The Brothel Deadwood** (610 Main St., 605/559-0231, www.deadwoodbrothel.com, 11am-7pm daily May-Sept., 11am-7pm Wed.-Sat. Oct.-Apr., $15) tells, through stories, the history of prostitution in Deadwood. The industry existed in Deadwood from 1876 until the last of the houses were closed in 1980. The tour is on the second floor of the building, above the Eagle Bar. The tour contains adult content, and visitors must be at least 16 years of age to participate.

RECREATION

Head for the **Deadwood Recreation Center** (105 Sherman St., 605/578-3729, www.cityofdeadwood.com, 5am-7pm Mon.-Fri., 7am-5pm Sat., adult $4, senior and child

18 and under $2, family $7) for fun and fitness the morning after a late night of dining and gambling. The price can't be beat, and the facility includes a waterslide, lap pool, indoor running track, racquetball/squash court, basketball court, fitness equipment, weights, and a sauna. Call when you are in town for the pool schedule and information about activities.

The **Mickelson Trail** (day-use fee $4, annual $15) is 109 miles (175 km) of a "rails-to-trails" project. The trail runs between Edgemont in the south and Deadwood in the north. The most strenuous route is the 19-mile (31-km) stretch between Deadwood and Dumont. Dumont is the highest point on the trail, so it might be a good idea to pick up a shuttle to Dumont and ride back to Deadwood. **Rabbit Bike** (175 Walnut Ave., Hill City, 605/574-4302, www.rabbitbike.com, 8am-5pm Mon.-Sat. and 9am-4pm Sun. summer, 9am-4pm Mon.-Sat. spring) is happy to pick up folks in Deadwood and shuttle them to any of the Mickelson Trail trailheads. They will also deliver rental bikes to Deadwood. With an extensive inventory of bikes in stock, there are comfort bikes and hardtail bikes, recumbent bikes, as well as bikes for kids. Bicycle gear is available as is a full-service repair shop. Bike rental rates depend on the length of the trip and the bike selected (non-electric bikes: half-day adult $40-50, child $25, full-day adult $75-85, child $35; electric bikes: half-day adult $75, full-day adult $125). Rentals include tire repair kits (no charge if unused) and helmets. The shuttle for two people from Deadwood to Dumont is $60. If there are more folks in your party, give them a call for rates, as they vary based on the number of people in the group.

TOURS

Boot Hill Tours (3 Siever St., 605/800-8687, www.boothilltours.com, May-Oct., adult $20, child ages 6-12 $15) offers one-hour tours daily. Learn about local lore and history, the gold rush, Chinese people in Deadwood, the lives of the wilder characters who lived in Deadwood, and the future of mining in the hills. The tours wind through the historic downtown streets of Deadwood and travel up to Mount Moriah Cemetery. Six tours are scheduled daily (9:30am, 11am, 12:30pm, 2pm, 3:30pm, and 5pm) as long as weather permits.

Kevin Costner's **Original Deadwood Tour** (675 Main St., 605/578-2091, May-mid-Oct., ticket booth 9am-1:30pm Thurs.-Tues., adult $18, child ages 7-12 $9) provides a one-hour tour focusing on the history of the town and its major characters. There are three tours daily (10:30am, noon, 1:30pm). Learn about the Fort Laramie Treaty and the Custer Expedition, which started the gold rush explosion. Obtain tickets at the ticket booth and board in front of the building. Admission to Mount Moriah Cemetery is included in the tour fee.

Discovery Tours (605/431-1200 or 605/920-1020, www.blackhillsdiscoverytours. com, adult $99, child $79) services the Northern Hills area, providing year-round tours daily to Mount Rushmore, Crazy Horse, and Custer State Park via Iron Mountain Road and Needles Highway. In addition to picking up passengers in Deadwood, they will pick up in Spearfish and Lead, among other locations. Transportation for the tours are 14 passenger vans.

GAMING

Small stakes gambling was legalized in Deadwood in 1989 and revitalized the entire region. With over 80 gaming establishments in town, most of which are side by side on the two central streets of town, there are plenty of options. Technology has brought some changes to the casino floor in the form of coinless slot machines. Today the days of buckets filling with cascading coins is almost gone. Most casinos have only paper vouchers to pay out winnings.

The age limit for wagering in South Dakota is 21. Smoking indoors is banned in Deadwood, although smoking right outside the buildings is still allowed. It does clean up the air inside, though. It is hard to separate dining from lodging and gaming in Deadwood, since many of the gaming "resorts" offer all three. If the draw to Deadwood is to enjoy gaming, consider making reservations at the hotel hosting the casino!

Historically, gambling was limited, with a $5 bet the top wager amount allowed in 1989. That was increased to $100 in 2000 and then $1,000 in 2012, though only the larger casinos have adopted the higher limit. Games initially offered included slot machines, blackjack, and poker. In 2015, the repertoire of available games expanded to include roulette, craps, and keno. An amendment on the November 2020 election officially legalized sports betting in South Dakota. **Dale's Bar & Grill** in the **Deadwood Mountain Grand** (1906 Deadwood Mountain Dr., 605/559-0386 or 877/907-4726, www.deadwoodmountaingrand.com) was the first casino to implement sports betting. Twelve 85-inch (216-cm) and seven 65-inch (165-cm) displays will allow patrons to watch 19 games at once. The casino at the Grand is already very popular, offering roulette, craps, table games, and slots, along with several places to dine, drink, and stay on-site.

Continuously voted the best casino in Deadwood by local area residents, **The Lodge at Deadwood** (100 Pine Crest Ln., 605/584-4800 or 877/393-5634, www.deadwoodlodge.com, 24 hours daily, high stakes) is an elegant facility about 0.75 mile (1.2 km) from the downtown district. Nestled into the side of Mount Roosevelt, the lodge is best described as classy. Lots of natural stone, tile, and wood highlight all areas of the facility. The casino floor is spacious, with plenty of elbow room for gamblers, and features table games and slot machines. Over 300 games are available. Beer and well drinks are complimentary for players at the table games and complimentary draft beer and coffee is free for players at the slot machines. Though the site is not in downtown Deadwood, the complex (casino, restaurants, and hotel) offers trolley rides to Main Street, which is just a minute away.

The **Mineral Palace** (601 Main St., 605/578-2036 or 800/847-2522, www.mineralpalace.com, 24 hours daily, high stakes) has over 350 slot machines. Blackjack, live three-card poker, and double-deck blackjack are the featured table games. In addition to the table games, poker, and slot machines, the Mineral also offers roulette tables. The property has a restaurant and a 75-room hotel. The **Tin Lizzie Gaming Resort** (555 Lower Main St., 605/578-1715 or 800/643-4490, www.tinlizzie.com, 24 hours daily, high stakes) is another local favorite. When asked what makes it a local hangout, the most common response is "great people." There are plenty of state-of-the-art slot machines and live blackjack games. It is also one of just a few complexes offering craps, keno, roulette, and sports betting. The complex now includes **Starbucks, Paddy O'Neill's Irish Pub** (sister to a pub of the same name in Rapid City), two restaurants, and a Hampton Inn.

A favorite of gamblers is the **Silverado-Franklin** (709 Main St., 605/578-3670 or 800/584-7005, www.silveradofranklin.com, 24 hours daily, high stakes), the largest casino on Main Street. The building doesn't have the historic background of some of its neighbors since it was built in 1933 by businessman W. E. Adams to house Hills Chevrolet. It was purchased and renovated by Silverado after the legalization of gambling. The casino offers 225 slot machines, several variations of blackjack and live poker, craps, and roulette. The buffet downstairs from the casino has a great atmosphere and good food.

ENTERTAINMENT

The entire city of Deadwood *is* essentially an entertainment venue, and there are many events that occur on a daily basis. Stop by the **Deadwood History and Information Center** (3 Siever St., 605/578-2507, www.deadwood.com, 9am-5pm daily) or **Deadwood Welcome Center** (501 Main St., 605/578-1876, www.deadwood.com, 9am-5pm daily) to pick up information about events on the day of your visit. Keep in mind, though,

that some activities require reservations at least 24 hours in advance and that hours may shift during special event weekends, the Sturgis Rally (10 days in August beginning on the first Friday), and on holidays.

Deadwood Alive

The Wild West vibe maintains its reign in this old gold-mining community, thanks in part to **Deadwood Alive** (800/344-8826, www.deadwoodalive.com), which manages a troupe of actors in full historic regalia performing in shoot-outs, reenactments, narrated walking tours of historic Deadwood, and stagecoach rides.

Shoot-outs are free to the public and occur three times Monday-Saturday in summer (with reduced showtimes in fall and spring): at 2pm at Outlaw Square (703 Main St.), 4pm in front of the Buffalo Bodega Complex (658 Main St.) and the Holiday Inn Express (1906 Deadwood Mountain Dr.), and 6pm at the Wild Bill Bar at the Celebrity Hotel (624 Main St.). At 4:30pm, the "shootists" will be hanging about in Gold Street Courtyard (the alley across from Main St. and Lee St.), ready to answer questions or even give autographs to folks who enjoyed the show.

Reenactments include the shooting of Wild Bill Hickok at **Saloon No. 10** (657 Main St.), where poor Wild Bill meets his maker several times a day during the summer months (1pm, 3pm, 5pm, and 7pm Mon.-Sat. summer, free). It's a quick little scene but fun, especially for those members of the crowd who volunteer to play cards with Bill. After Wild Bill dies for the last time that day, watch Jack McCall, the low-down cowardly scoundrel who keeps on killing Bill, get captured in front of the saloon at 7:35 pm.

To complete the saga of the killing of Wild Bill, head to the **Silverado-Franklin** (709 Main St.) to watch the **Trial of Jack McCall** (8pm Mon.-Sat. summer, adult $8, senior $7, child ages 6-12 $4, child 5 and under free).

1: view of Deadwood from Mount Moriah 2: Days of '76 Rodeo 3: gaming in Deadwood 4: downtown Deadwood

This show is one of the longest-running staged plays in the nation, having been performed in Deadwood since the mid-1920s. And it's another audience participation, family-fun show. Reservations must be made at least 24 hours before the show.

The troupe also narrates a walking tour of historic Deadwood called the **Lawman's Patrol** (noon Mon.-Sat. summer, noon Fri.-Sat. spring and fall, $15 pp). The walking tour departs from the Midnight Star (677 Main St.) and makes multiple stops through town while old cowboy sheriffs talk about the brothels, the gold rush, the saloons, and the famous and infamous characters who populated the community. Fires and floods are also part of Deadwood's history. The tour lasts 45-60 minutes. Reservations online or by phone must be made at least 24 hours in advance of the walk.

There is another option available for spending time with these raucous characters of the Old West: Take a **stagecoach ride** (9am-1:30pm on the half hour in summer, adult $12, child ages 6-12 $7, child ages 3-5 $3), one of the iconic modes of transportation in the West. Tickets are available at the Lucky Horse Stage Stop near the Celebrity Hotel (629 Main St.). Reservations online or by phone must be made at least 24 hours in advance.

Events

Deadwood is the most "weekend event" community in the hills, with special events lined up all year. Events can affect lodging prices, so reserve early! Exact dates and other information can be found through the **Deadwood Chamber of Commerce** (800/344-8826, www.deadwood.com/events).

Deadwood has big celebrations for Mardi Gras, St. Patrick's Day, and July 4th weekend, as well as local events like **Wild Bill Days** (mid-June), named after one of Deadwood's infamous gunslingers and featuring activities including gold panning, sluice demonstrations, a book fair, a dock-diving dog competition, and several outdoor concerts.

The **Days of '76 Rodeo** (late July) is another major weekend celebration. The rodeo was selected by the Professional Rodeo Cowboys Association as the Midsize Rodeo of the Year for 2004-2008. The Days of '76 Rodeo has been kicking up heels for almost 100 years.

After the rodeo ends, the chaos begins as the **Sturgis Rally** literally brings thousands of motorcycles and their riders to Sturgis—about 14 miles (22.5 km) east of Deadwood—and the Black Hills for 10 days beginning the first Friday of August.

Kool Deadwood Nights is a weeklong celebration held in late August that brings a wide variety of classic cars to town. There are races, a show and shine, a parade, and scenic cruises throughout the hills, including a poker run.

And then there's **DeadWeird** around Halloween, a local favorite.

Outdoor venue **Outlaw Square** (703 Main St., 605/578-1876, www.outlawsquare. com) hosts both free and ticketed events. In addition to the shoot-outs, free and family-friendly activities are on offer in the square all summer long (except during the Sturgis Rally and bad weather). Activities include movie nights, a farmers market, sunrise yoga and Zumba, and family-oriented history nights. In the evenings, the square plays host to the **Deadwood Open Air Music Series** (605/717-7016, www.deadwoodlive.com, general admission $39-49, reserved seating $69-89, multi-seat tables $149-159), which features live performances by musicians from across the nation. Performers have included folks like Clay Walker and Dwight Yoakum.

Nightlife

TOP EXPERIENCE

★ SALOON NO. 10

Saloon No. 10 (657 Main St., 605/578-3346, www.saloon10.com, 9am-2am daily) is an Old West saloon with a great bar and restaurant in addition to gaming rooms. Billed as the only museum with a bar, the saloon is filled with historic artifacts and photos that line the walls and hang from the ceiling. The bar offers over 171 bourbons, scotch, and whiskeys as well as lots of beer on tap. It bears the name of the place where Wild Bill Hickok was killed while playing poker in 1875. Self-designated the "party center of Deadwood," it has live music on tap from 2pm-5pm on summer weekend afternoons. Live bands perform nightly 9pm-1:30am. And free reenactments of the shooting of Wild Bill happen multiple times a day at the saloon in summer (page 191). Poor Bill.

LIVE MUSIC

With 2,500 seats, the event center at the **Deadwood Mountain Grand** (1906 Deadwood Mountain Dr., 605/559-0386 or 877/907-4726, www.deadwoodmountain grand.com, $25-55, make reservations early for the best price) brings a wide variety of acts to town, including the likes of Tanya Tucker, Trace Adkins, Three Dog Night, and Hairball. Tickets purchases are automatically directed to the www.ticketmaster.com site from the Mountain Grand website. The Holiday Inn (877/666-3243 for reservations) is part of the Deadwood Mountain Grand complex, should you elect to stay the night.

If you'd rather participate in music than listen to it, visit the **Buffalo Bodega Complex** (658 Main St., 605/578-1162, www. buffalobodega.com) and join the community of karaoke singers. A DJ is on hand and karaoke starts at 9pm. There's also live music is in the afternoon on most weekends 4pm-8pm. The complex has a large stage and an outdoor venue and occupies pretty much a whole block of historic Main Street. It also includes the **Buffalo Bar** (11am-10pm Sun.-Thurs, 11am-2am Fri.-Sat.), **Bodega Casino and Bar** (9am-noon Sun.-Thurs., 9am-2am Fri.-Sat), and the **Buffalo Steak House** (11am-9pm Sun.-Thurs., 11am-10pm Fri.-Sat.). Ask to be seated in the rooftop Crow's Nest for a great view of town!

SHOPPING

While there are souvenir shops galore in Deadwood (since every casino sells *something*, particularly branded items), there are a few great specialty shops in town that are not casinos. The place to buy jewelry in Deadwood is at **Shankar Jewelry** (29 Deadwood St., 605/578-3808, www.deadwoodjewelry.com, 10am-6pm Mon.-Sat.), a family-owned business that is one of the few that returned after a huge fire in 1987. The owners travel the world looking for the best in striking and unusual jewelry pieces, and they succeed. Their jewelry is stunning. Jewelry repair is available on-site.

The published mission statement of **Chubby Chipmunk** (420 Cliff St., 605/722-2447, www.chubbychipmunk.com, 10am-5pm daily summer) is "to provide the most decadent truffles you will ever experience." This is an honorable goal, and one we can all get behind. All the chocolates are homemade and hand-dipped in Deadwood by owner and chocolatier Mary "Chip" Tautkus. It's a must-stop when visiting or passing through Deadwood.

Dakota Sky Stone (671 Main St., 605/717-0100, www.dakotaskystone.com, 9am-9pm daily summer, winter hours vary) is a family-owned business that has been in the Black Hills for over 50 years. The store specializes in Native American-made turquoise jewelry and one-of-a-kind pieces.

Miss Kitty's Mercantile (649 Main St., 605/559-0599, 9am-9pm Mon.-Thurs., 10am-10pm Fri.-Sun.) is a fun shop that displays and sells the works of 3D artists and also carries Montana Silversmiths jewelry, Prairie Soap Company products, and Western apparel and gifts. Look for the beautifully hand-beaded jean jackets and lots of custom-designed gifts.

Mind Blown Studio (73 Sherman St., 605/571-1071, www.mindblownstudio.com, 7am-5pm daily summer, call for hours in winter) is a working glassblowing studio and sells beautiful handblown vases, ornaments, bowls, paperweights, and glass tumblers, among other items. After selecting a unique and beautiful gift, grab a cup of coffee at the Pump House, which shares the same space as the studio. In addition to coffee, the Pump House has wine, beer, pastries, and other snacks that can be enjoyed on the outside patio.

An interesting combination of offerings can be found at **Jacobs Gallery Shop** (670 Main St., 605/559-1876, www.jacobsgalleryshop.com, 10am-7pm daily summer), where works of art and a Vintage Motorcycle Museum mingle. The art is heavily (though not entirely) focused on motorcycles and autos and includes photographs, pen-and-ink work, and paintings. Scott Jacobs, owner of the gallery, is a licensed Harley-Davidson artist, and it shows in his work. It's a beautiful shop that's well worth the stop.

FOOD

Truth be told, it is almost impossible to separate food from lodgings and casinos in Deadwood. Almost all establishments offer all three. Parents can feel comfortable bringing the whole family to the hotel restaurants as in all cases the restaurants are separate from the casino floor. Most of the food is reasonably priced. No one wants you to leave.

Casual Dining

Bully's Restaurant (633 Main St., 605/578-1745, www.historicbullock.com, 7am-11am daily, $9-13) is inside the historic Bullock Hotel and one of the nicest spots in town for an early and tasty breakfast. The menu is limited, but the restaurant, tucked into the small bar, is away from the hustle and noise of the casino. Breakfast offerings include a 6-ounce (170-g) sirloin; bacon or sausage with two eggs, hash browns, and toast; and the daily special. It's small, it's cozy, and the food is good.

For the best buffet in Deadwood, check out the **Silverado Grand Buffet** (709 Main St., 605/578-3670 or 800/584-7005, www.silveradofranklin.com, prime rib lunch buffet 11am-2:30pm Mon.-Sat., $15; prime rib breakfast buffet 7:30am-10:30am Sat., $15; prime rib brunch 8am-2:30pm Sun., $18; prime rib dinner buffet 4:30pm-9pm Sun.-Thurs., $21; crab and prime rib buffet 4:30pm-10pm Fri.-Sat., $34). The restaurant is inside

Sturgis Motorcycle Rally

In 1938, nine Sturgis motorcyclists and their families got together for the first Black Hills Motor Classic and camped on a lawn belonging to one of the participants. Today, approximately 400,000-500,000 bikers converge annually on the Black Hills beginning on the first Friday of August and lasting 10 days through the subsequent Sunday, filling every campground, hotel, and motel in the Northern and Central Hills.

Thousands of bikes line the streets of Sturgis. Bikers and nonbikers alike shuffle along the sidewalks admiring paint jobs, leatherwork, gleaming chrome, and each other. Wild hats, bikinis, leather, and not much else adorn more than a few of the celebrants. Beautiful young women, hired by the large motorcycle companies, stroll by in branded leathers and little else. Tattoos and piercings, food on a stick, rally T-shirts, and beer are the purchases of choice. It's crowded. It's noisy. It's a party. And for the most part, it's a jovial, fun-loving, and friendly crowd.

There are races and poker runs and daily rides into the hills. Every motorcycle manufacturer in the world is there, from the smallest custom bike creator to Harley-Davidson. At night, there are world-class concerts, and the parties lean toward the raucous. It's the biggest event in South Dakota, doubling the population of the state for about 10 days. Some of the venues that are synonymous with or unique to Sturgis include the following:

- The **Sturgis Motorcycle Museum** (999 Main St., 605/347-2001, www.sturgismuseum. com, 9am-5pm daily summer, 10am-4pm daily winter, 1 person $10, 2 people $15, $5 for each additional person) has a great collection of vintage motorcycles dating back to the early 1900s and a hall of fame to honor those who have contributed to the sport of motorcycling.

- The **Buffalo Chip Campground** (20622 131st Ave., 605/347-9000, www.buffalochip.com) is a small city unto itself, about 5 miles (8 km) east of Sturgis. In May 2015 (75th anniversary of the rally), they actually became a town . . . that no one really lives in, which is why in 2019 a

the Silverado-Franklin Hotel and Gaming Complex. The buffet includes over 80 feet (24 m) of buffet items. Look for made-to-order items, wood-fired pizzas, and soup, salad, and dessert selections. The highlight of the week is the all-you-can-eat crab buffet and prime rib on Friday and Saturday nights. The restaurant is downstairs and away from the noise and light of the casinos.

The Lodge at Deadwood has two restaurants. **Oggie's Sports Bar** (100 Pine Crest Ln., 605/571-2120, www.deadwoodlodge.com, 7am-10pm Mon.-Thurs., 7am-11pm Fri.-Sat., 7am-9pm Sun., breakfast $10-13, lunch and dinner $11-29) is the casual offering. The breakfast menu has all the standards, such as pancakes and egg dishes, but most have a creative edge to them. There are three different varieties of eggs Benedict, and the Wrangler burrito (scrambled eggs, chorizo sausage, cheddar cheese, home fries, and sour cream) sounds delicious. Lunch and dinner share a menu that features pizzas, soups and salads, burgers, sandwiches, and signature dishes. A nice touch is a lighter-side menu, off of which patrons can order a half sandwich and soup or a smaller portion of meat. A favorite signature dish seems to be the steak tips burrito, but it all looks good. The decor is paneled wood walls festooned with TVs, a wood-beamed ceiling, black tabletops, and a light and long full-service bar—overall, exactly what a sports bar and grill should look like.

A newer establishment with a great environment and food is **Jacob's Brewhouse & Grocer** (79 Sherman St., 605/559-1895, www. jacobsbrewhouse.com, 11am-10pm Mon.-Sat., 11am-9pm Sun., lunch $13-15, dinner $16-32), which has a limited but interesting menu including smoked pork, ahi tuna, chimichurri chicken, and grilled wild salmon over truffle fettuccine. The historic building is beautiful and feels modern thanks to the creative steel panels and the lovely artwork on the walls.

Fourth Circuit judge ruled that it is not a municipality. It's a story that is likely not yet over. Famous for both its campground and concerts, the Buffalo Chip provides several different on-site dining options, tent camping, RV camping, cabin camping, four pay-as-you-go shower houses, and restrooms. Concerts in the past have included acts like Lynyrd Skynyrd, Alice Cooper, and George Thorogood and the Destroyers. Weekly passes or daily admissions are available; both include camping and concerts.

- **The Knuckle Saloon** (931 1st St., 605/347-0106, www.theknuckle.com, 11am-2am daily) is filled with Sturgis memorabilia and antiques from the town's early days. With the longest bar in town, live music, and poker and pool tournaments, it's the hottest spot downtown. In addition to the bar, the venue has a restaurant on-site. It seems there might be new owners on the horizon.

- The **Full Throttle Saloon** (19950 Hwy. 79, 605/423-4584, www.fullthrottlesaloon.com) earned its reputation as the world's largest biker bar, hosting concerts and contests with an R rating. Unfortunately, in 2015, it burned to the ground. It has risen from the ashes in this new location, but it'll take a while to rebuild its reputation. It has a full roster of concerts coming up and a huge campground today.

- After the rally, when things calm down, visit **Bear Butte State Park** (605/347-5240, http://gfp.sd.gov/parks, $8 per vehicle daily), about 6 miles (9.7 km) northeast of Sturgis off of Highway 79. The land here is sacred to Native Americans. Find hiking trails, as well as fishing and camping across the highway at the park's Bear Butte Lake.

The best information about the rally, including lodgings and schedules of events, can be found at the website created by the **Sturgis Chamber of Commerce** (2040 Junction Ave., 605/347-2556, www.sturgisareachamber.com).

Coffee, baked goods, a good meal, and great beer is provided in a comfortable environment with great service.

Fine Dining

The ★ **Deadwood Social Club** (657 Main St., 605/578-3346 or 800/952-9398, www.saloon10.com, 11am-9pm Sun.-Thurs., 11am-10pm Fri.-Sat., lunch $11-26, dinner $17-41) is on the second floor of **Saloon No. 10** and features Northern Italian cuisine in a cozy, wood, brick-lined atmosphere. If there is such a thing as Western elegance, the Social Club has mastered it with a rough-and-tumble version of Victorian style. The restaurant has an extensive wine list (and you can purchase wine to go) and a menu that includes a wide variety of pasta dishes in addition to steaks. They have a wonderful chicken Wellington. Although the offerings include the standard pasta, chicken, fish, seafood, and steaks, the preparation is a refreshing change from the

standard fare in the hills: both handcrafted and delicious. Think tortellini with butternut squash, ricotta, hazelnuts, honey, and sage, or buffalo ravioli. The lunch menu is much like dinner but adds sandwiches and burgers. Look for seating on the rooftop patio; enjoy your meal in the cool evenings and watch the people below walking about the historic district. In addition to the menu, every evening the restaurant presents a dinner feature.

If you are looking to break away from the flashing lights and ringing bells of the downtown district, head up the hill on U.S. 14A, take a left on Pine Crest Road, and step inside the Lodge at Deadwood. Here you'll find the **Deadwood Grille** (100 Pine Crest Rd., 605/571-2121 or 877/393-5634, www.deadwoodlodge.com, 4:30pm-10pm daily, $15-36). The restaurant is spacious and attractive with faux leather and wood booths, tile floors, brick walls, and nice lighting. It is a casual fine dining establishment. The fish selections include halibut, salmon, walleye, and shrimp; steaks include hand-cut rib eye, filet mignon, or top sirloin steaks and buffalo rib eye. There are also pork and chicken-based menu items. On the lighter side there are beef or buffalo burgers and salads.

The folks from one of the best-liked restaurants in the hills (the Alpine Inn in Hill City) have opened a restaurant in Deadwood called **Flyt** (372 Main St., 605/571-1263, www.flytdeadwood.com, 6:30am-9pm daily, breakfast $12-16, lunch $13-17, dinner $16-24) that serves up a whole new concept. They have taken the best of the Alpine menu and added a twist, which they have called a "flyt." Any item on the menu that has "flyt" in the title will have three different but complementary taste sensations in one "flight"—essentially three tapas. The idea is an adaptation of ordering a flight or tasting sampler of craft beers. For example, the "frommage a trois flyt tapa" includes a cream cheese shrimp cocktail, artichoke dip, and an olive tapenade with baguette. Not all items come in flights. The lunch menu features a schnitzel sandwich, a variety of burgers, filet mignon, and rib eye. The dinner menu adds chicken and shrimp entrées. The Alpine is as famous for its desserts as it is for its steaks, and the Deadwood extension continues the service. There are currently 12 desserts on the menu. They can be ordered à la carte or as a flyt of three. I'll have the bread pudding, the cheesecake with strawberry sauce, the lemon cream cheese mousse with blueberry and the amaretto compote, please! The decor is not fancy, but it is cozy and the food is very good.

In the Franklin Hotel is the **Legends Steakhouse** (700 Main St., 605/578-3670 or 800/584-7005, www.silveradofranklin.com, 7am-11am and 5pm-9pm Sun.-Thurs., 7am-11am and 5pm-10pm Fri.-Sat., breakfast $10-22, dinner $18-34), an attractive restaurant with a long, warm, muted stone wall; lovely dark woodwork; and recessed lighting. Breakfast options include everything from pancakes and waffles to steak and eggs or lobster Benedict. Dinner entrées include a variety of steaks, chicken, and limited fish and seafood dishes.

ACCOMMODATIONS

The price of most accommodations in the Black Hills varies significantly from winter to summer, but in Deadwood, the difference is even more pronounced, rising and falling greatly from weekdays to weekends and even from weekend to weekend depending on events. The summer ranges noted here generally reflect the weekday to weekend variation for an average summer week. Rates noted do not include holiday weekends or rates during the Sturgis Motorcycle Rally (the first 10 days in August starting on Friday). During the Sturgis Motorcycle Rally, many rooms double in price.

Under $150

Just a few blocks from downtown Deadwood, the ★ **Cedar Wood Inn** (103 Charles St., 605/578-2725 or 800/841-0127, www.cedarwoodinn.com, summer $99-120, winter $39-69) is a well-maintained property that has been family owned for over 20 years. It is beautifully landscaped, and the rooms are large and uniquely decorated. There is no smoking in any of the rooms. Free Wi-Fi is available in all the rooms, and coffee and rolls are served in the morning. There are a limited number of rooms that allow pets for a fee of $25 per night.

The **Super 8 Deadwood** (196 Cliff St., 605/578-2535, www.super8.com, summer $130-170, shoulder season $90-160, winter $65-115) has some of the friendliest people in town at the front desk. It's a nice facility with a pool, a hot tub, and free Wi-Fi access. There's a beautiful deck available to guests that overlooks Whitewood Creek. A warm breakfast buffet is included with the room price, and the hotel houses a casino and pizzeria. For winter enthusiasts, the hotel is located on snowmobile Trail #7. Pets are not allowed with the exception of service animals.

$150-250

The 28-room **Bullock Hotel** (633 Main St., 605/578-1745 or 800/336-1876, www. historicbullock.com, summer $149-175, shoulder season and winter $109-139) was built by the man credited with bringing law and order to Deadwood. Seth Bullock moved to Deadwood one day before Wild Bill Hickok was shot to death. A former lawman, Bullock was appointed sheriff seven months after his arrival. Commerce is what brought Bullock to town, however, and his first endeavor, with his business partner Sol Star, was a hardware store. The building survived the fire of 1879, but wasn't so lucky in 1894, when a conflagration razed it. Bullock decided to replace the store and aimed to build the finest hotel in Deadwood. In 1895, the Bullock Hotel was built. Today, beautifully restored, it is one of the most photographed locations in town. It is also on the itinerary for folks who like to stay in haunted hotels. Reputedly, Seth Bullock, who died in 1919, still visits. According to most guests, his ghost is mischievous but friendly. The hotel offers a ghost tour (5pm Thurs.-Sat., adult $13, child 11 and under $7) that lasts about an hour. The rooms at the hotel are a bit spare, Victorian in style, and have the same feel to them as in most historic hotels. Colors are emerald green, red, and gold. All the furnishings are replicas. Amenities include free wireless Internet and coffeemakers. Breakfast is not provided, but the best breakfast can be found in **Bully's,** the hotel restaurant.

When the **Martin & Mason Hotel** (33 Deadwood St., 605/722-3456, www. martinmasonhotel.com, king room $180-240) was renovated in 2007, the owners went beyond the ordinary in restoring it to its Victorian splendor. Eight rooms are available for guests: Five are single king rooms and three are suites. All the rooms have authentic furnishings and decor from the 1890s. The hotel is elegant, and all of the rooms' accoutrements are first class, including 100 percent Egyptian cotton sheets, cable TV and wireless Internet, and fresh scones and coffee in the morning.

The **Lodge at Deadwood** (100 Pine Crest Ln., 605/584-4800 or 877/393-5634, www. deadwoodlodge.com, summer $219-249, off-season $119-189) is one of the more elegant facilities in town. The 140-room complex includes the hotel, a sports bar, a restaurant, an indoor water park, and a casino. The hotel has a natural feel, with lots of wood and stone incorporated into the decor. The artwork tends to wildlife paintings and scenic photographs of the Black Hills. The rooms are luxurious and spacious, with pillow-top beds, LCD televisions, refrigerators, coffeemakers, microwaves, minifridges, and free wireless Internet. Many have patios or balconies. There is an outside seating patio for guests, a fitness center, and a large pool and whirlpool. Pets are allowed at no additional charge. The lodge can be found just off Mt. Roosevelt Road, before you reach the city center. From exit 17 off I-90, take U.S. 85 south. The lodge is not in the Main Street historic district but does provide a trolley to the downtown area as well as to many of the attractions in town.

CAMPGROUNDS

Whistler Gulch Campground (235 Cliff St., 605/578-2092 or 800/704-7139, www. whistlergulch.com, May-Sept., tents sites $27, RV sites, tent sites with electricity $34, RVs with full hookups $55-75, sleeping cabin $81) is tucked away from the noise and the traffic of Deadwood but is still within walking distance of the downtown area. It has been family owned for over 15 years. In the beautiful lodge are guest laundry facilities and a shop that sells groceries, RV supplies, and other goods. There is a shower house, heated swimming pool, and a "sport court" where basketball, volleyball, or tennis can be played. The Deadwood Trolley stops here and will give free rides to the downtown area.

INFORMATION AND SERVICES

Home to the Deadwood Chamber of Commerce, the **Deadwood Welcome Center** (501 Main St., 605/578-1876, www.deadwood.com, 9am-5pm daily) provides free parking, public restrooms, and information about the daily schedule of events happening in town. It is also the location of a terminal for the City Trolley. The **post office** is at 68 Sherman Street. Emergency medical care can be obtained at **Monument Health Lead-Deadwood Hospital** (61 Charles St., 605/717-6000) and **Clinic** (71 Charles St., 8am-5pm Mon.-Fri.), where walk-in services are available.

GETTING THERE AND AROUND

Dakota Taxi (605/920-2020, www.dakotataxinow.com, 24 hours daily) provides taxi service in the Deadwood area, including shuttle service to any point on the Mickelson Trail and to the Rapid City Airport at reasonable rates. The **Deadwood Trolley** (605/578-2082, www.cityofdeadwood.com/transportation-facilities, 8am-midnight Sun.-Thurs. and 8am-2am Fri.-Sat. summer, 10am-10pm Sun.-Thurs. and 8am-2am Fri.-Sat. winter, $1 pp) is operated by the city of Deadwood. The trolley is designed, for the most part, to shuttle folks around town. It stops at most of the hotels and some of the campgrounds. The trolley runs 365 days per year. It's a great way to get around town without driving.

The Badlands

The Badlands are an eerie place. The twisted spires and pinnacles are striped pale yellow, burgundy, and light pink. In daylight the colors are pastel. In the early light of morning or dusk they deepen. A visit to the Badlands is like a visit to another planet, one that is starkly forbidding and strikingly beautiful. Gazing over the plains from the high ridges of the park is not unlike the sense you get while looking out to sea. Miles and miles of open plain lie before you, with little evidence of humankind. Though the dusty pale guise gives the landscape a barren appearance, the Badlands are filled with life. Host to bison, pronghorn, bighorn sheep, deer, fox, coyotes, prairie dogs, burrowing owls, and other prairie animals, including the rare black-footed ferret, the Badlands are a wildlife wonderland.

Highlights

Look for ★ to find recommended sights, activities, dining, and lodging.

★ **Badlands Loop Road:** This winding 23-mile (37-km), 60-minute drive showcases the otherworldly beauty of the Badlands, with plenty of turnouts and dramatic vistas (page 205).

★ **Sage Creek Rim Road:** This 22-mile-long (35-km) gravel road provides some of the best wildlife-viewing in the park, including its resident bison herd and Prairie Dog Town (page 208).

★ **Ben Reifel Visitor Center:** This is the place to learn about everything in Badlands National Park—with an award-winning video, exhibits, lots of books, maps, and knowledgeable rangers (page 208).

★ **Stargazing in Badlands National Park:** Discover the celestial skies during ranger-led Night Sky Programs. With access to high-powered telescopes and knowledgeable astronomers, participants will have the opportunity to enjoy a close-up look at the planets, constellations, and even the satellites that circle the earth above us (page 210).

★ **Wall Drug:** A sign advertising free ice water led to the creation of this 76,000-square-foot (7,060-m) roadside attraction that's like a world of its own (page 216).

★ **Minuteman Missile National Historic Site:** Learn the truth about Minuteman missiles and the "missileers" responsible for their deployment (page 217).

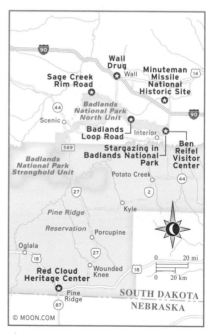

★ **Red Cloud Heritage Center:** Visit the cemetery where Chief Red Cloud, one of the great leaders of the Oglala Lakota people, is buried. Then browse a beautiful gallery of Native American art (page 225).

The town of Wall serves as the northern gateway to Badlands National Park and is a good choice for overnight stays, since services in the park are limited. Wall is most famous, however, for Wall Drug, the ultimate roadside attraction. Purchased in 1931 by the Hustead family, the drugstore languished until Dorothy Hustead thought to advertise free ice water, in verse, on road signs scattered along the highway. Hot and thirsty travelers began visiting the store the very first day the signs went up. Today, Wall Drug now serves upward of 20,000 people a day in a massive complex of shops and photo ops.

The White River Visitor Center of the South Unit of Badlands National Park is located on the Pine Ridge Reservation. Displays at the center include information about both the park and Lakota history and culture. The reservation is vast, encompassing over 3,400 sparsely populated square miles (8,806 sq km). In addition to the Badlands, the reservation lands include both mixed-grass and short-grass prairie. Visitors interested in Native American history and culture may want to plan ahead for a visit to the reservation, home to the Oglala Lakota people.

GEOLOGY

The vast area of the Great Plains was beneath an inland sea for almost 500 million years. The sedimentary layers beneath the sea are estimated to have been 5,000-10,000 feet thick (1,524-3,048 m), with many of the layers compressed to stone. Between 65-70 million years ago, an uplift in the continent created the Black Hills 70 miles (113 km) west of the Badlands. The uplift also caused the inland sea to drain, leaving the nearly flat floor of the sea exposed. The floor of that sea is the oldest formation now visible in the Badlands, called the Pierre Shale. Two geologic processes, deposition and erosion, working on the landscape for 65 million years, created the Badlands that we see today. As the wind eroded the sedimentary layers on top of the Black Hills uplift, it deposited those layers across the plains. Streams, sluggishly flowing over the relatively flat surface of the eastern plains, deposited more layers. Volcanic activity deposited yet more layers. As the uplift continued, the streams flowed more quickly and began to carve into the sediments initially deposited by the slower waters, leaving behind the spires, valleys, and fascinating formations we see today. The Badlands Wall, a towering range of spires that runs through the park, was once the northern bank of the White River that carved through the plains. To distinguish the South Dakota Badlands from other badlands areas in the West, they are frequently referred to as the White River Badlands. The spires of the wall average 800 feet tall (244 m) and separate the upper prairie flats from the lower grassy prairie of the south and east.

PLANNING YOUR TIME

There are four sites in this area east of Rapid City that encompass a lot of territory: Badlands National Park, the Minuteman Missile National Historic Site, Wall Drug, and the Pine Ridge Indian Reservation. Not all sites will interest all travelers, but at the very least, a visit to this region of the state is likely to require a full day including travel time. To visit all four without exhaustion would take an overnight stay.

It is worth visiting the Badlands area at any time of year, but the best seasons to visit the park are the spring or early summer. The grasses are still a luscious green early in the year, and the daytime temperatures are milder than the very hot days that occur more frequently in July and August. By the end of summer, the grasses are brown, removing a bit of color from the view, but the spires, buttes, and tables of the area are no less beautiful.

Badlands National Park is open 24 hours a day, seven days a week. The park is divided

Previous: the Badlands; a telescope for stargazing; the Notch Trail.

The Badlands

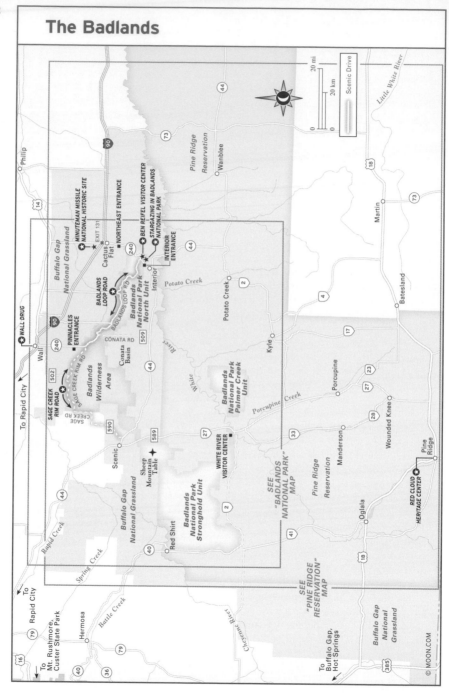

© MOON.COM

into two units: the North Unit and the Stronghold District, or South Unit, which includes the Palmer Creek area.

Getting to the North Unit of Badlands National Park is an easy day trip from Rapid City or a great detour on the I-90 drive across the state on a trip to the Black Hills. Keep in mind, however, that viewing a sunset or sunrise in the park is one of the peak experiences of a visit. While accommodations are limited, there are primitive campsites and a lodge within the park boundaries. Backcountry camping is allowed. The town of Interior at the southern edge of the North Unit of the park has limited accommodations. The town of Wall 8 miles (13 km) north of the Pinnacles Entrance on the north side of the park has several accommodations and restaurants.

The Stronghold District of the park is on the Pine Ridge Reservation but managed by the Park Service with the cooperation of the Oglala Sioux Nation at the White River Visitor Center. This area, with the exception of Sheep Mountain Table, is not accessible by road, and there is a lot of private land interspersed with the park lands. The Palmer Creek Unit can be reached by backcountry hiking only, and in order to get there, visitors must get permission to cross private property.

One tour option may include the Badlands, the Minuteman Missile National Historic Site, and Wall Drug: a perfect mix of scenic beauty, fascinating history, and a goofy roadside attraction. This would be a full day of activity. Another option is to start with Pine Ridge and a night in the Badlands, followed the next day by the missile site and Wall Drug before returning to Rapid City.

Getting There and Around

There are three different access points to **Badlands National Park.** For visitors traveling west on I-90, the **Northeast Entrance** is the closest and is located south off the exit for Highway 240. (Note that the Minuteman Missile National Historic Site is also off this exit, just north of the interstate). The **Interior Entrance** is at the southern end of the park

and takes its name from the nearby town of Interior, located off Highway 44. But for most visitors from the Black Hills region, the **Pinnacles Entrance** is the easiest and fastest way to the Badlands. From Rapid City, it's just 63 miles (101 km) of 80-mph (129-kph) driving east via I-90. If you are planning on spending the night in or near the park, this is the best option. Visit the town of Wall for breakfast and a peek at Wall Drug, and then head into the park through the Pinnacles Entrance. Get a schedule of events at the entrance gate and then travel the Badlands Loop Road headed south. The loop is just 23 miles (37 km), but should take some time. (If you have some extra time, a quick detour from the loop, a short distance down the gravel Sage Creek Rim Road just south of the Pinnacles Entrance to the park, is where some of the oldest layers of park formations are visible and where much of the wildlife, including Rocky Mountain sheep, the bison herd, and a prairie dog colony, are located.) There are many scenic overlooks and short walking trails along the way. Stop at the Ben Reifel Visitor Center at the south end of the park, do some hiking on trails near the center, enjoy the evening program sponsored by the park, and stay at the lodge (advance reservations are highly recommended) or in the town of Interior. In the morning, exit the park via the Northeast Entrance, visit the **Minuteman Missile National Historic Site** (advance reservations mandatory for visiting the launch site but not the visitor center), and then loop back to Rapid City via I-90.

Visitors who are planning to visit the **Pine Ridge Reservation** after their visit to the North Unit of the park may well want to make a stop at Sheep Mountain Table in the Stronghold District. This area is only readily accessible in dry weather. Do not attempt to visit this area if it is wet or snowy. To find Sheep Mountain Table, take Highway 44 West to the town of Scenic and head south on Bombing Range Road (aka Bureau of Indian Affairs Road 27, or BIA 27/County Road 589). Travel about 4 miles (6 km) and look for Sheep Mountain Table Road on the right. This 7-mile (11-km) gravel road will bring you to the top of the table with spectacular views. Head back to the main road to continue south into the reservation. An alternate route to the reservation would be to head east and south on Highway 44 from Interior and then turn west on BIA 2 toward Kyle on reservation land.

Note that many tour companies will do the driving for you, if desired. **GeoFunTrek** (605/923-8386 or 605/430-1531, www.geofuntrek.com) and **Affordable Adventures** (605/342-7691, www.affordableadventuresbh.com) offer narrated tours of the Badlands, with pickup locations in Rapid City.

SAFETY

The scenic highways are delightful ways to tour the park, but getting out and hiking the region has its own rewards. The region is beautiful but remote, so visitors need to consider safety when thinking about leaving the car behind and walking the wilderness areas of the park. During the summer months, the temperatures in the Badlands can reach over 100°F, and once hikers are on the trails, there is no drinkable water available. Pack in plenty to drink, wear sunglasses, and use sunscreen.

Be aware that bison are free-roaming in the park and very fast and dangerous. Keep at least 100 yards (90 m) away from them. You cannot outrun them should they decide to charge. Hikers in the backcountry may find that the bison here are not used to visitors and somewhat curious. Keep an eye on their location and drift away from them if they decide to approach. Do not stare at them, as this would be interpreted as aggressive behavior on your part.

Exercise caution when hiking anywhere in the Badlands. The soil can be very loose and cause sliding. The most common injury in the park is a sprained ankle, so wear good sturdy footgear. The weather in the park can change dramatically on short notice, and thunderstorms are common during the summer. At a minimum, a good windbreaker is mandatory gear. For longer hikes, consider carrying rain gear. Remember, also, that cell phone service in this remote area is sporadic at best. If you are planning a long hike or an overnight stay in a wilderness area, let the park rangers know your plans.

The South Unit of the Badlands was used as a bombing practice range during World War II. It is possible (though unlikely) that you could find unexploded ordnance (bullets, etc.) if you hike in that region. Do not pick up any of these items, but please do report your findings to the Park Service. If you have a GPS unit, please note the location of the items found.

Badlands National Park and Vicinity

A place of otherworldly beauty, the Badlands are also a paleontologist's dream. Each layer of the Badlands has a story to tell about the plants, animals, and climate of the region at the time of the deposit. The oldest layer, the Pierre Shale, contains the fossilized remains of clams, ammonites, and sea reptiles, proving the existence of the inland sea that once covered the area. As the sea receded, the area became a lush tropical environment, as evidenced by the Chadron Formation. Deposits in this formation are 35-37 million years old and contain evidence of alligators and palm-type plants in the region. Also commonly found in this layer are many ancient mammals, including a rhinoceros-like creature called the titanothere. Different kinds of fossils began to appear when the climate cooled and became drier. Evidence of herd animals, including a sheeplike mammal, have been found. Should you discover any fossils in the park, report them to park personnel. It is illegal to take any fossils, plants, or rocks out of a national park; they are to be left where found.

The **entrance fee** to the park is $30 per car, $25 per motorcycle, and $15 per pedestrian or bicyclist. Entrance fees allow access for seven days. The cost for an annual pass just for the park is $55. All interagency government passes are accepted here, including the **America the Beautiful Annual Pass** ($80), **Annual Senior Pass** ($20), and **Senior Lifetime Pass** ($80). The passes can be purchased at the gate (ages 62 plus are eligible for Senior passes; Military and Access passes are free). The "Every Kid Outdoors" pass allows fourth-grade students and their families free access to the national parks as well. (More information about that program and certificates for entrance can be obtained at www.everykidoutdoors.gov.) The park is open 24 hours a day, seven days a week. The hours of the park buildings vary by season.

Pets are allowed in the Badlands but only in "developed" areas, which include campgrounds, roads, picnic areas, and parking lots. They are not allowed on hiking trails, in the visitor centers, or in the Badlands Wilderness Area. They must be on a leash when in the park and cannot be left unattended anywhere in the park.

HISTORY

In 1872, Yellowstone National Park was created, the first of many areas set aside for the enjoyment of the people. From that time, a system of national parks, national monuments, and other sites has been set aside for scenic, historic, prehistoric, or scientific interest. Peter Norbeck, as a U.S. senator from South Dakota, was the chief instigator for getting the Badlands declared a national monument, and that designation was given to the park in 1939. When the park entered into a joint-operating agreement with the Oglala Lakota people in 1976 for the South Unit of the Badlands, known as the Stronghold District, the managed area grew to over 244,000 acres (98,700 ha) with 64,000 acres (25,900 ha) of

wilderness. In 1978, it was reclassified from a national monument to a national park.

Paleontologists have been doing research in the park since the first published record of a fossil jaw found in 1846, and the Park Service intends to continue that tradition into the future. In 1993, two visitors to the Badlands discovered a large backbone protruding from the ground and notified park personnel. For 15 years, the Park Service and the South Dakota School of Mines worked together at "Big Pig Dig," the site where the backbone was found. Over 19,000 bones were recovered from the site, including those of three-toed horses, tiny deerlike creatures, turtles, and a saber-toothed tiger. (No ancient pigs were found at the site, which was closed in 2008.) In 2010, a seven-year-old girl participating in the Junior Ranger Program discovered a fossil and reported it. The skull was determined to be that of a saber-toothed tiger.

SIGHTS

TOP EXPERIENCE

★ Badlands Loop Road

The Badlands Loop Road is the only paved road through the Badlands. It is a 23-mile (37-km) road that runs between the Pinnacles Entrance in the north to the Ben Reifel Visitor Center in the southeast. The road winds between the ridges of the Badlands Wall, literally a wall of spires and pinnacles that was once the northern bank of the White River. As the river cut into the sediments of the plains, the wall was left behind. Several scenic turnouts along the road provide dramatic vistas of the Badlands and **Buffalo Gap National Grassland,** which borders the park. Carry your binoculars and keep an eye out for wildlife. From the north, heading to the southeast, stop at the **Pinnacles Overlook,** the **Ancient Hunters Overlook,** and then, if you've packed a lunch, keep an eye out for Conata Road, which is near Dillon Pass. There are picnic tables about 0.5 mile (0.8 km) south on the road. Several other

Badlands National Park

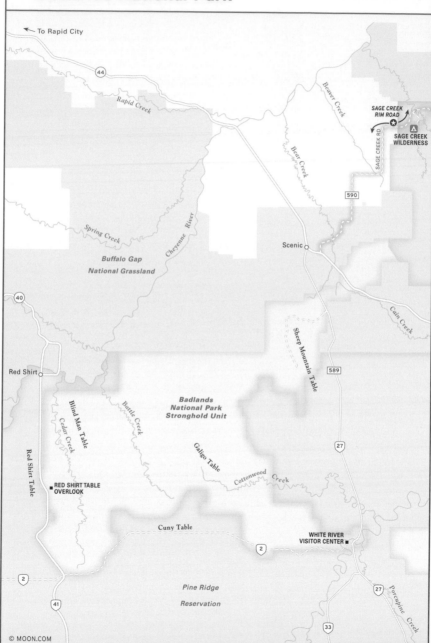

To Rapid City

44

Rapid Creek

Beaver Creek

SAGE CREEK
RIM ROAD

SAGE CREEK RD

SAGE CREEK
WILDERNESS

Bear Creek

590

Spring Creek

Cheyenne River

Buffalo Gap
National Grassland

Scenic

Cain Creek

40

Sheep Mountain Table

589

Red Shirt

Badlands
National Park
Stronghold Unit

Blind Man Table

Cedar Creek

Battle Creek

Galigo Table

27

Red Shirt Table

RED SHIRT TABLE
OVERLOOK

Cottonwood Creek

Cuny Table

WHITE RIVER
VISITOR CENTER

2

2

Pine Ridge

27

41

Reservation

33

Porcupine Creek

© MOON.COM

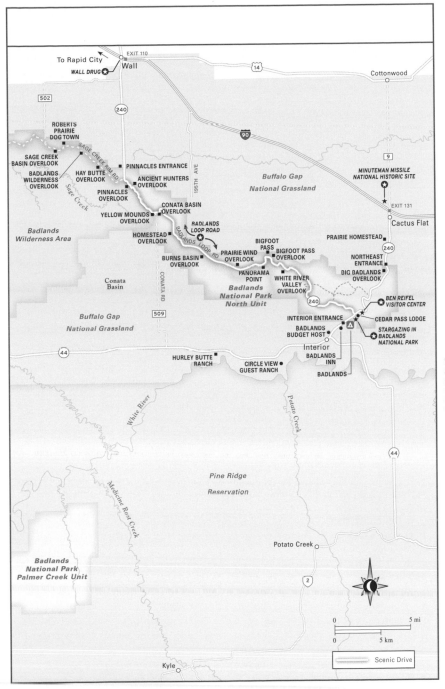

turnouts are found between Dillon Pass and Big Foot Pass, and more picnic tables are at the **Big Foot Pass Overlook.** Park signs along the route announce activities in the area. The **Fossil Exhibit Trail** marked with interpretive signs and fossil displays is an easy, wheelchair-accessible path that can be traversed in 20 minutes or less. It provides a nice stop for a good stretch. It also has humorous (but also rather sad) signs about the fate of some of the historic creatures that lived in the area over time. The theme? "Adapt, Move or Die." The road ends at the Ben Reifel Visitor Center.

TOP EXPERIENCE

★ Sage Creek Rim Road

The Sage Creek Rim Road is a gravel road just south of the northern Pinnacles Entrance to the park. The road travels north and west through the park and circles the Badlands Wilderness Area. Look for the **Hay Butte Overlook,** where Rocky Mountain bighorn sheep are commonly seen, and the **Badlands Wilderness Overlook.** The formations here are a little softer and less craggy than the spires along the Badlands Loop Road, but wildlife is more abundant. The park's bison herd is usually seen in this area. About 5 miles (8 km) down the road, look for the **Roberts Prairie Dog Town,** a large colony of black-tailed prairie dogs. They're rodents, but very cute ones, and the barking and social antics of these small animals are fun to watch. At dusk, keep an eye out for the rare black-footed ferret. Prairie dogs are the ferret's main food source. Just past Roberts Prairie Dog Town is the **Sage Creek Basin Overlook.** This is a great place to head into the park for hiking because it has easy access without the sharp and steep cliffs common off the Badlands Loop Road. Heading south along this road, you will cross a bridge over Sage Creek. At this point, examine the riverbank and you'll be able to see the Pierre Shale—the oldest visible sedimentary layer in the park, dating back over 70 million years. Seven miles (11 km) past

Roberts Prairie Dog Town, a left-hand turn on another gravel road will bring you to the **Sage Creek Campground.** There are picnic tables and pit toilets here. This is another good starting point for off-trail hiking. This is also where Sage Creek Rim Road officially ends. To return to the park, turn around and follow the road back. Past this point, it becomes Sage Creek Road, and terminates at Highway 44 outside of the park. Heading east on Highway 44 from here would return you to the park; however, it is over 30 miles (48 km) to the Interior Entrance.

★ Ben Reifel Visitor Center

The **Ben Reifel Visitor Center** (25216 Ben Reifel Rd., Hwy. 240, 605/433-5361, www.nps.gov/badl, 7am-7pm daily May-Sept., 8am-4pm daily Oct.-Apr., closed Thanksgiving, Christmas, and New Year's) is at park headquarters on the south edge of the Badlands Loop Road. Watch the award-winning video *Land of Stone and Light* in the adjacent theater as a great introduction to the park. It is 20 minutes long and plays every 25 minutes during the day. The video features superb photography of the park, along with a narrative discussion of the wildlife, geology, paleontology, early peoples, and history of the park. Exhibits at the visitor center examine the history, ecology, geology, and paleontology of the Badlands and include samples of fossils found in the park. There is also a bookstore on-site and restrooms.

For kids ages 7-12, there are Junior Ranger booklets filled with activities to do in the park. And during the summer months, ask at the visitor center for information about park ranger talks that might include a hike into the prairie, a game, or another activity for those working on Junior Ranger status. A completed activity book will earn the participant a Junior Ranger badge.

The Paleontology Prep Lab inside the Ben Reifel Visitor Center is used to prepare

1: the layers of the Badlands **2:** Rocky Mountain sheep off Sage Creek Rim Road

fossils and open 9am-4:30pm daily Memorial Day through late September.

White River Visitor Center

The **White River Visitor Center** (Hwy. 27, Pine Ridge, 605/455-2878, 9am-5pm daily June-Aug. as staff are available, closed in off-season; check with rangers upon arrival to see if the center is open) is 20 miles (32 km) south of the town of Scenic off Bombing Range Road (Hwy. 27) on the **Pine Ridge Reservation.** It is a remote location that services people interested in Pine Ridge and serious back-country camping and hiking. Exhibits at the center include fossils and Lakota artifacts, as well as some information about historic events in Lakota history. The **South Unit,** or Stronghold District, of the Badlands is not easily accessible, with just one road and no hiking trails. The **Palmer Creek Unit** of the South Unit is surrounded by private property, and hikers must get permission to cross private lands to get there. The center has a list of property owners and maps to help hikers plot their routes and gain permissions. The Stronghold District was used as a bombing range during World War II, and there is un-exploded ordnance in the area. Hikers are asked to report any finds (unlikely!) to the Park Service. Do not touch!

Rangers at the center give talks on Oglala Lakota history and culture, geology, and public land management when staff are available.

RECREATION

Vast distances, pastel-colored spires, bright sun, rocks, fossils, fragile flowers, and a fascinating geological and paleontological history make the park one of the most awe-inspiring sites in South Dakota. Over 64,000 acres (25,900 ha) in the park are designated wilderness areas. The two wilderness units in the park are the **Sage Creek Wilderness,** accessible from the Sage Creek Rim Road or the Sage Creek Campground, and the **Conata Basin,** which is accessible via Conata Road and the Conata picnic area south of Dillon Pass.

There are no established trails in the wilderness areas, though hiking is encouraged. Feel free to rely on the paths carved by the bison or follow personal whimsy as you wander the grasslands and the Badlands formations. Enjoy the beauty of the region, but be careful of drop-offs. Erosion has left a lot of loose, unstable soil, and you could find yourself sliding off the edge of a cliff. If you are planning on spending some time in the park, camping is allowed anywhere that is at least 0.5 mile (0.8 km) away from any road or trail and not visible from park roads. Keep in mind that prairie grasses grow tall, and with hot temperatures and strong winds, fire danger in the park is frequently high. Campfires are not allowed anywhere in the park. Backpacking stoves can be used. Backpacking in this region is best in spring and fall, but those are also times when park usage is pretty low, and there won't be many folks in the vicinity should you run into difficulty. The Badlands are remote and surrounded by high pinnacles that frequently block cell phone signals. For your safety, stop by the visitor center and let the rangers know your plans. Note that pets are not allowed in the wilderness areas or on any of the park's hiking trails.

Ranger-Led Programs

During the summer months, generally Memorial Day through Labor Day, there are several ranger-guided programs offered at the park. The time and locations of the talks can be found in the park newspaper, which can be picked up at the Pinnacles Entrance and at the Ben Reifel Visitor Center. All the programs are free.

TOP EXPERIENCE

★ STARGAZING

In the evening, look for the **Evening Program** (begins at 9pm-9:45pm in the spring, 8:30pm-9:15pm Aug.-Sept.) for a ranger talk followed by the popular 40-minute **Night Sky Program,** which affords participants the opportunity to view the spectacular night sky through large telescopes. Expect to see an astonishing view of the Milky Way as rangers point out different constellations. Both programs are held at the amphitheater at the Cedar Pass Campground, within walking distance of the Ben Reifel Visitor Center.

In 2012, the park held its first **Annual Astronomy Festival,** which is still going on. For three days, there are activities focused on the sky, with special programs on night skies, solar studies, and rocket launching, as well as classes in backyard astronomy and film presentations. The festival is held in July or August. Check the park website (www. nps.gov/badl) for exact dates the year you are visiting.

DAYTIME PROGRAMS

Program offerings may include a 45-minute **Geology Walk** at the Door/Window trailheads, 2 miles (3 km) northeast of the Ben Reifel Visitor Center off Highway 240; a 15- to 20-minute **Fossil Talk** at the Fossil Exhibit Trail on Badlands Loop Road about 5 miles (8 km) northwest of the Ben Reifel Visitor Center; **Fun in the Sun,** which starts at the Ben Reifel Visitor Center and includes discussions and activities focused on the sun,

including the opportunity to look at the sun through a special telescope; and the ranger-led **Junior Ranger Program** (11am daily) for children ages 7-12, which includes a hike, game, or other activity, at the conclusion of which participants earn a Junior Ranger badge.

Hiking

Day hiking in the Badlands is a joy. The vistas are grand in all directions, and the sharp-edged spires and rounded mounds of the Badlands formations are fun to explore. Remember that hiking is encouraged in the wilderness areas of the park even though there are no specific trails there. Wear good shoes, use sunscreen, carry water, and be aware that fire danger can be high in the prairie during hot dry summers. Bison roam free in the park and are to be avoided. Admire them from a distance and keep at least 100 yards (90 m) away from these dangerous and unpredictable animals. Twisted ankles are the most common injury in the park. Watch your footing on the loose sand eroding from the spires. That said, for those who prefer some guidance, there are also several marked trails within the park boundaries, most of which are easy to moderately strenuous.

hiker in the Badlands

DOOR TRAIL

Distance: 0.75 mile (1.2 km) round-trip
Duration: 30 minutes
Elevation Gain: 100 feet (30 m)
Effort: Easy
Trailhead: Door & Window parking lot
Directions: From the Ben Reifel Visitor Center, travel 2 miles (3 km) northeast on Highway 240 to the Door & Window parking lot. The trailhead is on the north end of the parking lot.

The first 150 yards (137 m) are on a boardwalk that is wheelchair accessible. Once the boardwalk ends, the trail slopes upward and travels through a "door" in the Badlands Wall to give great views of the grasslands and the outer wall of the Badlands. On the other side of the door, the trail is not maintained.

WINDOW TRAIL

Distance: 0.25 mile (0.4 km) round-trip
Duration: 20 minutes
Elevation Gain: 100 feet (30 m)
Effort: Easy (wheelchair accessible)
Trailhead: Center of the Door & Window parking lot

The entire trail is boardwalk. It leads to a window in the Badlands Wall where views of the grasslands, an erosion-carved canyon, and the spires of the Badlands Wall are visible.

NOTCH TRAIL

Distance: 1.5 miles (2.4 km) round-trip
Duration: 2 hours
Elevation Gain: 100 feet (30 m)
Effort: Moderately strenuous
Trailhead: South end of the Door & Window parking lot

The trail starts in a canyon, climbs a rope and log ladder, and follows a narrow ledge to the "notch," through which a sweeping view of the White River Valley is revealed. Parts of this trail can be steep, and the narrow ledge can be intimidating for anyone afraid of heights. Do not attempt if there has been recent rainfall.

CASTLE TRAIL

Distance: 10 miles (16 km) round-trip
Duration: 5 hours
Elevation Gain: None
Effort: Moderate
Trailhead: Across the road from the Fossil Exhibit Trail, 5 miles (8 km) northwest of the Ben Reifel Visitor Center on Badlands Loop Road

This is the longest marked trail in the park. On the north end, the trail winds down through some of the park spires and mounds. Most of the trail is level and crosses the grasslands with views of the Badlands formations to the west and south. Watch for cacti and rattlesnakes. The trail ends on Highway 240, on the west side across from the Door & Window parking lot.

Biking

There are no bike rental places in the Badlands, so you have to bring your own or rent bicycles in Rapid City and haul them to the park. Bikes are not allowed on the hiking trails or in the backcountry wilderness areas, but they can be used on the paved and gravel roads in the park. A brochure on loop trips on combined park and county roads is available at the visitor center.

During peak season in the summer, bikers should be cautious on the **Badlands Loop Road,** since it is not a wide road and there can be a lot of traffic. It can be an exhilarating ride, however, and from the Pinnacles Overlook to the visitor center, it is 22 miles (35 km) of mostly downhill riding.

Slightly off the beaten path is the **Sage Creek Rim Road.** This 22-mile (35-km) gravel road skirts the northern edge of the wilderness area, runs past Roberts Prairie Dog Town, and passes though the lowest and oldest layers of the Badlands formations.

For the adventurous, a less-traveled and equally beautiful road open to bicyclists can be found in the South Unit of the park. **Sheep Mountain Table Road** is about 4 miles (6 km) south of the town of Scenic off BIA 27/County Road 589. It is a 7-mile-long (11-km), dead-end dirt road with spectacular views of the South Unit of the park and the Black Hills 70 miles (113 km) to the west. Check for the road's status when you arrive; due to weather or other conditions, it may be closed. It is a moderately strenuous ride with a total elevation gain of about 400 feet (122 m). The most strenuous part of the ride is a 250-foot (76-m) climb at the end to the top of Sheep Mountain Table. To shorten the ride, it is possible to drive in with a vehicle, pull off the road, and park. The road can be impassable when wet. There are no services here, so bring plenty of water.

Horseback Riding

Horses are allowed in the park, although there are no commercial horse rental facilities. If you are bringing your horses with you on your trip to the hills, prime horseback riding country can be found in the Sage Creek Wilderness. The **Sage Creek Campground** has a section designated for horse use, and a watering hole is about 0.5 mile (0.8 km) southwest of the campground. This is an easy place to park trailers and ride into the Badlands. Horses are not allowed on marked trails, roads, and highways in the park, but are otherwise allowed. Horse trailers can be parked at any overlook for day use, but are not allowed to remain at overlooks and parking lots overnight.

For $55, visitors to the region can experience a one-hour private ride at **Hurley Butte Ranch** (19651 E. Hwy. 44, 605/450-1683), along the edge of the Badlands. There are never more than five people on a ride, and frequently it will be just you and a guide!

SHOPPING

While in Interior look for the **Native West Trading Company** (251 Hwy. 44, Interior, 605/433-5003, www.nativewest-trading.com, 9am-6pm daily May-Sept.), an authentic store promoting Native American arts in South Dakota. The inventory includes materials needed for powwow regalia, including an extensive bead collection, jingles, and more. There is also a varied collection of how-to books on subjects such as beading, jewelry design, and saddle repair. In addition to art and craft supplies, the store carries the works of many Lakota and other Native plains artists and craftspeople, used boots and saddles, quilts, jewelry, and sage bundles. It's a beautiful collection, artfully displayed.

FOOD AND ACCOMMODATIONS

Dining options in the park are limited, and the on-site restaurant is closed in winter. If visiting off-season, purchase food in Wall or pack a picnic lunch.

The only lodging, gift store, and restaurant in Badlands National Park is at **Cedar Pass Lodge** (20681 Hwy. 240, 605/433-5460 or 877/386-4383, www.cedarpasslodge.com, mid-Apr.-mid-Oct., new cabins $185, no pets). The facility opened in 1928, and by 2012 the historic cabins were showing signs of age. The resort company began building new cabins, and now all the cabins have been replaced or renovated. The new cabins were constructed to resemble the historic ones but extensively upgraded. The interiors are lined with fallen beetle-kill pine from the Black Hills. The blue streaking on the wood is the result of the trees' defense system kicking in. The cabins have air-conditioning, televisions, refrigerators, microwaves, and coffeemakers. They also have small decks, and the furnishings are made of lodgepole pine. Situated close to the Ben Reifel Visitor Center, the cabins can't be beat for location. It's a short walk to the summer evening astronomy programs put on by the park rangers. If you're looking to experience a park sunrise or sunset, this is the place to stay. The lodge is very popular, so reservations should be made long before you arrive.

The **Cedar Pass Lodge Restaurant** (20681 Hwy. 240, 605/433-5460, www.cedarpasslodge.com, 7am-10am and 11am-8pm daily Memorial Day-Labor Day, call for hours mid-Apr.-Memorial Day and Labor Day-Oct., $9-14) has grab-and-go as well as dine-in options. While the classic Indian taco on fry bread is the signature dish, there are also healthier choices, including a salads, sandwiches, and burgers. Adjacent to the restaurant is a lovely gift shop featuring jewelry, books, camping supplies, travel mugs, and souvenirs. The reservation desk for the lodge

THE BADLANDS
BADLANDS NATIONAL PARK AND VICINITY

and the campground is located in the gift shop area. The campground, lodge, gift shop, and restaurant are all run by the concessionaire **Forever Resorts** (877/386-4383, www.foreverresorts.com).

Limited lodging is available in the small town of Interior, which is just outside of the southern entrance to the North Unit. The 20-room **Badlands Inn** (20615 Hwy. 377, Interior, 605/433-5401, 605/433-5460, or 877/386-4383 www.badlandsinn.com, mid-May-mid-Oct., $135) is within a mile of the park boundary in the town of Interior. The inn is run by the same people who manage the Cedar Pass Lodge. The rooms are double queens and basic. There is a television, a coffeepot, and air-conditioning. The room rate includes a continental breakfast.

The **Badlands Budget Host** (900 Hwy. 377, Interior, 605/433-5335 or 800/388-4643, www.badlandsbudgethostmotel.com, summer $80-140, spring and fall $70-90) is another hotel with location, location, location. About 1.5 miles (2.4 km) from the southern entrance to the North Unit of Badlands National Park, the hotel is plain, but the rooms are clean and reasonable and the view wonderful. The hotel offers free wireless Internet, and a small restaurant is on-site. Pets are allowed for a one-time fee of $25. There is an outdoor pool, laundry facilities, and a small grocery store here, too. Adjacent to the motel and run by the same folks is a small campground. Sites include 30-50 amp hookups ($35-50 daily) to no hookups ($22), which can be for tents or RVs. The campground includes restrooms and a shower house.

The ★ **Circle View Guest Ranch** (20055 E. Hwy. 44, 605/433-5582, www.circleviewranch.com, guesthouse rooms $150-200, bunkhouse rooms $80-125, cabins $165-225, original homestead cabin $55-75) is a working cattle ranch situated on 3,000 acres (1,214 ha) just 6 miles (10 km) west of the park headquarters. The ranch is a year-round bed-and-breakfast and provides visitors in the guest rooms and bunkhouse with a full breakfast, wireless Internet, a fully equipped shared kitchen, private baths, and a game room with foosball, table tennis, and a collection of games. The eight guest rooms have Western decor, with colorful quilts and wood furniture. There are burros to visit and free-range chickens roaming about. The views are gorgeous and the hosts treat guests like family. The bunkhouse has four bedrooms and two baths, one of which is shared. The cabins do not include breakfast. One of the cabins has a full kitchenette and sleeps up to six (price depends on number of guests), and the second cabin has a fridge and microwave and sleeps four. The original homestead cabin is sited on the White River. It has no amenities except an outhouse and a real sense of what living on the prairie used to be like. Homestead cabin visitors may add breakfast for $13 for adults and $7 for children. Additionally, as is the case in many ranch communities, neighbors are frequently family, and the owner of the Circle View is happy to set guests up for horseback rides at the nearby **Hurley Butte Ranch** (19651 E. Hwy. 44, 605/450-1683), which is owned by her brother. For $55, guests and other visitors to the region can experience a one-hour private ride at the ranch along the edge of the Badlands. There are never more than five people on a ride, and frequently it will be just you and the guide.

Camping
Cedar Pass Campground (20681 Hwy. 240, 605/433-5476 or 605/433-5460, www.cedarpasslodge.com, full-service season Apr.-Oct., tent sites $23 for two persons, $4 for each additional person, RV sites with electrical hookups $38 for two, $4 for each additional person, dump station $1; winter $15 for any site with no services) is near the Ben Reifel Visitor Center. In the summer, the campground has cold running water, flush toilets, and picnic tables, and pay-per-use showers are available. In the winter, only picnic tables and trash containers are available. The 96 sites are filled on a first-come, first-served basis. Open campfires are not allowed; however, small propane grills may be used for cooking.

The four group campsites available can be reserved. The cost is $40 for 10 people, plus $5 for each additional person, with a maximum occupancy of 26.

Located off Sage Creek Rim Road, the **Sage Creek Wilderness Campground** is the perfect place to begin an overnight stay in the park. The price is definitely right—camping here is free—but the facilities are primitive. There are picnic tables and pit toilets. Pack in water, because none is available at this location. A portion of the campground is set aside for horse use. Motor homes and pull-behind trailers longer than 18 feet (5.5 m) are not allowed (except for horse trailers). Due to fire danger, campfires are not allowed, but charcoal grills and cookstoves can be used. It's available on a first-come, first-served basis. The maximum stay is 14 days.

INFORMATION AND SERVICES
Information

For information about Badlands National Park, contact park headquarters at the **Ben Reifel Visitor Center** (25216 Ben Reifel Rd., Hwy. 240, 605/433-5361, www.nps.gov/badl, 7am-7pm daily May-Sept., 8am-4pm daily Oct.-Apr., closed Thanksgiving, Christmas, and New Year's).

Tour Companies

Several tour companies make day trips out to the Badlands from Rapid City and other communities in the Black Hills. Each company has a slightly different offering. **Affordable Adventures** (5542 Meteor St., Rapid City, 605/342-7691, www.affordableadventuresbh.com, $145 pp) is a small-group tour company that provides standard narrated van tours through the Badlands. The tour includes information about geology, history, and local lore. The fee includes admission to the park but not the price of meals. The Badlands tour includes the Badlands Loop Road, Ben Reifel Visitor Center, and Wall Drug (for shopping and for lunch), as well as the Minuteman Missile National Historic Site and Prairie Homestead sod house, and takes 7-8 hours. Departure time from Rapid City is at 8:30am. This tour is offered year-round. The company is more than happy to design custom tours as well.

Black Hills Adventure Tours (550 Berry Blvd., Rapid City, 605/209-7817, www.blackhillsadventuretours.com, $325 pp, minimum 2 people) offers a scenic tour of sites in and around the Badlands as well as an adventure hiking and exploring tour in the prairies near the park. The tours are for private groups only. The "Prehistoric Bones & Stones" hike is a full day (8-9 hours) with a local expert who discusses the prehistoric creatures that roamed the prairie near the Badlands, while pointing out fossils in the region that most of us wouldn't see on our own. (They must stay where they lay.) In addition, the group will search for prairie agates and (rare) Fairburn agates which, if found, can be kept. The sightseeing tour of Badlands National Park includes a wildlife tour, the Badlands Loop Road, time to browse the Ben Reifel Visitor Center and have lunch at the Cedar Pass Lodge Restaurant, a stop at the Minuteman Missile National Historic Site, and a visit to Wall Drug. Transportation is provided in sport utility vehicles or small vans, depending on the number of participants. Lunch is not included in the fee. Tours are offered year-round.

GeoFunTrek (605/923-8386 or 605/430-1531, www.geofuntrek.com, $550 for 2, $100 each additional person, all admissions paid, snacks provided) provides custom private tours for families or groups of friends. All of the tours are guided by the owners of the company. One of the owners of the company loves geology and paleontology, and his knowledge base adds a lot to what visitors learn about the region. Since the Badlands are a land of deposition and erosion, and fossils, it is great to have an expert on board.

For an entirely different experience, **Black Hills Aerial Adventures** (21020 SD-240, I-90, exit 131, at Cactus Flats, look for the helicopter stand just before the park entrance,

605/673-2163, www.coptertours.com, May-Sept., $49-255) offers five different flying tours over the Badlands. View the spires and buttes from an entirely different perspective. The tours are distinguished by miles covered and flight time. The introductory tour ($49) is 6 miles (10 km) and takes 5-6 minutes of flight time. Other choices include 9 miles (15 km, $110), 12 miles (19 km, $135), and 17 miles (27 km, $155). The longest tour ($255) circles about 35 miles (56 km) of the Badlands and provides about 25 minutes of flight time.

Other Services

Campers and backpackers can find groceries at the **Wall Food Center** (103 South Blvd. W., Wall, 605/279-2331). Remember that there is very little in the way of food available in Badlands National Park at any time—and nothing is available October-early May—so the grocery store might be a good option for creating a picnic lunch. Pick up water while you are there.

The **post office** is at 529 Main Street in Wall.

Wall

The town of Wall is just 8 miles (13 km) north of the Pinnacles Entrance to Badlands National Park, and it's the largest service provider of food and accommodations for park-goers in the region. The community is even named for one of the park formations, the wall of spires that runs for miles on the north end of the Badlands. Geologically, the Badlands Wall is the ancient northern bank of the White River which, partnered with the wind, carved out the Badlands formations.

HISTORY

Founded in 1907, the town of Wall was, like many of South Dakota's prairie communities, built on railroad expansion, cattle, and homesteading. In 1931, Wall was a dusty, flat-out broke town with a little over 300 residents. Ted Hustead, a fairly recent graduate of pharmacy school at the time, searched the plains looking for a good place to buy or build a pharmacy of his own and settled on the town of Wall. It was not the best choice, or so it seemed. Cars would chug by the little town on their way to Rapid City, 55 miles (89 km) to the west, but no one stopped in Wall. Ted and his wife, Dorothy, decided to give it five years. As the end of the fifth year drew near and success had still not graced the small pharmacy, Dorothy came up with the idea of enticing motorists off the highway with the promise of free ice water. Ted figured it couldn't hurt and put signs up for miles advertising the free water with jingles that automobile riders could read as they drove. It was an instant hit, and Wall Drug has been the driving force of tourism in Wall ever since. Today, Wall Drug is the largest employer in town, followed by Badlands National Park.

SIGHTS
★ Wall Drug

Wall Drug (510 Main St., 605/279-2175, www.walldrug.com, 8am-8pm daily June-Aug., 8am-5:30pm daily Sept.-May) is the ultimate roadside attraction. Occupying over 76,000 square feet (7,060 sq m), Wall Drug sells all the tourist paraphernalia your heart could desire, and the backyard is home to unlimited photo opportunities—including a giant jackalope saddled up and ready to ride, a roaring, smoke-spewing T. rex, and a splashing water feature to keep the kids cool on hot summer days. But all is not plastic and tack at Wall Drug. The complex is divided into several small shops. A fine art gallery sells paintings, art prints, pottery, and bronze sculptures, and there is a great little bookstore with a fine collection of regional books. Look for Western clothing, leather goods, a rock shop, camping supplies, a jewelry store, a doughnut shop, an espresso bar, and a restaurant. With over

50,000 square feet (4,645 sq m) of shopping space, there is something on hand to fill every need, including camping and cooking supplies, toys for the kids, fossil replicas, magnets, and mugs. It's a long list. And, there is a drugstore. Coffee is still five cents (though better coffee is available for a bit more), and ice water is still free.

Wall Drug still uses highway signs to advertise its offerings. The scope of the sign placement has expanded along with the store's success. Today, you can find signs advertising free ice water at Wall Drug along the highways in many outlying states, including Colorado and Wyoming. Ever visionary, there is even a Wall Drug sign in a London Underground station. And yes, even there, the advertising was successful. Curious Londoners have called the store asking about the signs, and some have come to visit!

National Grasslands Visitor Center

Wall is home to the **National Grasslands Visitor Center** (708 Main St., 605/279-2125, www.fs.usda.gov, 8am-6pm daily summer, 8am-4:30pm Mon.-Fri. off-season). The center features over 20 exhibits highlighting the history of the Great Plains, prairie plants, and animals, including the endangered black-footed ferret and its food source, the prairie dog. A 25-minute film called *America's Grasslands* is shown upon request. The center also has information and maps about recreational opportunities in the grasslands.

★ Minuteman Missile National Historic Site

It is ironic that one of the most frivolous of roadside stops, Wall Drug, is just down the street from one of the most ominous and serious. After World War II, relations between the United States and the Soviet Union became hostile as differences in political ideology and the shadow of atomic warfare loomed over both countries. Fear of nuclear attack created an arms race between the two that resulted in nuclear weapons stockpiles that could have

eliminated life on earth many times over. The Minuteman missile, named after the Minutemen of the Revolutionary War, was the deterrent of choice for the United States. The missile could be launched in less than six minutes and reach its target, up to 6,000 miles (9,660 km) away, in less than 30. Even if the Soviet Union made a first-strike nuclear attack, the United States could respond quickly enough to "take them down with us." Minuteman missiles were armed with the equivalent of over one million tons of dynamite. This is 60 times more powerful than the bomb that was dropped on Hiroshima, Japan, that killed over 140,000 people. It was a devastating scenario. Minuteman missiles were developed in 1950, though the Minuteman II missiles of South Dakota were built in 1960. In South Dakota, there were 150 launch silos and 15 launch control centers, all of which were operational by 1963.

In 1991, President George H. W. Bush and Soviet leader Mikhail Gorbachev signed the Strategic Arms Reduction Act Treaty (START) to reduce those stockpiles. All Minuteman II missile sites in South Dakota were deactivated. The START agreement did allow for one launch facility to serve as an interpretive location, and Launch Facility Delta-09 in South Dakota was designated to be that place.

Three sites within miles of each other comprise the historic site. There is the visitor center, the launch control facility, and the missile launch site. The **Minuteman Missile Visitor Contact Center** (I-90, exit 131, on the north side of the highway, 605/433-5552, www.nps.gov/mimi, Wed.-Sun. 8am-4pm daily summer, 9am-3pm Wed.-Sun. off-season, free) is right off I-90 at exit 131. It is impossible to miss. Don't call and ask for the address to feed to your GPS system, however, because you will be misdirected (the rangers specifically asked that I mention that). The visitor center has several exhibits that provide a frightening view of what the Cold War was all about. The center exhibits include the history of the Cold War, the resulting "family basement bomb shelter" trend, a feature on the missileers,

and the scope of the destruction that would have ensued if the missiles had ever been used. All visitors planning on taking the Launch Control Facility Delta-01 tour will need to stop at the visitor center before heading out on the ranger-guided 40-minute survey. **Reservations** (adult $12, youth 6-16 $8) are required and can be made by calling 605/717-7629 or online at www.npsreservations.com/minuteman-missile. They can be made 90 days in advance, and for the summer season it's highly recommended that reservations are made early.

Launch Control Facility Delta-01 (advance reservations required) off I-90, exit 127, about 4 miles (6 km) from park headquarters, is the control facility for the missile launch. It is here that the missileers—those responsible for the firing of the missile, should the need arise—lived and worked (in three-day-on, three-day-off shifts). The upper floors of the site housed the living quarters for the eight personnel required to maintain the site. Basketball courts were installed outdoors, and a television room, library, and weight room were installed inside. The work of the missileers involved hours and hours of boredom, since their only real task was to wait for a signal to launch a nuclear attack. Underneath the living quarters, 31 feet (9 m) down, was the launch control facility. There were two missileers in the underground facility at all times. Should an emergency war order come through, the missileers would decode it, agree to its authenticity, and then both missileers would open their personal combination safes to retrieve their own keys. Two keys, turned simultaneously, were required to launch the missile. The key slots were set more than 12 feet apart so that one person could not launch the missile alone. Debunking the Hollywood myth, there never was a red phone or a red button to push for missile launch.

Launch Facility Delta-09 is the actual missile silo. The silo is off I-90 at exit 116. It is

1: the Wall Drug complex 2: Wall Drug T-rex 3: the secret to Wall Drug's success 4: Minuteman Missile National Historic Site

an outside exhibit, and the site is open year-round, weather permitting. There is no charge to visit. After exiting the highway, head south for about 0.5 mile (0.8 km), and the silo will be visible on the right side of the road. The silo that housed the missile is composed of an underground launch tube, 12 feet (4 m) in diameter and 80 feet (24 m) deep. It was capped by a 90-ton overhead door that would blow off when the missile was activated. Today, the door has been pulled partially off, and a glass viewing window has been installed. An unarmed missile sits in the site, and the glass window affords a view straight down into the silo at the warhead. Rangers are stationed at the facility only intermittently, but a self-guided cell phone tour is available April-October. The telephone number is posted at the site.

There are several misconceptions about the missile program that get cleared up on the tour, including the use of dual keys versus a red button. Another misconception was that the missile sites were "top secret." In fact, since the missiles were intended to be deterrents to nuclear war, their existence was highly publicized, and the sites themselves were never hidden. Many, like the silos in South Dakota, were located right next to interstate highways in plain view.

FOOD

The **Red Rock Restaurant** (506 Glenn St., 605/279-2388, 10am-10pm Tues.-Sun., $12-32) is a family style restaurant that serves pies, soups, and salads—all made from scratch. The menu also features a variety of burgers and other sandwiches. Favorite dinner items include locally grown South Dakota beef, and prime rib dinners are served every Saturday night. The decor is comfortable, with pine walls accented with a dark woodsy green. Beer and wine are available.

The **Badlands Saloon & Grille** (509 Main St., 605/279-2210, 10am-2am daily summer, lunch $13-17, dinner $20-33) is a bright and cheerful bar and grill with light wood booths throughout and seating at the bar. The menu is basic with burgers, sandwiches, and pizza the prime items for lunch, which can also be selected for dinner. The pizza comes personal size if desired so that not everyone needs to get pizza if someone in the party is looking for a burger. (But the pizzas are very good.) In the evening the menu includes rib eye, country-fried steak, and fried chicken. The best place to sit for fast service is at the bar.

The **Wall Drug Cafe** (510 Main St., 605/279-2175, www.walldrug.com, 8am-8pm daily June-Aug., 8am-5pm daily Sept.-May, $10-17) offers cafeteria-style dining and seats over 500 people. It's not fancy, but there are some great choices. In the morning, the cake doughnuts are especially delicious, as are the pecan rolls. The hot roast beef sandwich is as good a sandwich as you'll find anywhere. While the vegetarian options are limited, the vegetarian burger was one of the best sampled in the region. Finally, the folks at Wall Drug know how to serve large numbers of folks quickly. While you have your meal, take time to enjoy the huge collection of Western art displayed on the walls. The café is set up with two lines: an express line with limited menu selections and a second line with broader choices. If you are in a hurry, go express!

For packing a picnic without worrying about having the right equipment to do so, there is a **Subway** (218 South Blvd., 605/279-2722, 9am-9pm daily, $6-10) sub shop in town.

ACCOMMODATIONS

The town of Wall has a population hovering just over 800. On any given evening, though, the town can host more than 2,000 visitors. Thanks to Wall Drug and the proximity of Badlands National Park, Wall is full of lodging choices. Many of the chains are there and close to the highway, including **Best Western Plains Motel** (712 Glenn St., 605/279-2145), **Days Inn** (212 10th Ave. N, 605/279-2000 or 800/329-7466), **Travel Lodge** (211 10th St., 605/279-2133), **Americas Best Value Inn** (201 S. Boulevard, 605/279-2127), as are several locally owned establishments.

The ★ **Frontier Cabins Motel** (1101

S. Glenn St., 605/279-2619 or 888/200-8519, www.frontiercabins.net, Memorial Day-Sept. cabins $135-157, tipis $79, Apr.-May and Sept. cabins $95-130, Oct.-Nov. cabins $65-80, add $10 for meadow view) is just off exit 110 on I-90. The motel has 33 rustic cabins with a long list of amenities, including free wireless Internet, microwaves, refrigerators, coffeemakers, air-conditioning, and ceiling fans in every room. There are laundry facilities on-site, and the cabins are all smoke-free. No pets are allowed. There is a nice-size gift shop here, as well as a picnic area, a hot tub, and a playground for the children. The cabins are pine-paneled and nicely decorated in basic hunting lodge/Western style. The tipis are not heated or air-conditioned, but include two cots, two sleeping bags, and a small table. A bath and shower are available to tipi guests.

For basic accommodations, check out **Sunshine Inn** (608 Main St., 605/279-2178 or 800/782-2613, www.wallsunshineinn.weebly.com, May-mid-Oct., $70-85). Owned by the same family since "sometime in the '70s," the inn offers 26 clean rooms, free Wi-Fi, and coffee and juice in the morning. Pets are allowed for an $8 per pet per night. It's the perfect spot for a really reasonable stay near the park.

Campers should check out the **Sleepy Hollow Campground** (118 W. 4th Ave., 605/279-2100, www.sleepyhollowsd.com, mid-Apr.-mid.-Oct., tent sites $30, RV sites $43-54). The campground is off I-90, exit 109, and within easy walking distance of downtown Wall. All 59 RV sites are pull-through. Facilities include a laundry and a small pool. There are free showers on-site, pets are welcome (there is even a fenced-in dog park!), and free Wi-Fi is available. It's a nicely treed, lovely spot to stay.

INFORMATION AND SERVICES

Contact the **Wall Chamber of Commerce** (501 Main St., 605/279-2665 or 888/852-9255, www.wall-badlands.com, 8am-5pm Mon.-Fri.) for additional information about the town of Wall. Campers and backpackers can find groceries at the **Wall Food Center** (103 South Blvd. W., 605/279-2331). For any medical issues that arise, there is a **Monument Health Wall Clinic** (112 7th Ave., 605/279-2149, 7:30am-5pm Mon.-Thurs.) in Wall. Remember that there is very little in the way of food available in Badlands National Park at any time, and nothing is available October-early May, so the grocery store might be a good option for creating a picnic lunch. Pick up water while you are there. The **post office** is at 529 Main Street.

Pine Ridge Reservation

The Pine Ridge Reservation in the southwest corner of South Dakota is home to the Oglala Sioux Nation. One of the largest reservations in the United States, it encompasses 3,468 square miles (8,982 sq km) of land of varying attributes. In the northwest corner, the multihued peaks, spires, grassy tables, and valleys of the South Unit of the Badlands occupy 160,000 acres (64,750 ha). The land just south of the Badlands, west and central in the reservation, touches the outer spurs of the Black Hills, with low rolling hills, stands of ponderosa pine, and mixed-grass prairie. The southern and eastern areas of the reservation are prairie grasslands.

Life for the Oglala Sioux (Lakota) has not been easy. Forced to move onto reservation land at the end of the Indian Wars of 1876, stripped of their lands and livelihood, their language, and, in many cases, their culture, the Lakota people still have a long road of healing ahead of them. In terms of relative time, the wounds are recent, though the damage is deep. There are signs, however, that out of the poverty and pain a new nation of Oglala Lakota leaders have emerged, who will work to bring the community to spiritual and economic health.

Today, the people of Pine Ridge work to share their culture with the world outside the reservation boundaries. Their lands are beautiful, their history important. Visit the Red Cloud Indian School and learn about them. Stop at Prairie Wind Casino, one of the first ventures to bring visitors to the reservation, and test your luck. Honor those who were massacred at Wounded Knee. Seek out a powwow. Go hiking near the Badlands and visit the art galleries and shops of the small communities of the Pine Ridge Reservation.

PLANNING YOUR VISIT

With the exception of the South Unit (Stronghold District) of Badlands National Park, the Pine Ridge Reservation is privately owned land. It is a good idea to plan ahead for a visit to the reservation. The area is vast and the towns are small. A visit to Pine Ridge is more about the culture and history than sightseeing. A large part of the experience is meeting people. Some restaurants are in people's homes, and bed-and-breakfasts are in backyards. The powwows are community ceremonies. There isn't much in the way of tourist services on Pine Ridge. Some of the lodges and inns will contact local guides if you're interested in a tour of the reservation, horseback riding excursion, or other community events.

There are sights to see without making arrangements through lodgings, but planning ahead is highly recommended. Many of the art galleries on the reservation are run by the artists themselves, and they aren't always available. The reservation is large, and a long drive should end with more than an empty studio. Call before you leave. And once you get started? Tune your radio to KILI, 90.1 FM, and enjoy listening to the best in community-oriented radio broadcasting.

A suggested route specifically for a visit to the Pine Ridge Reservation from Rapid City will bring you past some beautiful overlooks into the Badlands located on the reservation, as well as to the Red Cloud Indian School,

Pine Ridge Reservation

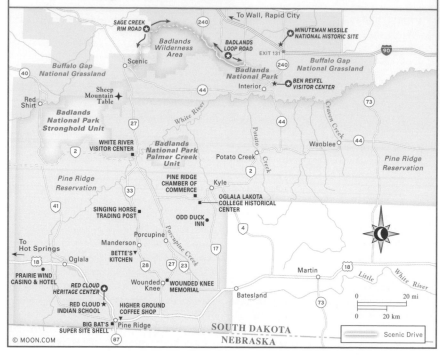

To Wall, Rapid City

SAGE CREEK RIM ROAD

MINUTEMAN MISSILE NATIONAL HISTORIC SITE

Badlands Wilderness Area

BADLANDS LOOP ROAD

EXIT 131

Buffalo Gap National Grassland

Scenic

Badlands National Park

BEN REIFEL VISITOR CENTER

Interior

Sheep Mountain Table

Red Shirt

White River

Badlands National Park Stronghold Unit

Potato Creek

Wanblee

Pine Ridge Reservation

Craven Creek

WHITE RIVER VISITOR CENTER

Badlands National Park Palmer Creek Unit

Potato Creek

Pine Ridge Reservation

PINE RIDGE CHAMBER OF COMMERCE

Kyle

OGLALA LAKOTA COLLEGE HISTORICAL CENTER

SINGING HORSE TRADING POST

ODD DUCK INN

Porcupine

Porcupine Creek

Manderson

BETTE'S KITCHEN

Martin

Little White River

To Hot Springs

Oglala

PRAIRIE WIND CASINO & HOTEL

RED CLOUD HERITAGE CENTER

Wounded Knee

WOUNDED KNEE MEMORIAL

Batesland

0   20 mi

0   20 km

RED CLOUD INDIAN SCHOOL

HIGHER GROUND COFFEE SHOP

BIG BAT'S SUPER SITE SHELL

Pine Ridge

SOUTH DAKOTA

NEBRASKA

Scenic Drive

© MOON.COM

Red Cloud Heritage Center, the Wounded Knee Memorial, and Oglala Lakota College Historical Center. Take Highway 79 South to Hermosa. Head east on Highway 40 (which turns into BIA 41). Turn left on U.S. 18 to Pine Ridge. Continue on U.S. 18 until you arrive at the intersection with BIA 27 and turn left. Continue on until the intersection with BIA 2 and take a right on it to Kyle. Turn left on Highway 44 to Interior and the southern entrance to Badlands National Park. This route takes about 3.5 hours without stops, but plan on this being an all-day trip. Spend the night at a hotel in Interior or at the Cedar Pass Lodge or Campground in Badlands National Park. If coming from Hot Springs, follow U.S. 385/18 to Pine Ridge and continue from there. That will cut out an hour from the drive time.

HISTORY

The Fort Laramie Treaty of 1868 defined the **Great Sioux Nation** as including all the lands from the Nebraska line to the 46th parallel between the Missouri River and the 104th meridian. That definition encompasses the entire Black Hills region. Settlers in the Dakota Territory were unhappy with the treaty. It had always been assumed that there might be a great deal of mineral wealth in the region, and as early as 1872, the editor of the Sioux City newspaper began publishing stories about the prospects for gold in the hills, as well as openly soliciting recruits for an expedition. The expedition didn't happen, thanks to military commands to abandon the project, but support for an excursion clearly existed in high levels of government. The secretary of the interior openly proclaimed that the Black

Hills were not necessary to the happiness and prosperity of the Native peoples.

Not all the Native Americans in the Black Hills region had agreed to sign the 1868 treaty, and so it was decided that an exploratory expedition should head into the hills, ostensibly searching for a good location for a military post. **Lieutenant Colonel George A. Custer** was assigned to command the enterprise. The Custer Expedition set out for the hills in July 1874. It was an unusual expedition from the get-go. Over a thousand military troops were part of the group. Native scouts, newspaper correspondents, miners, a scientific corps, a musical band, and many civilian employees were also included on the roster of personnel. The expedition never reported on a good location for a military post, but it did publicize the discovery of gold in the hills. Dispatches confirming gold in the Black Hills were sent in early August. By August 12, 1874, the news was released to the general public.

The first few gold-seeking parties were escorted out of the Black Hills by the military. But the trespassing prospectors came from all directions, and by 1875, at least 800 miners had eluded the government patrols and were working in the Black Hills. While the military was trying to keep the prospectors out, local communities to the east were demanding that the hills be opened to settlers. The government decided to open negotiations and arranged for a delegation of Native American chiefs to visit the capital in 1875. The chiefs refused to give up the Black Hills and returned home. But despite this refusal, the government held a Grand Council with the tribes in late 1875 and offered $400,000 annually for mining rights to the hills, or, alternatively, $6 million for the outright purchase of the land. This offer was also refused. The government's response was to withdraw the cavalry from the hills, essentially allowing trespassers free access. Instead of stopping provision trains carrying food and supplies to the mining camps, the freighters were advised to arm themselves against "hostile natives." The result of that

decision was the beginning of another round of Indian Wars.

By the end of the year, continual skirmishes were occurring in the Bighorn Mountains and Powder River regions of Wyoming to the north and west of the Black Hills. Military leaders decided that the appropriate action would be a show of force that would bring the tribespeople into the agencies. General Crook initiated a campaign against the tribes in early 1876 from Fort Fetterman in Wyoming, heading for the Powder River country with only 900 troops. After an unsuccessful attack against a band of Cheyenne and a band of Oglala Lakota under the leadership of Lakota warrior **Crazy Horse,** General Crook and his troops returned to the fort with plans to wait until spring before taking further military action. As spring approached, an attack strategy was designed to overwhelm the Native people with three columns of troops: one led by General Crook, heading north from Fort Fetterman; one led by Colonel Gibbon, heading south from Montana and following the Yellowstone River; and one led by General Terry, moving west from the Little Missouri. Lieutenant Colonel Custer was in command of the 7th Cavalry under General Terry. Custer did not wait for Crook and Gibbon to arrive once he discovered a Native American camp. He divided his small army into three segments, keeping just 223 men by his side. While the other two segments of his command had to retreat from their attack positions and were able to join up, they were not able to go to the aid of Custer, whose forces were completely annihilated. Known as "Custer's Last Stand," it was the last of the major battles to be won by Native American forces.

Offensive attacks on the Sioux resumed in August 1876. At several of the agencies, friendly Natives were disarmed and their ponies taken as a preventative measure. Led by Crazy Horse, two-thirds of the Lakota, who had taken part in the Battle of the Little Bighorn, spent the winter of 1876-1877 in the Powder River area. The military alternately skirmished and attempted negotiations. In

The Wounded Knee Massacre

In 1877, the Oglala Sioux surrendered to military forces, and in 1878, in accordance with the treaty, they moved onto the Pine Ridge Reservation. It was a complete departure from their historical and cultural traditions. The nomadic life became sedentary. The hunting life ceased to exist, both with the demise of the bison and the enforced attempts at agriculture on the reservation. The mission of the government was to push the Lakota to give up their culture completely and assimilate into mainstream U.S. culture. Reservation schools and boarding schools were established, and the Lakota language was banned. Traditional dances and ceremonies were also banned. And, just four years after the treaty that forced the people onto reservations, the government wanted to take more land. Justifiably, there was a lot of unrest on the reservation.

In the midst of all this unrest, a new movement, a new religion, was rising in Nevada. At the center of the religion was a ceremony called the **Ghost Dance.** At the heart of the religion was the belief that the ceremony would cause the encroaching settlers to go away and Native Americans would be able to return to their former lives. Hearing about this new movement, a delegation from the Cheyenne River Reservation and another from the Rosebud Reservation headed to Nevada to learn more. When they returned, they introduced the Ghost Dance to Pine Ridge and then to the Rosebud and Cheyenne Reservations. The newly appointed Pine Ridge administrator panicked and called in the military.

When the soldiers arrived, the Ghost Dancers, fearing for their lives, fled into the Badlands. Rumors started that Sitting Bull, who had returned from Canada and was living near Standing Rock, was going to join the dancers in the south, and his arrest was ordered. When his band was found, they resisted, and Sitting Bull and several of his warriors were killed on December 15, 1890. A band of dancers traveling with Chief Big Foot on their way to surrender heard about the death of Sitting Bull and fled. They were intercepted by units from the 7th Cavalry and escorted to upper Wounded Knee Creek. On the morning of December 29, cavalry members entered Big Foot's camp to search for weapons and disarm the Native Americans. But before they entered the camp, several Hotchkiss machine guns were set up on the ridge, trained on the camp below. In the course of the search, a shot was fired, and the cavalry retaliated with the Hotchkiss guns and other weapons. The number of dead is disputed, but at least 200 men, women, and children, including Big Foot, either died on the battlefield or later from their wounds or hypothermia. The bodies were found as far as 2 miles (3 km) away, as people were killed while they were trying to flee. It was the last major encounter between tribespeople and the military in the West.

The Wounded Knee Massacre was brought to national attention again in 1973 when a group of activists involved in the American Indian Movement (AIM) took over the village of Wounded Knee, laying siege to it for 71 days. Their demands were for hearings to be held on violations by the U.S. government regarding land use and treaty rights and investigations of other grievances. Their cause elicited a lot of support, but their violent means created conflict not only between the outside and reservation communities, but between tribal factions, as well. Shots were also fired at this Wounded Knee conflict, resulting in two deaths and nearly a dozen other gunshot wounds. Subsequently, charges brought against the AIM members were dismissed when the court judge found the FBI guilty of gross misconduct for its part in the skirmish.

February 1877, the military went to Spotted Tail, a chief at one of the friendly camps that had not been disarmed, for assistance. Spotted Tail convinced many of his people to surrender. Some headed into Canada under the leadership of Sitting Bull, but by May 1877, nearly 4,500 people went to the agencies. Crazy Horse and his band were the last to come in.

They went to the Red Cloud Agency, where Crazy Horse was killed when he resisted being placed in confinement.

The tragic events of the 1876 battles gave Congress the power and popular support to pass an appropriations bill that dictated that the Sioux would not receive any further appropriations unless they gave up the Black Hills.

Commissioners went to several agencies of the Sioux carrying the new agreement. Without horses or weapons, the Lakota gave in. Under the terms, they sacrificed the Black Hills and all hunting rights in Montana and Wyoming. In lieu of money, the government committed to providing rations until the Lakota could support themselves. The tribes were to be relocated to reservation lands. Many of those that had previously surrendered fled north to join Sitting Bull in Canada. Of those that remained, Spotted Tail's Brule band relocated to Rosebud Creek, and the Oglala Lakota picked their site at Pine Ridge, a few miles north of the Nebraska border.

SIGHTS
Wounded Knee Memorial
On a dusty hilltop overlooking the grassy plains of the Pine Ridge Reservation, the Wounded Knee Memorial is a small fenced-in cemetery, within which a tall stone stands as quiet testimony, covered with the names of some of the many Lakota who were killed at the Wounded Knee Massacre of 1890. The memorial has no real address, no telephone number, no hours, and no admission fee. It sits at the junction of BIA 27 and BIA 28 just south of the community of Porcupine.

★ Red Cloud Heritage Center
The **Red Cloud Heritage Center** (100 Mission Dr., Pine Ridge, 605/867-5491, www.redcloudschool.org, 8am-noon Mon.-Fri., free, donations accepted) is on the grounds of the Red Cloud Indian School off U.S. 18, just west of the community of Pine Ridge. The Red Cloud Indian School started its affiliation with the Pine Ridge Reservation as the Jesuit Holy Rosary Mission. The reservation was deemed an Episcopal reservation by the U.S. government, but Chief Red Cloud chose the Jesuits (the "Black Robes") to provide Native American children with the education they would need to survive in both the outside and tribal worlds and requested that they be allowed on the reservation. The mission was built in 1888. Today, the school teaches over

600 students from kindergarten through high school and has moved out of the old mission into larger classroom buildings on campus.

The Red Cloud Heritage Center opened in 1982 and is housed in the old mission building. The museum's fine arts collection has over 10,000 pieces, including paintings, drawings, and sculptures. The tribal arts collection focuses on Native American artifacts reflecting Oglala culture and history. For 10 weeks every summer (June-mid-August) the Heritage Center hosts the **Red Cloud Indian Art Show,** which brings together the work of artists from Native American tribes across the United States and Canada. Started in 1969, it is one of the longest-running Native American art shows in the country and includes some truly exquisite pieces. There is a **gift shop** adjacent to the museum where the works of local Lakota artists are available for sale. Choose from an extensive collection of porcupine quillwork, beadwork, and a variety of traditional plains art including jewelry, pottery, glassware, star quilts, buffalo hides, and other specialty items.

Just to the left of the Heritage Center building, you will see a path that heads up a small hill and ends at the cemetery. It is in this cemetery that **Chief Red Cloud** lies buried. Red Cloud was one of the great Lakota chiefs and one of the signers of the original Fort Laramie Treaty.

Be sure to visit the **Holy Rosary Church** on the school property. The original structure burned to the ground in 1996. The new building, opened in 1998, contains beautiful Lakota-designed stained-glass windows.

Red Cloud Indian School
The **Red Cloud Indian School** (100 Mission Dr., Pine Ridge, 605/867-5491, www.redcloudschool.org) offers campus tours (10am Mon.-Fri, adult $12, child 12 and under free). The narrated tour takes about one hour and includes a walk about the campus while learning about Lakota history. Tour guides are Red Cloud graduates. The tour also includes a visit to Red Cloud's memorial gravesite and

Powwows

powwow on the plains

The powwow (*wacipi*) is a Native American celebration enjoyed throughout the United States. It is a time to celebrate, to honor, and sometimes to mourn. It is a time to sing and dance and a time to renew friendships. Powwows are colorful and rhythmic, an art form with historic roots that continues to evolve in contemporary culture.

Powwows are generally two to three days long. Passes can be purchased for a single day or for the weekend. The grand entry is a highlight not to be missed. Several large annual powwows throughout the Black Hills welcome visitors (fees vary):

- The **Black Hills State University Lakota Omniciye Wacipi** (1200 University St., Spearfish, 800/255-2478 or 605/642-6578, www.bhsu.edu) is held annually in mid-April. It is organized through the BHSU Center for Indian Studies and has been held for over 35 years.

- The **Oglala Lakota College Graduation Wacipi** (Pine Ridge Reservation, powwow grounds in Kyle, call Oglala Lakota College for details 605/454-6000, www.olc.edu) is held in mid-June as a graduation ceremony for students and the community.

- The **Oglala Nation Wacipi Rodeo & Fair** (Pine Ridge Reservation, powwow grounds in Pine Ridge, call Pine Ridge Chamber of Commerce for details 605/455-2685, http://oglalanationpowwow.com) is held the first full weekend in August and includes a rodeo.

- The **Black Hills Pow Wow** (Rushmore Plaza Civic Center, 444 N. Mt. Rushmore Rd., Rapid City, 605/394-4111 or 605/341-0925, www.blackhillspowwow.com) has been held for over 40 years and is one of the premier gatherings in the country. It is held over the weekend of Native American Day in early October.

In addition to the large celebrations, community powwows are held most weekends at various locations in the hills early spring-late fall. Check with the local chamber of commerce to see where an open powwow may be held during your visit. If in Rapid City, check with Prairie Edge Galleries for a powwow listing.

the Holy Rosary Church. After the tour, participants will have time to visit the Red Cloud Heritage Center to view the artwork on display and access the gift shop where Native American-made jewelry and other gift items may be purchased.

Pine Ridge Chamber of Commerce Visitor Center

The **Pine Ridge Chamber of Commerce Visitor Center** (7900 Lakota Prairie Dr., Kyle, 605/455-2685, www.pineridgechamber.com, typically 9am-5pm Mon.-Fri., call to confirm hours) hosts a different Lakota artist every week from early June to late August. Check the website for virtual introductions. It's also a good place to call and check on local powwows and other events on the reservation.

Oglala Lakota College Historical Center

On the campus of the Oglala Lakota College, the **Historical Center** (490 Piya Wiconi Rd., Kyle, 605/455-6000, ext. 6139, www.olc.edu/about/historical_center.htm, 9am-5pm Mon.-Fri. June-Aug.) chronicles the history of the Lakota with historic photos, displays, and artwork. The history covered dates from the early 1800s to the Wounded Knee Massacre in 1890. An audiotape is available for greater understanding of the displays. In addition to historical exhibits, a different artist is featured every week throughout the summer.

Prairie Wind Casino

The **Prairie Wind Casino** (112 Casino Dr., 12 mi/19 km east of Oelrichs on U.S. 18, 605/867-6300 or 800/705-9463, www.prairiewindcasino.com, 9am-1am Sun.-Thurs., 24 hours Fri.-Sat.) started as a couple of double-wide trailers, graduated to a tent-like building, and, in 2007, opened its current complex, which includes the casino, a hotel, and a restaurant. Blackjack, poker, and video and slot machines are the order of the day. In addition, craps and roulette can be played at the casino. Tournaments are held on a regular basis. Call the casino for information about the schedule. No alcohol is served on reservation land. There is a hotel and a restaurant on-site.

RECREATION
Horseback Riding

Horseback riding is available year-round at the **Singing Horse Trading Post** (1210 BIA 33, Porcupine, 605/455-2143, www.singinghorse.net, $45 for the first hour and two hours for $80). The trading post is about 7 miles (11 km) north of Manderson on BIA 33, about 0.5 mile (0.8 km) past the intersection with BIA 14, on the right. Ask about other options, including half-or full-day rides, overnight rides, and rides into the Badlands. Please call in advance to arrange your ride and for additional pricing information.

EVENTS

The **Oglala Nation Wacipi Rodeo & Fair** is held the first weekend in August at the powwow grounds at Pine Ridge. There is a gate fee set by the Tribal Office early in the year. Call the **Pine Ridge Chamber of Commerce** (605/455-2685, www.pineridgechamber.com) or the **Tribal Office** (605/867-5821, ext. 222 or 227) for directions and more information. The event includes powwows and the rodeo.

A **powwow** is a community celebration and dance competition. Be sure to be on time for the grand entry, which is the opening ceremony for the powwow. It is a swirl of color and movement as contestants from each dance category enter the powwow grounds. Watch for the incredibly beautiful beadwork on the deerskin dresses of the traditional women dancers. Listen to the chiming of the hundreds of tiny bell-like jingle cones sewn on each dress of the jingle dancers. Enjoy the sinuous movements of the grass dancers and the flashing swirl of color and movement that announce the arrival of the fancy dancers. The dances are performed to drums, and the dancers are judged on their poise, footwork, demeanor, and showmanship. The powwow is held outside and chairs are not provided, so bring something to sit on.

SHOPPING

The **Singing Horse Trading Post** (1210 BIA 33, Porcupine, 605/455-2143, www.singinghorse.net, noon-8pm Mon.-Sat., noon-6pm Sun. summer, noon-6pm Mon.-Sat. winter) started out as a supplier for Lakota arts and crafts, an enterprise it continues to this day. The trading post now also carries finished Lakota-made arts and crafts, as well. They have a wonderful collection of pieces adorned with beautiful beadwork, quillwork, star quilts, and paintings. The trading post is about 7 miles (11 km) north of Manderson on BIA 33, about 0.5 mile (0.8 km) past the intersection with BIA 14, on the right.

FOOD

Every community needs a great morning meeting place, and Pine Ridge has the ★ **Higher Ground Coffee Shop** (U.S. 18, Pine Ridge, 605/867-5685, 7am-1pm Mon. and Wed.-Fri., breakfast $5, lunch $9-13). In downtown Pine Ridge, across the street from Pizza Hut on U.S. 18, look for a rose-colored building with coffee beans stenciled on the walls just below the roofline. This is a warm, welcoming place with a fireplace and a wraparound deck that serves pastries and breakfast burritos in the morning and creates a luncheon special every day. The daily special varies from sandwiches to casseroles to whatever the owner is in the mood to create. All the pastries and breads are made from scratch, and homemade pies are served seasonally. And, of course, there is a full menu of hot and cold coffee and other specialty drinks including smoothies. Free wireless Internet is available.

The **Food Stop** (100 Main St., Kyle, 605/455-2866, 8am-4pm Mon.-Fri., $5-10) is located in the oldest building on the reservation. It looks a little rough on the outside, but it's fine on the inside, with a few tables and booths, wood paneling, and Native American artifacts on the walls. Breakfast choices include eggs, biscuits and gravy options, omelets, pancakes, and French toast. Lunch presents a wide selection of burgers and sandwiches. Other choices include chicken strips and drumsticks, hot wings, and finger steaks, all at very reasonable prices.

Not only will you get home cooking at **Bette's Kitchen** (101 Black Elk Rd., Manderson, 605/867-1739, 11:30am-2pm daily, $7-9), you'll be served in Bette's home. She is a descendant of Black Elk, and her home is on historic Black Elk land. She is also a former nutritionist. The specialty of the house is soup made from scratch with homemade bread. Bette is happy to accommodate vegetarians with veggie burgers or vegetarian soup. Relax and enjoy this little center of community activity. The kitchen is 1 mile (1.6 km) south of Manderson, or 7 miles (11 km) north of the Wounded Knee Memorial, off BIA 28. Look for the signs, as the driveway can be hard to see. Bette's home sits on a ridge on the left as you go up the hill. Large groups can be accommodated, but call ahead!

Twelve miles (19 km) east of Oelrichs or 30 miles (48 km) west of Pine Ridge, off U.S. 18, the **Stronghold Restaurant** (U.S. 18, 605/867-8956, www.prairiewindcasino.com, 9am-11pm Wed.-Sun., lunch $9-15, dinner $15-30) is on the grounds of the Prairie Wind Casino & Hotel. Patrons can dine-in or take out. The dining room is large but cozy with wood floors and muted wall colors highlighted by original paintings from local artists. Breakfast includes doughnuts, breakfast burritos, biscuits and gravy, and breakfast sandwiches. The lunch menu features a wide selection of burgers and hot sandwiches, and adds T-bone steak, grilled chicken, chicken-fried steak, and fish-and-chips for dinner.

Big Bat's Super-Site Shell (junction U.S. 18 and Hwy. 407, Pine Ridge, 605/867-5077, 24 hours daily, limited grill items available to 11pm, breakfast $9, lunch and dinner $12) is part museum, part gift shop, part gas station, and part restaurant, all rolled into one. It is the center of a lot of Pine Ridge activity. The store is named after Baptiste Gene Pourier (Big

---

1: Wounded Knee Memorial **2:** Lakota stained-glass windows at the Holy Rosary Church

Bat), a Frenchman born in 1834 who married a Lakota woman named Jean Richards. With his ability to speak French, English, and Lakota, Big Bat worked as an interpreter for the negotiation of the Fort Laramie Treaty in 1868. The current owners, Bat and Patty Pourier, are Big Bat's great-great-grandchildren. The restaurant serves a full breakfast menu, including egg dishes, waffles, and pancakes. Lunch and dinner include a variety of sandwiches including buffalo burgers, burritos, and subs, as well as a daily lunch special. The ceilings are high and the acoustics are poor, so it can be a little loud inside. Look for some special touches. Don Montileaux, a Lakota artist, was hired to do all the artwork for the building. Montileaux created a 108-foot (33-m) mural based on Lakota oral history, telling stories related by his grandfather, including "Buffalo Calf Woman" and "The Horse Story." There are historical photos on the wall, and many Lakota symbols and beliefs are displayed and explained throughout the store. After lunch, you can fill your gas tank while you're there!

ACCOMMODATIONS

Located in the southwest corner of the Pine Ridge Reservation, the **Prairie Wind Casino & Hotel** (U.S. 18, Pine Ridge, 605/867-6300 or 800/705-9463, www.prairiewindcasino. com, summer $95-125, off-season $65-90) is 12 miles (19 km) east of Oelrichs, or 30 miles (48 km) west of the town of Pine Ridge on U.S. 18. Amenities include an indoor swimming pool, a hot tub, a laundry facility, and a fitness center. Some of the rooms (first floor) include microwave ovens, small coffeemakers, and small refrigerators. Guests may ask for larger coffeemakers at the front desk. All 78 rooms are decorated in Native American style, and all are nonsmoking. The hotel has a restaurant on-site.

The **Singing Horse Trading Post** (1210 BIA 33, Porcupine, 605/455-2143, www. singinghorse.net, mobile home and cabin from $175, cowboy cabins $40 pp per night) has an eclectic mix of offerings for guests. The newest addition is a cozy cabin with a separate bedroom, kitchenette, and bath. Linens and towels are provided. There are two "cowboy cabins" on the property; designed in a Western style, the cabins each have two sets of bunk beds. The bath and shower for the cowboy cabins are located in the main building. Linens and towels are provided. There is also a three-bedroom mobile home on the property with full kitchen, bath, and shower. Camping is allowed in specific areas on-site but there are no hookups of any kind, though the bath and shower at the main house are available to campers.

The **Odd Duck Inn** (Kyle, 605/455-2972 or 605/890-6280 www.oddduckinn.com, $75) is owned and operated by Oglala Lakota tribe member Tilda Long Soldier-St. Pierre and her husband, renowned author Mark St. Pierre. Their inn is north and east of Kyle. Take BIA 2 east from Kyle to the junction of BIA 17. Head south about 2 miles (3 km) and watch for the signs. The Odd Duck Inn is about 4 miles (6 km) down a gravel road. The inn has two homes available for guests—a total of eight rooms. There are three shared kitchens, but you need to bring your own food. Four bathrooms are available. The homes are also equipped with central air, laundry, dishwashers, and wireless Internet. If you are interested in learning about Lakota culture, this is a great place to start. Mark and Tilda are willing to arrange or conduct arts, Lakota culture, Western and Native American, or wildlife tours for guests ($225 base cost, plus $25 pp up to a maximum of four participants, for an eight-hour day).

INFORMATION AND SERVICES
Information

The **Pine Ridge Chamber of Commerce** (7900 Lakota Prairie Dr., Kyle, 605/455-2685, www.pineridgechamber.com, typically 9am-5pm Mon.-Fri., call to confirm hours) has information on powwows and other community events, reservation maps, and business directories. The chamber also keeps a list of local tour guides to the Pine Ridge Reservation.

Medical services can be found at **Pine**

Ridge Hospital (E. U.S. 18, Pine Ridge, 605/867-5131), **Kyle Health Center** (Wapiyapi Ave., Kyle, 605/455-2541), and **Wanblee Health Center** (210 1st St., Wanblee, 605/462-6155).

There are groceries at **Kyle Grocery** (Kyle, 605/455-2824, 7:30am-7:30pm Mon.-Sat., 10am-6pm Sun.) as well as gas pumps and an ATM machine. In the Pine Ridge area, groceries are available at **Buche Foods** (560 S. 1st St., Pine Ridge, 605/867-5183, 8am-10pm Mon.-Sat., 10am-10pm Sun.), which also has a hardware store and ATM services.

Be sure to listen to **KILI Radio** (605/867-5002, www.kiliradio.org, 90.1 FM Reservation, 88.7 Rapid City) while you are visiting the reservation, and pick up a copy of the **Lakota Times newspaper** (605/685-1868, www.lakotatimes.com). The paper is published weekly and can be found at convenience stores and grocery stores throughout the reservation.

Tour Companies

If staying on or visiting the reservation, tours can be arranged through some of the local businesses. Check with the **Odd Duck Inn** (Kyle, 605/455-2972 or 605/890-6280) or the **Singing Horse Trading Post** (Porcupine, 605/455-2143) to make arrangements for tours with local guides or to get information about current events.

Access to the Pine Ridge Reservation is primarily by car. It is possible, however, to arrange a tour with **Affordable Adventures** (5542 Meteor St., Rapid City, 605/342-7691, www.affordableadventuresbh.com, $185 pp, limited availability), a small-group tour company that provides narrated tours in small vans. The tours start in Rapid City, travel to the town of Scenic, and then head south to the South Unit of the Badlands and to the Pine Ridge Reservation on BIA 27. The tour varies, depending on the weather, but generally includes visits to the South Unit's Sheep Mountain Table and the White River Visitor Center, Oglala Lakota College Historical Center, Wounded Knee Memorial, Red Cloud Heritage Center, and Red Shirt Table. Tours will sometimes include a step-on narration by Native American guides and takes 8-10 hours. Lunch is in Manderson or Kyle.

Background

The Landscape

The Black Hills of South Dakota are frequently referred to as an "Island in the Plains," and the description is an apt one. The Cheyenne River sets the southern border while the Belle Fourche River (pronounced Bell Foosh) defines the northern edge. The Thunder Basin National Grassland of Wyoming to the west and the Buffalo Gap National Grassland to the east complete the circle around the hills. The hills rise over 3,000 feet (914 m) above the plains, reaching their pinnacle of 7,242 feet (2,207 m) at Black Elk Peak, one of the highest points in North America east of the Rocky Mountains. About two-thirds of the hills are

within the confines of the Black Hills National Forest. The southern region is mixed-grass prairie. The north is lush with ponderosa pine, and even the ridges of the rolling hills of the south sport pine silhouettes. Seen from a distance, the deep green trees appear as a dark band on the horizon, giving the area its name. From east to west, about two-thirds of the hills are located in South Dakota, and one-third spills into Wyoming. Several small rivers cut through the hills—most notably Spearfish Creek in the north, Rapid Creek in the central region, and the Fall River in the south—and bring additional recreational and scenic beauty to the area.

GEOLOGY

The Black Hills were formed by an uplift that occurred near the end of the Cretaceous period or the beginning of the Paleogene period, 65-70 million years ago. The uplift created an elliptical dome, at the center of which is a crystalline core, composed of the oldest rocks in the hills. This core is Precambrian, dating back over two billion years. The granite peaks near Mount Rushmore, dominated by the 7,242-foot (2,207-m) Black Elk Peak, are at the center of the uplift. At the time of the uplift, it is estimated that the hills reached an elevation of over 15,000 feet (4,572 m), and the work of wind and water over the last 65 million years has created the hills we see today.

Encircling the Precambrian core of the Black Hills are progressively younger rock layers. Time in the Black Hills looks much like a topographic map, each band a different geological period, marching downward and outward and around the hills, from oldest to youngest through the Precambrian, Paleozoic, Mesozoic, and Cenozoic eras.

Unlike the Black Hills, in the Badlands, the youngest formations are on the top and time marches straight down. Formed primarily by the two geologic processes of deposition and erosion, the oldest exposed (and lowest) layers were created 69-75 million years ago, when the surface area was covered by a warm inland sea. When the hills uplifted, the sea drained away and was replaced by a river floodplain that deposited a new layer every time a flood occurred. A drier period followed, bringing sediments deposited by the wind, the colors varying with time and volcanic activity. As the uplift to the west continued, the water current increased and began to carve into the very deposits earlier streams had left behind. Some 65 million years later, we have the eroded spires and valleys of the Badlands today.

CLIMATE

The Dakotas have the reputation for harsh winters with frequent blizzards and scorching summers, but weather in the Black Hills is much less dramatic. The hills are semiarid, and residents can expect to see an average of 275 days of sunshine per year. Rainfall is generally less than 17 inches (43 cm) per year, and annual snowfall hovers around 40 inches (102 cm), most of which is deposited in the upper elevations. There are regional climate differences in the hills, with temperatures a few degrees cooler and snowfall a few inches greater in the higher elevations of the Central and Northern Hills. The southern fringe of the hills, just south of Custer State Park, is frequently referred to as the "banana belt," with weather generally milder than that of the Northern Hills. Open to the southern chinook winds generated by the Rocky Mountains and protected by the higher peaks to the north from the cold Arctic winds heading south from Canada, Southern Hills weather is not unlike that of Denver, drier and warmer than the regions around it. Like most areas of the world now, the weather has become a little less predictable. The winters fluctuate from mild to incredibly cold, and the summers go from never-ending June rains to drought. Still, late June and the

---

Previous: Spring Creek in the Central Hills.

month of September continue to promise the most delightful weather.

The major determinate of climate is latitude, modified by regional variations in topography, elevation, precipitation, and other factors. The Black Hills, roughly situated at 43.4-44.5° latitude, share this position with sister cities Corvallis, Oregon; Jackson, Wyoming; Stowe, Vermont; Portland, Maine; and Nice, France.

The climate of the hills varies greatly month by month. January and February are the coldest months of the year. Daytime temperatures average in the 30s (-1.1 to 3.9°C), and snowfall averages from 5 inches (18 cm) in the Rapid City area to 15 inches (38 cm) in the higher elevations. Nights can bring temperatures down to 10-20°F (-12.2 to -1.7°C), though single-digit and subzero days can occur, particularly in the higher elevations. Frequent sunny days and chinook winds from the Rocky Mountains, however, can result in temperatures climbing into the 50s and 60s (10-20.6°C). March is the snowiest month of the year, and April is not far behind, but temperatures start to warm up (with average daytime temperatures hovering around 40°F/4.4°C in March and 50°F/10°C in April, and lows in the 20s

and 30s/-6.7 to 3.9°C, respectively). In May and June, precipitation changes to rain and then thundershowers, which generally arrive midafternoon, move quickly to the plains, and disappear by evening. Temperatures start to rise dramatically, with daytime highs averaging in the 60s in May and 70s by June (15.6-26.1°C). Nights remain chilly, still in the 30s and 40s (-1.1 to 9.4°C) in May, but nighttime lows climb in June to the 40s and 50s (4.4-15°C). Summers are warm, dry, and sunny, with daytime temperatures reaching into the 70s and 80s (21.1-31.6°C) and nights averaging in the 50s (10-15°C). Remember that these are averages, and actual temperatures on any given day can be significantly higher or lower than average. Pack those sweaters, but keep in mind that at elevations of 4,000-7,000 feet (1,219-2,134 m), the sun can be intense. Don't forget the sunscreen and sunglasses, and don't rule out bringing along a brimmed hat for sun protection. September and October traditionally experience mild days, with temperatures in the 60s and 70s (15.6-26.1°C) in September and the 50s and 60s (10-20.6°C) in October. At night, temperatures drop to the 30s and 40s (-1.1 to 9.4°C) in September, and by October, you can subtract another 10°F (5-6°C) from

the sharp edges of erosion in the Badlands

the low. November and December mark the beginning of winter, with the number of mild versus cool days reversing. Daytime temperatures hover in the 30s (-1.1 to 3.9°C), though milder days are frequent. Nights bring readings in the teens, with occasional Arctic air from Canada bringing subzero temperatures. Sun and warmer temperatures always return quickly, though. Snowfall averages about 5 inches (18 cm) a month during this period, with early storms generating heavy, wet snows and later storms bringing light and drier snow. The short days of winter cut sharply into the available sunshine and, by the end of this period, everyone is looking forward to spring.

The Badlands, situated in the middle of the plains, have no protection, no shade, and no windbreak. As a result, winters there can be very cold, with brisk winds and frigid weather arriving from the north. Summers are hotter than the neighboring regions. At a lower elevation and, again, with little shade, temperatures are not infrequently at least 10 degrees (5-6°C) higher than in the hills to the west.

All of that being said, remember that the difference between climate and weather is a function of time. Climate is the result of years of studies of the averages and patterns of daily weather. Weather is short term. It's what you confront when you wake up in the morning. Be prepared

Plants and Animals

The Black Hills occupy an area of approximately 65 by 125 miles (105 by 201 km); while the area is small, the diversity is great. In the middle of the country, surrounded by grasslands and plains, the Black Hills form the ecological junction of many regions, where you will find wildlife and plant species typical of the Rocky Mountains, the Great Plains, and northern and eastern forests.

PLANTS

There are over 1,500 plant species in South Dakota, and of those, over 1,200 species can be found in the Black Hills. The ponderosa pine is the dominant tree in the Black Hills, and it grows in every region and habitat in the hills. Companion vegetation, however, is dictated by variations in moisture, elevation, temperature, and soil conditions. Species common to prairie grasslands, coniferous forests, deciduous forests, and mountainous forests can all be found in the region. It is estimated that of the 1,200 species of plants in the Black Hills region, 30 percent originated in the plains, 25 percent in the Rockies, 5 percent in deciduous forests, and 1 percent in northern forests.

Grasslands

Wind Cave National Park, the Badlands, and the southern area of Custer State Park contain both ponderosa pine forest and mixed-grass prairie environments. In yet another example of how east meets west in the Black Hills, the area west of the Black Hills is shortgrass prairie, and lands east of the Missouri are tallgrass prairie. Plants that grow in shortgrass or in tallgrass prairies can both be found in the mixed-grass prairie of western and central South Dakota. In a rainy year, tallgrass prairie plants will be the most evident. In an arid year, the shortgrass prairie plants will thrive. Tallgrass prairie plants require more moisture than shortgrass plants and can usually be located, even in dry years, in valleys, where drainage adds moisture to the fields.

Cacti thrive in shortgrass prairies, and prickly pear and pincushion cactus are common in this region on the drier southern-facing slopes. Other common shortgrass plants in this area includes bluegrasses, buffalo grass, wheatgrass, and little bluestem. Shrubs include rabbitbrush, sage, mountain mahogany, buffaloberry, dogwood, snowberry, and coralberry, among others.

About 25 percent of Wind Cave National Park is tree-covered; ponderosa pine is the most common tree. There are also scattered groves of elm, aspen, bur oak, box elder, and birch in the park, which are usually found in drainage areas.

Deciduous Forest

A deciduous tree is one that sheds its leaves in the winter, enters a dormancy phase in cold weather, and then, when warmer temperatures return, experiences regrowth. This process allows the tree to withstand extremes of temperature. There are several pockets of deciduous trees in the hills, most of which are migrants from the east. On the eastern side of the hills near streambeds, deciduous trees include the box elder, ash, American elm, eastern cottonwood, dogwood, and willows. The northeastern foothills, at lower elevations and with relatively dry slopes, host bur oaks with an understory (plants that grow in the shade or beneath the canopy of higher trees) of sumac, coralberry, and poison ivy. In the northwest corner of the hills, more quaking aspens and paper birches can be found. Understory plants include chokecherry, beaked hazelnut, and wild rose.

Coniferous Forest

Ponderosa pine is everywhere in the Black Hills. There are regional variations in the understory of the forest depending on many factors, including moisture levels, temperature, and elevation. In the Southern Hills, where the environment is generally warmer and drier than the rest of the region, the understory of the ponderosa pine forest is composed of little bluestem, yucca, sagebrush, sand lily, and various grama and needlegrasses. In areas that are at elevations over 7,000 feet (2,134 m), the understory is composed of juniper, Oregon grape, buffaloberry, and blue wild rye. At the moister elevations of 4,000-5,000 feet (1,219-1,524 m), the forest canopy includes both the ponderosa pine and the bur oak, with an understory of chokecherry, Oregon grape, and melic grasses. On the western edge

of the hills, skunkbrush and American black currant appear. White spruce is also found in the higher and moisture-rich elevations of the Black Hills. A variant of the white spruce, the Black Hills spruce is the state tree of South Dakota.

Wildflowers

At first glance, the prairie grasslands appear to be a sea of soft green or gold, depending on the season. A closer look reveals vibrant color scattered throughout the fields. There are literally hundreds of wildflower species that grow in the prairie grasslands. The American pasque, a beautiful light-violet flower, is one of the first of early spring and is also the state flower. Many species of milk vetches, asters, milkweeds, penstemons, and evening primroses are common.

Beautiful to look at, flowers in the Black Hills were also used for practical and medicinal purposes by many Native American people. The sap of the bright-yellow false dandelion was used to clean teeth, wild blue flax seeds were used to flavor food, purple clover made a flavorful tea, and the purple coneflower (echinacea) was used for headaches, stomachaches, and sore throats.

ANIMALS

The mixed habitat of the Black Hills, the rolling plains of the Southern Hills, and the wooded hills and stream valleys of the area all provide homes for a wide variety of wildlife. The South Dakota state bird is the **ring-necked pheasant** (an import), and the state animal is the **coyote.**

Mammals

It has been estimated that when Europeans first arrived on North American soil, 40-60 million **bison** roamed the Great Plains. A century after the Lewis and Clark Expedition, less than 1,000 bison were alive in the country.

Conservationists and hunters both realized that bison could disappear from the prairie environment forever if action wasn't taken. In 1911, the American Bison Society began searching for places to establish a protected habitat for the bison. Wind Cave National Park was one of the first places where bison were restored to the wild. In 1913, 20 animals were donated to the park; six came from a small herd left near Yellowstone, and 14 were donated by the New York Zoological Society. Today, the herd numbers around 500, a quantity over the estimated optimal number of 350 bison for the available 33,851 acres (13,699 ha) of range in the park. However, the herd is rounded up and culled and checked for overall health yearly. In recent years, traces of cattle genes have been found in most bison herds. Through testing, however, it has been determined that the Wind Cave National Park herd is pure American bison, untainted by any cattle genes.

Other animals, including the **pronghorn** and the **elk,** were also reintroduced to Wind Cave National Park in the early 1900s. Today, the pronghorn herd is estimated at 50 animals, and the elk have an estimated population of 250 animals. With the onset of chronic wasting disease, the elk herd is continually monitored for health, and the numbers are kept low to prevent more contagion. Conservation work continues at the park. The endangered **black-footed ferret** was reintroduced to the park beginning in 2007. Currently the population is estimated to be between 25 and 40 animals, a self-sustaining number.

The bison at Wind Cave National Park are not the only bison in the region. Bison were reintroduced to Custer State Park in 1914, shortly after the Wind Cave herd was established, with the purchase of 36 bison. By 1940, the herd size at Custer State Park had increased to over 2,500 animals. At that size, the herd was overgrazing the rangeland, and it was determined that a healthy sustainable herd should number around 1,500 animals. Currently an estimated population of 1,400 animals roam through the 73,000 acres (29,542 ha) of the park today. The annual **Buffalo Roundup,** which occurs in Custer State Park in late September, is open to the public and the time when the herd

is vaccinated against disease and culled if necessary.

Bison are confined within these large range areas, but most of the wildlife of the Black Hills come and go as they please through the parks and are found throughout the hills. Easily visible animals include **white-tailed deer** and their large-eared relative, the **mule deer.** The beautiful snowy-white **mountain goat** can be seen in the northern corners of Custer State Park and is also frequently spotted around Mount Rushmore National Memorial and Crazy Horse Memorial. The mountain goat is unique to North America but not a species native to the Black Hills. Stocked in the region in 1924, it has since thrived. The original bighorn sheep species in South Dakota, the Audubon subspecies, became extinct in 1920. A herd of **Rocky Mountain bighorn sheep** was introduced to Custer State Park and can still be seen, generally north of Blue Bell Lodge in the park. The **prairie dog** never suffered the threat of extinction and is prolific in Custer State Park and Wind Cave National Park, as well as the prairie regions surrounding the hills. It has been discovered, however, that a virulent strain of plague is threatening colonies in the Badlands, in the Conata Basin, and in Wind Cave. Many of these areas have been dusted with insecticide (to kill fleas that carry the disease), though some of the prairie dog acres are still at risk.

Much of the wildlife of the Black Hills is not as easily viewed. Elk are shy animals and only infrequently spotted without research. The elk is a majestic animal, with heavy, wide antlers. They can stand 5 feet (1.5 m) at the shoulder and weigh over 700 pounds (318 kg). Even in the briefest flash of a headlight, the sheer size of an elk makes its identity unmistakable. The region's only remaining large predator is the **mountain lion,** which has been spotted somewhat more frequently in recent years, likely due to an increase in active hunting, which drives the animal out of its hidden den areas. Other seldom-seen inhabitants of the hills include the flying squirrel,

Lewis and Clark and a Lucky Prairie Dog

Thomas Jefferson was a visionary armchair explorer. In January 1803, even before the Louisiana Purchase had been suggested, before the United States officially took possession of the territories north and west of the Mississippi River, he requested that Congress fund an expedition that would cross the Louisiana Territory regardless of who owned it. It was his wish that the territory become part of the United States, however, and by April 1803, an agreement had been reached (but not yet ratified) for the United States to purchase 875,000 square miles (2.3 million sq km) of land for $15 million, doubling the size of the country. By December 1803, the United States had taken possession of the Louisiana Territory. In 1804, Jefferson's request for a mission to explore the territory became the Lewis and Clark Expedition. The expedition had three missions, one of which was to discover and document new wildlife. The expedition arrived in South Dakota in late 1804. Many of the prairie animals discovered on the trip had never been seen by explorers before, and in keeping with the expedition's mandate, several live species were sent back to Washington DC. A prairie dog was captured, wintered with the crew in Fort Mandan, and then survived the trip downriver and east to Washington DC. Not all of the live specimens were as lucky. (I'm not sure I'd have wanted to be the one receiving Jefferson's mail at the time.) A sharp-tailed grouse made the trip, but didn't arrive alive. Only one of four magpies survived the trip. Lewis and Clark were also the first to provide detailed scientific descriptions of the pronghorn (which they erroneously called a goat), jackrabbit, mule deer, and coyote. The bounty of the prairies was also revealed. Meriwether Lewis wrote, "Vast herds of Buffaloe deer Elk and Antilopes were seen feeding in every direction as far as the eye of the observer could reach."

opossum, raccoon, weasel, mink, skunk, badger, fox, coyote, bobcat, and marmot.

Birds

The Black Hills are as far west as most eastern birds travel, and as far east as most western birds fly. As a result, you'll want to bring your field guide to North America, or to the Great Plains, and forget packing guides to just eastern or western birds. Add to the mix the unique environment south of Hot Springs, where a warm-water stream and a cold-water stream come together. It's an unusual ecological combination that results in an interesting collection of birds, plants, and insects. Bird lists for the region include over 400 different species in South Dakota, most of which can be found in the Black Hills.

In the southern mixed-grass habitat, look for the **sharp-tailed grouse, long-billed curlew, burrowing owl,** and diminishing populations of **sage grouse, sage thrasher,** and **Brewer's sparrow.** The Badlands region hosts **white-throated swifts,** and juniper groves are home to **long-eared owls** and **mountain bluebirds.** The ponderosa pine forests that dominate the Black Hills provide rich habitat for **three-toed woodpeckers, ruby-** and **golden-crowned kinglets,** and **Swainson's thrushes.** Waterside, the **western tanager, black-headed grosbeak, lazuli bunting,** and **Bullock's oriole** can be found.

The South Dakota Ornithologists' Union has identified several birding "hot spots" in the Black Hills, including Sylvan Lake in Custer State Park; the Boles and Redbird Canyons, which are near Jewel Cave; the Fort Meade Recreation Area; Canyon Lake in Rapid City; Hot Brook Canyon, just outside of Hot Springs; Angostura Recreation Area, south of Hot Springs; Edgemont, with its sage-rich habitat; and Spearfish Canyon and Roughlock Falls in the Northern Hills.

Reptiles and Amphibians

Amphibians fall between fish and reptiles on the evolutionary scale, and many have changed little from their ancestors that roamed the earth up to 270 million years ago.

Cold-blooded amphibians, at the early stages of their development, live in water and breathe through gills. As they mature, amphibians will usually lose their gills, develop legs, and many become terrestrial. Appropriately, the word *amphibian* means "double life."

South Dakota has a total of 15 species of amphibians. Of these, just about half can be found in the Black Hills region, including two species of true frogs (the **northern leopard frog** and the **bullfrog**), two species of true toads (the **Great Plains toad** and the **Woodhouse's toad**), one tree frog (the **chorus frog**), one spadefoot (the **plains spadefoot**), and one salamander (the **tiger salamander**). While some amphibians are completely terrestrial, all of South Dakota's amphibians must return to water to lay their eggs.

Reptiles are also cold-blooded, but unlike amphibians, they never had gills or breathed water in any stage of their development. Reptiles in the Black Hills include turtles, snakes, and lizards. Turtles have been with us since the Triassic period, dating back over 200 million years. In winter, all South Dakota turtles hibernate in burrows or in the mud underwater. There are seven species of turtle in South Dakota, of which four are found in the Black Hills region: the **western painted turtle,** the **snapping turtle,** the **spiny softshell turtle,** and the **smooth softshell turtle.** Both the softshell turtles are classified as rare. The snapping turtle is the largest, most aggressive, and most common turtle in South Dakota, and it can grow to over 40 pounds (18 kg). It is not wise to try and pick one of these up. With sharp claws and strong jaws, a snapper can inflict a great deal of damage on ill-placed fingers. The western painted turtle lives up to its name with a gorgeous red, orange, and yellow plastron (lower shell).

Ten different species of snake inhabit the Black Hills. The biggest in the region is the **bull snake,** which can range 37-72 inches (183 cm) in length. The **Black Hills redbelly snake,** once thought to be rare, may well be just super-shy. A subspecies of the redbelly snake, it prefers high, moist elevations, like the conditions near Mount Rushmore and Black Elk Peak. The **prairie rattlesnake** is the only venomous snake in the Black Hills. A member of the pit viper family, the prairie rattler has a triangle-shaped head, with a pit on both sides of the head between the eye and nostril. Light brown in color, the snake is marked by dark oval blotches with light borders that become rings near the tail section. Rattlers range 30-40 inches (76-102 cm) in length and have a rattle on the tail. Remember that any snake with a pointed tail is not a rattlesnake. Also remember that snakes are secretive by nature, not aggressive, and will leave you alone if you leave them alone, unless trapped or endangered in some way.

Insects and Arachnids

The **western black widow spider** is one of the few venomous arachnids in the state, though it's uncommon for people to be bitten by the spider. A reclusive spider, it is known for the bright-red hourglass shape on its lower abdomen.

In the early spring, the **wood tick** is one of South Dakota's more annoying arachnids. (Ticks are not insects; they are closely related to spiders.) The wood tick can carry Rocky Mountain spotted fever and Colorado tick fever. The deer tick, which carries Lyme disease, is rare in South Dakota.

The insect posing the most problems in South Dakota is not a threat to humans, but does pose a danger to the ponderosa pine forest that dominates the flora of the Black Hills. The **mountain pine beetle** has inhabited the Black Hills as long as there has been a pine forest here. The beetle population is cyclical. At times, the beetle is fairly rare, but every 10 years or so, numbers increase, and beetles attack healthy as well as stressed trees. These outbreaks last 5-20 years, and then the population declines again. Pine beetle infestation in the Black Hills reached epidemic proportions beginning in 1996 and returned to normal by 2016. It is thought that epidemics are due to a combination of factors, including drought, fire suppression, and mild winters. (Pine beetles will die out if subjected to extreme cold for several days in the midst of winter.) You can see the effects of the beetle in the large number of rust-colored trees in the forest. Measures taken to prevent the spread of the pine beetle include thinning tree stands and prescribed burns. The area around Black Elk Peak includes the Elk Creek Wilderness and is a place that has high visitation. No logging or burning is allowed in the wilderness. Pine beetle infestation near Black Elk Peak prompted the Forest Service to take action. Logging in the area will be noticeable for quite some time.

Fish

South Dakota is home to over 100 fish species, and, of these, nearly 30 species are of interest to anglers. The mountain lakes and fast-moving streams of the Black Hills contain populations of **walleye, salmon, bluegill, crappie, perch, bass, pike, trout,** and **catfish.**

ENVIRONMENTAL ISSUES

Several environmental issues confront the various agencies charged with stewardship of the public lands of South Dakota. Employees of the national forests and the national grasslands, both under the auspices of the National Park Service (in turn under the Department of Agriculture), and the South Dakota Department of Game, Fish, and Parks, all have management responsibilities over large tracts of land in the Black Hills. The national parks and monuments are recreational in nature. The national forests and national grasslands are oriented to mixed-use with decisions to be made regarding issues such as grazing, mining, and logging, balanced against recreational use. The South Dakota Department of Game, Fish, and Parks regulates hunting and fishing and also manages several large parks, including Angostura Recreation Area and Custer State Park.

Fire

An environmental concern common to every land management agency in the Black Hills is how to respond to fire. The climate most favorable to ponderosa pine forests includes high spring vegetation followed by conditions favorable to frequent summer fires, including drought and thunderstorms. Fire is important to the ecology of the grasslands and the ponderosa pine. Fire suppression in the Black Hills was started initially to protect the timber industry. The effect of fire suppression over many years, however, was to create a high density of trees, which resulted in far more destructive fires when they occurred. The fires are hotter and likelier to exhibit crowning behavior. Crowning behavior is just what it sounds like—fire burning high in the crowns of the trees and traveling quickly from tree to tree, instead of burning slowly and low to the ground. These fires are more difficult to contain once started. As homes are built closer and closer to national parks, grasslands, and forests, fire suppression becomes an important issue for the citizens of the region. All of the agencies involved have tried to balance fire suppression with fire management, frequently with controlled fires called prescribed burns.

Logging

One of the responsibilities of the Black Hills National Forest is to ensure that economic interests and forest health are well balanced. Studies indicate that the current rate of logging in the Black Hills is not sustainable for the long-term health of the forest. The debate has not been settled, but the Rocky Mountain Research Center of the Department of Agriculture has suggested a significant cut in the logging volume taking place in the hills.

Mountain Lions

Predators have never fared well in South Dakota. Wolves and bears, once active in the region, have been eliminated. Coyotes, on the predator/varmint list, can be hunted year-round; there is no daily or possession limit, and the cost of a license is just $5. In 2005, the mountain lion, the last big predator remaining in the hills, with no history of attacks on humans, was declared a game animal by the state, and the hunts began. The number of allowable kills each season increased dramatically until 2015, when it was noted that the limits were no longer being filled during the season. It is suspected that the original estimates of the mountain lion population were in excess of the actual population. The hunting fee for mountain lion is $28, one of the least expensive licenses offered.

Hunters and ranchers, both powerful coalitions in South Dakota, are strong supporters of mountain lion hunting. Conservation groups are not as enthusiastic. Many believe that trophy hunting the last small population of lions left in the region is not a reasonable management philosophy. The first hunt limited the kill to a total of 25 animals, with an additional restriction of five breeding-age females. A few short years later, the number of allowable kills increased to 40 animals total, out of which 25 could be breeding females. The South Dakota Department of Game, Fish, and Parks set the mountain lion kill for the 2013 season at 100 lions, or 70 female lions. By 2018, the limit was lowered to 60 total, or 40 female lions, and remains at this level to date. Conservationists are concerned that the department's estimate of the lion population is too high.

Hunting caused the near demise of the bison, the pronghorn, and the elk in this region, but contemporary hunting organizations are generally inclined to keep populations healthy enough to allow for continued hunting. The mountain lion does not have any such protective organization. The more mountain lions are hunted, the more mountain lions will be visible as they are driven from their dens. The more visible they are, the more they will be hunted. The future of the mountain lion in South Dakota appears grim.

Uranium and Gold

After World War II, uranium became the hot ticket for mining companies. Nuclear power plants were being built, and uranium was a crucial element for the power supply of the future. As a result, the price of uranium went up enough to make mining feasible. Mining in the southern Black Hills began near the Fall River County community of Edgemont. Uranium was mined and milled here beginning in 1956 and continuing through 1974, when economic factors caused owners to keep the mines closed. In recent years, due to environmental concerns about global warming caused, in part, by the use of fossil fuels, interest in nuclear energy has rebounded. New nuclear reactors built in China and India have increased the demand for uranium, as well. In 2002, the price of uranium was $9.60 per pound. By September 2008, it had risen to over $60 per pound. The 2011 earthquake and tsunami in Japan, however, which caused the Fukushima nuclear reactor to fail, led to uranium prices tumbling to around $45 per pound. In 2020-2021, prices fluctuated between $28 and $38 per pound. That price is apparently still high enough to make uranium mining in South Dakota economically feasible.

Exploratory holes are already being drilled near Edgemont, but not without protest. Three groups—Defenders of the Black Hills, Action for the Environment, and South Dakota Clean Water Alliance—are fighting the reemergence of mining in the area. The major concern regionally is the possible contamination of groundwater. However, the state legislature does not support those concerns. In 2011, a bill that suspended state rules over how uranium is mined was passed. The process has been slow, but it probably won't be long before uranium mining is once again an active industry in the Black Hills.

In recent years, with high gold prices, interest has also been revived in gold mining in the hills. Controversy has erupted over this possibility, since one of the sites selected for new mining permits is along the ridge of scenic Spearfish Canyon. In an area prized for its natural beauty, the specter of mining in the canyon has many in the tourism industry nervous. Lawrence County has already approved a conditional-use permit for the mine proposal. Generally speaking, legislation in South Dakota has consistently been for industry over environment. There is no reason to believe that policy will change anytime soon.

Oil

South Dakota is not an extractive site for oil, but it is an area over which controversial pipelines have been established. Protests in South Dakota have been minimal compared to the well-publicized protests near the Standing Rock Reservation in North Dakota over the Dakota Access pipeline in 2016. The Keystone XL pipeline, another phase of the same plan, was given the go-ahead with the resurgence of governmental support for the extractive industries. South Dakota, an ultraconservative state with little regard for environmental issues, readily gave permits to the pipelines in 2010. The pipeline path would have crossed Nebraska over the Ogallala Aquifer, which supplies water for millions of Plains states residents. For years Indigenous tribes, conservationists, and Nebraska ranchers fought the building of the pipeline. In June of 2019 the project was terminated by its developers. With a new administration in 2021, the Keystone XL pipeline federal cross-border permit was revoked.

The latest environmental threat noted in 2021 was the application of oil companies to drill in South Dakota. It is likely that the drilling, if approved, will be for "waste water disposal," the contents of which are unknown.

History

FIRST PEOPLES

It is thought that the first people to make their way into what is now South Dakota came across a land bridge from Asia, through Alaska, and then migrated south. They traveled to North America sometime 15,000-20,000 years ago. Evidence of our first peoples, Paleoindians, here in South Dakota can be traced to around 11,500 years ago. The Clovis peoples were hunters and gatherers of the Old Stone Age. Their weapons were stone and bone, and they lived with and hunted giant bison, mammoths, camels, and saber-toothed tigers. Evidence of their life on the plains was uncovered on what is now the Pine Ridge Reservation. The **Clovis peoples** appeared just as the ice age was coming to a close. As ice age animals became extinct, hunting tools changed, and a new era of hunters, called the Folsom hunters, appeared. Folsom spearpoints, longer and finer than Clovis points, have been found in South Dakota, though no campsites have been located. It was with these spearpoints that the long-lasting tradition of the bison hunt began.

Archaeological evidence has determined that about 7,000 years ago, the climate of South Dakota began to change. It had been relatively warm and comfortable, but it got much drier, with frequent droughts. Hunting expanded to include smaller game, and plant foods were incorporated into the people's diet. Communities were very small. By 3,000 years ago, the weather on the plains was about the same as it is today. Bison hunts, by then, had become fairly sophisticated, with larger bands of Native Americans coming together to use traps and drives to kill larger numbers of animals. It was possible to sustain more people in a single community as the ability to procure food improved. This period, as tribes became larger, was known as the Woodland period. In the west, the Woodland hunters are believed to be the predecessors to the Shoshone, Kiowa, Crow, and Cheyenne. Over time, spears gave way to the bow and arrow, pottery came into use, and the first traces of true agricultural practices appeared around AD 900. In AD 1250-1450, an agricultural people migrated from southern Minnesota. These people, believed to be the predecessors to the Mandan, Arikara, and Hidatsa, were planting corn, beans, squash, and sunflowers.

One of the most successful early tribes of the Dakotas was the **Arikara.** The Arikara migrated up the Missouri River basin from Kansas and Nebraska in the 1500s. They settled in central South Dakota, near the current location of Pierre. The Arikara built earth lodges and lived in small villages. At one time, it is believed, there were as many as 32 villages and as many as 4,000 warriors scattered along the river. The Arikara were non-nomadic and had an advanced system of trade with other tribes. They were responsible for many of the horses that were traded to the Teton Sioux, initially located to the east. Horses were brought up from the southwest by the Kiowa, Arapahoe, Comanche, and Cheyenne, and the Arikara would travel to the Black Hills on their hunting trips and pick them up for trading with other tribes.

The earliest recorded reference of the **Sioux** was in 1640, as recorded by French priests. The French were referring to the people who called themselves the Oceti Sakowin, or the Seven Council Fires of the **Lakota, Dakota,** and **Nakota** tribes. At the time, the tribe living near the headwaters of the Mississippi River, as recorded by the priests, was the Dakota. The Teton Sioux (Lakota) tribe was recorded as the first to be encountered near the Black Hills in the late 1700s. At that time, the Black Hills were occupied by the Cheyenne. The Brule were the next to move west, settling south of the Badlands. During 1776-1825, life was good for the tribes in their new location. Guns and horses had been added to their lifestyle; tipis replaced the stationary dwellings they occupied in the east; and game, particularly bison, was plentiful.

THE EUROPEANS

In the late 1600s and early 1700s, the British were developing their trading companies in the Hudson Bay area, and the Spanish were active in the Southwest. The upper Missouri River Valley was part of the French colonial

empire until 1763. Very little attention was paid to the region, however, as the French concentrated their efforts in the Mississippi River Valley.

While the Europeans were developing their holdings elsewhere, their trade goods were making an appearance on the plains near the Black Hills, as intertribal trading brought horses north to the hills and plains, and other goods west from Minnesota. Beads, knives, and other iron tools were found in early Native American campsites. There were several French excursions into the Missouri River Valley, but a number of factors kept further development at bay, including run-ins with the Sioux. The first documented European exploration of South Dakota was in 1743, when French explorer Pierre Gaultier de Varennes, Sieur de La Verendrye, may have gotten to within sight of the Black Hills.

In 1763, the French ceded their interests in lands west of the Mississippi to Spain. The Spanish ownership of the lands west of the Mississippi had little impact on the region. In an attempt to oust the British incursions into the area from the north, several excursions were sent upriver from St. Louis to set up a Spanish post near the Mandans in what is now North Dakota. They met with little success. In 1800, Spain ceded the area back to France, and in 1803, France sold it to the United States.

LEWIS AND CLARK

Thomas Jefferson had long wanted to explore the West and to find a water route to the Pacific Ocean. Before the land belonged to the United States, he had asked Meriwether Lewis if he would be interested in leading an exploration expedition to the Missouri River basin with the intent of finding passage to the Pacific. Negotiations with France for the purchase of the Louisiana Territory began early in 1803; by April, an agreement was signed, and by October, this constitutionally questionable purchase was ratified by Congress. The lands purchased were bordered by the Mississippi River on the east and extended west to the Rocky Mountains and north into

British North America. Virtually all of what would become South Dakota was included in the purchase. By May 1804, Lewis and Clark were on their way up the Missouri River. They stuck with the river and didn't head into the Black Hills, but the successful expedition to the Pacific Coast fired the imagination of the American people, affirmed the United States' ownership of the Missouri River basin, served as the starting point of negotiations with the Native American inhabitants of the West, and opened the country to the fur trade. The American expeditioners now confronted the same issues the Spanish had before them, specifically how to establish friendly relations with the Native American tribes and how to stave off any further invasion by the British into U.S. soil. Unfortunately, the relationship between explorers and the Teton Sioux was not improved upon by the Lewis and Clark Expedition. Clark wrote in his journal:

> These are the vilest miscreants of the savage race, and must ever remain the pirates of the Missouri, until such measures are pursued, by our government, as will make them feel a dependence on its will for their supply of merchandise.

Unfortunately, this set the precedent for the way the tribes were treated for the next 100 years.

THE FUR TRADE

In the early 1800s, the upper Missouri River Valley was a virtually untapped resource for fur traders. As long as the Mississippi River provided enough bounty for all, there was little motivation to tread deeper into Native American country. But as the pelts became harder to find, traders looked farther west for new resources.

Early fur trading, east of the plains, included very few buffalo hides. Introduced to the market as traders moved west, demand for the hides increased exponentially over the next few years. Safe passage through the area required the cooperation of the Native American tribes that inhabited the region—the Arikara, the Mandans, and the Sioux. When the fur trade was focused on the smaller pelts of the mink, otter, and beaver, the tribes were not particularly interested in trapping. But as demand for buffalo hides increased, the Native people, particularly the Teton Sioux, joined the hunt and were active participants in their procurement. The success of the fur trade was intimately tied to relationships with the Native American tribespeople and to peaceful interactions between their tribes. There were several skirmishes between tribes, however, and between the tribes and the traders, including a war in the 1820s with the Arikara, whom the traders and the Teton Sioux fought together. In 1825, the Atkinson-O'Fallon Commission traveled up the Missouri River charged with the task of negotiating treaties with the upper Missouri tribes. It was a successful expedition. The fur trade initially brought wealth to the Native American people in the form of cooking utensils, guns, and other material goods, but it also eliminated their economic stability and introduced whiskey to a population vulnerable to its abuse. By the 1850s, the heyday of the fur trade was over.

MANIFEST DESTINY

The first time the term "manifest destiny" was seen in print was in 1839, and the idea of American expansion all the way to the West Coast became popular in the 1840s. (In fact, many of the supporters of manifest destiny saw the United States occupying all of North America and Cuba.) By the 1850s, there was a steady stream of settlers heading west. The constant river of migrants through the central plains caused tension with the Teton Sioux, who hunted from the White River region south to the North Platte. Tension turned to skirmishes, and military outposts started to crop up throughout the West. First Fort Kearny in Nebraska Territory, then Fort Laramie in Wyoming, and finally Fort Pierre in what was to be Dakota Territory were bought from failing fur companies and populated with soldiers. When it was determined that Fort Pierre was not in good enough condition to house a large military contingent, another post, Fort Randall, was established in Nebraska. These were the first military posts established in the region. Once they were in place, exploration of the region began. Lieutenant G. K. Warren explored the country above the North Platte River and decided that continued military presence in Sioux country was important for the protection of traders and settlers.

While the military was moving into the region west of the Missouri River, settlers in the east managed to push a bill through Congress establishing Dakota Territory in March 1861. Everything north of the 43rd parallel became part of this territory, which included the entire upper Missouri River Valley. There was no great rush to settle the territory, however, as the nation was involved in the Civil War and trouble with the Native American inhabitants did little to make the lands inviting. The white population of the Dakota Territory in 1860 was estimated to be about 500 people, most of whom were located in the southeastern corner of the state.

In the early 1860s, however, gold camps began to spring up in Montana, and Congress authorized three roads through Dakota Territory. One of these roads was planned to cross along the southern base of the Black Hills, and one would pass by the edge of the northern Black Hills. Neither project was successful, but as a result of the gold camps, river traffic up the Missouri increased significantly. The western territories started to clamor for railroads.

In 1863, Native American tribes were becoming agitated by all the activity in their regions. In 1863-1868, several skirmishes caused increased military activity in Dakota Territory. Beginning with the Minnesota Santee Sioux, who fled west across the Dakota Plains, unrest spread all the way to the Teton Sioux, who roamed between the Missouri River and the Powder River Valley, northwest of the Black Hills. The Cheyenne and Arapahoe tribes moved into the Powder River

region, as well. The military was determined to defeat these tribes and to build a wagon road through the region. What ensued was later called Red Cloud's War, for the Oglala chief who led the fight to keep the hunting grounds free of intrusion. While the military did not want peace, the civilians did, and in 1868, the Fort Laramie Treaty was signed. Under the terms of the treaty, the United States abandoned the Powder River country, the military posts were shut down, and the Bozeman Trail leading to the Montana mines was closed. It was one of the few success stories for the Native American tribes. But it didn't last.

The terms of the treaty also allowed for the construction of a central agency to be built on agency land within the reservation lands. The agency would include a warehouse for Native American goods, a residence for the government-appointed Indian agent responsible for ensuring that all parties followed the terms of the treaty, and additional residences for a physician, carpenter, miller, blacksmith, farmer, and engineer. The agency would also build a schoolhouse or mission building and a sawmill. Any tribal member who wished to could select land with the guidance of the agent, if the intent was to farm it. The land would be removed from the common ownership of the tribe and transferred to the individual, as long as that individual continued to cultivate the land. Clothing, food, and financial payments were also promised to the tribes that signed the treaty.

The treaty of 1868 was not signed by all of the Native American tribes in the region, and most of them did not live on agency lands. Many of the unsigned tribes would come to the agency, however, collect rations, and, on occasion, raid nearby settlers. In response, the military decided that an outpost was needed somewhere in the Black Hills.

THE CUSTER EXPEDITION

In what was purported to be a response to raids by Native American tribes that had not signed treaties, **Lieutenant Colonel George A. Custer** was placed in charge of an expedition to find a good location for a military post in the Black Hills. Custer took 1,000 men with him and approached the hills from the north. In addition to military members, there were scientists, miners, newspaper journalists, and even musicians along on what must have been one of the best provisioned expeditions in U.S. history. The expedition headed for the hills in July 1874. By July 30, two miners found traces of gold in French Creek. By August 12, the news was released by the military headquarters in St. Paul. By the time Custer returned to headquarters, just 60 days after he left, prospectors were already getting ready to violate the 1868 treaty and invade the tribal lands.

While the military was trying to keep trespassers out, the settlers were demanding that the hills be opened, and popular sentiment in Washington was with the settlers. Arrangements were made to bring many of the Native American chiefs to Washington to persuade them to part with the area. The chiefs were noncommittal and returned home. A scientific expedition was then sent to the hills to determine their value for the purpose of negotiation. A Grand Council was held in September 1875. Thousands of Sioux showed up for the council and promptly rejected the $6 million offered for the Black Hills. They also rejected the proposal for an annual rental payment of $400,000 a year for the mining rights to the hills. In addition to the hills, the government asked the Native American tribes to cede the Wyoming Bighorn country. When the tribes rejected the offer, the government removed the cavalry from the region, opening the hills to the invasion of the prospectors and to a new round of Indian Wars.

THE INDIAN WARS

In late 1875, continual skirmishes with the Native American tribes were occurring in the Bighorn Mountains and Powder River regions of Wyoming, to the north and west of the Black Hills. The "hostile population" was estimated to be about 3,000 strong. Military leaders decided that the appropriate action would be a show of force that would bring the tribespeople into the agencies. General Crook initiated a campaign against the tribes in early 1876 from Fort Fetterman in Wyoming, heading for the Powder River country with only 900 troops. After an unsuccessful attack against a band of Cheyenne and a band of Oglalas under the leadership of Lakota warrior **Crazy Horse,** General Crook and his troops returned to the fort for the winter. As spring approached, an attack strategy was designed to overwhelm the Native people with three columns of troops, one led by General Crook, one by Colonel Gibbon, and one by General Terry. Lieutenant Colonel George A. Custer, serving under General Terry, was in command of the 7th Cavalry.

In May 1876, the three military columns set out from their respective bases. One of the columns, under General Crook, was attacked early on by a group led by Crazy Horse, which prevented Crook from meeting up with Terry and Gibbon. When Gibbon and Terry met, it was decided to divide the troops into two groups and attack the Native American camp from the north and south simultaneously, trapping the tribespeople between the two forces. Gibbon and Terry traveled together to attack from the south. Custer's cavalry headed out on a different path to attack from the north.

Custer arrived at the Little Bighorn River ahead of Terry and Gibbon and did not wait for them, which resulted in disaster. Dividing his cavalry into three segments, Custer began his attack. Two sections of Custer's troops survived the battle, but Custer and the men who stayed with him were wiped out.

Known today as the **Battle of the Little Bighorn,** or alternately as "Custer's Last Stand," it was also the last of the major battles to be won by tribal forces. Attacks against the Native people resumed in August 1876. At several of the agencies, friendly tribespeople were disarmed and their ponies taken away from them as a preventative measure. Skirmishes alternated with attempts to negotiate. In

The Lakota

The peoples called the "Sioux" by French trappers and traders collectively call themselves the "Oceti Sakowin" or "Seven Council Fires." The first Council Fire was located in east-central Minnesota, near Mille Lacs. As the population grew and members migrated west, the Oceti Sakowin created six additional Council Fires. Each Council Fire is, in turn, one of three divisions: Dakota, Nakota, or Lakota.

The people who were most a part of western South Dakota's history were the Titonwan Council Fire of the Lakota Division of the Oceti Sakowin. There are seven distinct groups (oyates) of the Titonwan Council Fire: the Hunkpapa, Itazipco, Mniconjou, Oglala, Oohenunpa, Sicangu, and Sihasapa. The Oglalas claim the Pine Ridge Reservation, located just south of Badlands National Park, as home. The Hunkpapa settled on the Standing Rock Reservation, located on the Missouri River on the northern border of South Dakota. Just south of the Standing Rock Reservation, the Cheyenne River Reservation is home to the Mniconjou, Itazipco, Oohenunpa and Sihasapa oyates.

Many famous Lakota leaders are from the Titonwan Council Fire:

Oglala chief **Red Cloud** successfully led the Native American campaign to close the Bozeman Trail, which passed through the hunting grounds of the Oceti Sakowin.

Hunkpapa chief **Sitting Bull** led his people in the Battle of the Little Bighorn, also known as "Custer's Last Stand." Sitting Bull died when an attempt to arrest him was made during the days of the Ghost Dance, a ceremony intended to resurrect the traditional lifestyle and culture of the Native Americans.

Mniconjou chief **Big Foot** was an early practitioner of the Ghost Dance. Many of his people were massacred at Wounded Knee in 1890.

The controversial Sicangu chief **Spotted Tail** believed that the westward migration of easterners was inevitable. Along with Red Cloud, he signed the Fort Laramie Treaty of 1868. The U.S. government soon violated the treaty, leading to the Indian Wars of 1875-1876. Spotted Tail convinced many Native people to surrender and move to reservations and agency lands.

The great Oglala warrior **Crazy Horse** refused to sign any treaty. When he was killed after his surrender at Fort Robinson, many blamed Spotted Tail.

early 1877, the military went to Spotted Tail, a chief at one of the friendly Native American camps that had not been disarmed, for assistance. Spotted Tail convinced many of the Native people to surrender. Some headed into Canada under the leadership of Sitting Bull, but many went to the agencies. Crazy Horse, reputed to be Spotted Tail's nephew, and his band were the last to return. They went to the Red Cloud Agency, where Crazy Horse was killed when he resisted being placed in confinement.

The Battle of the Little Bighorn gave Congress the power and popular support to pass an appropriations bill that dictated that the Sioux would not receive any further appropriations unless they gave up the Black Hills. Commissioners carried the new agreement to several agencies of the Sioux, where,

without horses or weapons, the tribespeople acquiesced. Under the terms, the tribes sacrificed the Black Hills and all hunting rights in Montana and Wyoming. The Native people were to be relocated to reservation lands. Many of those who had previously surrendered fled north to join Sitting Bull in Canada. Of those who remained, Spotted Tail's band relocated to Rosebud Creek, and the Oglala Lakota picked their site at Pine Ridge, just west of Rosebud.

STATEHOOD

The eastern border of South Dakota was its population, agricultural, and trade center until the discovery of gold. Prospectors flocked to the Black Hills, first to Custer, then north to Deadwood and Lead. For about two years, the rush was on as prospectors filed claims and began a frenzied search for the metal that would make their fortunes. As the search for gold turned into the industry of mining, commerce and government expanded to serve the emerging communities. Freighters brought provisions, timber companies provided building materials, and farmers produced the food. Mining expanded from gold to other minerals including silver, galena, mica, feldspar, tin, lithium, and beryllium. Recognition of the increased population and impact on Dakota Territory came in 1883, when the legislators voted to move the regional capital to Bismarck, a central location that could serve both the eastern and western corners of Dakota Territory. By this time, efforts were already underway to admit Dakota Territory to statehood. The selection of Bismarck as the new capital, however, caused much resentment in the southern parts of the territory, and a divisionist movement began, with the desired outcome being the establishment of a separate state of South Dakota. This proposal was rejected in 1883, but voters in southern Dakota Territory approved a state constitution and elected state officers, even choosing senators for the new state. This effort was also rejected at the nation's capital.

The northern sections of Dakota Territory, much less populous than the southern sections, were initially anti-divisionist because they were concerned that separating the territory would result in the south becoming a state, and the north being doomed to territorial status. The two began to work together, however, with the south willing to share the Dakota name and promising to actively promote the admission of two states to the Union at the same time. This was the winning strategy, and North Dakota and South Dakota became the 39th and 40th states admitted to the Union, respectively, in 1889. The city of Pierre was appointed the temporary new capital of the state of South Dakota until 1890, when its status was finalized, and Bismarck retained its position as the capital of the state of North Dakota.

WOUNDED KNEE

The boom in population and growth of Dakota Territory, particularly the area of what became South Dakota, still had one big deterrent to growth: the separation of the eastern and western sections of the state by large reservations. Settlers pushing ever westward along the Missouri River wanted to press farther into Sioux territory. Three attempts were made to renegotiate the treaties. The first two attempts, one in 1882 and another in 1883, clearly ignored the three-fourths signature requirements of the 1878 treaty and were rejected by the U.S. Senate. It wasn't until the Crook Commission of 1889, led by General George Crook, who was trusted by the tribes, that more lands were opened to settlement. The Sioux agreed to move onto reservation lands that included specific boundaries. To obtain this agreement, Crook promised the tribes many things, including reparations for the horses that had been confiscated from them in earlier years.

The tribes were never paid for the horses and, at the same time that the new treaty went into effect, rations were cut. This contributed to the general unrest on the reservations, particularly among the Sioux tribes at the Pine Ridge and Cheyenne Reservations, who were among the last to be forced onto reservation lands. At the same time, word was reaching the tribes of a new Native religion arising in Nevada, a religion punctuated by the **Ghost Dance** as a ceremony that was supposed to bring back the buffalo and return the plains to the Native people. A band of Cheyenne headed to Nevada to meet with Wovoka, the new messiah of the religion, and upon its return, introduced the dance to the Pine Ridge Reservation.

The Ghost Dance frightened settlers and the Indian agent in charge at Pine Ridge, who called for military assistance. In 1890, remnants of the 7th Cavalry that was defeated at Custer's Last Stand entered reservation land to stop the dance. Their first act was the attempted arrest of Sitting Bull, who resisted and was killed. Word of Sitting Bull's death spread quickly, and Chief Big Foot and his band fled south to the Badlands fearing attack. When the cavalry caught up with them, they had already flown the white flag and the cavalry escorted the band to the small village of Wounded Knee. That night, Hotchkiss guns (an early form of machine gun) were set up on the ridge overlooking the valley. In the morning, the cavalry entered the camp with the intent of disarming the band. A shot was fired and, though no one was injured and most of the tribespeople had already surrendered their weapons, the cavalry attacked, killing at least 200 Native people, many of whom were women and children.

The **Wounded Knee Massacre** created much public outcry, and a review was made of many of the policies in place regarding the hiring of agency personnel, the distribution of rations, and other issues. Assimilation of the Native people into mainstream culture remained the predominant policy approach. The Dawes Act of 1887 was designed to introduce the concept of private property to the tribes. It was also a way for the government to seize more Native lands. Dawes believed that private property, a concept alien to Native American culture, would serve to civilize the tribes. The act gave the government the power to survey the land and then to allot it to tribe members, essentially eliminating tribal lands and creating private property within the reservation boundaries. The underbelly of the new act was that once the allotments were doled out, the remainder of the reservation land was considered to be surplus and would be available for sale. The end result of the Dawes Act was dramatic. The amount of land held by Native people on reservations nationwide decreased from 138 million acres (55.8 million ha) in 1887, when it was enacted, to just 48 million acres (19.4 million ha) by the time it was repealed in 1934.

CONTEMPORARY TIMES

The early 20th century saw the state of South Dakota fall in with national trends. When World War I began, South Dakota created a State Council of Defense that encouraged increases in food production and set quotas for fundraising for the war effort, primarily through the sale of war bonds. South Dakota did quite well in both regards, far exceeding food production requests and fundraising quotas.

The 1920s and '30s brought economic disaster to South Dakota, particularly to the east. In the early 1920s, income from farming

mass grave of Lakota people killed in the Wounded Knee Massacre

decreased significantly, and as a result, farm properties lost value. Farmers were unable to service their debts. Bank failures were not uncommon by 1923, and when the stock market crashed in 1929, South Dakota was already reeling. The Great Depression of the 1930s was not the only disaster to strike the Dakotas at the time. Grasshoppers, drought, severe winter weather, and crop failures added to the already impossible circumstances of farmers. Over 30,000 farm foreclosures occurred in the 1920s and early 1930s. The population of the state declined more than 7 percent as people abandoned their property. Workers in the Black Hills, tied more to mining than agriculture, particularly in Deadwood and Lead, saw shorter hours, but miners were still working and rode through the Great Depression relatively unscathed.

Implemented in the early 1930s, the New Deal farm legislation brought relief in the form of government subsidies and rewards for low production in order to raise prices. It also brought some interesting projects to life. The Works Progress Administration (WPA) put over 3.5 million Americans back to work. One of the projects administered by the WPA was the Federal Writers' Project, which employed over 6,500 people to write about the geography, history, and culture of each state. The WPA guide to South Dakota is still in print today. The Civilian Conservation Corps (CCC), another New Deal project, was also active in South Dakota. There were over 26,000 South Dakotans who worked in the camps at one time or another. The majority were put to work on projects in the Black Hills. Some of the major projects of the camps included the fire towers at the top of Black Elk Peak (formerly Harney Peak) and Mount Coolidge and Dinosaur Park in Rapid City. (The buildings used to house the actors and staff of the Black Hills Playhouse in Custer State Park originally comprised a CCC camp.) At the end of the Great Depression, the need for the CCC no longer existed, and the program was discontinued in 1942.

World War II had long-term effects on South Dakota. Deadwood and Lead suffered during the war, when the Homestake Mine was ordered to stop producing gold while the war was on. Many of the miners left to work in the copper mines or join the armed forces, and populations declined severely in these towns. After the war, however, mining techniques were upgraded and gold mining resumed. Several military installations created in the state remained as permanent bases after the war was over. In the Black Hills area, Ellsworth Air Force Base in Rapid City and the Black Hills Ordnance Depot in Igloo, south of the town of Edgemont, brought increases in population and employment.

National trends in the 1950s and '60s affected South Dakota and its rural and urban communities. The search for hydroelectric power brought four large dams to the Missouri River in the 1950s and provided much work for South Dakotans. However, the dams swallowed 500,000 acres (202,343 ha) of land, about half of which was owned by the Native American tribes located on the Missouri, and once again, reparations were minor. In the 1960s, the heightening Cold War kept Ellsworth Air Force Base in Rapid City fully occupied as over 150 intercontinental missile silos were installed and managed by base personnel. The 1960s also brought two interstate highways to the state, one of which, I-90, was of major import to the Black Hills region, connecting as it did the more populous eastern cities, including those in Nebraska and Minnesota, to the Black Hills. With the increase in automobile travel and truck freighting, however, the importance of the railroad for passenger travel disappeared. By the late 1960s, there were no longer any passenger railcars traveling to South Dakota.

Lakota Activism
The early 1970s brought a nationwide air of discontent and the creation of many social organizations, many of them militant, to the United States. The Students for a Democratic Society, the Black Panthers, and the **American Indian Movement (AIM)**

all were known to use violent means to bring awareness to social issues of the day. In 1973, the American Indian Movement came to South Dakota. In February 1973, members of AIM took over the community of Wounded Knee, protesting corrupt government. FBI agents were sent to remove the AIM occupiers and a siege ensued. For 71 days, AIM held the community; two people were killed, 12 were wounded, and 1,200 were arrested. The event attracted worldwide attention to the plight of Native Americans in the United States. A subsequent trial of AIM leadership relating to the events at Wounded Knee resulted in the acquittal of all charges of wrongdoing.

For over 100 years, the Sioux argued that the 1877 act ratified by Congress was an illegal one, breaking the Fort Laramie Treaty of 1868, and that the Black Hills should be returned to the Lakota. The Sioux filed a lawsuit in 1920, the soonest this avenue was open to them, claiming that the Black Hills were taken without just compensation and triggering a legal battle that continues, on the strength of continuous appeals, to this day. In July 1980, however, a small victory was handed to the Oglala Lakota. The Supreme Court of the United States ruled as follows:

> In sum, we conclude that the legal analysis and factual findings of the Court of Claims fully support its conclusion that the terms of the 1877 Act did not effect "a mere change in the form of investment of Indian tribal property." ... Rather, the 1877 Act effected a taking of tribal property, property which had been set aside for the exclusive occupation of the Sioux by the Fort Laramie Treaty of 1868. That taking implied an obligation on the part of the Government to make just compensation to the Sioux Nation, and that obligation, including an award of interest, must now, at last, be paid.

The amount due was to be $17.1 million plus interest from 1877. The settlement was rejected by the Sioux. Today the value of the settlement is estimated to be 1.3 billion dollars.

The money has never been collected, and the Sioux believe the Black Hills should be returned to them. The lawsuits continue, and Lakota activism is on the rise. Some Lakota activists are explicitly calling for the closure of Mount Rushmore. The tribes have filed lawsuits against pipelines and uranium mines to protect water supplies and protested against fireworks that threatened the forests. They continue to negotiate and have made some progress in receiving restitution for egregious treatment in the past. They also continue negotiating to have public lands returned to the Native American tribes.

South Dakota Today

In 1930, the state of South Dakota had a population of about 690,000. The Great Depression, the droughts, and the grasshoppers that attacked the state in 1930-1940 reduced that number by 50,000 people. It wasn't until 1990 that the state population regained its 1930 numbers. Today, the state of South Dakota has a population of approximately 885,000 people, 29 percent of whom live in either Sioux Falls or Rapid City. Demographically, according to the 2020 census site, the population is 80.7 percent White, 8.8 percent American Indian and Alaska Native, 2 percent Black or African American, 1.5 percent Asian, 1.8 per cent other, and 5.3 percent two or more races. There are nine Indigenous reservations and tribal land areas in the state.

While the state continues to increase in population, the growth is primarily in the urban areas. Rural counties are getting older, and young people are leaving the state. A conservative state, South Dakota has voted Republican in the last 11 presidential elections. However, this does not make the state predictable on all conservative issues. In the decade ended in 2009, voters twice rejected attempts to make abortion illegal in the state, and passed legislation to ban smoking in all public establishments including casinos and bars. In 2020, by a grassroots initiative, both medical and recreational marijuana were legalized (the Republican-dominated legislature, however, has determined that "rules" need to be set to determine how the initiative should be implemented). It is a state where independents are likely to be conservative and unpredictable. Still, the state's economy remains entwined with the industries of its past: agriculture, ranching, mining, government services, and tourism.

Economy

The Black Hills developed as a natural resource-rich island surrounded by the grasslands of South Dakota and Wyoming. Early industries, including mining, logging, farming, ranching, and tourism, remain major sources of revenue for Black Hills communities to this day. The community of Rapid City, the only major urban area in the Black Hills region, continues to provide the bulk of the area's services, including health care, retail sales, and financial services. Rapid City is also host to the only commercial airport in the area.

MINING

The early 1900s saw most of the activity related to the mining of gold disappear in the Black Hills. Mining did not disappear entirely, however. In addition to gold, the Black Hills region is rich in other minerals; into the 1950s, the Black Hills led the nation in the production of mica, feldspar, and beryl. As of 2011, there were 47 active mines in the state. Gold remains the leading mineral commodity, in terms of value, even though there is only one active gold mine. In 2015, Wharf Resources, with a mine located near Lead in the Northern Hills, estimated production for the next year to equal 85,000 to 90,000 ounces (2,551 kg) of gold. Wharf Resources has been mining in South Dakota since 1982.

The last detailed information about mining in South Dakota was provided in May 2012 for 2011 mining results. In 2012, the state legislature repealed the requirement to publish these reports. Published by the State Department of Environment and Natural Resources, the reports historically contained information about the number of mining permits (and who requested them), the acreage reclaimed, the status of the cleanup at Superfund sites, and the gallons of water and pounds of cyanide used by the mining companies. None of this information is now readily available to South Dakota residents. In addition, in 2011 the state legislature set aside regulations pertaining to in situ mining. The state has decided to allow the EPA to regulate mining in South Dakota with no state oversight.

TOURISM

In 1875, the Bureau of Indian Affairs sent an expedition into the Black Hills that explored the region south of the areas visited by the Custer Expedition of 1874. Reports of warm-water springs in the area of what is now Fall River County began to circulate in the hills. As the gold rush slowed in the Northern Hills, many of the successful individuals in Deadwood began to look for opportunities elsewhere in the hills, and the idea of a warm-water resort appealed to many of them. By 1881, an investment group dedicated themselves to the development and marketing of the community. As word got out, a steady stream of travelers came to the area to enjoy the mineral waters. At the time, medical tourism—visiting mineral spas—was a popular pastime, and drinking and soaking in the water were said to cure just about every possible ailment. Most of the beautiful sandstone buildings that exist today in Hot Springs were built in 1890-1910. The railroad brought travelers to the town by 1891. Hot Springs was the first tourist town in the hills. Today, Evans Plunge, built in 1890, remains one of Hot Springs' major attractions. In the late 1800s, the State Soldiers' Home and the Battle Mountain Sanitarium were built in Hot Springs, due primarily to the healing properties attributed to the mineral water. Today, the Soldiers' Home is the State Veterans' Home, and the Battle Mountain Sanitarium is the Veterans' Hospital. Spas, massage therapy, and natural foods are still a part of the Hot Springs economy today.

As miners prospected for gold and other minerals in the Black Hills, a second element for tourism arose: caves. Both Jewel Cave and Wind Cave were not mineral-rich enough to mine, but the caves themselves were interesting, and cave tours became the second tourist attraction in the hills.

In 1916, Peter Norbeck was elected governor of South Dakota. Norbeck was a progressive and a conservationist, and during his tenure, he was able to convince the legislature to create a state park board. As chairman of that board, Norbeck was able to work with the committee to ensure that Custer State Park would be one of the largest state parks in the nation. He also designed scenic highways through the park to make the land accessible to the public.

The crowning achievement of South Dakota tourism was the hiring of Gutzon Borglum to carve a mountain in the state. The idea was instigated by Doane Robinson, state historian, who believed that South Dakota could benefit from the increased use of automobiles if it could come up with a great attraction. Reading about the Stone Mountain carving of Confederate heroes in Georgia, Robinson contacted the carver on that project, Gutzon Borglum, to see if he might be interested in a project in the Black Hills. Initially, Robinson envisioned several carvings in the spires of the Needles formation, honoring both Native American and white heroes. Borglum determined that the spires were too fragile for that kind of work and selected Mount Rushmore instead. He also decided that a more national theme was needed to attract people to the area, and he picked the presidents who would grace the mountain. The carving started in 1927 and was completed in 1941. Today, over three million visitors a year come to the monument. In addition to the attraction itself, the carving brought new economic life to the defunct mining communities of Hill City and Keystone, which now service visitors with retail shops, dining establishments, and accommodations.

Today, tourism is a growing industry in the

Tourism is a large part of the Black Hills economy.

state of South Dakota. By 2008, state tourism dollars reached $967 million. In 2010, income from tourism topped 1.059 billion. Today, travel and tourism make up the second-largest industry in the state and the third-largest private sector employer.

CATTLE RANCHING

The relocation of the Oglala and Brule Sioux tribes to reservation land, and the near extinction of the bison herds as a result of the fur trade, opened the front range of the Black Hills to cattle. The range cattle industry began in Texas, where huge herds roamed the plains. As rail lines made their way into the Midwest, the cattle were driven north to the rail yards where they were shipped east. Demand for cattle as provisions in the Black Hills region increased, as well, both for the rations provided to the reservation tribes and for the growing communities. In 1880, the Black Hills Live Stock Association was founded, and by the end of 1882, it was estimated that over 250,000 head of cattle were grazing along the front range of the hills. Farther north, there were still enough bison to halt cattle grazing. In 1880-1886, professional hunters engaged in the slaughter of most of the remaining bison on the plains, allowing the cattle companies to expand into the northern plains. By 1884, the number of cattle on the plains that surrounded the Black Hills was estimated at over 700,000 head.

The fortunes of the great cattle companies changed dramatically during the winter of 1886-1887, when early storms struck the region. Heavy snows were followed by days of subzero weather. The storms caused huge losses, driving many of the cattle companies out of business. Northern companies lost as much as 90 percent of their herds. Custer County and Fall River County, protected by the hills, saw negligible losses.

Another problem facing cattle companies was the movement of homesteaders into South Dakota. While the Homestead Act of 1862 started migration into South Dakota, most homesteaders were initially limited to the eastern corners of the state, and most were coming from neighboring states. With the completion of the railroad to Rapid City from the East in 1883, and from Nebraska in 1886, homesteaders trickled into the Black Hills region, claiming what had previously been public domain lands and putting up fences. Cattle owners frequently found their herds fenced out of watering holes, and the land available for open range grazing was diminishing rapidly. At first, the cattle companies leased lands from the reservations, but soon, with the Crook Commission, more lands were open to settlement and the available range diminished even further. The population of "West River" increased from about 45,000 in 1900 to over 135,000 by 1910. By 1911, the herd law, which held owners of livestock responsible for damages to crops, was applicable everywhere, and the open range period in South Dakota history was over.

While the huge cattle ranches of the past are no longer with us, ranching with agriculture remains an important industry in western South Dakota.

NEW INDUSTRIES

The towns of Deadwood and Lead were long dependent on the mining industry for their survival. By the early 1900s, most of the gold mines in the region were closed or working on limited production schedules. During World War II, all gold mining was shut down temporarily under orders from the U.S. government, and miners left to work in copper mines elsewhere or enlisted to help in the war effort. Mining resumed after the war, but both production and employment numbers continually declined. Deadwood's population decreased from around 3,000 in 1960 to 1,800 by 1990. As the population shrank, local businesses were shuttered. In 1986, a community group called "Deadwood U Bet" was created, advocating for small stakes gambling in Deadwood. The group was successful, and in November 1989, small stakes gambling was legalized. The community, designated a National Historic Landmark in 1961, was determined to use a portion of the revenue earned to save the historic structures in town. As a result of that commitment, most of the historic buildings in the community have been completely renovated. It is estimated that the legalization of gambling in the community created nearly 2,000 new jobs. Approximately 27 percent of the new jobs were held by residents of Lead, but the bulk of the benefit of the gambling initiative has gone to Deadwood. The population decline continues in the county, however, with a decrease of 4.5 percent between 2000 and 2008. However, with the tax revenue generated by the casinos, Deadwood has been able to save its heritage and work on establishing the town as a center of tourism. Lead has not yet found the key to economic growth, except as a bedroom services city for Deadwood.

Another new industry coming to the hills is scientific research. After the Homestake Mine in Lead closed in 2002, the National Science Foundation (NSF) selected it as the location for the Deep Underground Science and Engineering Laboratory. Eventually the NSF declined to fund the building of the lab, but the Department of Energy took over. The lab is now called the Sanford Underground Research Facility, named after philanthropist T. Denny Sanford, who donated 70 million dollars to its construction. Here, experiments in physics (dark matter) will be performed, and the site will be a center for mining research as well as research in geology and biology. The community and many surrounding communities are hoping this facility will pave the way for more science and research facilities in the future.

Essentials

Transportation

The best way to get around the Black Hills region is by car. For those who don't want to do all the driving, it is possible to arrange for day trips to the Badlands, Deadwood, Custer State Park, and Mount Rushmore through several small tour companies in the region. For visitors planning just 1-3 days in the hills, the tours may be all you need.

AIR

There is one commercial airport in the Black Hills region and that is the **Rapid City Regional Airport** (RAP, 605/393-9924 airport information, 605/393-2850 flight information, www.rapairport.com). There are

several auto rental agencies at the airport (although almost all are divisions of the same company), including **Alamo** (833/445-1504), **National** (833/445-1503), **Hertz** (605/393-0160), **Avis** (605/393-0740), **Budget** (605/393-0488), and **Enterprise** (833/445-1502). Shuttle service is available through **Airport Express Shuttle** (605/399-9999 or 800/357-9998, www. rapidshuttle.com), which will pick up and drop off at any location in Rapid City or in the Black Hills.

CAR

The entire Black Hills region is about 65 miles (105 km) from east to west and 125 miles (201 km) from north to south. Any two points within the hills is an easy day trip, though traveling through the hills can take twice as long as traveling around the edges due to the two-lane, winding roads.

Major transportation routes include **I-90,** which enters the hills region at Rapid City; skirts along the Northern Hills past Sturgis, Deadwood, and Spearfish; and then heads off into Wyoming. **Highway 79** runs north-south along the eastern edge of the hills and connects Rapid City to the southern community of Hot Springs. **U.S. 18** in the south connects Hot Springs and Edgemont and then continues west into Wyoming and **U.S. 85,** which travels up the western and Wyoming section of the Black Hills and cuts into the northwestern corner of the South Dakota Black Hills, joining up with I-90 near Deadwood.

Within the boundaries of the Black Hills, major routes include **U.S. 16,** which is the direct route south from Rapid City into the Central Hills, including Mount Rushmore. **U.S. 385** follows the western edge of the developed portion of the hills and runs from Hot Springs through Custer and Hill City, and winds up halfway between Deadwood and Lead.

While you are never far from a **gas station** within the confines of the Black Hills, you should keep your tank full when you head out to the Badlands or the Pine Ridge Reservation. Cell phone service is sporadic, towns are far apart, and a wrong turn can lead to miles and miles from nowhere. It's best to err on the side of caution and fill up whenever the tank is less than half full.

BUSES AND TOURS

Rapid City has limited city-to-city bus service. **Jefferson Lines** (605/348-3300 or 800/451-5333, www.jeffersonlines.com) has one departure headed east and one departure headed west daily. The line is the contract carrier in the Midwest for Greyhound and covers the route between Minneapolis and Billings, Montana. **Greyhound** (800/231-2222, www. greyhound.com) can get you to Rapid City, but travel times are exceedingly long. There is one bus a day from the Denver area to Rapid City, for instance, and travel time is over 13 hours. The distance from Denver to Rapid City is a little over 350 miles (565 km) and can be driven in about 6.5 hours.

There are several tour companies that will arrange day trips by bus or van into the hills. Standard large-bus daylong driving tours are limited. Day trips to Mount Rushmore are offered by **Mount Rushmore Tours** (605/343-3113 or 888/343-3113, www. mountrushmoretours.com, mid-May-mid-Oct.). **Dakota Trailways** (605/642-2353 or 800/499-2652, www.mydakotatrailways.com) is available for group charter tours.

There are also several smaller tour companies willing to customize private tours to suit visitors' needs. These companies typically use 7- to 14-passenger vans as transportation. Look for **GeoFunTrek** (605/923-8386 or 605/430-1531, www.geofuntrek.com) or **Affordable Adventures** (605/342-7691, www.affordableadventuresbh.com). In addition to van tours of the region, **Black Hills Adventure Tours** (605/209-7817, www. blackhillsadventuretours.com) also offers hiking, biking, and kayaking tours.

Recreation

The Black Hills of South Dakota are an outdoor enthusiast's paradise. There are plenty of fast-running streams and reservoirs for fishing and water sports. The national parks and state parks are great for hiking, biking, and horseback riding, and you can also enjoy great rock climbing and exciting spelunking tours.

In particular, there are two special trails for hikers and bicyclists worth exploring on a visit here. The **George S. Mickelson Trail** winds 109 miles (175 km) along the historic Deadwood-Edgemont Burlington Northern rail line, which was abandoned in 1983. The trail is gravel and, with a grade of less than 3 percent, accessible to most users with mobility issues. The fee to use the trail is $4 per day or $15 per year. It's maintained by the South Dakota Department of Game, Fish, and Parks. Trail information, including details on hunting and fishing licenses and downloadable maps, can be found at http://gfp.sd.gov.

The **Centennial Trail,** Trail #89, is a cooperative project of several governmental agencies. The trail is 111 miles (179 km) long and winds through much of the scenic beauty of South Dakota. The trail starts in the prairies south of Bear Butte, near Sturgis, and winds through Black Hills National Forest land, the Black Elk Wilderness Area, Custer State Park, and Wind Cave National Park. The trail is open to hiking, biking, and horseback riding (except for portions located in Wind Cave, where only hiking is allowed). The easiest place to find information is on the Black Hills National Forest website (www.fs.usda.gov/blackhills). Select "Maps & Publications," then "Recreation Publications & Maps." On the website, under the Black Hills National Forest Non-Motorized Trail System header, select "Trail Brochures" and, finally, number 89, "Centennial."

In addition to private campgrounds, the Black Hills National Forest and the South Dakota Department of Game, Fish, and Parks offer several **campgrounds.** Some of the campgrounds are on a first-come, first-served basis, and some take reservations. Some are open all year, and some are seasonal. For listings and information about all the Black Hills National Forest campgrounds, visit www.fs.usda.gov/blackhills and select the options "Recreation" and "Camping & Cabins." Information includes fees, reservation requirements, whether or not the campground is open all year, and if there is drinking water available; for some, maps are available. For campgrounds that take reservations, they can be made by calling 877/444-6777 or going online at www.recreation.gov. Information about South Dakota state campground facilities, which include Angostura Recreation Area and Custer State Park, can be found by visiting http://gfp.sd.gov and selecting the "State Parks" option. To research state campgrounds, access the same site and click on "Camp," then "Camping Options." To make reservations at a South Dakota state campground, call 800/710-2267 or visit http://reservations.gooutdoorssouthdakota.com.

PARK PASSES

The federal government offers an annual pass, called the **America the Beautiful—National Parks and Federal Recreational Lands Pass,** to the public that allows entrance to any national park or federal recreation lands with an entrance fee or standard amenities fee. There are six different passes. The Annual Pass is $80 per year for adults under the age of 62. Seniors have two pass options: the Annual Senior Pass for $20 or Lifetime Senior Pass for $80. To get a senior pass, a U.S. citizen or permanent resident must 62 years or older. The remaining passes are free and include a Military Pass for active military and their dependents, veterans, and Gold Star families; a 4th Grade Pass, which is in effect from September-August (the school year through the following summer) for all 4th grade students who attain a valid paper pass from everykidoutdoors.gov; an Access Pass for U.S. citizens or permanent residents with disabilities; and a Volunteer Pass for folks who have completed 250 hours of service at a federal agency that participates in the Interagency Pass Program. While the Black Hills and the Badlands contain a lot of federal lands—including Jewel Cave, Wind Cave, Mount Rushmore, the Minuteman Missile National Historic Site, and Badlands National Park—standard passes will only be honored at Badlands National Park. (The entrance fee to the park is $30 per car, $25 per motorcycle, and $15 per pedestrian or bicycle. Entrance fees allow access for seven days.) There are no entrance fees at any of the other sites. There is a parking fee at Mount Rushmore and for tours at the cave sites. If this is the only area in

which you are planning to visit national recreation lands in the current year, the price of the pass may not be cost-effective.

Several picnic areas in the **Black Hills National Forest** include day-use fees of $5-7 (half price for America the Beautiful Senior Pass holders) or sell standard annual passes for $25 or a premium annual pass for $40 (half price for Senior or Access Pass holders). The premium pass grants access to all of the sites accessible with the standard pass and adds Sheridan Lake, Pactola Reservoir, and the Calumet Trailhead.

Custer State Park is also a fee area. A temporary pass is available for $20 per vehicle and is good for seven days. The annual pass is $36. The Mickelson Trail, a walking/biking path that runs Edgemont-Deadwood, requires a trail pass, which costs $4 per day or $15 a year.

Travel Tips

ATTENDING A POWWOW

A powwow is a gathering of Native Americans to sing and dance, to compete, and to reconnect with old friends. They are a part of Native American culture. Powwows are held throughout the Black Hills, with annual ceremonies in both Spearfish and Rapid City. On Pine Ridge Reservation, powwows are a part of community life. Visiting Pine Ridge is literally a visit to another country—the reservation is a sovereign nation within the borders of the United States. It is also a place where there are a lot of people willing to share their culture with outsiders.

While attending a powwow is a wonderful way to experience Native American culture, it is **important** to respect the ceremony and the celebration of the tribes and remember that you are a guest. The participants in the dance will be wearing their finest regalia. Honor this and refrain from wearing grungy, torn clothing.

Many powwows, particularly on reservation lands, are held outdoors where there is very little in the way of public seating. Bring lawn chairs or blankets to sit on. There are sometimes benches set up around the arena. These benches are reserved for dancers only. Sometimes the areas just behind the benches are reserved for family members, so ask before you set up chairs.

Some of the outfits worn by the dancers are breathtakingly beautiful. Remember to ask permission before you take pictures. Listen to the master of ceremonies for cues. Certain songs and ceremonies require the attendees to stand with heads uncovered while they are played. The Grand Entry Song, Flag Songs, Veteran Songs, and Memorial Songs all require that you stand. Attendees are free to participate in intertribal dances whether wearing regalia or not, but should not try to dance at any other time. Blanket dances are held at traditional powwows to help defray the costs of the powwows and the travel costs of some of the drums. If you see a blanket placed on the grounds and dancers start leaving money on the blanket, feel free to contribute by asking a dancer to place money on the blanket for you. If a dancer drops or loses something off their regalia, particularly an eagle feather, do not pick it up. There are ceremonies for retrieving items that have touched the ground. Ask a dancer or other person in authority for assistance.

It sounds like a lot of rules, but the guiding principle behind attending a powwow is respect. Enjoy the dance, enjoy the food, meet people, and celebrate the beauty of a Native American powwow.

INTERNATIONAL VISITORS

International visitors to the United States must clear U.S. Customs and Border Protection (CBP) to enter the United States. There is valuable information available to foreign travelers on the CBP website at www.cbp.gov/travel/international-visitors, including what paperwork is required to enter the United States and sample customs declaration forms that will need to be filled out on arrival.

Many banks in South Dakota are not able to exchange foreign currency. In Rapid City, **Great Western Bank** (14 Saint Joseph St., 605/343-9230, Mon.-Fri. 8:30am-5pm) is one of the few that can exchange most foreign currencies. If you are traveling on weekends, consider exchanging funds before you leave home or at major airport connections like Denver or Chicago.

ACCESS FOR TRAVELERS WITH DISABILITIES

South Dakota is an accessible state for travelers with disabilities. Most attractions, hotels, and restaurants are equipped to accommodate visitors in wheelchairs and have set aside parking spaces and provide ramps. All of the federal parks and monuments have provided for some level of access for travelers with disabilities, including wheelchair-accessible

trails. Mount Rushmore has a 27-page Braille guide to the monument available upon request from the information desk, and many of the films about the monument are both captioned for the hearing impaired and narrated for the visually impaired. Note that some of the historic buildings in some communities may not be as accessible as desired. If you have any questions about accessibility, particularly with historic accommodations, be sure to call and ask.

LBGTQ TRAVELERS

South Dakota is a conservative and religious state. Overt displays of physical affection are likely to make residents a little uncomfortable. This is true for both straight and LGBTQ travelers. Be respectful of local reserve. For the most part, as a community deeply involved in hospitality, the people are extremely friendly and welcoming to everyone.

SENIOR TRAVELERS

Most attractions, museums, and many of the restaurants in the Black Hills region offer discounts to seniors, so feel free to ask about discounts even if there are no posted signs. The state also offers a discount on senior fishing licenses if you are planning a fishing outing while in the hills. Many of the hotels in the hills offer discounts to members of **AARP** (American Association of Retired Persons, www.aarp.org), as well. For a $20 annual fee or $80 lifetime fee, seniors (ages 62 and up) should consider purchasing the America the Beautiful—National Parks and Federal Recreational Lands Pass. In the Black Hills, it will allow you to enter Badlands National Park for free. Other benefits may include discounts for fee-based activities. Check with the recreation area to determine if discounts are in place.

Road Scholar (800/454-5768, www.roadscholar.org) has historically offered reasonably priced educational tours to seniors over the age of 55. The organization has lifted most of its age restrictions, but still provides activity-level requirements for the tours, to assist seniors in selecting a tour that will match their individual level of fitness.

TRAVELING WITH CHILDREN

The Black Hills region of South Dakota has a strong orientation toward family-style vacations. There are plenty of attractions geared toward children, and many of them, like Dinosaur Park and Storybook Island in Rapid City, are free. There are lakes to swim and boat and trails for hiking, biking, and horseback riding. There are miniature golf courses and trout to feed. It really is a wonderland for kids.

There are a few things to consider if you are traveling with the kids. First, if you are planning on staying at a bed-and-breakfast, check to make sure that children are welcome there, as in some instances, they are not. Second, the environment in the Black Hills region is fairly arid, so make sure that children carry and drink enough water to avoid dehydration and wear sunscreen to avoid sunburn. And finally, keep an eye on the kids when hiking in the higher elevations of the Northern Hills. Very few of the trails have guardrails, and some of the drop-offs can be steep and long. This is also true in the Badlands. The soil is loose and the cliffs are high, so make sure the children are forewarned to stay away from the cliff edges.

TRAVELING WITH PETS

Pets are allowed in many of the public parks in the Black Hills area, but the rules are sometimes very restrictive. In the Badlands, for instance, pets are allowed only in developed areas of the park (that is, on roads and in campgrounds). Pets must always be on a leash and cannot go on hiking trails or enter any of the wilderness areas of the park. At Mount Rushmore, pets, with the exception of service animals, are not allowed anywhere in the memorial. The Black Hills National Forest sites allow pets on the trails, but they must be leashed or under strict voice control. There is an additional $2 charge for animals in national forest campgrounds. Custer State Park allows pets in campgrounds, but pets are not allowed in any of the camping cabins, lodges, or other park buildings.

You are allowed to leave your pet in an unattended vehicle, but this could be very dangerous and is not recommended. Temperatures in the summer can soar to over 100°F (37.8°C), and even on a day where the temperature reaches just 80°F (26.7°C),

Traveling with pets can be a challenge.

the interior of a car can reach temperatures far above those safe for your pet. There are many pet-friendly lodgings in the Black Hills. On a day when you expect to spend a great deal of time at a site that restricts pets, confer with your host to see if you might be permitted to leave your animal for the day, or check with a local vet or kennel. It is a good idea to call a local veterinarian and ask for a kennel recommendation.

Lodgings that do allow for pets have various methods of determining the charge. Some venues charge a single dollar amount for the length of your stay. Some have a per pet per night charge. Some don't allow large dogs, and most don't allow cats. Always, when making reservations, ask about pet policies and mention that your reservation should be for a pet-friendly room. Most accommodations only have a few rooms set aside for travelers with pets. If you don't mention it, you may find that there are no rooms available for you.

HEALTH AND SAFETY
Wind, Water, and Sun

High altitude, a semiarid climate, lots of sunshine, and summer thunderstorms can affect your health and safety when visiting the Black Hills. First and foremost, always use sunscreen and wear sunglasses. The high altitudes of the Central and Northern Hills combined with the sunshine can cause **sunburn** in a fairly short period of time. Second, carry water. Hikers, bikers, and others who spend extended periods outdoors need to worry about both **dehydration** and **hyperthermia.** There is no water available on most hiking trails, and where there are streams or lakes, it's not safe to drink the water due to mining chemicals, farm and ranch fertilizers, and pesticides. **Hyperthermia** (overheating) can occur with too much exposure to the sun and can be a medical emergency. Symptoms can include red skin, dizziness, and vomiting. Severe cases may result in confused or even hostile behavior. Mild cases can be treated by getting out of the sun and drinking water. In more severe cases, remove restrictive

clothing and splash cool water on the victim. Immersion in cool water, if there is a stream or lake nearby, will also help. Immersion in very cold water is not recommended. The best course of action is prevention. Stay hydrated, monitor your temperature, and rest in the shade frequently on days of high heat.

Conversely, **hypothermia** (overcooling) can also be a problem in the hills, though it's not as common as overheating. Evenings in the hills, especially in the higher elevations, can be relatively cool. If you are out hiking and are caught in a late-afternoon thunderstorm, wet clothing and cool temperatures can bring on hypothermia. Be prepared and carry a windbreaker or light poncho with you when hiking. Symptoms of hypothermia include shivering, slurred speech, and cold pale skin. Older adults, infants, young children, and people who are very lean are at particular risk. If you suspect hypothermia, remove wet clothing and cover up with something warm and dry. Make sure to stay out of the wind and cover the victim's head to maintain body heat. Do not give a victim any alcoholic drinks or attempt to massage them into warmth. Hypothermia, like hyperthermia, can be a medical emergency.

Ankle injuries are the most common injuries sustained in the Badlands. The soils are eroding constantly and can cause sliding. Wear good footgear with strong ankle support if you expect to engage in any backcountry hiking. Be especially careful not to get too close to the edges of buttes and spires. The soil is very loose in places and/or may be slippery due to leaves or mud. You don't want to find yourself sliding off the side of a cliff.

Insects and Animals

The **West Nile virus** is carried by mosquitoes, and there have been several cases of the virus diagnosed in the Black Hills. Mosquitoes are found near standing water and are most active in the morning and at dusk; use insect repellent if planning to hike in marshy areas or if you are camping near water.

Another disease-carrying pest commonly

found in both the Black Hills and the Badlands is the **wood tick.** Ticks in South Dakota can transmit **Rocky Mountain spotted fever** and **Colorado tick fever.** With ticks, the best defense is to be watchful. Repel ticks by tucking your pants into your socks when outdoors in the spring and spraying clothing and exposed skin with a tick repellent. Wear light colors so that any ticks that may land are easily visible. It takes several hours of feeding before a tick can transmit disease, so check frequently for ticks when you are outdoors. To remove ticks, use tweezers and pull slowly and steadily up and away from your skin. Matches do not encourage ticks to back out, contrary to common mythology. Ticks are most common in the early spring. Remember that ticks like pets too, so if you are traveling with pets, give them a good going-over and remove any ticks you find. Some pet owners use tick collars or powders on pets and that works well.

There are few toxic creatures in the Black Hills. However, the **prairie rattlesnake** is a local resident. Keep an eye on where you are putting your feet and hands when hiking and scrambling through rock formations. Rattlesnakes are not aggressive and are as loath to see you as you are to see them. If you hear any rattling or hissing, back off and head in a different direction. If bitten by a rattlesnake, seek medical attention immediately. In the interim, try to stay calm and minimize physical activity to slow the venom's circulation throughout the body. Do not try to remove the venom with cutting or suction, as both actions could be more dangerous than the bite itself.

The **western black widow spider** is one of South Dakota's few venomous arachnids. It is uncommon for people to be bitten by the spider. The bite of this spider can cause a wide variety of reactions depending on the age and condition of the person bitten. Symptoms include sharp pain at the time of the bite, which may be followed by muscle cramps, weakness and tremor. In severe cases, nausea, vomiting, fainting, dizziness, and chest pain may result.

Bites are rarely fatal, though they can be dangerous to seniors and to children. The decision to seek emergency care should be made early. If the person who was bitten by a black widow spider has more than minor pain or has whole-body symptoms, seek care at a hospital emergency room.

Problems with predatory animals are near nonexistent in the hills. Mountain lions and coyotes are present, but both are very shy of humans. There are no records of either attacking a human in the state. **Bison,** on the other hand, tend to attract trouble. Bison are free-roaming in Custer State Park, Wind Cave National Park, and Badlands National Park. This majestic animal enthralls visitors, who have a tendency to get too close to them in their quest for better photos. But, as bulky as they are, these animals are remarkably quick and agile. Keep your distance. An aggravated bison can accelerate quickly and reach speeds up to 45 miles per hour (72 kph). You cannot outrun them. Be especially wary during the rut season, which overlaps tourist season, occurring late July-September. Sadly, there are cases of visitors being gored by bison almost every year. Try to keep a distance of at least 100 yards (91 m).

Medical Care

There are small hospitals and medical clinics in most regions of the Black Hills. Most will provide emergency services and then transfer patients to Rapid City.

- **Central Hills: Monument Health Rapid City Hospital** (353 Fairmont Blvd., Rapid City, 605/755-1000) and **Monument Health Urgent Care Centers** (2116 Jackson Blvd., Rapid City, 605/755-2273; 1303 N. LaCrosse St., Rapid City, 605/755-2273) allow walk-in patients for nonemergency treatment and are generally viewed as doctor's offices by insurance companies.

- **Southern Hills: Monument Health Custer Hospital & Urgent Care Center** (1220 Montgomery St., Custer, 605/673-9400); **Fall River Health Services**

Coronavirus in South Dakota's Black Hills

At the time of writing in 2022, South Dakota had been moderately impacted by the effects of the coronavirus, but the situation is constantly evolving. The government of South Dakota is extremely conservative and has determined that safety precautions should be taken by individuals and not government entities. There are no state mandates of any kind, and the state has regulated against local communities establishing mandates as well. However, federal entities—such as the National Park Service, which oversees Mount Rushmore and the Badlands—follow the guidelines set by the CDC, and national chain stores and lodgings apply the same safety protocols in South Dakota as they do in all other states.

Now more than ever, Moon encourages its readers to be courteous and ethical in their travel. Be respectful to local residents and mindful of the situation in your chosen destination when planning your trip.

BEFORE YOU GO

- Check websites (listed below) for **local restrictions** and the **overall health status** of the destination and your point of origin. If you're traveling to or from an area that is currently a COVID-19 hot spot, you may want to reconsider your trip.

- Moon encourages travelers to **get vaccinated** if their health status allows and to take a **coronavirus test** with enough time to receive the results before departure if possible.

- If you plan to fly, check with your airline and the local health authorities for updated **travel requirements.** Some airlines may be taking more steps than others to help you travel safely; check their websites before buying your ticket. Check limitations on local airports as well. Consider a very early or very late flight to limit exposure. Flights may be more infrequent, with increased cancellations.

(1201 Hwy. 71 S., Hot Springs, 605/745-8910); **Pine Ridge Hospital** (E. U.S. 18, Pine Ridge, 605/867-5131); **Kyle Health Center** (Wapiyapi Ave., Kyle, 605/455-2541); **Wanblee Health Center** (210 1st St., Wanblee, 605/462-6155).

- **Northern Hills: Monument Health Lead-Deadwood** (61 Charles St., Deadwood, 605/717-6000); **Monument Health Spearfish Hospital** (1440 N. Main St., Spearfish, 605/644-4000) and **Urgent Care** (1420 N. 10th St., Spearfish, 605/717-8595).

- **Badlands: Monument Health Wall Clinic** (112 7th Ave., Wall, 605/279-2149).

CRIME

Crime rates are low in South Dakota, but keep safety in mind when traveling and follow standard safety procedures. Don't leave valuable items in hotel rooms or in clear sight on the seat of your car. Make sure cars are locked at trailheads and parking lots of local attractions. Women and others traveling alone should exercise the same caution that they would on a downtown street in any city. Be alert.

- Check the website of any venues you wish to patronize to confirm that they're open, if their hours have been adjusted, and to learn about any specific visitation requirements, such as **mandatory reservations** or **limited occupancy.**

- Pack **hand sanitizer,** a **thermometer,** and plenty of **face masks.** Consider packing **snacks, bottled water,** a **cooler,** or anything else you might need to limit the number of stops along your route. Be prepared for possible closures and reduced services over the course of your travels.

- Assess the risk of entering **crowded spaces,** joining **tours,** and taking **public transit.**

- Expect **general disruptions.** Events may be postponed or canceled. Some tours and venues may require reservations, enforce limits on the number of guests, or operate during different hours than the ones listed. Some may be closed entirely. Federal entities follow the guidelines as set by the CDC and are most likely to be impacted by updates to them; affected sites would include Minuteman Missile National Historic Site, Mount Rushmore, Jewel Cave, Wind Cave, and the Badlands. Small performance venues including the Custer State Park Playhouse and Performing Arts Center of Rapid City have set up outdoor stages for performances, which may result in weather cancellations or a cut in reservations in order to maintain social distancing in their small theaters.

RESOURCES

- **Centers for Disease Control and Prevention:** www.cdc.gov

- **South Dakota Department of Health:** www.doh.sd.gov

- **COVID-19 in South Dakota:** http://covid.sd.gov

Information and Services

TOURISM INFORMATION

The **South Dakota Department of Tourism** (800/732-5682, www.travelsouthdakota.com) is a great resource. Free visitor packages can be obtained by calling or making contact through the website. The state of South Dakota is dedicated to increasing tourism to the state and has committed a great deal of resources to accomplish that end.

The **South Dakota Department of Game, Fish, and Parks** (http://gfp.sd.gov, customer service 605/223-7660) can provide information about parks and recreation facilities, as well as hunting and fishing licenses (605/223-7660), and can help make reservations at state campgrounds (800/710-2267).

MAPS

It is easy to become directionally impaired in the hills, particular in the Central Hills, where the roads wind around the peaks. Almost all businesses in the Black Hills carry a regional map created by the Black Hills, Badlands and Lakes Association. This relatively simple map is a great help, so keep one in your glove compartment or travel pack. In addition to the regional map, most of the towns in the hills have street maps available at chamber of commerce offices.

For hikers, bikers, and other recreation fans, some of the best trail and recreational information can be downloaded for free from the websites of the **National Forest Service** (www.fs.usda.gov/blackhills) and

National Park Service (www.nps.gov/state/sd). In addition to hiking and biking guides, the National Forest Service has campground guides, recreation area guides, snowmobile trail guides, and other information about recreation opportunities in the Black Hills National Forest. **National forest offices** in the Black Hills are in Spearfish (605/642-4622), Rapid City (605/343-1567), and at Pactola Reservoir (605/343-8755, Memorial Day-Labor Day). The **Forest Supervisor's Office** (605/673-9200) is in Custer. Regional hiking and biking maps are also available at the visitor centers in all the national recreation spots in the hills, including Jewel Cave, Mount Rushmore, Wind Cave, Custer State Park, and Badlands National Park.

BUSINESS HOURS

Most restaurants, attractions, and retail shops geared toward tourism are open a minimum of six days a week Memorial Day-Labor Day. Closing times vary, but most attractions are open until 8pm, retail shops until 6pm, and restaurants generally until 8-10pm. In some of the smaller towns, however, Sunday can be iffy for retail. If you are planning on a day of shopping, try to fit that in Monday-Saturday to avoid disappointment. There are still locations in the hills that do not accept credit cards, so be sure to ask before you eat!

The shoulder of the tourist season—comprising early May, September, and October—generally brings shorter hours for all tourist-related industries and Sunday and occasionally Monday closures for retail. Most restaurants, hotels, and attractions remain open through at least October 15. In winter, in the smaller communities, a lot of places close. It is always a good idea to call for information before you head to any particular location October-April. Season's end can vary with weather or traffic patterns.

MONEY

There are still a few locations, particularly in the smaller towns, that do not take credit cards. Glance at an establishment's doors and windows for stickers that identify the kinds of charge cards a store or restaurant will accept; if there is nothing in the window, be sure to ask. Cash works best in those spots, and you'll find that most towns have ATMs. In most locations in the Black Hills, out of state personal checks are not accepted.

Prices marked on all goods for sale in South Dakota generally do not reflect sales

heading to the Badlands

taxes. The state sales tax is 4.5 percent, there is a 1.5 percent tourism tax for many industries during the summer months, and there are city sales taxes, as well, which add another 1-2 percent.

There are many categories of personal service workers who receive monetary tips for their services. Restaurant workers and taxi drivers typically receive 20 percent of the bill, and bellhops and airport porters expect to receive $1 per bag. If you elect to take a tour, it is appropriate to tip tour guides and/or drivers. For van tours, a nice tip is $5 per person, though don't be afraid to contribute more if the tour was exceptionally fun and informative. For large motorcoach tours, a reasonable tip is in the range of $3 per person.

CELL PHONES

Cell phone reception in the Black Hills is sporadic. While reception is fine in most of the local communities, once you get into some of the remoter locations, like the Badlands and the wilderness areas of the region, signals can frequently be blocked. If you are planning to do any backcountry hiking or camping, remember to notify rangers of your plans. If you run into trouble, you may not be able to call anyone. GPS will work most of the time for navigation, but not always. The remoter the location, the less likely that GPS will get you there.

ELECTRICITY

Most electrical outlets in the United States use a voltage rate of 110 or 220 volts. Most outlets are three-pronged with two flat and one round grounding prong. Older buildings may have just two-pronged plugs. In those circumstances, most hardware stores carry a converter that will allow you to use a three-pronged appliance in an older outlet.

Resources

Suggested Reading

There are several small presses in the West that publish interesting books about South Dakota and the plains. Two of the best include the **South Dakota State Historical Society Press** (605/773-6009, www.sdhspress.com) in Pierre and the **University of Nebraska Press** (402/472-3581, www.nebraskapress.unl.edu).

The Internet has made it possible for just about anyone to find just about any book, even if it is out of print. A few of the books listed here have gone out of print but are still readily available online, either new or used. If a book is out of print or hard to find, it's noted.

RECREATION
Hiking and Mountain Biking

Gildart, Bert. *Hiking the Black Hills Country: A Guide to More Than 50 Hikes in South Dakota and Wyoming (Hiking the Black Hills Country).* Guilford, CT: Globe Pequot (Falcon Guides), 2021. Plenty of hikes in the Black Hills, for the avid fan.

Gildart, Bert, and Jane Gildart. *Best Easy Day Hikes Black Hills Country.* Guilford, CT: Globe Pequot (Falcon Guides), 2022. A pocket-size, compact guide to some very nice hiking in the hills.

Golis, Aleen M. *The Mickelson Trail Guidebook.* CreateSpace Independent Publishing Platform (an Amazon company), 2013. An all-inclusive guide to the 109-mile (175-km) Mickelson Trail with maps, photographs, and descriptions of distinctive features along the trail. Lodging suggestions for the eight towns along the trail are included, as are general interest notes about the history of trains, the trail, and mining.

Knapp, Andy. *Mountain Biking the Great Plains States.* Guilford, CT: Globe Pequot (Falcon Guides), 1996. Included in this guide are 12 Black Hills mountain biking trails with good maps to the trailheads. The book is currently out of print, but easily obtained online.

Rogers, Hiram. *Exploring the Black Hills & Badlands: A Guide for Hikers, Cross-Country Skiers, and Mountain Bikers.* Boulder, CO, Johnson Books, 1999. The book is a little dated, but the trails don't change much. The Mickelson and Centennial Trails are included as well as 45 trails throughout the South Dakota Black Hills and additional Black Hills trails in Wyoming and North Dakota.

Rock Climbing

Busse, Andrew, and Andrew Burr. *Needles of Rushmore: Climbing in South Dakota's Mt. Rushmore National Memorial.* Boulder, CO: Fixed Pin Publishing, 2012. This book includes over 900 detailed routes, with fabulous photography, ascending the granite spires of South Dakota.

Cronin, Mikel. *South Dakota's Spearfish Canyon, the VC and other South Dakota*

Limestone. Boulder, CO: Sharp End Publishing, 2011. This book includes over 700 detailed routes for climbing in scenic Spearfish Canyon and other limestone climbing sites in the Black Hills.

NATURAL HISTORY

Dunn, Jon, and Jonathan Alderfer. *National Geographic Field Guide to the Birds of North America*, Washington DC: National Geographic, 2017. The Black Hills region is the western outpost of eastern birds and the eastern outpost of western birds. To find them all, you'll need this guide.

Kirkpatrick, Zoe. *Wildflowers of the Western Plains*. Lincoln, NE: University of Nebraska Press (Bison Books), 2008. A great little guide to wildflowers, organized by color for easy identification.

Larson, Gary, and James Johnson. *Plants of the Black Hills and Bear Lodge Mountains*. Brookings, SD: South Dakota State University Publications, 2007. The definitive guide to plants in the Black Hills region, with over 600 listings.

Tekiela, Stan. *Birds of the Dakotas*. Cambridge, MN: Adventure Publications, 2021. This is a great compact guide that will fit in a jacket pocket and has good color photos for identifying most of the common birds of the region. It's great for beginners.

GENERAL HISTORY

Ambrose, Stephen. *Crazy Horse and Custer: The Parallel Lives of Two American Warriors*. New York, NY: Penguin/Random House, 1996. From boyhood to manhood, Ambrose compares the lives of two military leaders of the Indian Wars of 1876. The book is available in audio and paperback.

Federal Writers' Project. *The WPA Guide to South Dakota*. St. Paul, MN: Minnesota Historical Society Press, 2006. Originally published in 1938, this is a fascinating combination of history and road-trip guide, written by out-of-work writers during the Great Depression.

Grafe, Ernest, and Paul Horsted. *Exploring with Custer: The 1874 Black Hills Expedition*. Custer, SD: Golden Valley Press, 2002. Follow in the final footsteps of Lieutenant Colonel George Armstrong Custer as he explored the Black Hills of South Dakota with 1,000 men, a band, miners, and newspaper correspondents. The book traces the expedition and is illustrated with fascinating then and now photographs. The hills haven't changed that much!

Hasselstrom, Linda. *Roadside History of South Dakota*. Missoula, MT: Mountain Press Publishing Company, 1998. Instead of being organized on a timeline, this history book is geographically oriented and offers a little history and a tale or two about smaller communities frequently overlooked in other history books.

Laskin, David. *Children's Blizzard*. New York, NY: HarperCollins Publishers, 2005. In January 1888, a late-afternoon blizzard struck the eastern plains of South Dakota and Nebraska, catching children headed home. The blizzard killed over 500 settlers. The story is told through interviews and journals of the people who lived through it.

Schell, Herbert. *History of South Dakota*. Pierre, SD: University of South Dakota State Historical Society Press, 2004. A great overview of the history of the state and the early years of the Black Hills.

NATIVE AMERICAN HISTORY AND CULTURE

Amiotte, Arthur, Louis Warren, and Janet Berlo. *Transformation and Continuity in Lakota Culture: The Collages of Arthur Amiotte, 1988–2014*. Pierre, SD: South Dakota State Historical Society Press, 2014. The work of Arthur Amiotte is funny, insightful, surprising, and thoughtful, just like the man who created them. This book shares his wonderful collages with a story to tell about Lakota culture as it navigated the changes brought on by the European invasion.

Flood, Renee Sansom. *Lost Bird of Wounded Knee*. New York, NY: Perseus Books (Da Capo Press), 1998. This is the story of the only survivor of the massacre at Wounded Knee. Lost Bird was an infant when the massacre occurred, and she was found alive underneath the frozen body of her mother.

Larson, Robert. *Red Cloud: Warrior-States-man of the Lakota Sioux*. Norman, OK: University of Oklahoma Press, 1999. Red Cloud was one of the great, though controversial, leaders of the Lakota tribes of the Great Plains. A ferocious warrior, Red Cloud, seeing the nonstop influx of settlers, eventually came to believe that a good treaty was the only way to save his people. Unfortunately, there was no such thing as a good treaty. He lived for many years on the Pine Ridge Reservation, where his status as hero or sellout is still debated. He lived to the age of 88, and his gravesite is located near the Red Cloud School in the community of Pine Ridge.

Lazarus, Edward. *Black Hills, White Justice: The Sioux Nation Versus the United States, 1775 to the Present*. New York, NY: HarperCollins Publishers, 1991. When Native Americans were forced to sign a new treaty after the Indian Wars of 1876, the Black Hills were taken illegally from the Great Sioux Nation. This book traces the history of an event that ended up being one of the longest-running court cases to be heard by the Supreme Court of the United States. You'd think it would be on the dry side? It's not. It's a headshaking tale of treachery. This book is out of print, but available used.

Marshall, Joseph, III. *The Lakota Way: Stories and Lessons for Living*. New York, NY: Penguin Books, 2002. A wonderful book of storytelling and philosophy of the Lakota culture. The book focuses on the 12 core qualities crucial to the Lakota way of living: bravery, fortitude, generosity, wisdom, respect, honor, perseverance, love, humility, sacrifice, truth, and compassion.

Niehardt, John. *Black Elk Speaks: Being the Life Story of a Holy Man of the Oglala Sioux*. Lincoln, NE: University of Nebraska Press, 2014. With an introduction by Philip DeLoria and annotations by Raymond J. DeMalli, this is a powerful story of the life of Lakota healer Nicholas Black Elk and the tragic history of his people as told to John Niehardt.

Pope, Dennis. *Sitting Bull, Prisoner of War*. Pierre, SD: South Dakota State Historical Society Press, 2010. For 20 months, Sitting Bull was held at Fort Randall in South Dakota. This book fills in the gaps in his life story and reveals the day-to-day experience of Sitting Bull as a captive who maintained his leadership role and his dignity in the worst of circumstances.

Sandoz, Mari. *Crazy Horse: Strange Man of the Oglalas*. Lincoln, NE: University of Nebraska Press, 2008. An in-depth look at one of the Lakotas' greatest warriors, who knew that signing a treaty with the white man was an exercise in meaninglessness.

St. Pierre, Mark. *Madonna Swan: A Lakota Woman's Story*. Norman, OK: University of Oklahoma Press, 2003. Written by a current-day resident of the Pine Ridge Reservation of the Oglala Lakota, the book combines traditional culture with contemporary problems when a Lakota woman is diagnosed with tuberculosis.

Welch, James. *Killing Custer: The Battle of Little Bighorn and the Fate of the Plains Indians*. New York, NY: W. W. Norton & Company, 2007. The Battle of the Little Bighorn from the tribal perspective.

RANCHERS AND PIONEERS

Blasingame, Ike. *Dakota Cowboy*. Lincoln, NE: University of Nebraska Press (Bison Books), 1964. Every South Dakota cowboy I've talked to cites this as the best true story of ranchers to be found.

Hasselstrom, Linda. *Feels Like Far: A Rancher's Life on the Great Plains*. Guilford, CT, Globe Pequot (Lyons Press), 1999. An insightful look at ranch life on the plains, written by one of South Dakota's best and most prolific writers.

Kohl, Edith Eudora. *Land of the Burnt Thigh*. St. Paul, MN: Minnesota Historical Society Press, 1986 reprint. Originally published New York, NY: Funk & Wagnalls, 1938. A lively tale of single women homesteaders in the plains.

O'Brien, Dan. *Buffalo for the Broken Heart*. New York, NY: Random House, 2002. A self-disclosing and fascinating look at one rancher's attempt to convert his cattle ranch to a buffalo ranch in the Black Hills of South Dakota.

Wilder, Laura Ingalls, and Pamela Smith Hill. *Pioneer Girl: The Annotated Biography*. Pierre, SD: South Dakota State Historical Society Press, 2014. Wilder is known best for the Little House book series on which the television series *Little House on the Prairie* was based. This annotated autobiography of one of South Dakota's most famous former residents is a must-read for all fans.

OTHER NONFICTION

Norris, Kathleen. *Dakota: A Spiritual Geography*. Boston, MA: Houghton Mifflin Harcourt (Mariner Books), 2001. An autobiography with thoughtful reflections on the changes in climate, population, and atmosphere of the state of South Dakota in the author's lifetime.

FICTION OF THE PLAINS AND THE WEST

Looking for the flavor of the West or just looking for a great read? I can't help myself. I am a voracious reader and former bookstore owner with a weakness for fiction. Here's a list of some absolutely wonderful Western reads.

Doig, Ivan. *The Whistling Season*. Boston, MA: Houghton Mifflin Harcourt, 2007. A man assigned the task of deciding whether or not to close Montana's one-room schools thinks back to his student days in a one-room school, taught by two of the most eccentric characters you'd ever hope to meet.

Haruf, Kent. *Plainsong*. New York, NY: Random House (Vintage), 1999. Written with the rhythm of the plains, this book explores how a place, a region, or a town can affect a life, a relationship, and a family.

Johnson, Craig. *The Cold Dish*. New York, NY: Penguin, 2004. The first in the Sheriff Walt Longmire series, an absolutely wonderful series about a small-town Wyoming sheriff. This flawed, good-hearted, honest man is a character you just have to love.

Meyers, Kent. *The Work of Wolves*. Boston, MA: Houghton Mifflin Harcourt, 2005. I don't think anyone could better depict small-town South Dakota, ranch life, and local humor better than Kent Meyers. Read this one before you visit.

Spragg, Mark. *An Unfinished Life*. New York, NY: Random House (Vintage), 2005. A story of family, friendship, and forgiveness on a Wyoming ranch.

CHILDREN'S BOOKS

Anderson, William. *M Is for Mount Rushmore: A South Dakota Alphabet*. Florence, KY: Gale-Cengage Learning (Sleeping Bear Press), 2005. A cute alphabet book and souvenir for the little ones . . . or the grandkids left at home.

Bruchac, Joseph. *A Boy Called Slow: The True Story of Sitting Bull.* New York: Penguin (Paperstar Books), 1998. The story of how Sitting Bull got his name, for children ages 4–8.

Horner, Jack. *Digging Up Dinosaurs.* Helena, MT: Farcountry Press, 2007. Written by Montana's state paleontologist, the book is beautifully illustrated and a fun introduction to fossil finding for kids.

Montileaux, Don. *Tatanka and the Lakota People.* Pierre, SD: South Dakota State Historical Society Press, 2009. A beautifully illustrated children's book about the creation story of the Lakota people.

Robson, Gary, and illustrator Robert Rath. *Who Pooped in the Black Hills? Scats and Tracks for Kids.* Helena, MT: Farcountry Press, 2006. This one is a big hit with the kids.

SCENERY AND PHOTOGRAPHY

Kettlewell, Dick. *Black Hills Impressions.* Helena, MT: Farcountry Press, 2004. This is a book to look for once you arrive. It's a great souvenir for every visitor.

MAGAZINES AND JOURNALS

There aren't very many magazines published in the Black Hills, but the statewide *South Dakota Magazine* (www.southdakota magazine.com) contains interesting specialty articles on the towns and people of South Dakota. The magazine is published bimonthly.

Internet Resources

RECREATION

National Park Service
www.nps.gov

Find a national park site by state anywhere in the country. A search on South Dakota will allow you to select Jewel Cave, Wind Cave, Mount Rushmore, the Badlands, and the Minuteman Missile National Historic Site. Choosing any of these selections will bring you to websites with all kinds of information about the history, ecology, and recreational opportunities of the parks as well as updated fee and hours of operation information.

Black Hills National Forest
www.fs.usda.gov/blackhills

This is a great source of information about national forest recreation areas and campgrounds, as well as trail maps and information about the flora and fauna of the Black Hills.

South Dakota Department of Game, Fish, and Parks
http://gfp.sd.gov

Make state campground reservations, find out about hunting and fishing licenses, and learn about South Dakota wildlife here. This is a great website with a lot of free publications, including hunting and fishing handbooks, campground maps, and trail guides.

www.recreation.gov

This website is the creation of 12 different organizations. It was established to help users discover just about everything about public lands in the United States. There is information about what public lands are near you and what activities are available—down to the level of where to hike, bike, swim, or camp. Partners in the site include the Army Corps of Engineers, Forest Service, National Park Service, Bureau of Land Management, Bureau of Reclamation, Fish and Wildlife Service, and the National Archives.

NATURAL RESOURCES

United States Geological Survey
www.usgs.gov
Look for topographical maps of anywhere in the United States. Buy maps online. Research the natural sciences, including biology, geology, and geography. Download USGS publications. Do an advanced search on publications and input South Dakota. You'll find everything and more about minerals in the state. Take a look at the social media tab and follow the USGS on Facebook or Twitter. Download USGS wallpapers.

National Speleological Society
www.caves.org
South Dakota is a land of caves. Explore this otherworldly realm at this website. Look for some gorgeous videos of underground earth. While you're at it, give a listen to Jan Conn (explorer and early mapper of Jewel Cave) singing "Never Go Caving with Someone Smaller than You." Find her by using the website search page—look for the 1999 NSS Cave Salon Ballad results.

NATURAL HISTORY

South Dakota Ornithologists' Union
www.sdou.org
Everything you need to know about birds in South Dakota, including state checklists, birding hot spots, and links to other birding websites pertaining to South Dakota birds.

PUBLICATIONS

South Dakota Magazine
www.southdakotamagazine.com
This is a great bimonthly magazine with searchable archives online. If you are interested in a specific topic or community, download the full index of articles and then order back issues. The website is a great resource for researchers and writers.

Rapid City Journal
www.rapidcityjournal.com
The only daily newspaper in the region has a good online calendar of events, some restaurant reviews (check under entertainment), and information on book signings, art galleries, and shows. This website will give you some great ideas for joining in on local cultural events and entertainment.

TOURISM

South Dakota
www.travelsouthdakota.com
The state of South Dakota is committed to increasing tourism, and this website is a great overview of the attractions, history, and culture of the state. While the site offers reservations online, it's a bit slow and includes a very limited number of lodgings. Reservation services are also provided by the Black Hills and Badlands site (www.blackhillsbadlands.com) below.

Black Hills and Badlands
www.blackhillsbadlands.com
This website offers a lot of the same information as the South Dakota tourism website (www.travelsouthdakota.com), but the central reservation service here is easier to use and seems to offer a few more lodging choices. As with the state-offered site, be aware that not all accommodations are listed.

Index

List of Maps

Photo Credits

All photos © Laural A. Bidwell except page 2 © travelsouthdakota.com; page 3 © travelsouthdakota.com; page 6 © (top left) travelsouthdakota.com; (bottom) travelsouthdakota.com; page 8 © (top) travelsouthdakota.com; page 9 © (top) travelsouthdakota.com; page 10 © travelsouthdakota.com; page 12 © travelsouthdakota.com; page 13 © (top) travelsouthdakota.com; (bottom) Jason P Ross | Dreamstime.com; page 14 © (bottom) travelsouthdakota.com; page 15 © (top) travelsouthdakota.com; (bottom) travelsouthdakota.com; page 16 © (bottom) Crazy Horse Memorial; page 28 © (bottom) travelsouthdakota.com; page 30 © (top) The Termesphere Gallery; page 31 © Oocoskun | Dreamstime.com; page 41 © (top left) National Park Service; (bottom) National Park Service; page 49 © travelsouthdakota.com; page 66 © (top) travelsouthdakota.com; page 78 © (top) National Park Service; (left middle)travelsouthdakota.com; page 95 © travelsouthdakota.com; page 96 © (top left) travelsouthdakota.com; (top right) travelsouthdakota.com; page 99 © Crazy Horse Memorial Foundation; page 107 © (top) National Park Service; (bottom) travelsouthdakota.com; page 118 © John Minium; page 125 © (top) travelsouthdakota.com; (left middle) travelsouthdakota.com; (bottom) travelsouthdakota.com; page 147 © (top) travelsouthdakota.com; (bottom) travelsouthdakota.com; page 173 © travelsouthdakota.com; page 179 © (top) travelsouthdakota.com; page 190 © (right middle)travelsouthdakota.com; (bottom) travelsouthdakota.com; page 211 © Kesi Irvin; page 218 © (top) travelsouthdakota.com; page 226 © travelsouthdakota.com; page 228 © (top) travelsouthdakota.com; page 249 © travelsouthdakota.com; page 253 © travelsouthdakota.com; page 256 © travelsouthdakota.com; page 266 © travelsouthdakota.com

Acknowledgments

To my mother, Barbara Bidwell, who inspired me with the travel tales of her youth and the many cross-country road trips well into her seventies: Mom, you're my road warrior role model. Thank you for always believing in me.

To James—my partner and best friend—thanks for your love, humor, patience, and encouragement.

ACADIA
NATIONAL PARK

SEASIDE TOWNS · FALL FOLIAGE
CYCLING & PADDLING

HILARY NANGLE

ARCHES &
CANYONLANDS
NATIONAL PARKS

HIKING · BIKING
SCENIC DRIVES

JUDY JEWELL & W. C. MCRAE

BANFF
NATIONAL
PARK

HIKE · CAMP
SEE WILDLIFE

ANDREW HEMPSTEAD

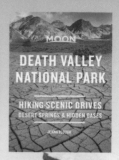

DEATH VALLEY
NATIONAL PARK

HIKING · SCENIC DRIVES
DESERT SPRINGS & HIDDEN OASES

JENNA BLOUGH

GLACIER
NATIONAL PARK

HIKING · CAMPING
LAKES & PEAKS

BECKY LOMAX

GRAND
CANYON

HIKE · CAMP
RAFT THE
COLORADO RIVER

TIM HULL

GREAT SMOKY
MOUNTAINS
NATIONAL PARK

HIKING · CAMPING
SCENIC DRIVES

JASON FRYE

JOSHUA TREE
& PALM SPRINGS

HIKING · SCENIC DRIVES
DESERT GETAWAYS

JENNA BLOUGH

ROCKY
MOUNTAIN
NATIONAL PARK

HIKE · CAMP
SEE WILDLIFE

ERIN ENGLISH

SEQUOIA &
KINGS CANYON

HIKING · CAMPING
WATERFALLS & BIG TREES

LEIGH BERNACCHI

YELLOWSTONE
& GRAND TETON

HIKE · CAMP
SEE WILDLIFE

BECKY LOMAX

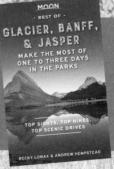

YOSEMITE
SEQUOIA &
KINGS CANYON

HIKING · CAMPING
REDWOODS & WATERFALLS

ANN MARIE BROWN

ZION &
BRYCE

WITH ARCHES, CANYONLANDS, CAPITOL REEF,
GRAND STAIRCASE-ESCALANTE & MORE

HIKING · BIKING
SCENIC DRIVES

JUDY JEWELL & W. C. MCRAE

Spending only
a few days in
a park? Try
Moon's Best of
Parks guides.

- BEST OF -
GLACIER, BANFF,
& JASPER
MAKE THE MOST OF
ONE TO THREE DAYS
IN THE PARKS

TOP SIGHTS, TOP HIKES,
TOP SCENIC DRIVES

BECKY LOMAX & ANDREW HEMPSTEAD

ROAD TRIP GUIDES

MOON
BLUE RIDGE PARKWAY
Road Trip

WITH SHENANDOAH & GREAT SMOKY
MOUNTAINS NATIONAL PARKS

JASON FRYE

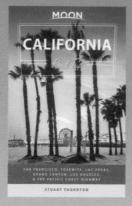

MOON
CALIFORNIA
Road Trip

SAN FRANCISCO, YOSEMITE, LAS VEGAS,
GRAND CANYON, LOS ANGELES,
& THE PACIFIC COAST HIGHWAY

STUART THORNTON

MOON
NASHVILLE TO NEW ORLEANS
Road Trip

NATCHEZ TRACE PARKWAY • MEMPHIS •
TUPELO • MISSISSIPPI BLUES TRAIL

MARGARET LITTMAN

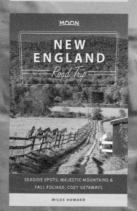

MOON
NEW ENGLAND
Road Trip

SEASIDE SPOTS, MAJESTIC MOUNTAINS &
FALL FOLIAGE, COZY GETAWAYS

MILES HOWARD

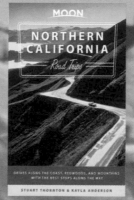

MOON
NORTHERN CALIFORNIA
Road Trips

DRIVES ALONG THE COAST, REDWOODS, AND MOUNTAINS
WITH THE BEST STOPS ALONG THE WAY

STUART THORNTON & KAYLA ANDERSON

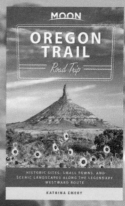

MOON
OREGON TRAIL
Road Trip

HISTORIC SITES, SMALL TOWNS, AND
SCENIC LANDSCAPES ALONG THE LEGENDARY
WESTWARD ROUTE

KATRINA EMERY

MOON
PACIFIC COAST HIGHWAY
Road Trip

CALIFORNIA,
OREGON & WASHINGTON

IAN ANDERSON

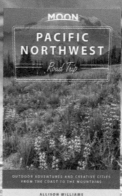

MOON
PACIFIC NORTHWEST
Road Trip

OUTDOOR ADVENTURES AND CREATIVE CITIES
FROM THE COAST TO THE MOUNTAINS

ALLISON WILLIAMS

MOON
ROUTE 66
Road Trip

JESSICA DUNHAM

MOON.COM | ROADTRIPUSA.COM

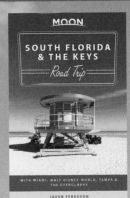

MOON
SOUTH FLORIDA & THE KEYS
Road Trip

WITH MIAMI, WALT DISNEY WORLD, TAMPA &
THE EVERGLADES

JASON FERGUSON

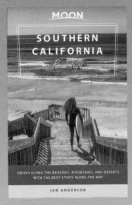

MOON
SOUTHERN CALIFORNIA
Road Trips

DRIVES ALONG THE BEACHES, MOUNTAINS, AND DESERTS
WITH THE BEST STOPS ALONG THE WAY

IAN ANDERSON

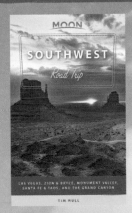

MOON
SOUTHWEST
Road Trip

LAS VEGAS, ZION & BRYCE, MONUMENT VALLEY,
SANTA FE & TAOS, AND THE GRAND CANYON

TIM HULL

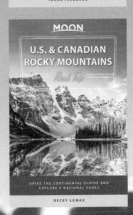

MOON
U.S. & CANADIAN ROCKY MOUNTAINS
Road Trip

DRIVE THE CONTINENTAL DIVIDE AND
EXPLORE 9 NATIONAL PARKS

BECKY LOMAX

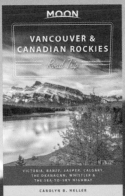

MOON
VANCOUVER & CANADIAN ROCKIES
Road Trip

VICTORIA, BANFF, JASPER, CALGARY,
THE OKANAGAN, WHISTLER,
THE SEA-TO-SKY HIGHWAY

CAROLYN B. HELLER

MOON
YELLOWSTONE TO GLACIER NATIONAL PARK
Road Trip

JACKSON HOLE, CODY, THE GRAND TETONS
& THE ROCKY MOUNTAIN FRONT

CARTER G. WALKER

MOON
BASEBALL
Road Trips

TIMOTHY MALCOLM

THE COMPLETE GUIDE
TO ALL THE BALLPARKS,
WITH BEER,
BITES,
AND SIGHTS
NEARBY

the OPEN ROAD

50 BEST ROAD TRIPS *in the* USA

From Weekend Getaways
to Cross-Country Adventures

JESSICA DUNHAM

MOON
Road Trip USA
25TH ANNIVERSARY EDITION

CROSS-COUNTRY ADVENTURES ON
AMERICA'S TWO-LANE HIGHWAYS

Jamie Jensen

MAP SYMBOLS

▭	Expressway	○	City/Town	✈	Airport	⚲	Golf Course
▭	Primary Road	◉	State Capital	✗	Airfield	P	Parking Area
▭	Secondary Road	⊛	National Capital	▲	Mountain	▱	Archaeological Site
▭	Unpaved Road	✪	Highlight	✚	Unique Natural Feature	▮	Church
----	Trail	★	Point of Interest			▯	Gas Station
•••••	Ferry	•	Accommodation	⍲	Waterfall	◔	Glacier
▬▬	Railroad	▼	Restaurant/Bar	▲	Park	▨	Mangrove
▭	Pedestrian Walkway	▪	Other Location	▯	Trailhead	▱	Reef
▥	Stairs	▲	Campground	⛷	Skiing Area	▱	Swamp

CONVERSION TABLES

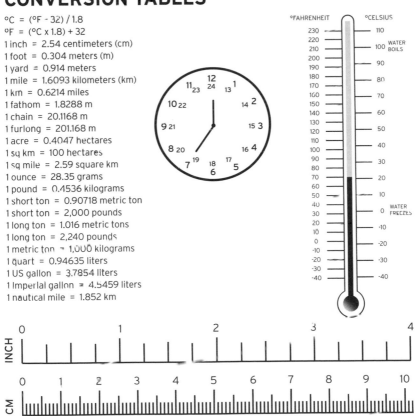

°C = (°F - 32) / 1.8
°F = (°C x 1.8) + 32
1 inch = 2.54 centimeters (cm)
1 foot = 0.304 meters (m)
1 yard = 0.914 meters
1 mile = 1.6093 kilometers (km)
1 km = 0.6214 miles
1 fathom = 1.8288 m
1 chain = 20.1168 m
1 furlong = 201.168 m
1 acre = 0.4047 hectares
1 sq km = 100 hectares
1 sq mile = 2.59 square km
1 ounce = 28.35 grams
1 pound = 0.4536 kilograms
1 short ton = 0.90718 metric ton
1 short ton = 2,000 pounds
1 long ton = 1.016 metric tons
1 long ton = 2,240 pounds
1 metric ton = 1,000 kilograms
1 quart = 0.94635 liters
1 US gallon = 3.7854 liters
1 Imperial gallon = 4.5459 liters
1 nautical mile = 1.852 km

MOON SOUTH DAKOTA'S BLACK HILLS

Avalon Travel
Hachette Book Group
1700 Fourth Street
Berkeley, CA 94710, USA
www.moon.com

Editor: Kristi Mitsuda
Series Manager: Kathryn Ettinger
Copy Editor: Ashley Benning
Graphics and Production Coordinator: Darren Alessi
Cover Design: Toni Tajima
Map Editor: Kat Bennett
Cartographers: John Culp, Brian Shotwell
Indexer: Greg Jewett

ISBN-13: 9781640496132
Printing History
1st Edition — 2010
5th Edition — November 2022
5 4 3 2 1

Front cover photo: Sylvan Lake, Custer State Park © Greg Vaughn / Alamy Stock Photo
Back cover photo: Badlands National Park © Kelsey Mcquisten | Dreamstime.com

Printed in Malaysia for Imago